U.S. STAMP YEARBOOK 2005

A comprehensive record of technical data, design development and stories behind all of the stamps and postal cards issued by the United States Postal Service in 2005.

By
George Amick

Published by *Linn's Stamp News*, the largest and most informative stamp newspaper in the world. *Linn's* is owned by Amos Press, 911 Vandemark Road, Sidney, Ohio 45365. Amos Press also publishes *Scott Stamp Monthly* and the Scott line of catalogs and albums.

ISSN 0748-996X

ACKNOWLEDGMENTS

It would be impossible to produce the Linn's U.S. Stamp Yearbook series without the help of many people. I deeply appreciate the generosity with which they give of their time and information.

For the concept sketches and other art-in-progress developed by the U.S. Postal Service in creating 2005's stamp and stationery designs, and for many hours of conversations on how the stamps and the designs came about, I thank Terrence McCaffrey, manager of stamp development for the U.S. Postal Service, and his art directors: Carl Herrman, Phil Jordan, Ethel Kessler, Derry Noyes, Howard Paine and Richard Sheaff. Year after year, they enthusiastically recall for me the stories of how these remarkable stamps were planned and created.

Willing assistance came from USPS officials David Faillor, Bill Gicker, Faustino Romero, Mark Saunders, Lauren Sposato and many others. At PhotoAssist, Louis Plummer, Sidney Brown and their associates are always available to answer my questions, often in the same phone call or by return e-mail.

Thanks also to the illustrators, designers and photographers who shared their experiences in creating stamp art, including Sally Andersen-Bruce, Mark Anderson, John Boyd, Carl Purcell, Bill Phillips, Victor Stabin and Will Wilson; to Laura A. Miller of the Little Rock Central High Visitors' Center and Debra Schwartz of StudioEIS for their information on design sources for the To Form a More Perfect Union pane; and to Joe Sheeran of Ashton-Potter (USA) Ltd., and to Sandra Lane and Don Woo at Sennett Security Products.

I'm indebted to many philatelic colleagues, including Bob Dumaine, Rita Dumaine, Lloyd de Vries, Steve Esrati, John Larson and the entire editorial staff of *Linn's Stamp News*. I again owe special thanks to Angie Stricker, who was responsible for the layout of *Yearbook 2005*.

I end these acknowledgments, as usual, with a bow to the two Donnas: Donna Houseman, the superb editor at *Linn's* who has been creating books out of the words, facts and pictures I send her for more than 20 years, and my number one fan, researcher, computer expert and wife, Donna Amick.

George Amick

CONTENTS

Legend for Linn's Yearbook Specification Charts

The following is an explanation of the terminology used in the charts that appear at the beginning of each chapter in this *Yearbook*:

Date of Issue: The official first-day-sale date designated by the Postal Service.

Catalog Number: The number or numbers assigned to the stamp or other postal item by the Scott *Specialized Catalogue of United States Stamps & Covers.*

Colors: The color or colors in which the stamp is printed. A number in parentheses preceded by the letters PMS refers to the color's designation under the Pantone Matching System.

First-Day Cancel: The post office location that is identified in the official first-day cancellations.

FDCs Canceled: This figure represents the total number of first-day covers hand-canceled and machine-canceled for collectors and dealers by Stamp Fulfillment Services in Kansas City, Missouri. It does not include covers canceled at the first-day site on the day of issue.

Format: The number and arrangement of stamps in the panes and printing plates.

Perf: The number of teeth or holes per 2 centimeters, as measured with a perforation gauge, and the type of perforator or die cutter used.

Selvage Inscriptions: Informational or promotional material printed in the selvage of certain sheet stamps.

Selvage Markings: Standard markings, other than plate numbers, of the kind found on most sheet stamps.

Cover Markings: Material printed on the inside and outside of booklet covers.

Illustrator or Photographer: The person commissioned by USPS to provide the artwork for the stamp.

Designer: The specialist who adapts the illustration or photograph to a stamp design.

Art Director: The USPS staff member or private-sector graphic arts specialist assigned to work with the illustrator and designer. Often the art director is also the designer.

Typographer: The specialist who selects and arranges the kind and size of type for the letters and numbers in the stamp design.

Engraver: The person who engraves the die for a stamp with an intaglio component.

Modeler: The specialist who takes the artwork and typography and makes any adaptations that are necessary to meet the requirements of the printing process. After completing this work, the modeler makes a stamp-size, full-color model of the design, which must be approved by USPS before production begins.

Stamp Manufacturing: The agency or company that manufactured the stamp, and the process by which it was made.

Quantity Ordered: The number of stamps or other postal items ordered by USPS.

Plate/Sleeve/Cylinder Number Detail: The number and location of plate, sleeve and/or cylinder numbers on the selvage of sheet stamps, on the peel-off strips, covers or stamps of booklet panes, and on coil stamps at constant intervals along the strip.

Plate/Cylinder Numbers Reported: The numbers or combinations of numbers of plates or cylinders used to print the stamp.

Counting Number Detail: The progressive numbers that are printed on the back of some coil stamps or their liner paper at constant intervals for counting purposes.

Tagging: The method used to add phosphor to the stamp or postal stationery in order to activate automated mail-handling equipment in post offices.

Corrections for *Linn's Stamp Yearbook 2004*

Page 2 (Acknowledgments): The name of the director of the USS Constellation Museum is Christopher Rowsom.

Page 8 (Introduction): Two 2004 stamps incorporated Scrambled Indicia in their designs: the Air Force Academy and World War II Memorial commemoratives.

Page 77: The vignettes of all three of the Lewis and Clark commemorative stamps were printed by offset lithography.

Page 291: The sixth and seventh lines and the words "On individual cards" on the eighth line should be eliminated.

Correction for *Linn's Stamp Yearbook 2002*

Page 286: The item illustrated under the heading "Nondenominated (37¢) Flag/Vending Booklet of 20" actually is the item that is correctly illustrated on page 284 under the heading "Nondenominated (37¢) Flag/Double-Sided Convertible Booklet of 20."

INTRODUCTION

In 2005, the Postal Service issued 161 collectible varieties of stamps and postal stationery, more than the 148 of 2004 but far fewer than the record 242 varieties that poured forth in 2002.

The 2005 output was heavy on commemoratives, with 107, the largest number in that category since the 140 of 2000. Ninety-eight of the 107 were issued in blocks or panes containing four or more designs.

Unique formats marked some of these large multiples. A 12-stamp pane featured Masterworks of American Architecture. Key events in the Civil Rights movement were commemorated with 10 stamps depicting existing artworks and arranged in a U-shape on a pane titled "To Form a More Perfect Union." And a pane honoring Jim Henson, the Man Behind the Muppets, contained 10 stamps depicting Muppet characters, plus an 11th stamp set apart from the others with a portrait of Henson himself.

A desire to cater to a growing market of Hispanic-American collectors led the Postal Service to issue its first bilingual block of four stamps, "Let's Dance/Bailemos," celebrating dances of Latin-American origin. The initiative led to a costly error: After finding that the accent marks in the Spanish text on the back of the pane liner were incorrect, USPS ordered the destruction of the entire first run of 70 million printed stamps and 974,000 associated picture postal cards containing similar mistakes at a cost of $172,000.

Several multiple-stamp sets, while not parts of ongoing series, were related to previous issues.

A 10-variety pane, American Advances in Aviation, that pictured aircraft representing innovation and technological development, was designed by the same team that created the 1997 Classic American Aircraft pane of 20 varieties. A block of four Constellations stamps was a logical follow-up to the 15 Cloudscapes stamps of 2004; both sets were issued for National Stamp Collecting Month and found their subject matter in the skies overhead.

Another block of four, honoring Distinguished Marines, was a comrade-in-arms to the Distinguished Soldiers quartet of 2000. A convertible booklet of five varieties depicting Sporty Cars of the 1950s was a sequel to two previous five-stamp sets featuring bygone automobiles. Four stamps honored American Scientists and recalled similar blocks for American Inventors (1983) and Pioneers of Communication (1996).

Meanwhile, a half-dozen commemorative series, long-running and recent, were extended in 2005: Nature of America, American Treasures, Art of Disney, Black Heritage, Literary Arts and Legends of Hollywood. A smiling President Ronald Reagan was shown on a single stamp issued close to his birth date following the year of his death, which is standard procedure for stamps for deceased presidents. The year's only intaglio-printed stamp honored film actress Greta Garbo and was a joint issue with Sweden.

Many of the commemoratives, including some of the more innovative ones, had a short shelf life because of the increase in the first-class rate from 37¢ to 39¢ that took place a few days after the end of the year. Issued on August 30 or later were To Form a More Perfect Union, Let's Dance, Greta Garbo, Jim Henson and the Muppets, Constellations and Distinguished Marines. The latter stamps, issued November 10, saw less than two months of stand-alone service.

In December, the Postal Service anticipated the rate change by issuing 11 varieties of a nondenominated Lady Liberty and Flag definitive stamp that sold for the new first-class rate, 39¢. These helped boost the number of definitives for 2005 to 27. The year also saw 13 new special stamps, one letter sheet and 13 picture postal cards. No postal card in the Historic Preservation series appeared in 2005.

Stamp Fulfillment Services continued to offer uncut press sheets of selected new commemoratives, a practice that began in 1994. Four such sheets were available in 2005. The year saw the Postal Service discontinue its use of Scrambled Indicia, which are design elements that can only be seen through a special decoder lens and had been part of selected commemoratives and high-value definitives since 1997.

In 2005, the private sector completed its takeover of the U.S. stamp printing business. On June 10, workers at the Bureau of Engraving and Printing in Washington, D.C., pulled a final roll of 37¢ Flag stamps from the Andreotti gravure press, an act that concluded 111 years of stamp production by the Bureau.

37¢ LUNAR NEW YEAR DOUBLE-SIDED PANE (12 DESIGNS)
LUNAR NEW YEAR SERIES

Date of Issue: January 6, 2005

Catalog Number: Scott 3895, full pane; 3895a-3895l, individual stamps

Colors: magenta, yellow, cyan, black

First-Day Cancel: Honolulu, Hawaii

First-Day Cancellations: 139,475

Format: Double-sided pane of 24, 12 on each side, horizontal, 3 across, 4 down. Gravure printing cylinders printing 576 stamps per revolution (24 across, 24 around) manufactured by Armotek Industries.

Gum Type: self-adhesive

Overall Stamp Size: 1.56 by 0.99 inches; 39.21 by 25.14 mm

Pane Size: 7.25 by 5.937 inches; 184.15 by 150.799 mm

Perforations: 10¾ (die-cut simulated perforations) (Comco Custom rotary die cutter)

Selvage Markings: "© 2004 USPS"

Selvage Inscription: "HAPPY NEW YEAR!" in English and Kanji characters

Designer, Illustrator and Typographer: Clarence Lee of Honolulu, Hawaii

Art Director: Terrence McCaffrey (USPS)

Modeler: Donald H. Woo of Sennett Security Products, Chantilly, Virginia

Stamp Manufacturing: Stamps printed for Sennett Security Products by American Packaging Corporation, Columbus, Wisconsin, on Ceruti Roto 5 gravure press. Stamps finished by Unique Binders of Fredericksburg, Virginia.

Quantity Ordered: 9,000,000 panes (108,000,000 stamps)

Cylinder Number Detail: none

Paper Supplier: Mactac

Tagging: unphosphored paper, block tagging over stamps

The Stamps

Between 1993 and 2004, the Postal Service commemorated each of the 12 years in the modified lunar (lunisolar) calendar used in China and other parts of Asia with a stamp depicting the animal for which the year is named. Each stamp was issued in advance of the New Year celebration and was dedicated in a city with a significant Asian-American population.

The 12th stamp in the series commemorated the Year of the Monkey and had its first-day sale January 13, 2004, in San Francisco, California.

On January 6, 2005, in Honolulu, Hawaii, and nationwide, the Postal Service issued a double-sided pane — which it called a souvenir sheet — reproducing all 12 designs in their original colors in two matching blocks of 12 stamps, one block on each side. Postmaster General John E. Potter described the pane as "a spectacular grand finale" to the series when he unveiled its design December 30, 2003.

The original stamps were denominated to cover the first-class rate at the time they were issued, from 29¢ to 37¢. They were printed by various methods by several different printing firms and distributed in panes of 20. The first nine had water-activated gum and conventional perforations. The new pane, like the three final stamps in the series, is self-adhesive with die-cut simulated perfs. It was printed by the gravure process by American Packaging Corporation for Sennett Security Products. All the stamps on the pane bear a 37¢ denomination, to make them practical for use in 2005, and all include a black "2005" year date beneath the design.

Although USPS had produced double-sided panes for convertible booklets before, the Lunar New Year was the first flat pane to be made that way. The reason, said Terrence McCaffrey, manager of stamp development, had to do with the stamps' 37¢ face value.

A pane of 12 37¢ stamps, which was the format originally planned, would sell for $4.44, which, according to ancient Chinese superstition, would mean "death-death-death," McCaffrey said. The word "four" is read as "si" in Chinese Mandarin and "shi" in Japanese, a close homonym for the word for death in both languages and in the Cantonese dialect spoken in Hong Kong. Because of the belief, the number four often is omitted in numbering hotel and hospital rooms in China and Japan, and many residents of those countries are willing to pay extra to avoid being assigned telephone numbers or automobile license plates that include fours.

On the other hand, the word "eight" sounds like "fa" ("prosperity") in Chinese and is highly favored.

"We had long discussions internally, trying to decide how to get around that problem," McCaffrey said. "Some people were saying, 'Well, that's the old school; the older people in the Chinese community still think that way but the younger generations don't, so we shouldn't have a problem.' I said, 'Yes, but we're dealing with a lot of traditionalists here.'

"We thought about making the stamps postcard rate (23¢) or international rate (80¢) to get a total that would get rid of those fours. Finally we came up with the solution of doing a double-sided souvenir sheet, which would

give us a face value of $8.88 and convert a bad-luck symbol to its opposite. The printers had told us they could do that format, and we were thinking about using it for a future project, so we decided to use it now.

"We then deliberated long and hard over whether we would be accused of gouging the public. But we positioned the double-sided sheet as something that was new and unique."

When the first stamp in the series was issued, the year it commemorated was the Year of the Rooster, which is the 10th year in the traditional cycle. However, the stamps on the new pane are in the proper order, with the blocks of 12 starting with the Year of the Rat — the first year in the sequence — and ending with the Year of the Boar. Another Year of the Rooster commenced February 9, 2005.

The original 12 stamps, their dates of issue, printing contractors and printing processes were:

29¢ Year of the Rooster, December 30, 1992 (Scott 2720), American Bank Note Company-Los Angeles, offset-intaglio combination.

29¢ Year of the Dog, February 5, 1994 (Scott 2817), Stamp Venturers, gravure.

29¢ Year of the Boar, December 30, 1994 (Scott 2876), Stamp Venturers, gravure.

32¢ Year of the Rat, February 8, 1996 (Scott 3060), Stamp Venturers, gravure. This stamp was the first in the series to bear a year date beneath the bottom frameline; all subsequent stamps have included this design feature, in either black or the stamp's background color.

32¢ Year of the Ox, January 5, 1997 (Scott 3120), Stamp Venturers, gravure.

32¢ Year of the Tiger, January 5, 1998 (Scott 3179), Stamp Venturers, gravure.

32¢ Year of the Hare, January 5, 1999 (Scott 3272), Sennett Security Products, gravure.

33¢ Year of the Dragon, January 6, 2000 (Scott 3370), Ashton-Potter (USA) Ltd., offset.

34¢ Year of the Snake, January 20, 2001 (Scott 3500), Ashton-Potter (USA) Ltd., offset.

34¢ Year of the Horse, February 11, 2002

(Scott 3559), Banknote Corporation of America, offset.

37¢ Year of the Ram, January 15, 2003 (Scott 3747), Banknote Corporation of America, offset.

37¢ Year of the Monkey, January 13, 2004 (Scott 3832), Sennett Security Products, gravure.

The editors of the Scott catalogs assigned number 3895 to the double-sided pane. Originally, they gave 11 of its stamps, Year of the Rat through Year of the Boar, the small-letter designations 3895a through 3895k. The Year of the Monkey stamp from the pane was listed with the Year of the

Monkey stand-alone stamp of 2004 (Scott 3832) and designated 3832a, on the assumption that the only difference between the two stamps was in their year dates, a black 2005 on one and a green 2004 on the other.

In March, however, the editors determined that there were other design differences that justified listing the 2005 Year of the Monkey

stamp with the other 11 stamps on the pane. For example, the dark outlines of the monkey's right paw and left leg are wider on the 2004 stand-alone stamp than on its 2005 counterpart. The latter's number was changed to 3895i, and the numbers for the Rooster, Dog and Boar stamps became 3895j, 3895k and 3895l, respectively.

Collectors of used stamps found that stamps from the Lunar New Year pane are particularly difficult to soak from their envelopes. The pane's soak-resistant laminated paper was manufactured by Mactac Printing Products of Stow, Ohio.

The Designs

All 12 stamps were designed by Clarence Lee, a Honolulu graphic designer, who depicted each animal in a way that suggests traditional Chinese cut-paper art. He cut each figure from paper with an Exacto knife, photographed the cutout and overlaid the negative on an airbrushed background so the background color showed through the transparent parts of the figure. The inscriptions on each stamp in Kanji, which is a Japanese adaptation of Chinese characters, were created in grass-style calligraphy by Lau Bun of Honolulu.

Seeing the 12 stamp images together makes clearer the scheme for the background colors that was worked out early in the process by Lee and McCaffrey, who served as art director for all the stamps except the first. Their plan was to move through the dark colors of the spectrum for the

Clarence Lee's first essay for the Lunar New Year pane showed the 12 stamps with their original denominations and in the order in which they were issued. On the finished pane, all the stamps have a face value of 37¢ and the top row of stamps has been moved to the bottom of the block, putting the animals representing the years in their proper sequence.

first six stamps, beginning with bright red for the Rooster stamp and ending with blue-green for the Tiger, then repeat the sequence for the final six.

The selvage design for the pane also was designed in cut-paper style by Clarence Lee, with calligraphy by Lau Bun. It consists of stylized bamboo stalks in blended hues of yellow, green, orange, blue and purple against a solid red-orange background. The message "HAPPY NEW YEAR!" with dots, or bullets, between the words, is in dropout white at the top, and the same message, in four Kanji characters, is dropped out of the wide lateral selvage, which is to the left of the block of stamps on the front side of the pane and to the right of the stamps on the reverse side.

The two sides differ in appearance because the stamps are not centered on the pane. If both sides had been identical, the blocks would not have lined up back to back. "That would have created the possibility that some faint die-cut lines might have come through on the selvage of one or both sides," McCaffrey explained. "Even though the die cuts aren't supposed to penetrate the liner, we were afraid they might show, and we didn't want that to happen."

Varieties

On March 23, 2005, auctioneer Jacques C. Schiff Jr. of Ridgefield Park, New Jersey, sold a pane of Lunar New Year stamps with shifted die cuts on the reverse side that caused the three stamps in the top row to be imperforate. The error pane brought $990, including the 10 percent buyer's premium.

The vertical shift between the printed web and the flexible die-cutting mat, which occurred during the finishing stage of production, measured about 1½ inches and led to the trio of stamps without die cuts, as well as production freaks among the remaining nine stamps on the pane.

Five days after the Schiff auction, a New Hampshire collector contacted *Linn's Stamp News* to report that he bought four similarly miscut panes at a local post office shortly after the issue date.

First-Day Facts

Azeezaly S. Jaffer, USPS vice president for public affairs and communications, dedicated the Lunar New Year pane in a ceremony in the Coral

The top three stamps on the back of this double-sided pane of Lunar New Year stamps are die-cut-missing errors. Linn's Stamp News *electronically enhanced the positions of the horizontal and vertical die cuts to make them easier to see.*

Ballroom of the Hilton Hawaiian Village in Honolulu.

Speakers were Winifred Pong, president, Chinese Chamber of Commerce of Hawaii; Dr. Ming Chen, chair, Narcissus Festival; Ginny Gong, national president, Organization of Chinese Americans; and Clarence Lee, designer of the stamps and the pane.

Edward L. Broglio, Honolulu District manager for USPS, was master of ceremonies. Peter Schall, the host hotel's managing director, gave the welcome. Honored guests were Frank J. Santos, Honolulu postmaster, and Thomas P. McCarthy, postmaster of Holualoa, Hawaii; they were introduced by Steve D. LeNoir, president of the National League of Postmasters of the United States.

With this issue, USPS introduced first-day covers with digital color postmarks. Clarence Lee designed the Lunar New Year pane's postmark, which depicted two mirror-image stylized dragons. The cost was $1.50 for a random cover, or $18 for a set of 12. Stamp Fulfillment Services also offered a set of 12 covers with conventional black-ink cancellations for $9, and a canceled full pane, front and back, for $11.38. Stamped covers submitted by collectors to the postmaster in Honolulu received black-ink cancellations.

Michael Schreiber, editor of *Linn's*, wrote in his Open Album column that the color cancel "in effect is an official cachet (added design) in the disguise of a traditional pictorial postmark." He cited what he called "Laurence's Law," first stated in a 1993 column by then-editor Michael Laurence, that "official cachets drive out all other cachets." The new cancel "will drive the black cancels out of existence," Schreiber predicted, "and it will be the end of the U.S. private cachet industry."

The earliest known pre-release use of a Lunar New Year stamp (Year of the Dog) was on a cover machine-canceled in Portland, Oregon, January 5, one day before its official first day of sale.

Shown here is a digital color first-day cancellation on a stamp from the Lunar New Year pane. Stamp Fulfillment Services sold covers with this cancellation for $1.50 per random cover, or $18 for a full set of 12.

37¢ MARIAN ANDERSON
BLACK HERITAGE SERIES

Date of Issue: January 27, 2005

Catalog Number: Scott 3896

Colors: magenta, yellow, cyan, black

First-Day Cancel: Washington, D.C.

First-Day Cancellations: 75,513

Format: Panes of 20, vertical, 5 across, 4 down. Gravure printing cylinders printing 360 stamps per revolution (30 across, 12 around) manufactured by Southern Graphics Systems.

Gum Type: self-adhesive

Overall Stamp Size: 0.99 by 1.56 inches; 25.146 by 39.624 mm

Pane Size: 5.94 by 7.25 inches; 150.87 by 184.15 mm

Perforations: 10¾ (die-cut simulated perforations) (Comco Custom rotary die cutter)

Selvage Markings: '© 2004/USPS' '.37/x20/$7.40' 'PLATE/POSITION' and diagram.

Back Markings: On selvage liner: Universal Product Code (UPC) "458000" in 4 locations. On stamp liner: "Marian Anderson/1897-1993/was one of the greatest/classically trained singers/of the 20th century and a/central figure in the/struggle of black/Americans for racial/equality. She performed/internationally, singing a/varied repertoire in her/rich contralto."

Illustrator: Albert Slark of Ajax, Ontario, Canada

Designer, Art Director and Typographer: Richard Sheaff of Scottsdale, Arizona

Modeler: Donald H. Woo of Sennett Security Products, Chantilly, Virginia

Stamp Manufacturing: Stamps printed for Sennett Security Products by American Packaging Corporation, Columbus, Wisconsin, on Champlain

Roto 3 gravure press. Stamps finished by Unique Binders of Fredericksburg, Virginia.

Quantity Ordered: 150,000,000

Cylinder Number Detail: 1 set of 4 cylinder numbers preceded by the letter
S in selvage above or below each corner stamp

Cylinder Number Combination Reported: S1111

Paper Supplier: Mactac

Tagging: unphosphored paper, block tagging over stamps

The Stamp

On January 27, the Postal Service issued a stamp honoring contralto
Marian Anderson. The stamp, the 28th in the annual Black Heritage series,
was dedicated in Washington, D.C., at the Daughters of the American
Revolution Memorial Continental Hall at Constitution Hall.

The choice of dedication site was richly symbolic. In 1939, the DAR
denied Anderson permission to present a concert at Constitution Hall,
then the only large concert auditorium in the nation's capital, because of
her race.

In 2005, however, attitudes had changed. Presley Merritt Wagoner, president general of the DAR, said: "The beauty of Marion Anderson's voice,
amplified by her courage and grace, brought attention to the eloquence of
the many voices urging our nation to overcome prejudice and intolerance.
The Daughters of the American Revolution are proud to participate with
the U.S. Postal Service in celebrating the issuance of the Marian Anderson
commemorative stamp."

Anderson was the second consecutive concert and opera singer to be
featured in the Black Heritage series, but her selection brought none of
the controversy that had attended the 2004 subject choice, Paul Robeson.
Unlike Robeson, who had been bitterly critical of the U.S. treatment of
black Americans and had praised Stalin's Soviet Union as a country free
of racism, Anderson was noncontroversial and widely admired.

The self-adhesive stamp was printed by American Packaging Corporation for Sennett Security Products by the gravure process and distributed
in panes of 20. A paragraph of text about Anderson is on the back of the
liner paper behind each stamp.

Anderson, who died in 1993, had become eligible for stamp honors only
two years earlier under the Postal Service's rule that requires at least 10
years to elapse between a person's death and his or her appearance on a
U.S. stamp. The only exception is for presidents.

"She rose to the top of our list of potential Black Heritage subjects
because of her prominence," said Terrence McCaffrey, manager of stamp
development. "The [Citizens' Stamp Advisory] Committee is particularly
interested in identifying women to honor in the series." Anderson was the
eighth woman to be depicted on a Black Heritage stamp, joining Harriet

Tubman (on the first stamp in the series, in 1978), Mary McLeod Bethune (1985), Sojourner Truth (1986), Ida B. Wells (1990), Bessie Coleman (1995), Madam C.J. Walker (1998) and Patricia Roberts Harris (2000).

Marian Anderson was born February 27, 1897, in Philadelphia, Pennsylvania, and began singing at the age of 6 in the choirs of the Union Baptist Church. In her mature years, her voice was remarkable for its strength, clarity and range. Conductor Arturo Toscanini told her: "Yours is a voice such as one hears only once in a hundred years."

She studied violin and piano before concentrating on singing. At 15, she received free voice lessons from Mary Patterson, a prominent black soprano. After a local music school rejected her application for admission because she was black, her church held fundraisers to enable her to study privately with noted singer and voice teacher Giuseppe Boghetti. Boghetti taught her many of the operatic arias and art songs for which she would become known.

Anderson began to tour regionally in the South and East, performing mainly at black colleges and churches, and also recorded spirituals for the Victor Talking Machine Company. In 1925, she won a competition against 300 other singers that gave her an opportunity to sing with the New York Philharmonic Orchestra. The concert led to a Rosenwald Foundation fellowship for her and the opportunity to study in Europe.

She spent most of her time in Sweden, Norway and Finland, where she became an audience favorite, and Germany, where she worked on her language skills and added a body of lieder (traditional German songs) to her repertoire. Finnish composer Jean Sibelius dedicated his composition *Solitude* to Anderson. She returned to Europe several times for study and concert tours, including performances in the Soviet Union.

In 1935, American impresario Sol Hurok heard Anderson sing at a concert in Paris and signed her to a contract. Reviewing her homecoming concert December 30, 1935, at Town Hall in New York City, a *New York Times* critic wrote: "Let it be said at the outset: Marian Anderson has returned to her native land one of the great singers of our time." The next year, President Franklin D. Roosevelt invited her to sing for guests at a White House dinner party, and Eleanor Roosevelt praised her in her newspaper column.

When Hurok tried to book Constitution Hall for a Washington stop on Anderson's 1939 tour, he was turned down because of the DAR's "white artists only" policy. The incident provided the occasion for one of the few great affirmations of equality in America before World War II. It stirred widespread indignation, even in a largely segregated country that was still more than 20 years away from its civil rights revolution. Mrs. Roosevelt resigned from the DAR in protest, and Interior Secretary Harold Ickes offered the singer the use of the Lincoln Memorial for an outdoor recital that would be free to the public. Here, on April 9, Easter Sunday, Anderson stood at the base of the memorial to the Great Emancipator and sang for an estimated 75,000 people on the Mall and a nationwide radio audience in the millions.

Rebuked by public opinion, the DAR ultimately changed its policy for Constitution Hall. Anderson first appeared there in a concert for the benefit of wartime China relief — at her insistence, blacks were seated in the orchestra section of the hall for the first time — and performed in its auditorium in several regular performances thereafter. In her 1956 autobiography, *My Lord, What a Morning*, she wrote: "When I finally walked into Constitution Hall and sang from the stage I had no feeling different from what I have in other halls. There was no sense of triumph. I felt that it was a beautiful concert hall, and I was happy to sing in it."

Constitution Hall itself was pictured on a 15¢ picture postal card in the Historic Preservation series issued in 1990 to commemorate the DAR's 100th anniversary.

Anderson married architect Orpheus H. Fisher in 1943, and they settled on a farm near Danbury, Connecticut. During World War II and the Korean War, she toured bases and hospitals, giving concerts for American and Allied troops.

In 1955, Anderson debuted in Giuseppe Verdi's *A Masked Ball* at the New York Metropolitan Opera, becoming the Met's first black soloist. At 58, her voice was beginning to show signs of age, but she remained a sentimental and symbolic favorite.

She gave her final formal concert in 1956, but performed at the presidential inaugurations of Dwight D. Eisenhower in 1957 and John F. Kennedy in 1961. Eisenhower named her an official delegate to the United Nations in 1958.

After her husband's death, she moved to Portland, Oregon, to live with her nephew, orchestra conductor James DePreist. She suffered a stroke

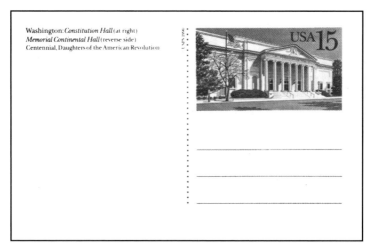

Constitution Hall, a building linked in history with Marian Anderson, was pictured on this 1990 picture postal card in the Historic Preservation series.

early in 1993 and died April 8, 1993, of heart failure at age 96.

Among the many honors she received were the NAACP's Spingarn Medal, presented to her by Eleanor Roosevelt in 1939; the Bok Award from the City of Philadelphia in 1941; the Presidential Medal of Freedom, presented by President Lyndon Johnson in 1963; New York City's Handel Medallion in 1972; the United Nations peace prize in 1977; the national medal of arts from President Ronald Reagan in 1986; and a Grammy award for lifetime achievement in 1991.

The Design

In 1996, USPS art director Richard Sheaff made a major change in the look of the Black Heritage series. He used a photograph of that year's subject, marine biologist Ernest E. Just, rather than a painting or engraving.

Future stamps in the series also would show photographs, Sheaff said at the time, as long as satisfactory ones could be found. "If we come to somebody for whom we can't find a good photograph, we'll paint a portrait," he said.

Following that plan, the subsequent Black Heritage stamps displayed photos of their subjects. Each was in monotone or duotone, with the predominant color varying from year to year. However, an unexpected objection arose.

Some black Americans complained that the men and women honored in the series were slighted by not being pictured in full color. The dissenting letters and e-mails came not from organizations but from individuals, and reflected the views of some Postal Service staff members as well, Terrence McCaffrey said.

On the other hand, he said, the minority-group members of CSAC have had no problem with the series' design style. "They were fine with it," he said. "They defended it. They felt it was a superb series, very elegant and dignified, but they understood the wants of the American public, and they were willing to entertain a change."

For the 2004 stamp honoring Paul Robeson, Sheaff developed several designs in the then-current format based on different black-and-white photographs, and CSAC chose one. However, to satisfy those who felt the Black Heritage portraits should be in full color, the committee asked Sheaff to commission a color painting based on the photograph they had selected. The work was done by Albert Slark of Ajax, Ontario, Canada, who specializes in book covers and advertising and also paints from life. His painting wasn't used, however, because Robeson's son, Paul Jr., preferred the photo version.

A similar process was followed in designing the Marian Anderson stamp. Sheaff created three designs with photographic sources, and CSAC chose one with a photo that was believed to have been made by Moise Benkow in Stockholm, Sweden, around 1934. The black-and-white photo is a head-and-shoulders portrait of the singer, who is wearing a formal

Shown here is Richard Sheaff's design for the Marian Anderson stamp using a photograph of the subject, in the style of the previous nine Black Heritage stamps. Artist Albert Slark painted a portrait of Anderson based on the same photograph, and his painting was used for the stamp.

gown, diamond earrings and a diamond necklace with a pendant. It was furnished to the Postal Service by the Annenberg Rare Book and Manuscript Library of the University of Pennsylvania from its Marian Anderson Collection of Photographs.

The art director developed the photo into a conventional duotone Black Heritage design. As an alternative, he again contracted with Slark to paint a full-color portrait based on the chosen photo.

"We showed only the painting to the family, not the photograph version," Terrence McCaffrey said. "They loved it."

Slark's painting followed the photograph closely. He made the singer's gown a dark burgundy in color and placed his subject against a complementary violet background.

"I spent about two weeks working on the portrait," Slark told the Postal Service. "The hardest part was getting the eyes and the smile just right. I also went to the library to find color photographs of Anderson so I could match the skin tones. I really had fun with it."

In fact, Slark made two versions of the painting. "On the first version, the likeness was a little bit off, so he redid it," said Sheaff. "The second one looked fine. But somehow, along the way, he forgot one of the ear-

Sheaff created these alternative stamp designs, based on other photographs of Anderson.

22

Marian Anderson

When artist Slark reworked his painting of Anderson, he accidentally omitted the earring on her left ear. Sheaff replaced the earring, using his computer.

rings. Probably what happened was that in redoing the background he painted over the earring and forgot to put it back in.

"We didn't notice the omission until the process was far along, and I replaced the earring using my computer. I actually changed the earring a bit from the way it looked in the photograph, where it was a little too faint and fell in sort of an awkward way. I changed it slightly to look better."

The typography is similar to that used on other recent stamps in the series. The words "BLACK HERITAGE" and "USA 37," in a font called Impact, are at the top, and "Marian Anderson," in uppercase and lowercase Futura Medium type, is dropped out of the design across the bottom.

First-Day Facts

John M. Nolan, deputy postmaster general, dedicated the Marian Anderson stamp at the Constitution Hall ceremony. He substituted for Postmaster General John E. Potter, who had been scheduled to officiate.

Mezzo-soprano Denyce Graves is shown performing music associated with Marian Anderson at the standing-room-only first-day ceremony in Constitution Hall's O'Byrne Gallery.

23

Speakers were Allan Keiler, author of the biography *Marian Anderson: A Singer's Journey*, and Anderson's nephew, James DePreist, director of conducting and orchestral studies at The Juilliard School. Presley M. Wagoner, president general of the DAR, gave the welcome, and apologized again for the DAR's rebuff of Anderson in 1939. "Historically, [it] represents a sad chapter in our country's history and the history of the DAR," she said. "…I stand before you today wishing that history could be rewritten, but knowing that it cannot. I want to assure you that the DAR has learned from the past."

The Rev. Walter E. Fauntroy, pastor of the New Bethel Baptist Church, delivered the invocation. Mezzo-soprano Denyce Graves, who had sung at the inauguration of President George W. Bush a week earlier, sang two songs associated with Anderson. Angela Russell, anchorwoman and reporter for Washington ABC 7, WJLA-TV and News Channel 8, was master of ceremonies. Guests included sopranos Kathleen Battle, Matti Wilda and Brenda Jackson, as well as Jukka Valtasaari, the ambassador from Finland, where Anderson had experienced great early success.

The venue turned out to be inadequate for the crowd. It was the O'Byrne Gallery, a small room at the opposite end of the block-long DAR headquarters building from the 3,702-seat auditorium, which was locked. The room had seating for only 100 people; an overflow crowd watched the ceremony on a TV screen in the nearby library.

"I couldn't understand why the Postal Service agreed to such crowded conditions," wrote *Linn's Stamp News*' Washington correspondent, Bill McAllister. "Better to move the entire event to postal headquarters. At least there, people would not have been forced to stand through what became an elaborate 90-minute program.

"As it turned out, the stamp dedication was one of the most detailed first-day ceremonies I had ever seen in Washington, a wonderful blend of entertainment and education."

The choice of rooms had been the Postal Service's, not the DAR's, DAR representative Bren Landon told McAllister. They picked it "because they thought the room was more elegant, and they wanted a more intimate setting," he said. USPS spokeswoman Francis M. Frazier confirmed his statement. Postal officials had opted for the smaller room, she told McAllister, because they thought the auditorium was too big and that the acoustics in the lobby, where smaller events are held, were unsuitable.

Stamp Fulfillment Services offered its standard uncacheted first-day covers of the Anderson stamp for 75¢. It also sold what it called a "Marian Anderson illustrated envelope" with stamp and first-day cancellation that appeared to violate postal officials' assurances that USPS wouldn't produce cacheted first-day covers that would compete with those sold by commercial dealers.

The envelope "is undeniably a cacheted first-day cover," wrote Michael Baadke, editor of *Scott Stamp Monthly*, "with a stylish professional design and gradient tinted background that extends along the entire envelope. Along with three photographs of Anderson, … the cachet includes her name in uppercase orange lettering across the bottom of the envelope. One image of Anderson is repeated on the reverse of the envelope, which is also printed in gradient brown.

"The stamp is postmarked with the standard black pictorial first-day cancel used for the Anderson issue. It shows a facsimile of the singer's signature, the issue date and city, the words 'FIRST DAY OF ISSUE,' and a musical staff with four notes."

The cover was sold with a pane of 20 Anderson stamps, plus an individual insert card that fits into another new USPS product, the Black Heritage Cultural Diary. The package, called the "Marian Anderson Cultural Diary Page and Illustrated Envelope Set," sold for $12.95.

This is the Marian Anderson "illustrated envelope" that USPS offered for sale with a pane of Anderson stamps and an illustrated page to be inserted in a new product called "Cultural Diary: Expressions of African Americans."

37¢ RONALD REAGAN

Date of Issue: February 9, 2005

Catalog Number: Scott 3897

Colors: magenta, yellow, cyan, black

First-Day Cancel: Simi Valley, California

First-Day Cancellations: 541,210

Format: Panes of 20, horizontal, 4 across, 5 down. Gravure printing cylinders printing 360 stamps per revolution (30 across, 12 around) manufactured by Southern Graphics Systems. Also available in uncut press sheets of 6 panes (2 across, 3 down).

Gum Type: self-adhesive

Overall Stamp Size: 0.99 by 1.56 inches; 25.146 by 39.624 mm

Pane Size: 7.25 by 5.94 inches; 184.15 by 150.87 mm

Uncut Press Sheet Size: 11⅞ by 21¾ inches

Perforations: 10¾ (die-cut simulated perforations) (Comco Custom rotary die cutter)

Selvage Markings: "© 2004/USPS" ".37/x20/$7.40" "PLATE/POSITION" and diagram. Part of diagram is printed on die-cut teeth of center stamp in bottom row.

Back Markings: Universal Product Code (UPC) "457800" in 4 locations.

Illustrator: Michael Deas of Brooklyn Heights, New York

Designer and Art Director: Howard Paine of Delaplane, Virginia

Typographer: John Boyd of New York, New York

Modeler: Donald H. Woo of Sennett Security Products, Chantilly, Virginia

Stamp Manufacturing: Stamps printed for Sennett Security Products by American Packaging Corporation, Columbus, Wisconsin, on Champlain gravure press. Stamps finished by Unique Binders of Fredericksburg, Virginia.

Quantity Ordered: 170,000,000

Cylinder Number Detail: 1 set of 4 cylinder numbers preceded by the letter S in selvage above or below each corner stamp

Cylinder Number Combination Reported: S1111

Paper Supplier: Mactac

Tagging: phosphored paper

The Stamp

On February 9, the Postal Service issued a 37¢ stamp honoring Ronald Reagan, 40th president of the United States, who died June 5, 2004.

Presidents are exempted from the Citizens' Stamp Advisory Committee's rule that 10 years must elapse after a person's death before he or she can be honored on a stamp. Stamps for presidents are issued on or after their next birthday following their passing. February 6 would have been Reagan's 94th birthday.

The stamp was placed on sale nationwide. Simi Valley, California, site of the Ronald Reagan Presidential Library and Museum, was the official first-day city. Ceremonies also were held in Dixon, Illinois, which Reagan considered his hometown; Sacramento, California, the state capital, where he lived when he was California's governor; and Washington, D.C., where he served two terms as the nation's chief executive. First-day cancellations were available from all four cities and from Tampico, Illinois, Reagan's birthplace.

On June 16, 2004, 11 days after Reagan died, USPS announced plans to issue a stamp honoring him in 2005. The stamp's design was unveiled November 9 at the Reagan library by the president's widow, Nancy Reagan, and Postmaster General John E. "Jack" Potter. The date was the 15th anniversary of the fall of the Berlin Wall in 1989, an event that Reagan foresaw when he stood at the site in 1987 and directed a challenge to Mikhail Gorbachev, the leader of the Soviet Union: "Mr. Gorbachev, open this gate! Mr. Gorbachev, tear down this wall!"

The stamp was printed by the gravure process by American Packaging Corporation for Sennett Security Products and distributed in panes of 20. It also was available in uncut press sheets of six panes, which Stamp Fulfillment Services sold by mail at face value, $44.40. Its print order, 170 million, was unusually large for a commemorative stamp.

The issue produced an unprecedented constant vari-

A Ronald Reagan stamp, position 18 on a pane of 20, with a plate-position diagram tab attached, showing how the upper part of the diagram encroaches on the simulated perf teeth.

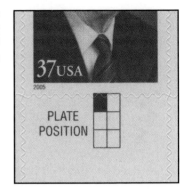

This enlargement of the bottom of a position 18 stamp shows the diagram encroachment in detail. The shading of the upper left box of the diagram indicates that the pane is from the upper left portion of the press sheet.

ety that was first reported February 9, only hours after the stamp went on sale nationwide, on the Virtual Stamp Club message board, located at www.virtualstampclub.com. On each pane, the center stamp in the bottom horizontal row — position 18 — shows a portion of the plate-position diagram in three of its die-cut simulated "teeth." Position diagrams have been printed in the selvage of U.S. stamps issued in pane format since 1992, but never before had a diagram encroached on the stamps themselves.

Postal officials figured out afterward what had happened, said Terrence McCaffrey, manager of stamp development for USPS. Dodge Color, which does the Postal Service's prepress work, makes a selvage template that includes a dummy plate-position diagram to guide the printer's placement of the actual diagram. The Reagan press plate was laid out two panes across by three panes down, resulting in a diagram that was deeper than the diagram on the template, and American Packaging Corporation failed to reposition or reduce it so that it would miss the die cuts of the stamp immediately above it. Officials at USPS checked and approved a proof of the pane, but because there were no die cuts on the proof, they didn't notice that the diagram was too close to the stamps.

On all plate-position diagrams, a single box is darkened to indicate the location of the pane on the plate. Thus, there are three subvarieties of the constant variety: left box dark, right box dark and neither box dark. One-twentieth of the total printing of 170 million stamps, or 8.5 million, will be a variety stamp. Of the 8.5 million, about 1.42 million will have the dark die-cut teeth on the left side, another 1.42 million will have the dark teeth on the right, and the balance of about 5.7 million will have no shading in the portion of the pane-position diagram that shows on the teeth.

The 2006 Scott *Specialized Catalogue of U.S. Stamps &*

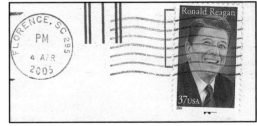

Shown here is a used example of the Reagan variety, mailed in April 2005.

Covers took note of the existence of the variety in its Reagan stamp listing, but didn't assign a minor number to it.

Reagan was born February 6, 1911, in a second-floor apartment in Tampico, a small town in northwest Illinois, to Nelle Wilson and John Edward "Jack" Reagan. An older brother, Neil "Moon" Reagan, was born in 1908. His father nicknamed Ronald "Dutch" because, he said, he "looked like a fat little Dutchman."

The family settled in Dixon, Illinois, in 1920. In 1928, Reagan graduated from Dixon High School, where he played football, basketball and track, acted in plays and was student body president. He also was student body president at little Eureka, Illinois, College, from which he graduated in 1932.

After holding sports broadcasting jobs in Iowa, Reagan took a screen test in Los Angeles that led to a seven-year contract with Warner Bros. His early films included *Brother Rat* (1938), *Dark Victory* (1940) and *Knute Rockne — All-American* (1940), in which he played the legendary Notre Dame halfback George Gipp and acquired a lifelong nickname, "The Gipper." He married actress Jane Wyman in 1940; their daughter Maureen was born the following year, and adopted son Michael was born in 1945. The marriage ended in divorce in 1949. Three years later, Reagan married another actress, Nancy Davis. Their two children, Patricia and Ronald Prescott, were born in 1952 and 1958, respectively.

World War II put Reagan's acting career on hold. In 1942, as a second lieutenant in the Army, he was assigned to the 1st Motion Picture Unit in Culver City, California, where he made more than 400 training films for pilots during the next three years. Reagan was discharged from the Army as a captain in 1945.

Reagan appeared in more than 50 films in his career. He was president of the Screen Actors Guild during 1947-1952 and 1959-1960, and worked to purge communist sympathizers from the film industry. During the 1950s, his concern over the growing geopolitical influence of communism caused him to move away from his long-time allegiance to the Democratic Party, and in 1962 he switched his registration to Republican.

Meanwhile, as a spokesman for the General Electric Company, Reagan toured the country giving motivational speeches to GE employees. He rose to national political prominence during Republican Barry Goldwater's unsuccessful presidential bid in 1964. Two years later, in 1966, he was elected governor of California, defeating incumbent Edmund G. "Pat" Brown in a landslide. Reagan won re-election in 1970 and left office in 1975.

Later that year, he announced his candidacy for the 1976 Republican presidential nomination against the Republican president, Gerald Ford. He lost, but his vigorous activity in the ensuing campaign laid a firm foundation for his successful run in the GOP presidential primaries in 1980. In the general election, he defeated Democratic President Jimmy Carter by some 8.4 million votes.

On March 31, 1981, Reagan was wounded in an assassination attempt. He fully recovered and served two terms, winning re-election in 1984 by some 16.8 million votes over Democrat Walter Mondale.

In the White House, he championed less government intervention in solving social problems, eased restrictions on business through free-market reforms, cut taxes and signed a comprehensive tax reform bill. During his presidency, the United States and the Soviet Union engaged in an intense arms race, which historians believe strained the Soviet economy and contributed to the U.S. victory in the Cold War. Despite Reagan's hatred of communism and his 1983 characterization of the USSR as "an evil empire," he developed a cordial personal relationship with the Soviets' reform leader, General Secretary Gorbachev, who would oversee a bloodless collapse of his country's communist regime after Reagan left office.

In 1994, almost six years after his departure from the White House, Reagan announced that he had been diagnosed with Alzheimer's disease. In a poignant letter to his fellow Americans written November 5, 1994, he wrote: "I now begin the journey that will lead me into the sunset of my life. I know that for America there will always be a bright dawn ahead." He remained mostly out of sight of the public during the decade in which the disease followed its inevitable course, and on June 6, 2004, he died of pneumonia.

His body lay in state in the rotunda of the U.S. Capitol in Washington, D.C., before the national funeral service, which was held in the National Cathedral June 11, 2004. The body then was taken to the Reagan library in Simi Valley for burial.

The Design

In the early 1990s, Terrence McCaffrey, then in charge of stamp design for USPS, asked his art directors to prepare stamps bearing the portraits of all the then-living presidents for possible issuance on short notice. Artist Daniel Schwartz was commissioned to paint Richard Nixon, and, on April 22, 1994, shortly after the artwork was completed, Nixon died. Schwartz made some minor changes in the painting requested by the late president's daughters, Tricia Nixon Cox and Julie Nixon Eisenhower, and the stamp was issued April 26, 1995.

Nearly 10 years elapsed before the next stamp, for Reagan, was required. This time it took several tries before USPS settled on the portrait that would be used on the stamp.

Two artists, Bill Nelson and Henry C. Casselli, made paintings in 1998 that art director Howard Paine developed into horizontal and vertical stamp designs, but these were turned down. Casselli's image was a "soft focus" one; Nelson, of Richmond, Virginia, who had illustrated the 1996 Big Band Leaders set in the Legends of American Music series, depicted a broadly smiling president.

Howard Paine made these horizontal layouts in 1998, using portraits made by Bill Nelson (left) and Henry C. Casselli. He also incorporated the portraits in vertical layouts. Both were deemed unsatisfactory; Nelson's painting of a broadly smiling Reagan was characterized by two former Reagan press aides as too "cartoonish."

Postal officials and CSAC liked the Nelson portrait, recalled McCaffrey. However, he said, "We shared it with Larry Speakes [a former Reagan press secretary] and Mark Weinberg [an assistant to Speakes]. Both knew the Reagan family, and both said, 'No, Mrs. Reagan would not like this. He looks too "cartoonish".' "

Next, Paine turned to an existing portrait by Daniel Schwartz, the illustrator of the Nixon stamp. For artistic effect, Schwartz had left a portion of Reagan's face, hair and one ear uncolored. "Daniel had done it years ago for a magazine and used it in his promotional literature," Paine said. "It's a light, sketchy thing. I loved it. I thought it would make a great stamp."

Weinberg, in a memo, told McCaffrey that the Schwartz portrait was "more in the right direction" than the Nelson portrait. However, he added, the painting had "too many lines near the eyes. Coloring is off — too much white on top and too much red on bottom of face."

Postal officials asked Schwartz to fill in the unpainted areas, and he did so, with reluctance. Further refinements were made by Dodge Color, the Postal Service's prepress-work contractor, which electronically softened

Shown here are stamp layouts incorporating two versions of an existing portrait of Reagan by Daniel Schwartz. On the left is the original, in which Schwartz left part of Reagan's face, hair and an ear unshaded for artistic effect, and a later version, after Schwartz had filled in the unpainted areas and the texture of the face had been electronically softened and smoothed.

At Nancy Reagan's request, Michael Deas based his painting of President Reagan that was shown on the stamp on this photograph made in 1981 by White House photographer Jack Kightlinger. In the painting, Deas changed Reagan's costume from an open-necked flannel shirt and denim jacket to a "presidential" blue suit and red and blue striped tie.

and evened out Reagan's complexion. Nevertheless, when Nancy Reagan ultimately saw the artwork after her husband's death, she was dissatisfied.

The widow relayed word through Reagan Foundation officials that she would prefer that the stamp be based on an altogether different image: a photograph that hangs in the conference room of the Reagan Foundation headquarters. The photo, of a smiling Ronald Reagan, was taken in 1981 by White House photographer Jack Kightlinger, and showed the president in an open-necked flannel shirt and denim jacket such as he frequently wore when at his ranch in Santa Barbara County, California.

"We liked the pose, but we felt it was too casual a portrait for a presidential stamp," McCaffrey said. "We said, 'We'll have to put a suit on him,' and they said, 'That's fine.' "

McCaffrey and Paine decided to call in yet another artist to translate the Kightlinger photograph into a painting. He was Michael Deas, one of the Postal Service's most reliable portraitists, whose stamp subjects have included numerous honorees in the Legends of Hollywood and Literary Arts series and, most recently, Meriwether Lewis and William Clark in 2004.

Deas, a perfectionist, tends to work slowly, and he uses oil paints, which require extra drying time. Time was short, however; it now was August 1, 2004, barely six months before the stamp's scheduled issue. After Paine asked Deas to deliver the finished painting in a month, Deas eliminated the usual color-sketch stage and went directly to finished art, and "I got it in a month and a day," Paine said.

"In fact, Michael did a second painting, 'while waiting for the first one to dry,' he said," Paine added. "The second one was based on a differ-

In addition to the painting depicted on the issued stamp, artist Michael Deas created a second painting of Reagan, using a different photograph as his source and showing the late president in a pensive mood. Howard Paine used it to create stamp designs in vertical commemorative, square and semijumbo formats. The latter is shown here.

ent photograph, showing Reagan with his hand to his chin. I had Dodge Color make proofs of both of them." Not surprisingly, CSAC approved the design with the pose Nancy Reagan had requested.

In Deas' portrait, Reagan wears a white shirt, red-and-blue striped tie and dark blue suit, all of which the artist copied from yet another photograph of the former president. Paine adapted it to fit a vertical commemorative-size stamp, and typographer John Boyd added the words "Ronald Reagan" across the top and "37 USA" in the lower left corner in dropout white Galliard type.

"We knew instantly that we had a winner," McCaffrey said. While in California in September 2004 for the first-day ceremony of the 37¢ John Wayne Legends of Hollywood stamp, he showed the Reagan design to Joanne Drake, the late president's chief of staff and a spokesperson for his family, and Duke Blackwood, executive director of the Ronald Reagan Presidential Library. They endorsed it with enthusiasm.

Nancy Reagan seemed to agree. At the design's unveiling, she said: "The stamp really captures Ronnie's humor and optimism, and I hope the American people will like it as much as I do." At her request, the Postal Service sent Deas' painting to Simi Valley, California, to be displayed at the Reagan Library.

First-Day Facts

The major event of the Reagan stamp's first day of issue was the Washington, D.C., ceremony, held at the Ronald Reagan Building and International Trade Center at 1300 Pennsylvania Avenue. Its cost to the Postal Service was $74,794.50, according to *Linn's Stamp News*, which had filed a Freedom of Information Act request for the amount. This sum paid in part for a reception for about 800 postal officials, members of Congress and other guests.

USPS officials who participated in the ceremony were James Miller, chairman of the Board of Governors, who dedicated the stamp, and Postmaster General Potter. Miller had been President Reagan's Federal Trade Commission chairman and director of the Office of Management and

Budget. Both men cited the thousands of handwritten letters Reagan wrote during his lifetime, with Ryan suggesting that "the Great Communicator" should also be known as "the Great Correspondent."

Edwin Meese 3d, who was President Reagan's chief policy adviser and later his attorney general, was master of ceremonies. Speakers were Kenneth M. Duberstein, who was Reagan's last presidential chief of staff; Frederick J. Ryan, chairman of the Ronald Reagan Presidential Library Foundation; Senator Ted Stevens, Republican of Alaska; Representative Danny K. Davis, Democrat of Illinois; and Andrew Card, chief of staff to President George W. Bush and a former Reagan administration official.

At the Simi Valley ceremony, William J. Brown, USPS vice president for Southeast Area operations, dedicated the stamp. The speaker was Thomas McClintock, California state senator from the 19th senatorial district. RoseMarie Calabrese-Fernandez, manager of the Sacramento Customer Service District for USPS, was master of ceremonies.

The Sacramento dedication ceremony was held on the west steps of the state capitol. In Dixon, Illinois, a ceremony was held at the Dixon Historic Center, which is the former Dixon High School that Reagan attended.

The first-day cancellations from Washington, Sacramento and Dixon contained a replica of Reagan's signature and the inscription "First Day of Sale." In Tampico, Illinois, where a special event was held at a bank restored to look as it did in 1991, Postmaster Judy Jacobson arranged to have a February 9 postmark made bearing the words "Birthplace Station." A museum adjacent to the bank has a large amount of Reagan memorabilia.

The earliest known pre-release use of a Reagan stamp was on a cover with a machine postmark from Los Angeles/Hollywood, California, dated February 8, 2005, one day before the official first day of sale.

This first-day cover bears postmarks from Tampico, Illinois, Reagan's birthplace, and Dixon, Illinois, his hometown. (Cover courtesy of Steven J. Bahnsen)

37¢ NORTHEAST DECIDUOUS FOREST (10 DESIGNS) NATURE OF AMERICA SERIES

Date of Issue: March 3, 2005

Catalog Numbers: Scott 3899, pane of 10; 3899a-3899j, stamps

Colors: yellow, magenta, cyan, black, brown (PMS 1805), green (PMS 5635)

First-Day Cancel: New York, New York

First-Day Cancellations: 235,593 (includes Garden Bouquet stamped stationery)

Format: Pane of 10, vertical and horizontal. Gravure printing cylinders printing 80 subjects per revolution, 2 panes across, 4 panes around, manufactured by Keating Gravure. Also sold in uncut press sheets of 8 panes (1 across by 2 down).

Gum Type: self-adhesive

Stamp Size: horizontal stamps, 1.56 by 1.225 inches (39.624 by 31.115 mm); vertical stamps, dimensions reversed

Pane Size: 9.125 by 6.75 inches (231.775 by 171.45 mm)

Uncut Press Sheet Size: 36¼ by 14¼ inches

Perforations: 10¾ (die-cut simulated perforations) (Comco Commander rotary die cutter)

Selvage Inscription: "NORTHEAST DECIDUOUS FOREST/SEVENTH IN A SERIES" "NATURE OF AMERICA"

Liner Back Markings: "NORTHEAST DECIDUOUS FOREST/Trees that shed their leaves each fall typify the deciduous/forests of the northeastern United States. In autumn their/vivid colors give these woodlands a unique beauty. The/region's temperate climate, with four distinct seasons and/ample precipitation, supports a complex forest community/of plants and animals./Mature forests have layers: a canopy of tall trees, an/understory of shorter trees, a shrub layer, an herb layer of/wildflowers and ferns, and a litter layer of decomposing/leaves and wood on the forest floor. This layering, called/stratification, allows a variety of plants to share the same/habitat. It also provides distinct niches for wildlife, as/different animal species forage and find shelter at each/level. Wild turkeys and ovenbirds feed and nest on the/ground. White-tailed deer browse among the herbs and/shrubs. In the canopy, red-shouldered hawks hunt from/exposed branches, while nocturnal red bats roost in/dense foliage."

Numbered illustration. "1. Northern Red Oak/Quercus rubra/2. Eastern Buck-moth/Hemileuca maia/3. Christmas Fern/Polystichum acrostichoides/4. Partridgeberry/Mitchella repens/5. Eastern Hemlock/Tsuga canadensis/6. Common Polypody/Polypodium polypodioides/7. Long-tailed Weasel/Mustela frenata/8. Ovenbird/Seiurus autocapillus/9. Eastern White Pine/Pinus strobus/10. Canada Mayflower/Maianthemum canadense/11. Red Eft (Eastern Newt)/Notophthalmus viridescens/12. American Beech/Fagus grandifolia/13. White-tailed Deer/Odocoileus virginianus/14. Honey Mushroom/Armillaria melea/15. Red Maple/Acer rubrum/16. Paper Birch/Betula papyrifera/17. Ground Pine/Lycopodium obscurum/18. Red-shouldered Hawk/Buteo lineatus/19. Eastern Chipmunk/Tamias striatus/20. Spinulose Woodfern/Dryopteris carthusiana/21. Wild Turkey/Meleagris gallopavo/22. Chicken Mushroom/Laetiporus sulphureus/23. Sugar Maple/Acer saccharum/24. Black Bear/Ursus americanus/25. American Chestnut sprouts/Castanea dentata/26. Eastern Red Bat/Lasiurus borealis/27. White Wood Aster/Aster divaricatus"

"©2004 USPS/NATURE OF AMERICA/THIS SERIES OF STAMPS FEATURES THE BEAUTY AND COMPLEXITY OF PLANT AND ANIMAL COMMUNITIES IN THE UNITED STATES." Universal Product Code (UPC) "459000."

Illustrator: John Dawson of Hilo, Hawaii

Designer, Typographer and Art Director: Ethel Kessler of Bethesda, Maryland

Stamp Manufacturing: Stamps printed by Avery Dennison Security Printing Division, Clinton, South Carolina, on a Dia Nippon Kiko gravure press. Stamps finished by Avery Dennison.

Quantity Ordered: 55,600,000 stamps

Plate Number Detail: no plate numbers

Paper Supplier: Fasson Division of Avery Dennison

Tagging: unphosphored paper, block tagging over stamps

The Stamps

On March 3, the Postal Service issued a pane of 10 commemoratives depicting the flora and fauna of a Northeast deciduous forest. The pane was the seventh in an annual series called "Nature of America" that features different biomes, or major ecological communities.

Like its predecessors, the pane displays a colorful murallike picture containing 10 self-adhesive, die-cut stamps that form part of the mural and can be peeled out of it. The stamps are laid out in a staggered fashion to correspond to the location of their subjects in the overall illustration. On this pane, one stamp stands alone, while each of the remaining nine stamps partially abuts at least one other stamp.

Each stamp has a design that bleeds off the tips of the simulated perforations and depicts at least one identifiable species native to a deciduous forest in the Northeastern United States. The only typography on each stamp is "USA 37" in two lines of dropout white Eras type (which helps the user locate the stamp on the pane) and the tiny 2005 year date in black in the lower left corner.

The stamps are semijumbo in size. Four are vertically oriented and six are horizontal. At no point on the pane does the die cutting run to the edges, and there are no cuts in the backing paper, which makes it somewhat difficult to extract individual stamps. The pane has no plate numbers.

The paper is unphosphored. Tagging was applied on press and covers each stamp, extending just beyond the tips of the die-cut simulated perfs.

As with the previous panes, the back of the liner displays an outline drawing of the scene on the front, with the species numbered and keyed to a list giving their common and scientific names.

Each of the Nature of America panes has been offered to collectors in uncut press sheets at face value through Stamp Fulfillment Services. The price of a press sheet of eight Northeast Deciduous Forest panes was $29.60.

For uniformity, it was decided that the entire series would be created by the same design team: illustrator John Dawson of Hilo, Hawaii, and Ethel Kessler, a Postal Service art director, designer and typographer. However, different printers and printing methods have been used. The Northeast

Deciduous Forest pane was printed by the gravure process by Avery Dennison Security Printing Division.

USPS ordered only 5.56 million panes, or 55.6 million stamps, the smallest print order for any pane in the Nature of America series. Previous printings have ranged from 100 million stamps for the first two panes, Sonoran Desert and Pacific Rain Forest, to 60 million for Arctic Tundra, the fifth in the series.

Postal officials originally had planned to issue six panes, with no underwater biome included. Later, they decided there were enough subjects, and sufficient marketing potential, for the series to be expanded to 12 panes, with a Pacific coral reef as one of the biomes. When the Citizens' Stamp Advisory Committee saw John Dawson's sketch for the latter pane, it asked him to put aside the nearly completed artwork for the Northeast Deciduous Forest pane — which had been scheduled for issuance in 2004 — and proceed to finished art on Pacific Coral Reef. The latter became part of the 2004 stamp program, and Northeast Deciduous Forest was pushed back to 2005.

Some of the species depicted in each Dawson painting lie outside the borders of the 10 stamps. When the stamps are removed, these species remain behind in the large selvage, which covers a total area of approximately 43 square inches, more than twice the approximately 19 square inches accounted for by the stamps. That ratio has remained constant through the series.

At the time the Sonoran Desert pane was issued in 1999, Terrence McCaffrey, manager of stamp development for USPS, acknowledged that there is "waste within the illustration area, but we felt it was a good trade-off." The alternative, he said, would have been to create five more stamps within the mural for a total of 15. Limiting the number of stamps on a pane to 10 prevents a large stamp program from becoming even larger.

In all, 27 species of wildlife are identified in the key on the back of the Northeast Deciduous Forest pane. The stamps and the species that appear on them in whole or part are (starting at the upper left): Scott 3899a (vertical), Eastern buckmoth, Northern red oak, Eastern hemlock; 3899b (horizontal), red-shouldered hawk, paper birch, red maple; 3899c (horizontal), Eastern red bat, sugar maple; 3899d (horizontal), white-tailed deer, American beech, red maple, Eastern white pine; 3899e (horizontal), black bear, American chestnut sprouts; 3899f (vertical), long-tailed weasel, common polypody; 3899g (vertical), wild turkey, paper birch; 3899h (vertical), ovenbird, Christmas fern, partridgeberry; 3899i (horizontal), red eft or Eastern newt, Canada mayflower, honey mushroom; 3899j (horizontal),

A large amount of John Dawson's illustration remains after the 10 stamps are removed from the pane.

Eastern chipmunk, spinulose woodfern, chicken mushroom, ground pine. Of the identified species, only the white wood aster, in the lower right corner of the picture, does not appear in whole or in part on any stamp.

Visible in the distance on the selvage portion, although not identified in the key, are a beaver swimming in the pond near its lodge and three swimming waterfowl.

To accompany the pane, John Dawson prepared a 24-page artist's sketchbook of text and drawings. Each two-page spread in the book is devoted to one of the 10 stamps on the pane and contains pencil and color sketches made by the artist before executing the finished painting for that stamp, along with his handwritten notes. With a pane of stamps included, the sketchbook was sold by the Postal Service for $14.95.

The Designs

John Dawson is a veteran wildlife and nature artist whose U.S. stamp credits, besides the first six Nature of America panes, include the Cats block of four of 1988, the Idaho Statehood commemorative of 1990 and the four Flowering Trees stamps of 1997. He paints with acrylics.

The Nature of America assignments call for him to crowd a large amount of detail into a relatively small space (8¾ by 5⅝ inches on the issued pane). The need to include flora and fauna of widely varying sizes requires that he position the small creatures in the foreground and the large ones in the distance, making their apparent size the same.

As the series has progressed, the design team has kept track of the various species of animals and plants that have been depicted to ensure against too much duplication of types that are native to more than one biome. The designers' aim is to show species whose principal habitat is the ecological community being portrayed.

PhotoAssist, the Postal Service's research firm, hired two experts from the Harvard Forest as consultants for the Northeast Deciduous Forest project: David Foster, the director, and Betsy Colburn, an aquatic ecologist. The Harvard Forest, a 3,000-acre ecological laboratory and classroom near Petersham in central Massachusetts that is operated by Harvard University, was chosen as a representative woodland for the purpose of designing the pane.

An exchange of correspondence between PhotoAssist's Carol Highsaw and the Postal Service's consultants that spanned 16 months is quoted over the next few pages as testimony to the commitment of the design team and the researchers to pictorial and textual accuracy.

One of the experts' initial recommendations was that the pane show a scene in late August, "which would allow the red maples … to be red or turning but the oaks and other deciduous trees would still be green. Shrubs … would also be turning purplish to provide additional color." The first week in October, when the foliage would be at its peak, would be too late for many of the species that ought to be shown, they said in a joint memorandum.

Shown here are some of John Dawson's pencil sketches from The Artist's Sketchbook: Northeast Deciduous Forest, *which the Postal Service offered as an ancillary product with the Northeast Deciduous Forest stamps. The sketches were among many made by Dawson before creating the finished acrylic painting reproduced on the pane.*

This is John Dawson's first pencil sketch for the Northeast Deciduous Forest pane, dated May 24, 2001. With its cutaway view of a beaver pond, it presents an altogether different scene from that on the finished painting. Among the creatures shown here but not featured on the issued pane of stamps are the beaver at the left, the great blue heron in flight, the wood duck swimming on the pond, the flock of red-winged blackbirds in the distance, the moose at right center, and, below the water's surface, pumpkinseed sunfish, a bullfrog and a pickerel.

Dawson's first pencil sketch for the Northeast Deciduous Forest pane, dated May 24, 2001, differs extensively from the finished product. In it, a beaver pond, rather than the forest floor, dominates the scene. The pond is cut away in the foreground to show fish, a bullfrog and other subterranean life below the surface; Dawson had provided a similar cutaway view of a stream in his painting for the second pane in the series, Pacific Rain Forest. Prominent in the Northeast Deciduous Forest sketch are a moose, a water snake, a great blue heron, a wood duck and a flock of red-winged blackbirds in flight, none of which remained in the final painting.

Foster and Colburn questioned this design approach. "The entire scene has more the appearance of a pool in the woods, e.g. a vernal pool or small beaver pond, than a larger water body that would be expected to support pickerel and larger fish species," they wrote. "There was also a question as to whether there was too much emphasis on the water as opposed to the forest, especially since beaver ponds occur across North America." For a better balance among forest, wetland and water, they suggested that the pond be moved to one side or to the rear, with the viewer looking at it through the woods.

This later color sketch shows an arrangement and selection of plants and animals that is much closer to that on the issued pane. The focus now is on the forest itself, and the beaver pond has been moved to the background of the picture. Before creating his final painting, Dawson made numerous additional changes based on the consultants' recommendations. He reduced the size of the boulder at left rear, replaced the millipede near the bottom of the picture on the left side with a red eft and made significant alterations to the white-tailed deer (reversing its direction), black bear, ovenbird, red bat and much of the vegetation.

Dawson followed their recommendation, abandoned the cutaway view of the pond and placed the body of water behind the forest. That meant eliminating several of the flora and fauna shown in the cutaway, including a water arum, water lily, pickerel, water boatman (an aquatic bug), pumpkinseed sunfish, golden shiner, bullfrog and water snake. Dawson also replaced some of the other species shown in his first sketch, closely following the specific recommendations of the consultants.

He dropped the wood duck, red-winged blackbirds and great blue heron, which are wetland birds and widely distributed. He added the ovenbird and wild turkey, which the consultants called "signature species" of the deciduous forest; the red-shouldered hawk, another deciduous-forest breeder; the weasel; the buckmoth; and the white wood aster. He replaced the moose with the white-tailed deer, even though the deer has become common in much of the Eastern United States.

The consultants suggested that showing acorns on the oaks "would better characterize this species' fall appearance and would highlight an important linkage between the trees and animals: acorns as an important food source for forest wildlife." Dawson complied. On their recommendation, he also added American beech and paper birch trees to his painting, bringing the number of tree species depicted to seven.

In October 2001, the consultants reviewed Dawson's color sketch with his revised layout.

"They like the new design very much," Carol Highsaw wrote in a memorandum to Dawson and Ethel Kessler. "They said that it achieves good balance between the forest and pond. It 'looks quite natural and is effective in showing the forest and the pond in nice perspective.' The overall depiction of the forest is excellent. There is no problem with the placement of the species in relation to one another. All the species depicted could be present in this setting in late August.

"They like the pond, but they want to know: (1) what the purple plant is along the shore; (2) what the grassy things are above the deer's antlers; and (3) if there are cattails near the beaver lodge. (If so, they should have shorter heads.)

"They like the closer boulder in the woods, but the larger boulder at the shore is too conspicuous and large; they suggest eliminating it and just running the shore off to the left.

"The American chestnut leaves are too small.

"The white pine looks like a fir. They suggest changing it to a hemlock and making a small tree by the edge of the pond (left of the deer) a white pine.

"The bark of the paper birch should be a bit whiter. Change the largest birch to an American beech (smooth gray bark).

"The leaves of the red maple should be more crimson and less orange.

"The leaves of the sugar maple should be arranged in opposite pairs on the twigs. The leaf shape is too stocky and the leaves are too leathery looking. Look at a Canadian flag for shape.

"Change the Canada mayflower to the common form and put two to four of them on the ground; they tend to occur in groups.

"The treeclub moss is too large; shrink it by 50 percent. Use ground pine for the common name.

"The northern red oak, partridgeberry, wood aster, Christmas fern, rock polypody, wood fern, chicken mushroom and honey mushroom look fine. Use spinulose woodfern as the common name and Dryopteris carthusiana as the Latin name for the woodfern.

"It might be too difficult to illustrate the eastern buckmoth laying eggs (as the artist had wanted to show).

"The millipede is about five times too large and wouldn't be seen on the ground surface. They suggest replacing it with a red eft, which would be about the size of the millipede in the sketch. Including a red eft would also add an amphibian to the artwork.

"All the birds look fine. The ground under the wild turkey should look like plants, leaves or humus.

"The wake behind the swimming beaver should be V-shaped, not U-shaped. Only the nose and top of the beaver's head should show above the surface of the water. The [beaver] lodge is fine.

"Make the black bear beefier — in fall, even a small bear would be fairly hefty.

"Make the long-tailed weasel a bit skinnier.

"The red bat is out of scale with the maple leaves and the other animals in the foreground. It also stands out more prominently than it would in nature. The red bat is well hidden, generally, when roosting, with its wings well drawn in to the body and the head tucked in, so that overall it looks like a two- to three-inch dead leaf hanging off a branch. It is good to include the red bat, because it is unique among our bat species in its habit of roosting in trees. The artist did a good job of showing that a roosting red bat usually hangs by one foot.

"The Eastern chipmunk and white-tailed deer look fine."

Dawson made each of the recommended changes, including replacing the millipede at the bottom of his color sketch with the red eft. He also added a female buckmoth laying her eggs on a red oak twig in the upper left corner.

The consultants had been puzzled by a purple plant along the shoreline in Dawson's color sketch. In a follow-up memo, Highsaw informed them that the plant was meant to be a highbush blueberry, which they had suggested that Dawson include for an added dash of color. To this, Colburn commented that the plants "looked pretty airy to us, more as though they were purple loosestrife or some late-flowering herbaceous plant." "Maybe a patch or two, instead of being so densely placed along the shoreline, and a bit more reddish tone, instead of the strong purple in the sketch, would help," she added. Dawson made appropriate changes. (The plant, which can be found to the right of the white-tailed deer on the finished pane, is not identified in the key on the back.)

Later, when the consultants saw Dawson's final color sketch, Colburn initiated a lengthy discussion of the relationship between two of the creatures, the ovenbird and the red eft.

"The change in the ovenbird to have it looking at the eft now has the ovenbird looking like a slightly short-billed woodcock or some other kind of partridgelike bird," she wrote. "Before, it looked like a thrush, which is what it is …

"The things that caught my eye immediately were the bill shape and size relative to the head, and a subtle but clear increase in chunkiness. The pose looking at the eft is not natural — its head would be slightly cocked, to provide the bird with more of a 3-D perspective on the eft. (Think of a robin checking out something on the ground.

"Also, a bird that was looking 'threateningly' at a red eft (which is unlikely; red efts are unpalatable) would not just be sitting quietly on the ground, but rather would be in a much more active stance. (Again, think

The Postal Service's consultants disagreed among themselves over the way the ovenbird is shown and the "writhing posture" of the red eft in Dawson's final painting. One consultant felt that the eft would not be in a defensive mode because the species is inedible to birds and in no danger of being eaten. Others found no inaccuracies in the bird's appearance and the eft's contorted position, and their opinions carried the day. Despite the extended discussion of the two creatures' relationship to each other, they do not appear on the same stamp, but are on adjacent stamps.

of a robin preparing to spear a worm.)"

To resolve the question, Highsaw consulted two additional experts: one on birds, the other on efts.

Gary R. Graves, an ornithologist with the Smithsonian Institution's National Museum of Natural History, agreed that the ovenbird's bill "should be subtly thinner and more curved," but added, "The body shape is fine.

"I think part of the problem is perspective. The ovenbird is supposed to be in the foreground, but it still looks a bit too large in comparison to the surrounding plants (Christmas fern) and the eft. That might be what prompted the 'short-billed woodcock' comment from the consultant … I would reduce the size of the ovenbird by 10 to 15 percent, keeping the eft and fern at the current size."

Highsaw asked Graves whether ovenbirds do in fact cock their heads, like robins, when looking at potential prey, and whether the bird should be shown looking at the eft or at the viewer.

"Ovenbirds (with their good peripheral vision) do not often cock their heads," the ornithologist replied. "Most prey items are picked off the leaf litter and from low-growing vegetation. Robins do the head-cocking to listen for worms at or near the surface.

"Is the ovenbird supposed to be looking at the eft? Efts (larval newts) are not dietary items of ground-foraging songbirds. Eft skin is loaded with toxins. I suspect that a foraging ovenbird would largely ignore a brightly colored eft. So the posture of the ovenbird is probably best left as it is."

Highsaw's other specialist was Edmund D. Brodie Jr., a herpetologist at Utah State University who has extensively researched the toxicity of newts. She wrote to him: "Because the red eft is unpalatable, the ovenbird probably would avoid eating it. However, John [Dawson] and I think the eft might display defensively, even though the ovenbird is an unlikely predator. What do you think? Is this posture appropriate in this context or should John change it?"

"No question the ovenbird would avoid eating the eft," Brodie replied. "The eft, however, would posture to the presence of the bird. The posture is variable in efts — the one John has used is fully appropriate …

"I see no basis to question the proximity of the bird and the eft behavior."

Nevertheless, Colburn, who first raised the issue, continued to find this portion of the painting unsatisfactory. "The beak and turned head [of the ovenbird] still don't look really right to me," she wrote to Highsaw in September 2002. "It was much better in the earlier, small color picture, when the bird's head was in profile and the beak was long and slender. The curve at the top of the beak is too great in the painting."

As for the eft, it "really needs to be redone," she continued. "The shininess, color, pattern and stance are all wrong for this animal … I have never seen a red eft in the contorted position depicted here unless it had been stepped on or had been picked up/turned over and was writhing to right itself.

"They don't usually need to worry about predators — they are toxic and taste bad, and their bright color advertises the fact! The writhing posture in front of the ovenbird is too contrived and unnatural. I strongly recommend having the eft crawling along on the ground, perhaps with its head raised slightly and looking around, and maybe with the body curved slightly (as if changing direction), but not contorted as in the painting. My opinion, respectfully, is that it would be better artistically as well as more true to nature."

Highsaw agreed to consult the two specialists one last time. Neither saw a need for major changes.

Graves, the ornithologist, said the size of the ovenbird vis-à-vis the fern and eft were "OK" and the beak size and curvature were "acceptable." Brodie, the herpetologist, decreed the eft's posture to be "appropriate" for an encounter with "a predator, e.g., the bird." That was good enough for the design team, and no further revisions in the painting were made.

Ironically, after all the debate about the visual relationship of the ovenbird and the eft, the two creatures don't even share the same stamp, but are on adjacent stamps.

On the pane, Dawson's illustration is framed in white, with a colored stripe along the top edge. Above the picture, in a typeface called Didot, is the inscription "NORTHEAST DECIDUOUS FOREST." "SEVENTH IN A SERIES," in the upper right corner, and "NATURE OF AMERICA," across the bottom, are smaller and set in Eras type.

On each pane in the series, the marginal inscriptions and top stripe are printed in colors that complement the colors of the pane illustration. For Northeast Deciduous Forest, Avery Dennison used reddish brown (PMS 1805) ink for the stripe and larger inscriptions and green (PMS 5635) for the small type. The illustration itself was printed in the four standard process colors.

First-Day Facts

The Northeast Deciduous Forest pane was issued in a ceremony at the American Stamp Dealers Association's New York Postage Stamp Mega-Event in Madison Square Garden, Manhattan. Henry A. Pankey, USPS vice president for emergency preparedness, was the dedicating official.

Speakers were John Dawson, the illustrator of the Nature of America series, and Robert K. Davies, director of lands and forest/New York state forester. David E. Failor, executive director for Stamp Services, was master of ceremonies. Honored guests were Robert E. Lamb, executive director of the American Philatelic Society, and Vinnie Malloy, district manager/postmaster for the Postal Service's New York District.

For a limited time, Stamp Fulfillment Services sold uncacheted first-day covers of the full pane for $6.20.

Three of the stamp varieties are known to have been sold and used before the March 3 release date. The red-shouldered hawk, red eft and Eastern chipmunk stamps exist on covers with March 1 postmarks.

37¢ SPRING FLOWERS (4 DESIGNS)
DOUBLE-SIDED CONVERTIBLE BOOKLET OF 20

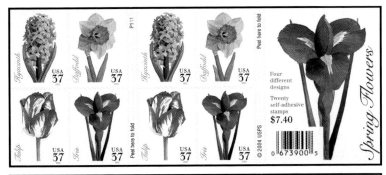

Date of Issue: March 15, 2005

Catalog Number: Scott 3900-3903, stamps; 3903a, block of 4; 3903b, convertible booklet of 20

Colors: black, cyan, magenta, yellow

First-Day Cancel: Chicago, Illinois

First-Day Cancellations: 191,201

Format: Convertible booklet pane of 20, vertical, arranged horizontally. Stamps on both sides, 8 (4 across by 2 down) plus label (booklet cover) on one side, 12 (6 across by 2 down) on other side, with vertical peel-off strips between blocks of 4 on each side. Offset printing plates printing 880 stamps per revolution.

Gum Type: self-adhesive

Overall Stamp Size: 0.91 by 1.19 inches; 23.114 by 30.226 mm

Pane Size: 5.76 by 2.38 inches; 146.304 by 60.452 mm

Perforations: 10¾ (die-cut simulated perforations), IDC custom rotary die-cutter. Backing paper rouletted behind peel-off strips.

Selvage Markings: "Peel here to fold" and plate numbers on 2 peel-off strips and "© 2004 USPS" "Peel here to fold" on other 2 peel-off strips

Back Markings: "Spring Flowers/Four/different/designs/Twenty/self-adhesive/stamps/$7.40" and Universal Product Code (UPC) "0 673900 5" on booklet cover

Illustrator and Typographer: Christopher Pullman of Cambridge, Massachusetts

Designer and Art Director: Derry Noyes of Washington, D.C.

Modeler: Joseph Sheeran of Ashton-Potter USA (Ltd.), Williamsville, New York

Stamp Manufacturing: Stamps printed by Ashton-Potter on Mueller Martini A74 offset press. Stamps finished by Ashton-Potter.

Quantity Ordered: 790,000,000

Plate Number Detail: 1 set of 4 plate numbers preceded by the letter P on 2 peel-off strips

Plate Number Combination Reported: P1111

Paper Supplier: Flexcon/Glatfelter

Tagging: phosphored paper with phosphor blocker on cover

The Stamps

On March 15, the Postal Service issued a set of four stamps depicting spring flowers: a blue hyacinth, a yellow daffodil, a red and white tulip and a purple iris. The first-day ceremony was held at the Chicago Flower and Garden Show in Chicago, Illinois.

The self-adhesive stamps are contained in a double-sided convertible booklet of 20, with five specimens of each variety. Ashton-Potter (USA) Ltd. printed them by the offset process. Three se-tenant blocks of four are on one side of the booklet and two blocks, with a label that serves as a booklet cover, on the other. All the stamps have at least one straight edge.

USPS ordered 790 million stamps, or 39.5 million booklets, an extremely large printing for a commemorative issue.

The watercolor paintings displayed on the stamps had been in the Postal

Service's design bank since 1993, when artist Christopher Pullman created them for art director Derry Noyes. Pullman provided an additional painting, showing a purple crocus, and from his artwork Noyes developed five vertical commemorative-size stamp designs.

However, their use was deferred because the illustrations and subject matter were considered too similar to paintings prepared by another artist, Ned Seidler, for a scheduled series of booklet stamps fea-

The Spring Flowers artwork was created in 1993 but held in the Postal Service's design bank for a dozen years, largely because it would have been too close in concept and design to four sets of booklet stamps featuring flowers of different seasons painted by Ned Seidler that were issued from 1993 to 1996. The 1993 set depicting spring flowers, shown here, included all four of the varieties on the 2005 pane — hyacinth, daffodil, tulip and iris, plus lilac.

turing garden flowers of the four seasons. The four booklets were issued from 1993 through 1996, one each year, each containing five varieties. The spring flowers stamps of 1993, with 29¢ denominations, depicted all four of the flowers that would be shown on the 2005 set — hyacinth, daffodil, tulip and iris — plus the lilac (Scott 2760-2764).

Later, when USPS was developing designs for new definitives to be used at the time of a rate change, Terrence McCaffrey, manager of stamp development, proposed that the Christopher Pullman paintings be brought out and put to use. "But the [Citizens' Stamp Advisory Committee] said, 'Let's try using photographs of flowers. We haven't done that before,' " McCaffrey said. "So the watercolors went back in the bank." Four se-tenant definitives in various formats, featuring photos of flowers by Robert Peak, were issued in 2000 for the increase in the first-class rate from 33¢ to 34¢.

Daffodils and tulips, two of the Spring Flowers of 2005, were depicted on stamps of the 6¢ Beautification of America block of four of 1969 (Scott 1365-1368). The iris, as the state flower of Tennessee, was shown on a 20¢ stamp in the 50-stamp State Birds and Flowers issue of 1982 (Scott 1994, 1994A).

"Spring flowers symbolize new beginnings, and their light, pastel colors give a hint of the summer colors to come," the Postal Service said in its press release. "The daffodil, or narcissus, with its wide range of yellow and white flowers, and the smaller hyacinth, one of the few true blue flowers, debut early in the garden. In addition, both are popular bulbs for blooming indoors.

"As the daffodil and hyacinth flowers fade outdoors, the elegant tulip and the long-blooming iris begin to appear. Valued as long-lasting cut flowers, both tulips and irises are used in many garden landscapes to provide height and color."

The Designs

Derry Noyes asked Christopher Pullman and his wife Esther, of Cambridge, Massachusetts, to prepare some stamp designs featuring spring flowers, possibly for a Love stamp or stamps. Both are designers, and Pullman had been a visiting professor at Yale, where Noyes, as an undergraduate, had taken his course.

"We started working on the project in the dead of winter, and the selection of fresh flowers was very limited," Pullman told the Postal Service. "Most of the early spring flowers that were available were bulbs, so that

In 1993, when Christopher Pullman made his watercolor flower paintings, Derry Noyes made design mockups of the illustrations in commemorative stamp size. The group of paintings included a purple crocus that wasn't used when the stamps were issued in special size 12 years later.

became the organizing idea for these stamps.

"With all the beautiful flowers in the house and the images we produced in the studio and found during our research, we were tempted to try other approaches. For example, we thought about the idea of tiny flowers that could be reproduced actual size on the stamps. We also collected many beautiful 18th-century and 19th-century botanical illustrations, which would have given the set a more historical feel."

"They came up with some rough concepts — just experiments, really," Noyes said. "They mocked up some flowers with letter forms, using the letters in LOVE, so that each stamp had a flower that started with that letter. They tried using the word LOVE in calligraphy, going across the pane of stamps. None of the ideas was viable, but it was sort of a fun exercise."

In the end, CSAC approved a hand-painted design by Pullman. "I've painted watercolors for many years," he said, "but I had almost never used any of these paintings in my professional work."

Pullman proceeded to paint six different flowers: the four that ended up as stamp subjects, plus a crocus and an all-red tulip. He based his paintings on photographs of blossoms purchased at a Boston flower market and images found in garden catalogs, the Postal Service reported.

Noyes mocked up designs using the paintings in commemorative stamp size, arranged vertically, and presented them to CSAC in booklet and pane-of-20 formats. When the decision finally was made to use the illustrations, however, McCaffrey decided that it would be more practical to issue the stamps in the special size that USPS uses for Love and Holiday Celebrations stamps and format them as a convertible booklet.

At the same time that she created the commemorative-size stamp designs, Noyes designed this booklet cover using a sixth Christopher Pullman painting, an all-red tulip.

"Chris reconfigured them — reproportioned them — with the help of Dodge Color [the Postal Service's prepress work contractor]," said Noyes. "That way we didn't have to crop the flowers. It looked as if the paintings still were intact where each green stem meets the base of the stamp. The difference isn't visible to the eye, really. I still liked them better in commemorative size, though."

Pullman placed the name of each flower vertically in the lower left, in black, in a delicate script typeface called Snell. The font for the black "USA 37" in the lower right corner is Walbaum.

Pullman also designed the non-stamp label that serves as the booklet cover, which bears an enlargement of the iris painting and the words "Spring Flowers" in Snell script. The Universal Product Code barcode covers a portion of the flower's stem and leaf. "He didn't seem to mind having the barcode cut into the flower that way, so I figured it was OK," Noyes said.

First-Day Facts

Jo Ann Feindt, USPS vice president for Great Lakes Area operations, dedicated the stamps in a ceremony at the Chicago Flower and Garden Show in Festival Hall at Chicago's Navy Pier. Collectors attending the ceremony were required to pay the admission fee to the show, which was $11 for adults and $5 for children.

Speakers were June Wood, president of the National Garden Club, Inc., and Anne-Marie St. Germaine, vice president for external affairs of the Chicago Botanic Garden. Kenton Morris, director of the Chicago Flower and Garden Show, was master of ceremonies. Honored guests were Denise Regent, Illinois state president of the National Garden Club; Akinyinka O. Akinyele, Chicago District manager for USPS; Mark Tovey, senior plant manager, Cardiss Collins Processing and Distribution Center, USPS; and Kelvin Mack, Chicago postmaster.

For a limited time, Stamp Fulfillment Services offered uncacheted first-day covers of the Spring Flowers stamps for $3 (set of four, conventional black cancellations), $6 (set of four, digital color cancellations) or $1.50 (random single, color cancellation).

37¢ ROBERT PENN WARREN
LITERARY ARTS SERIES

Date of Issue: April 22, 2005

Catalog Number: Scott 3904

Colors: yellow (PMS 129), magenta, yellow, cyan, black

First-Day Cancel: Guthrie, Kentucky

First-Day Cancellations: 66,515

Format: Panes of 20, horizontal, 4 across, 5 down. Gravure printing cylinders printing 360 stamps per revolution (30 across, 12 around) manufactured by Southern Graphics Systems.

Gum Type: self-adhesive

Overall Stamp Size: 1.56 by 0.99 inches; 39.624 by 25.146 mm

Pane Size: 7.25 by 5.94 inches; 184.15 by 150.87 mm

Perforations: 10¾ (die-cut simulated perforations) (Comco Custom rotary die cutter)

Selvage Markings: "© 2004/USPS" ".37/x20/$7.40" "PLATE/POSITION" and diagram.

Back Markings: On selvage: "Discover the universal language of stamps!/ Visit the Washington 2006 World Philatelic Exhibition May 27-June 3, 2006, in Washington, D.C." Universal Product Code (UPC) "458300" in 4 locations. On stamps: "Robert Penn Warren/(1905-1989)/America's first official poet laureate/received two Pulitzer Prizes for poetry/and one for the novel *All the King's Men,*/a 1946 work about the rise and fall/of a southern politician."

Illustrator: Will Wilson of San Francisco, California

Designer, Typographer and Art Director: Carl Herrman of Carlsbad, California

Modeler: Donald H. Woo of Sennett Security Products, Chantilly, Virginia

Stamp Manufacturing: Stamps printed for Sennett Security Products by American Packaging Corporation, Columbus, Wisconsin, on Cerutti 950 gravure press. Stamps finished by Unique Binders of Fredericksburg, Virginia.

Quantity Ordered: 45,000,000	

Cylinder Number Detail: 1 set of 5 cylinder numbers preceded by the letter S in selvage above or below each corner stamp

Cylinder Number Combination Reported: S11111

Paper Supplier: Mactac

Tagging: overall tagging

The Stamp

On April 22, the Postal Service issued a stamp in its Literary Arts series honoring American writer and educator Robert Penn Warren, the first official poet laureate of the United States and the only person to win the Pulitzer Prize for both fiction and poetry. The stamp had its first-day sale in Guthrie, Kentucky, two days before the 100th anniversary of Warren's birth there.

Warren was the 21st person to be depicted in the series, which began with a John Steinbeck stamp in 1979. He was placed on the list for stamp honors by the Subject Subcommittee of the Citizens' Stamp Advisory Committee as one of America's leading literary figures of the 20th century, and his stamp was scheduled for 2005 to coincide with his centennial.

American Packaging Corporation printed the self-adhesive commemorative by the gravure process and distributed it in panes of 20. A paragraph about Warren appears on the back of the stamp's liner paper, while two lines promoting the Washington 2006 World Philatelic Exhibition, scheduled for May 27 to June 3, 2006, are on the liner behind the bottom selvage. The same wording appeared on panes of stamps issued later in 2005, as well.

The print order, 45 million stamps, is comparable to those for Warren's recent predecessors in the series: James Baldwin, the 2004 Literary Arts subject (50 million); Zora Neale Hurston (70 million); Ogden Nash (75 million); Thomas Wolfe (53 million); and Ayn Rand (42.5 million).

Robert Penn Warren was born April 24, 1905, to Robert Franklin Warren, a banker, and Anna Ruth Penn Warren, a schoolteacher. In 1921, his left eye was injured when he was struck by a piece of coal that his younger brother, Thomas, tossed over a hedge. He eventually lost the sight of the eye, and his fear that he would lose the other eye as well was so strong and enduring that he once attempted suicide. The injured eye was removed in 1934.

The disability kept Warren out of the U.S. Naval Academy, where he had been scheduled to enroll, so he entered Vanderbilt University at the age of 16. Here, the red-haired young man acquired his lifelong nickname, "Red." A composition class taught by poet John Crowe Ransom helped Warren see his world as "the stuff of poetry." His early verse led to his membership in the Fugitives, a 1920s-era poets' group that included Ransom, Allen Tate and others who would go on to be successful writers.

Warren graduated summa cum laude from Vanderbilt, earned a master's degree from the University of California and did further graduate work at Yale and as a Rhodes scholar at Oxford. Later, he held academic positions at several universities, including Louisiana State, where he helped found and edit *The Southern Review*, a major literary quarterly with national readership. Outside the classroom, Warren was a prolific writer. His body of work eventually would span more than six decades and include 16 volumes of poetry, 10 novels, a collection of short stories and college textbooks on poetry and fiction.

Poetry was his greatest literary love. He once confided to a friend that while he had set out to write another novel, "nothing but poems would come." His poetic musings often were conversational or colloquial. Fusing fact with fiction, the poet wove his memories — of people and places, images and incidents — and his personal and political concerns into meditations on the meaning and significance of life. "What is a poem but a hazardous attempt at self-understanding?" he wrote in a 1985 essay.

Warren won two Pulitzer Prizes for poetry: in 1958, for the collection *Promises: Poems, 1954-1956*, and in 1979, for *Now and Then: Poems, 1976-1978*. He received his Pulitzer for fiction in 1947 for his most celebrated novel, *All The King's Men*, which was published the year before. Set in Louisiana in the 1930s, a time and place he knew well from his years at LSU, it was a tale of the rise and fall of several compelling characters. Foremost among them was Willie Stark, a Southern politician who achieved power but lost his ideals and ultimately his life. The story was suggested to Warren by the career of Huey "Kingfish" Long, the charismatic Louisiana governor and U.S. senator whose rise on the national stage was cut short by an assassin's bullet in 1935. However, "for better or for worse, Willie Stark was not Huey Long," Warren wrote. "Willie was only himself, whatever that self turned out to be, a shadowy wraith or a blundering human being." The novel was made into a film that won the Academy Award for best picture of 1949.

Other Warren novels include *At Heaven's Gate* (1943), which explored the conflict between agrarianism and big business in the 1920s; *World Enough and Time* (1950), based on a Kentucky murder trial of the 1820s; *Band of Angels* (1955), set in the Civil War-era South; *The Cave* (1959), based on a real incident in which a Tennessee hill resident becomes trapped in a cave; *Flood* (1964), which traced the reactions of the inhabitants of a small town that is soon to be flooded by the construction of a dam; and *A Place to Come To* (1977), about a 60-year-old classics professor reflecting on his life. His book-length poems include *Brother to Dragons* (1952) and *Audubon: A Vision* (1969).

Despite his eye injury, Warren led a life of constant activity. He swam miles before breakfast, climbed, skied and played basketball. In addition to his Pulitzer Prizes, he won virtually all the other major awards for American writers. He received the Presidential Medal of Freedom in 1980, and in 1986 he was appointed to the newly created post of poet laureate by Daniel

J. Boorstin, the librarian of Congress, for a one-year term.

In 1985 Warren was diagnosed with prostate cancer that had spread to the bones. He died September 15, 1989, in West Wardsboro, Vermont.

The Design

The design style of the Literary Arts series was established by artist Michael Deas in 1995 with the Tennessee Williams stamp. Each stamp is commemorative size, horizontally arranged, depicting a head-and-shoulders portrait of the subject against a background evocative of one of his or her major works, with the person's name superimposed on the portrait across the top in a variant of the Times New Roman typeface developed by USPS art director Richard Sheaff called Times a-Changin'.

Since then, all Literary Arts stamps except one (Ayn Rand, 1999) have incorporated that design style, although some of the subjects have been painted by artists other than Deas. Deas was too busy to undertake the Robert Penn Warren assignment, and Terrence McCaffrey suggested to art director Carl Herrman that he check on the availability of Will Wilson of San Francisco, California, a gallery painter whose work McCaffrey had seen in a publication of the Society of Illustrators.

Wilson paints in oils and creates an average of eight to ten pieces each year, working from life to create highly detailed figures, florals, still lifes, animals and portraits. "I thought, 'This guy is good,' " McCaffrey said. "He's in the same league with Michael Deas when it comes to incredible realism."

Although Wilson doesn't customarily take commercial clients, he agreed to illustrate the Robert Penn Warren stamp. Coincidentally, Wilson's paternal grandmother, like Warren, had been born and raised in Guthrie, Kentucky.

Finding a suitable photograph to serve as his model turned out to be difficult. "Later in life, Warren was almost completely bald," Herrman said. "He had very stringy hair which he combed terribly, and he didn't look very friendly." Another complication for the portraitist was Warren's artificial eye. "I didn't want to ignore the eye situation, because that was part of him, but I tried not to make it look like something that would draw attention to itself, either," Wilson said.

The photo the design team chose was a three-quarters view of the face from the right side, in which the artificial eye is not particularly noticeable. From the Center for Robert Penn Warren Studies of Western Kentucky University, it is black and white and was made in 1948, two years after the publication of *All the King's* Men, when Warren was in the prime of life.

Establishing the proper colors for the portrait wasn't a problem, Wilson said. He gave Warren red hair of the proper tint and "kind of a redhead's complexion." "Other than that, I just had to use my experience in painting portraits to get the flesh tones right," he said.

"Will did an incredible job of painting from the photograph, so that

Will Wilson based his painting of Robert Penn Warren for the stamp illustration on this black-and-white photograph made in 1948, two years after the publication of **All the King's Men.** *The photo was furnished by the Center for Robert Penn Warren Studies at Western Kentucky University.*

the family had no problem with accepting the portrait for the stamp," said Herrman.

Shown in the background on the left side of the portrait is Willie Stark, the protagonist of *All The King's Men*, with arms upraised as he gives a stump speech, while supporters display placards containing such slogans as "We Want Willie," "Win With Willie," and "Support Stark." The rest of the scene, to the right of the portrait, is of a Louisiana landscape, with trees and a body of water in the distance.

Wilson based the orator on a photograph of Huey Long, made on August 4, 1932, in Magnolia, Arkansas. Long was on a two-week speaking tour in Louisiana's neighboring state on behalf of a fellow U.S. senator and Democrat, Hattie Caraway, who had won a special election the preceding January to become the first woman elected to the U.S. Senate. Caraway was pictured on a 76¢ stamp in the Distinguished Americans series issued in 2001.

The people surrounding Stark in Wilson's painting were based on models whom the artist photographed in his studio, using appropriate lighting. The models posed, one at a time, each holding a pole to which Wilson had fastened a piece of cardboard. The slogans on the signs in the painting were from signs held by children in a movie still from *All The King's Men*.

The tree behind the political rally is an oak, while those on the right side of the painting are palms and cypress, all native to Louisiana. Wilson based the trees on photographs from books he found in a library.

At one point, Herrman and Wilson contemplated showing an illustration of the Louisiana governor's mansion at Baton Rouge in the background. However, because the building closely resembled the White House, upon which it reportedly was modeled, they concluded that its inclusion might confuse people who were unfamiliar with the author and his best-known work.

The author's name across the top of the stamp and "USA 37" in two

Will Wilson made this pencil sketch for the stamp design with an arrangement of elements close to that of his finished painting. His question and comments in the margin were directed to Carl Herrman, art director for the project.

lines beneath it on the right were printed in a gold self-color. The rest of the design was printed in the standard four process colors.

First-Day Facts

Ann Wright, Kentuckiana District manager for USPS, dedicated the stamp at the Robert Penn Warren Museum in Guthrie as part of a weeklong series of events celebrating the centennial of Warren's birth.

Speakers were Warren's children, Gabriel Warren and Rosanna Warren Scully, and Elaine Monroe of the Breathitt Veterinary Diagnostic Center. A. Scott Marshall, mayor of Guthrie, gave the welcome. Honored guests included Jeane Moore, director of educational, cultural and historic events for the Robert Penn Warren Birthplace Committee, and Tommie Lou Frey and Sandra Hughes, nieces of Warren.

Among those attending the ceremony were stamp illustrator Will Wilson's parents, Bonnie and Bill Wilson of Baltimore, Maryland.

For a limited time, Stamp Fulfillment Services sold uncacheted first-day covers for 75¢.

37¢ YIP HARBURG

Date of Issue: April 28, 2005

Catalog Number: Scott 3905

Colors: black, cyan, magenta, yellow

First-Day Cancel: New York, New York

First-Day Cancellations: 70,509

Format: Panes of 20, horizontal, 4 across, 5 down. Offset printing plates printing 240 stamps per revolution (20 across, 12 around).

Gum Type: self-adhesive

Microprinting: "USPS" on edge of cloud below coat lapel

Overall Stamp Size: 1.56 by 0.98 inches; 39.62 by 24.89 mm

Pane Size: 7.26 by 5.9 inches; 184.4 by 149.86 mm

Perforations: 10¾ (die-cut simulated perforations) (Heidelberg 102 Speedmaster rotary die cutter)

Selvage Markings: "© 2004/USPS" ".37/x20/$7.40" "PLATE/POSITION" and diagram.

Back Markings: On selvage: "Discover the universal language of stamps!/ Visit the Washington 2006 World Philatelic Exhibition May 27-June 3, 2006, in Washington, D.C." Universal Product Code (UPC) "457600" in 4 locations. On stamps: "E.Y. (Yip) Harburg/(1896-1981)/wrote the lyrics for more than 600/popular songs, including such classics/as 'Brother, Can You Spare a Dime?'/and 'Over the Rainbow.' "

Typographer: Greg Berger of Bethesda, Maryland

Designer and Art Director: Ethel Kessler of Bethesda, Maryland

Modeler: Donald H. Woo of Sennett Security Products, Chantilly, Virginia

Stamp Manufacturing: Stamps printed for Sennett Security Products by Banknote Corporation of America, Browns Summit, North Carolina, on Man Roland 300 offset press. Stamps finished by BCA.

Quantity Ordered: 40,000,000

Plate Number Detail: 1 set of 4 plate numbers preceded by the letter S in selvage above or below each corner stamp

Plate Number Combination Reported: S1111

Paper Supplier: Mactac

Tagging: block tagging over stamps

The Stamp

On April 28, the Postal Service issued a stamp honoring E.Y. "Yip" Harburg, a lyricist whose name is little known to the public but whose body of work includes some of the most popular and enduring songs of the Broadway stage and Hollywood screen.

Among Harburg's more than 500 published lyrics are *Brother, Can You Spare a Dime?*, *It's Only a Paper Moon*, *April in Paris*, *How Are Things in Glocca Morra?* and *Old Devil Moon*. In a class by themselves were his songs with composer Harold Arlen for the MGM film *The Wizard of Oz*, headed by a wistful ballad, *Over the Rainbow*, sung by a 17-year-old Judy Garland. *Over the Rainbow* won the Academy Award for best film song of 1939, was named the top song of the 20th century by the Recording Industry Association of America in 2001, and in 2004 was declared the greatest film song of all time by the American Film Institute.

Harburg had been overlooked by the Postal Service in the long-running Legends of American Music stamp series, missing the two sets for which he would have been eligible: Songwriters (1996), which included Arlen, his most frequent composer-collaborator, and Broadway Songwriters (1999). His principal advocate on the Citizens' Stamp Advisory Committee was film actor Karl Malden, who had met Harburg, was familiar with his Hollywood work and strongly believed he deserved a stamp. CSAC agreed to a stand-alone commemorative — the Legends series by then had ended — but, even after the stamp was designed, it waited for several years before finally gaining a spot in the 2005 program.

Banknote Corporation of America printed the self-adhesive stamp by the offset process for Sennett Security Products for distribution in panes of 20. A paragraph of descriptive text appears on the back of the liner paper behind each stamp. The print order was 40 million, a relatively small number for a single commemorative.

E.Y. Harburg was born Isidore Hochberg on April 8, 1896, to immigrant Russian Jewish parents on New York's Lower East Side. Remarkably, in the same city and same period (1895-1896), several other major figures in the small field of lyric writing were born, also to Jewish families: Oscar Hammerstein, Lorenz Hart and Ira Gershwin, all of whom would be pictured on U.S. stamps, plus Howard Dietz, Harry Ruby and Irving Caesar.

Possessed of great enthusiasm and energy as a young child, Harburg was called "Yipsl," the Yiddish word for squirrel, by his parents, and the nickname was picked up by his neighborhood friends. In 1923, he would change his name to Edgar Y. (for Yip) Harburg.

In school, he struck up a lasting friendship with Ira Gershwin. They shared a devotion to the verses of W.S. Gilbert, and Harburg was astonished when Gershwin told him that the verses were song lyrics and played for him recordings of the Gilbert and Sullivan operettas. "Gilbert and Sullivan tied Ira to me for life," Harburg wrote.

The two young men wrote for their school paper in high school and later at City College of New York. They also submitted poems to Franklin P. Adams' famous column "The Conning Tower" in *The New York World*, which has been described as "the finishing school for a generation of American humorists."

Harburg was a political radical who embraced socialism as a young man and avoided service in World War I by working as a journalist for three years in Uruguay. He described himself as "a rebel by birth," prepared to "contest anything that is unjust, that causes suffering in humanity." This social conscience emerges repeatedly in his verse, song lyrics and satires.

Despite his youthful disdain for capitalism, he started an electrical-appliance business, although he later would say he "hated every moment of it." The business failed, leaving Harburg deeply in debt. Ira Gershwin — by now joined with his composer brother George in a successful song-writing team — encouraged him to switch from writing light verse to lyrics, and recommended him to composer Jay Gorney, who was looking for a collaborator. Harburg and Gorney began writing songs together in 1929.

In 1932, for a revue called *Americana*, they caught the attention of the country with *Brother, Can You Spare a Dime?*, the disillusioned anthem of a worker and war veteran betrayed by the Great Depression. The song "has expressed the spirit of these times with more heartbreaking anguish than any of the prose bards of the day," wrote Brooks Atkinson in *The New York Times*.

Through the 1930s, Harburg wrote lyrics for musicals, revues and Hollywood films with Vernon Duke, Harold Arlen, Burton Lane and other composers. His great break was his assignment with Arlen to write the songs for the MGM production of L. Frank Baum's children's classic *The Wizard of Oz*, which premiered in 1939. By now the witty and evocative words and music are part of Americans' musical subconscious: *Ding, Dong, the Witch is Dead*; *If I Only Had a Brain* (*a Heart ... the Nerve*); *We're Off to See the Wizard*; *Follow the Yellow Brick Road*; and, of course, *Over the Rainbow*.

The word "rainbow" never appears in Baum's book. Yip Harburg introduced it to the film, a fact underscored by the title of his biography, *Who Put the Rainbow in The Wizard of Oz?*, written by his son Ernie Harburg and Harold Meyerson. The lyricist recalled the process to Hollywood historian Aljean Harmetz:

"This little girl thinks: 'My life is messed up. Where do I run?' The song has to be full of childish pleasures. Of lemon drops. The book had said Kansas was an arid place where not even flowers grew. The only colorful thing Dorothy saw, occasionally, would be the rainbow.

" 'Over the Rainbow is Where I Want to Be' was my [dummy] title, the title I gave Harold [Arlen]. A title has to ring a bell, has to blow a couple of Roman candles off. But he gave me a tune with those first two notes [an octave apart]. I tried 'I'll go over the rainbow,' 'Someday over the rainbow' or 'The other side of the rainbow.' I had difficulty coming to the idea of 'Somewhere.' For a while I thought I would just leave those first two notes out. It was a long time before I came to 'Somewhere over the rainbow.' "

It is part of cinema legend that Harburg and Arlen, along with producer Arthur Freed, had to fight to keep *Over the Rainbow* in the finished film after some of MGM boss Louis B. Mayer's advisers argued that it was slowing down the action. Harold Arlen told his biographer, Edwin Jablonski, that the song was axed after each of the movie's three previews, and each time Freed would go to Mayer and "argue it back into the film."

Among Harburg's later works were three musicals conveying strong political points of view, each with a different composer: *Bloomer Girl* with Arlen (1944), *Finian's Rainbow* with Burton Lane (1947) and *Flahooley!* with Sammy Fain (1951). *Finian's Rainbow*, which Harburg co-authored and directed, addressed issues of race, prejudice and oppression in the form of a fable featuring leprechauns, pots of gold and miraculous racial transformations in the fictitious southern state of Missitucky.

During the McCarthy era, Harburg was blacklisted by Hollywood, radio and television because of his associations with a number of organizations in which Communists played major roles. He denied any affinity for Communism — "I am outraged," he wrote to MGM's lawyer, "by the suggestion that somehow I am connected with, believe in, or am sympathetic with Communist or totalitarian philosophy" — but the blacklisting lasted a dozen years. Harburg stayed active in the theater, however, writing the songs with Arlen for *Jamaica* (1957) and with Jule Styne for *Darling of the Day* (1968).

As he aged, Harburg never stopped songwriting, working on shows or writing topical verse. On March 5, 1981, he died of a massive heart attack while driving near his old home in Brentwood, California. He had been on his way to a story conference for a film version of Robert Louis Stevenson's *Treasure Island*. Afterward, he was scheduled to fly to New York City to receive the Johnny Mercer Award of the Songwriters Hall of Fame.

The Design

When USPS art director Ethel Kessler was assigned to design the Harburg stamp in 1999, she was exploring ways to present stamp portraits of people who were not household names in a way that would convey some sense of their achievements. "I was trying to have a conversation about taking a visually and even by-name basically unknown person and put them on a stamp and have anybody care," she said.

She began by commissioning illustrator C.F. Payne to prepare a portrait of Harburg. Payne is a widely published caricaturist whose "Our America" artwork, reminiscent of the visual commentary of the late Norman Rock-

Ethel Kessler and CSAC considered using this C.F. Payne caricature of Harburg, with an elongated face and exaggerated ears and nose, but decided they wanted a more literal portrait for the stamp.

well, appears on the back cover of *Reader's Digest* each month. His initial pencil drawing of Harburg, based on a color photograph by Barbara Bordnick of New York City, lengthened the lyricist's face and exaggerated his ears and nose.

However, there were concerns that the caricature made Harburg look unsuitably "goofy," Kessler said, and that the Harburg family would be unhappy with such a non-literal portrait. They decided to try a different design direction, and the Payne essay never was developed into finished art.

They quickly settled on a photograph by Barbara Bordnick of New York City, which shows a smiling Harburg, in tweedy sport jacket and bow tie, resting his folded left hand against his face. Bordnick had shot the picture, an 8-by-10 color Polaroid, in 1978. "We worked together for two hours," the photographer told a Postal Service interviewer. "I told him my mother had sung his *How Are Things in Glocca Morra?* to me as a child, and he started to talk to me about his music. He even sang to me. He was so genuine, warm and imaginative — and wonderfully mischievous."

"Everybody was engaged by this photograph, so it seemed that using it was a good idea," Kessler said. "What's amazing is that he's 82 years old in the photo. You can just feel his love of life."

This 1978 color photograph of Harburg by New York City photographer Barbara Bordnick was used for this stamp.

However, the question of how to identify Harburg for the general public remained. "As a stamp buyer, I don't know who that is," Kessler said of the portrait. "You just show me a picture of this guy, he's somebody's grandfather or uncle, but what do I care? Why would I buy a stamp with his picture on it? What can we do to this portrait that will help people understand it?"

Simply showing the face with the words "Yip Harburg" and "Lyricist" wasn't enough, Kessler and CSAC decided. Their solution was to accompany the portrait with actual lyrics, and specifically those of *Over the Rainbow*. Kessler's long-time associate, Greg Berger, whose own stamp-design credits include the 33¢ Adoption commemorative of 2000, helped her explore several ways of doing this.

Kessler and Berger had been given a reproduction of Harburg's typed manuscript of the lyrics to *Over the Rainbow*, and they incorporated portions of the first two stanzas and the song's bridge as a backdrop to the portrait. However, the words were too small to be read comfortably at

Shown here are five essays created between 1999 and 2003 as part of the evolution of the design. One early effort merely identified Harburg as a "Lyricist," while the others used various amounts of the lyrics of Over the Rainbow.

stamp size. On the other hand, just using the four words "Somewhere over the rainbow" didn't seem adequate. They ultimately decided on a horizontal, commemorative-size design, with the Bordnick portrait on the right, a rainbow in the upper left corner, clouds at the lower left, and the words "Somewhere over/the rainbow/skies are blue…" in three curved lines of lowercase Frutiger condensed type.

"The words are kind of bouncing as if they are part of the rainbow or part of the clouds," Kessler said. "We were able to make the words larger. Since we had identified the song with his portrait, we decided that we didn't need the word 'Lyricist', and we left it off."

Kessler cropped the portrait across the upper part of Harburg's forehead, which allowed her to display his features at optimum size. She provided a solid blue background for the face, clouds and rainbow, and placed the name YIP HARBURG, in Frutiger condensed capitals, beneath the portrait. Greg Berger manipulated the photographed image on his computer to remove the wristwatch Harburg was wearing and bring the sleeve of his sport jacket down to cover the bare left wrist.

"I think, in the end, the stamp looks happy and inviting," Kessler said.

Because the printer used offset lithography, microprinting was included in the design as a security measure. The letters "USPS" can be found on the edge of the cloud just below Harburg's jacket lapel.

The letters "USPS" in microprinting can be found on the edge of the cloud just below Harburg's jacket lapel.

First-Day Facts

The first-day ceremony was held on the stage of the Kauffman Concert Hall at the 92nd Street Y in New York City, where Harburg had helped develop the well-known Lyrics and Lyricists American Songbook series and gave the inaugural lecture in 1970. David Solomon, vice president for operations for the Postal Service's New York Metro Area, dedicated the stamp.

Ernie Harburg, son of the songwriter and president of the Yip Harburg Foundation, was the speaker. David A. Failor, manager, Stamp Services, for USPS was master of ceremonies, and Sol Adler, executive director of the 92nd Street Y, gave the welcome.

Guests included the Harburgs' daughter, Marge Harburg; Deena Rosenberg Harburg, Harburg's daughter-in-law and founding chair of New York University's Musical Theatre Program; and Barbara Bordnick, the photographer whose portrait of Harburg appears on the stamp. Singer Maureen McGovern performed *Over the Rainbow,* grandson Ben Harburg sang *It's Only a Paper Moon,* and other performers presented live and filmed renditions of other Harburg songs. The husband-and-wife acting team of Eli Wallach and Anne Jackson offered some of Harburg's satiric verses in patter form.

For a limited time, Stamp Fulfillment Services sold uncacheted first-day covers for 75¢.

37¢ AMERICAN SCIENTISTS (4 DESIGNS)

Date of Issue: May 4, 2005

Catalog Numbers: Scott 3906-3909, single stamps; 3909a, block or horizontal strip of 4

Colors: blue (PMS 287), black, cyan, magenta, yellow

First-Day Cancel: Dallas, Texas

First-Day Cancellations: 241,517

Format: Panes of 20, horizontal, 4 across, 5 down. Offset printing plates printing 180 stamps per revolution (12 across, 15 around).

Microprinting: On Barbara McClintock stamp: a mutable allele (gene) on left collar. On Josiah Willard Gibbs stamp: the fundamental equation of thermodynamics on right collar. On John von Neumann stamp: a feedback loop on right collar. On Richard Feynman stamp: the equation alpha = 1/137 on left collar.

Gum Type: self-adhesive

Overall Stamp Size: 1.56 by 0.98 inches; 39.62 by 24.89 mm

Pane Size: 7.26 by 5.9 inches; 184.4 by 149.86 mm

Perforations: 10¾ (die-cut simulated perforations) (Heidelberg 102 Speedmaster rotary die cutter)

Selvage Inscription: "American Scientists"

Selvage Markings: "© 2004/USPS" ".37/x20/$7.40" "PLATE/POSITION" and diagram.

Back Markings: On selvage: "American Scientists." "Discover the universal language of stamps!/Visit the Washington 2006 World Philatelic Exhibition May 27-June 3, 2006, in Washington, D.C." Universal Product Code (UPC) "458100" in 4 locations. On stamps: "Richard P. Feynman/1918-1988/developed a new formulation of quantum/theory based, in part, on diagrams he invented/to help him visualize the dynamics of atomic/particles. In 1965, this noted theoretical/physicist, enthusiastic educator, and amateur/artist was awarded the Nobel Prize in Physics." "John von Neumann/(1903-1957)/made significant contributions in both pure/and applied mathematics, especially in the/areas of quantum mechanics, game theory,/and computer theory and design. In 1956, the/U.S. government presented the Enrico Fermi/Award to this eminent mathematician." "Josiah Willard Gibbs/(1839-1903)/formulated the modern system of/thermodynamic analysis. For this and other/extraordinary achievements, Gibbs received/some of the most prestigious awards of his/era, including the Rumford Prize from the/American Academy of Arts and Sciences." "Barbara McClintock/(1902-1992)/conducted maize plant research that led to/her discovery of genetic transposition — the/movement of genetic material within and/between chromosomes. In 1983, this/pioneering geneticist was awarded the/Nobel Prize in Physiology or Medicine."

Designer: Victor Stabin of Jim Thorpe, Pennsylvania

Art Director and Typographer: Carl Herrman of Carlsbad, California

Modeler: Donald H. Woo of Sennett Security Products, Chantilly, Virginia

Stamp Manufacturing: Stamps printed for Sennett Security Products by Banknote Corporation of America, Browns Summit, North Carolina, on Man Roland 300 offset press. Stamps finished by BCA.

Quantity Ordered: 50,000,000

Plate Number Detail: 1 set of 5 plate numbers preceded by the letter S in selvage above or below each corner stamp

Plate Number Combination Reported: S11111

Paper Supplier: Mactac

Tagging: unphosphored paper; large block tagging covering stamps

The Stamps

From time to time, a member of the Citizens' Stamp Advisory Committee will bring a proposal for a stamp issue to the panel and convince the other members that the idea should be approved for the U.S. stamp program.

So it was that CSAC member Michael Heyman, former chancellor of the University of California at Berkeley, successfully lobbied for a set of stamps that honored American scientists. "Michael felt that the sciences were underplayed in the stamp program and that we needed to do more science stamps," said Terrence McCaffrey, manager of stamp development.

With the blessing of the committee, Heyman consulted his former associates at Berkeley, asking them to list the top 10 individuals in each scientific discipline, and from their lists he chose four scientists from the 19th and 20th century for the set.

On May 4, four se-tenant stamps depicting these Americans were placed on sale at Yale University in New Haven, Connecticut. They were: thermodynamicist Josiah Willard Gibbs (1839-1903), geneticist Barbara McClintock (1902-1992), mathematician John von Neumann (1903-1957) and physicist Richard P. Feynman (1918-1988). McClintock and Feynman were Nobel laureates.

The stamps were printed by the offset process by Banknote Corporation of America for Sennett Security Products and distributed in panes of 20 containing five of each variety. A paragraph of text about each scientist is printed on the back of the liner paper for his or her stamp.

To advise on the project, PhotoAssist, the Postal Service's research firm, enlisted the help of these experts from academia: Judith Goodstein, California Institute of Technology's registrar and archivist; Eugene E.

The liner paper of each stamp contains a paragraph about the scientist shown on the stamp.

71

Haller, professor of materials science at the University of California at Berkeley; two of Haller's Berkeley colleagues, David B. Wake, a specialist in integrative biology and herpetology, and physicist Marvin L. Cohen; Nina Fedoroff, a molecular biologist at the Pennsylvania State University; Matthew Sands, professor emeritus of physics at the University of California at Santa Cruz, who had been a colleague of Richard Feynman; Silvan S. Schweber, professor emeritus of physics at Brandeis University; Kenneth R. Jolls, a chemical engineer at Iowa State University and an expert on the work of Josiah Gibbs; and William Aspray, an Indiana State University informatics professor and computer historian. Fedoroff, Sands, Jolls and Aspray were involved throughout the project, reviewing all the stamp art and text.

Barbara McClintock (1902-1992) was born in Hartford, Connecticut. At Cornell University, her enrollment in the school's only undergraduate genetics course set her on a career path that peaked when she received the 1983 Nobel Prize in the category "physiology or medicine" for discovering genetic transposition. She was the only woman ever to win an unshared Nobel in that category.

McClintock's research on maize led her to discover that genetic material can change positions on a chromosome or move from one chromosome

to another. The breakthrough took place at Cold Spring Harbor Laboratory in New York, where she was experimenting on mutations caused by broken chromosomes. She called her mobile genetic elements, which controlled the action of other genes during development, "transposable elements" or "jumping genes."

She remained at Cold Spring Harbor for 50 years. In 1944, she became only the third woman elected to the National Academy of Sciences. She received the National Medal of Science, the U.S. government's highest award for scientific achievement, in 1970.

Josiah Willard Gibbs (1839-1903) had been proposed for stamp honors as far back as 1940, when the American Chemical Society complained about his omission from the five Scientists stamps in the 35-stamp Famous Americans set (Scott 859-893), the first extended U.S. stamp issue to honor achievers outside of government and the military. Gibbs has been called one of the greatest scientists of the 19th century, whose discoveries were as fundamental in nature as those of Galileo and Newton. He made important contributions in vector analysis, electromagnetic theory and statistical mechanics, but he is best known for developing the modern method of thermodynamic analysis.

A native of New Haven, Connecticut, Gibbs graduated from hometown Yale University, where he earned the first doctorate in engineering to be conferred in the United States. After study in Europe, he returned to Yale and embarked on his career as an educator and researcher in experimental chemistry, applied physics and thermodynamics. He authored numerous papers, including *On the Equilibrium of Heterogeneous Substances*, in which Gibbs derived what would come to be known as the fundamental equation of thermodynamics, which elegantly relates the energy, pressure, volume, temperature and entropy (measure of disorder or uncertainty) in a system. "Many phenomena, which had never been within the domain of thermodynamics, were now annexed by this equation, including elastic and surface phenomena, changes of phase, and a great part of chemistry," wrote the American Institute of Physics.

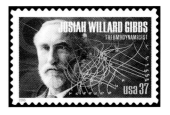

Gibbs wrote five papers on the electromagnetic theory of light, and prepared classroom notes that eventually became the first English-language work on modern vector analysis. In 1902, the year before his death, he published his classic *Elementary Principles in Statistical Mechanics*.

For his achievements, Gibbs received many awards, including the Rumford Prize of the American Academy of Arts and Sciences in 1880 and the Copley Medal of the Royal Society of London in 1901.

John von Neumann (1903-1957) made numerous scientific contributions in both pure and applied mathematics, and has been called the

father of the modern computer for his work on networks and parallel processes. Born in Budapest, he studied in Hungary, Germany and Switzerland before moving to the United States, where in 1933 he co-founded the Institute for Advanced Study in Princeton, New Jersey, with Albert Einstein and five other mathematicians. In 1937, von Neumann obtained U.S. citizenship, and during World War II, he was a consultant on the Manhattan Project to build an atomic bomb.

A *First Draft of a Report on the EDVAC (Electronic Discrete Variable Automatic Computer)*, written by von Neumann in June 1945, described a design based on the stored-program concept, meaning that operating instructions could be entered into a computer via punched cards and then stored internally. The machine, completed in 1952, became a prototype for almost every computer built since.

Von Neumann's two other landmark contributions were providing the mathematical foundations for quantum mechanics and, with Oskar Morgenstern, writing *Theory of Games and Economic Behavior* (1944). Game theory, which has applications in business and military strategies, analyzes situations involving conflicting interests in terms of the players' gains and losses.

President Dwight D. Eisenhower appointed von Neumann to the Atomic Energy Commission in 1955. In 1956, following a diagnosis of cancer that

John von Neumann was honored on this stamp (Scott 3354) of his native Hungary, issued in 1992.

would take his life the following year, he received the AEC's Enrico Fermi Award. In 1992, he was honored on a stamp of his native Hungary (Scott 3354).

Richard P. Feynman (1918-1988) was born in New York City and educated at the Massachusetts Institute of Technology and Princeton University. Like von Neumann, he worked on the wartime Manhattan Project. He won the Nobel Prize in physics in 1965 with Julian Schwinger and Shin'ichero Tomonaga for fundamental work in quantum electrodynamics, which the three carried out independently in the 1940s. His new formulation of quantum theory included innovative diagrams — now called Feynman diagrams — devised to help visualize the dynamics of atomic particles.

Feynman also made significant contributions to other areas of physics, including the computation theory, the fundamental theory for the weak nuclear force, which he developed with colleague Murray Gell-Mann, and superconductivity and superfluidity.

For 30 years he was a faculty member at the California Institute of Technology, where he overhauled the curricula and methods used to teach freshman physics. His classroom skills, outgoing personality and offbeat humor made him a teaching legend at Caltech, but he also developed a following in the general public, through two popular books in which he dealt with a wide range of subjects, *Surely, You're Joking, Mr. Feynman* (1985) and *What Do You Care What Other People Think?* (1988). His many fans included Microsoft founder Bill Gates, who has called Feynman one of the people he most admires.

A boyhood collection of the triangular and diamond-shaped stamps of Tannu Tuva inspired Feynman to learn all he could about what he called "a lost land." In 1981, his friend and fellow drummer Ralph Leighton founded the Friends of Tuva (www.fotuva.org), which dubbed Feynman the "patron saint" of Tannu Tuva. Feynman died before he could fulfill a dream to visit the remote Asian country, but Leighton made the trip, writing about it afterward in a book, *Tuva or Bust! Richard Feynman's Last Journey* (2000).

As a member of the presidential commission that investigated the space shuttle Challenger disaster in 1986, Feynman speculated that the rubber

O-rings used between sections of the shuttle's solid rocket boosters had lost their flexibility in an unusual freezing spell at Cape Canaveral and failed to properly seal the joints. This explanation for the shuttle explosion, which Feyman demonstrated in a televised experiment, was accepted by the commission and the public.

The Designs

Art director Carl Herrman had worked with artist Victor Stabin in designing the Henry Mancini stamp of 2004. He chose Stabin to illustrate the American Scientists stamps because of his skill as a portrait painter and his ability to expand and elaborate on the portraits through computer manipulation.

As it turned out, Stabin's talent with a brush wasn't required. After he had made one painting, of Richard Heyman in black and white, the decision was made to use photographs of the scientists instead. However, the artist's mastery of computer design turned out to be essential. As a bonus, he brought to the project a broad knowledge of science and its practitioners absorbed from his father, who had built scientific instrumentation at the Oak Ridge National Laboratory.

Early in the process, CSAC's design subcommittee had considered an alternative set of design concepts prepared by David Johnson, a Connecticut illustrator, at the request of art director Howard Paine. Johnson's detailed pen-and-ink portraits of the four scientists, with graphic illustrations meant to be representative of their work, were set against a parchment-colored background. However, the subcommittee opted to go with Victor Stabin's design treatments.

The photo of Heymann was furnished by the California Institute of

This alternative set of design concepts, with line-drawing portraits of the scientists against a parchment-colored background, was prepared by illustrator Daniel Johnson at the request of art director Howard Paine but not used.

Early in the design process, it was art director Carl Herrman's intention to have artist Victor Stabin paint the portraits of the four scientists. Stabin painted one portrait, of Richard Feynman, which Herrman incorporated in this stamp design. Later, it was decided to use photographs of the quartet instead. The background image shown here is taken from equations that Feynman chalked on his blackboard at Caltech shortly before his death, preserved intact by the university. However, consultants pointed out that it wasn't representative of the physicist's major contributions, and Stabin replaced it with examples of the diagrams devised by and named for Feynman.

Technology. It is undated, but is believed to show the physicist in his 30s. Gibbs' photograph, made near the end of his life, is from the collection of the Emilio Segre Visual Archives at the American Institute of Physics. McClintock's portrait, taken in 1983, came from the Cold Spring Harbor Laboratory, and Neumann's from the Los Alamos, New Mexico, National Laboratory.

More than portraits were wanted, however. "We didn't want the stamps to show just dead heads — heads chopped off — but to offer a bit of a background behind the portraits to suggest what the people were famous for," Herrman explained. Through Stabin's talent with computer image manipulation, the backgrounds would be blended with the portraits in montage fashion.

An early idea was to depict the scientists at work, but it proved impossible to find four suitable reference photographs. "Scientists are not like Hollywood stars who are followed around by publicists. They tend not to have particularly good photographs taken of them," said Herrman. "We didn't find many photos of these people doing anything other than lecturing, and four lecturing pictures would have been boring."

The designers' ultimate solution may have been no less boring to the layman, but it was one the scientific community would consider appropriate: to show formulas or diagrams representative of each scientist's work, against a dark surface suggestive of a classroom chalkboard. Stabin laid them into the design behind and, in some cases, overlapping the photo portraits.

In selecting these esoteric elements, Herrman and Stabin hoped to use examples that had been written in each scientist's own hand. For Richard

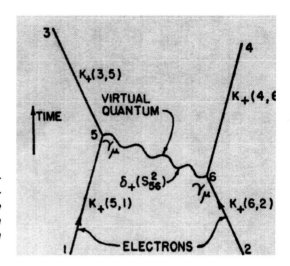

Shown here is a Feynman diagram, of the kind that Victor Stabin incorporated in the background of the Feynman stamp on the recommendation of consultant Matthew Sands.

Feynman, PhotoAssist found a series of equations, made by the physicist shortly before his death, on a blackboard at Caltech that the university has preserved intact. Stabin included a detail from the blackboard in his montage.

However, the consultants insisted that the background illustrations represent the scientists' principal contributions, and this became the controlling consideration. Feynman's blackboard was evocative, they agreed, but "what it shows demonstrates nothing meaningful," PhotoAssist's Mike Owens informed the design team in an e-mail. "They feel it [is] essential to show the Feynman diagram in this context," he added. Accordingly, Stabin replaced the equations with a series of Feynman diagrams.

For the McClintock design, Stabin drew a broken loop with crossed ends that was based on a historically significant figure that McClintock herself had drawn. McClintock's first recognition of genetic transposition was captured by this figure, which dates from the late 1940s and shows the position of chromosome breaks in a kernel of corn. Consultant Nina Fedoroff provided a copy of it that she had included in a book she had edited on McClintock, titled *The Dynamic Genome*.

The Gibbs device, a grid of curving, coiling lines, was furnished by the Gibbs expert on the consulting team, Kenneth R. Jolls. To an interviewer for the Iowa State University College of Engineering Web site, Jolls said: "I argued that the design had to be related to Gibbs' famous three-dimensional energy-entropy-volume surface, and we finally settled on the map of the USV surface that I dug out of the tombs at the Berkeley library from [Scottish physicist James Clerk] Maxwell's 1875 treatise on heat." Gibbs himself had stressed that to truly understand his ideas about thermodynamics, it was essential to use visual analogies, Jolls noted.

Another consultant, William Aspray, provided the background figures for the von Neumann design. They are reproductions of rough notes made by von Neumann in the 1940s for one of the first computer programs he wrote, and can be found in Aspray's book *John von Neumann and the Origins of Modern Computing* (MIT Press, 1990).

The stamps were printed in subdued tones of violet, brown and green, with different color combinations on each stamp. Herrman placed each scientist's name and specialty in white dropout Europa Grotesque letters in the upper right corner, while "USA 37," in a lighter shade of the stamp's predominant color, is in the lower right. In early versions, the dark backgrounds were allowed to bleed across the die-cut simulated perfs, but CSAC felt the result was too dark and called for standard white borders around the designs.

In refining the artwork on the computer, Stabin made some subtle modifications of the background. "It's hard to notice on the stamps, but he put in some little swirly circular motions and waves that gave the backgrounds a bit of dynamics without interfering in any way," Herrman said admiringly. "It's like a kind of cute little rhythm back there, with no particular meaning."

BCA printed the stamps in the standard four process colors, while a PMS blue was used for the words "American Scientists" that appeared on the pane header, or top selvage, also in Europa Grotesque type but with

In this version of the designs, the backgrounds bleed across the simulated perforations. CSAC deemed the effect too dark and called for conventional white borders around the stamps. The background diagram on the Barbara McClintock stamp later was replaced by one showing the position of the chromosome breaks in a kernel of corn. The description of Josiah Willard Gibbs as a "chemist" was changed to "thermodynamicist" at the urging of consultant Kenneth R. Jolls.

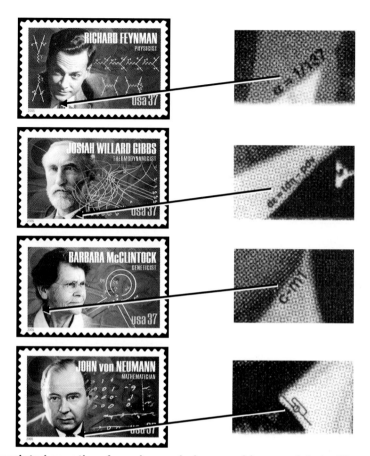

A microprinted equation, formula, symbol or graphic associated with each scientist can be found on his or her collar. For Feynman, it is the equation alpha = 1/137, the fine structure constant; for Gibbs, the fundamental equation of thermodynamics; for McClintock, a mutable allele (a form of gene) designation; and for von Neumann, a feedback loop.

a dropped shadow. The set's CSAC sponsor, Michael Heyman, had suggested that the title be "Notable American Scientists," but was persuaded to omit the adjective.

Although USPS does not require microprinting on its offset-printed stamps if they consist of multiple designs, Banknote Corporation of America included a novel form of microprinting on the collar of each of its American Scientists portraits. It consists of an equation, formula, symbol or graphic associated with the scientist and recommended by the consultants.

The microprinted material, with the names of the consultants, follows: for Feynman, the equation alpha = 1/137, the fine structure constant (Matthew Sands); for Gibbs, the thermodynamic fundamental equation, dU =

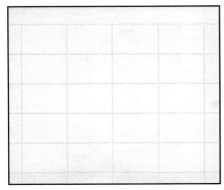

Shown here is a completely blank page of American Scientists stamps, identifiable by the text and bar codes on the back of the liner paper, which are intact. The serpentine die cuts have been computer-enhanced in this picture to make them easier to see.

TdS -PJV (Kenneth Jolls); for McClintock, a mutable allele (a form of gene) designation (Nina Fedoroff); for von Neumann, a feedback loop (William Aspray).

Varieties

Two panes of stamps with complementary errors were found. One is completely blank on the front; the other, on the back.

The first pane shows no trace of any of the five colors of printing ink on the surface of the paper. Its back is normal, with all the verso text in place on the stamps and the header type and bar codes in the selvage. Die cutting is normal on front and back.

According to *Linn's Stamp News*, auctioneer Jacques C. Schiff Jr. obtained the pane on consignment from a collector in Wisconsin who discovered it in a stack of American Scientists panes he had bought at a post office. Schiff offered it at his auction of October 26-27, 2005. The pane is listed as 3909b in the Scott *Specialized Catalogue of U.S. Stamps & Covers*.

The second pane, with no printing on the back of the liner-release paper, was purchased in California in February 2006 by collector John Barkdoll. It was scheduled to be listed in the 2007 Scott U.S. Specialized.

Ten vertical pairs of American Scientists stamps without die cuts are known, David Kols of Regency-Superior of St. Louis, Missouri, told *Linn's Stamp News* in August 2006. Two pairs (a Gibbs-Feynman and McClintock-von Neumann) were offered at auction by the company in late August, while another pair was offered by private treaty sale. The remaining seven pairs were owned by a Regency customer, Kols said.

Scott catalog editor James Kloetzel said the stamps would be listed as major errors in the 2007 Scott *Specialized Catalogue of United States Stamps & Covers*.

First-Day Facts

John F. Walsh of the USPS Board of Governors dedicated the stamps in a ceremony at Yale University's Henry R. Luce Hall.

The speakers were Michelle Feynman, daughter of Richard Feynman; Marina Whitman, daughter of John von Neumann; Marjorie M. Bhavnani, niece of Barbara McClintock; John Willard Gibbs M.D., a cousin of Josiah Willard Gibbs; John H. Marburger, director of the U.S. Office of Science Technology Policy; and Victor Stabin, the stamp designer. Opening and closing comments were offered by Paul A. Fleury, Yale's dean of engineering, and welcomes were extended by Richard C. Levin, president of Yale, and John DeStefano Jr., mayor of New Haven.

For a limited time, Stamp Fulfillment Services sold uncacheted first-day covers of the American Scientists stamps for $3 per set.

37¢ MASTERWORKS OF MODERN AMERICAN ARCHITECTURE (12 DESIGNS)

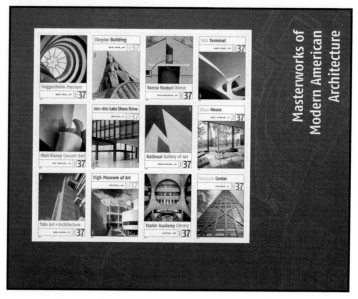

Date of Issue: May 19, 2005

Catalog Numbers: Scott 3910, pane of 12; 3910a-l, single stamps

Colors: black, red (PMS 485), purple (PMS 682), dark orange (PMS 716), light orange (PMS 7409), green (PMS 7489), blue (PMS 2726), stamps; black, back printing

First-Day Cancel: Las Vegas, Nevada

First-Day Cancellations: 451,241

Format: Pane of 12, vertical, 4 across, 3 down. Offset printing plates printing 144 stamps per revolution (12 across, 12 around).

Gum Type: self-adhesive

Stamp Size: 1.225 by 1.56 inches; 31.115 by 39.624 mm

Pane Size: 8 by 6.38 inches; 203.2 by 162.052 mm

Perforations: 10¾ by 11 (die-cut simulated perforations) (IDC two-station die cutter)

Selvage Inscription: "Masterworks of/Modern American/Architecture."

Selvage Markings: none

Back Markings: On selvage: "The drawing on the selvage by Richard Meier & Partners Architects LLP is a three-dimensional view of the High Museum of Art, Atlanta, Georgia." "© 2004 USPS." ".37 x 12 = $4.44." Universal Product Code (UPC) "566800." On stamps: "TWA Terminal/New York, NY

1962/Eero Saarinen initially planned/to study sculpture, so it's no/surprise that his architecture/shows a marked reliance/on sculptural forms. His curving/TWA terminal is one of the/first airport buildings to be/considered a great monument/of modern architecture." "Vanna Venturi House/Philadelphia, PA 1964/Architect Robert Venturi/designed what he characterized/as 'a little house with big scale,/symbolizing shelter' for his/mother. The house is centered/on the chimney and hearth;/the chimney splits the structure/and space extends outward/from the hearth." "Chrysler Building/New York, NY 1930/The Chrysler Building is frequently/praised as the greatest art deco/skyscraper; its distinctive peak/is a symbol of the Jazz Age/and one of the most recognizable/elements in the Manhattan/skyline, William Van Alen's design/incorporated many references/to Chrysler automobiles." "Solomon R. Guggenheim Museum/New York, NY 1959/With its circular ramp coiling/around a space topped by a glass/dome, the Solomon R. Guggenheim/Museum is one of the most/exhilarating interiors in modern/architecture. Frank Lloyd Wright/meant to design the perfect space/in which to contemplate an/art collection." "Glass House/New Canaan, CT 1949/As Philip Johnson once/observed, 'purpose is not/necessary to make a building/beautiful.' He designed his/famous house of steel and/glass more to be seen than to/be lived in. Serene proportion,/balance, and overall symmetry/distinguish this landmark." "National Gallery of Art/East Building/Washington, DC 1978/The East Building, known for/its triangular shapes and/light-filled atrium, is visually/linked to the museum's/original West Building in part/by use of the same marble./Its rigorously geometric design/is by I.M. Pei." "860-880 Lake Shore Drive/Chicago, IL 195l/Two identical 26-story apartment/towers of steel and glass designed/by Ludwig Mies van der Rohe/are prime examples of a new/approach to urban space./A pristine, spare elegance was/the hallmark of this architect's/famous principle that/'less is more.' " "Walt Disney Concert Hall/Los Angeles, CA 2003/Frank Gehry combined thrilling/curves with massive, unusual/shapes to create a home for the/Los Angeles Philharmonic./The stainless steel of the bold/exterior contrasts with the/hardwood panels in the main/auditorium, where patrons sit/on all sides of the orchestra." "Hancock Center/Chicago, IL 1970/This hundred-story, multiuse/tower, affectionately known as/'Big John,' was designed by/architect Bruce Graham and/engineer Fazlur Khan of the firm/Skidmore, Owings & Merrill./Crisscrossing braces stacked up the/side of the building carry most/of its weight." "Exeter Academy Library/Exeter, NH 1971/The central reading room in/this powerful school library/designed by Louis I. Kahn is circled/by balconies containing the/stacks. Study carrels are positioned/along the perimeter of the/building, where small windows/at eye level can be closed by/sliding wooden shutters." "High Museum of Art/Atlanta, GA 1983/The High Museum of Art,/like much of Richard Meier's/architecture, features white/enameled steel panels./It is composed of four quadrants,/including a monumental atrium/that houses the lobby and/provides a ceremonial center/for the museum." "Yale Art + Architecture Building/New Haven, CT 1963/This solid, textured structure/of concrete was completed/in 1963. Large skylights/illuminate the dramatic main/interior space, overlooked by/mezzanines and bridges./Architect Paul Rudolph intended/his bold urban building 'to excite/and challenge the occupants.' "

Designer and Typographer: Margaret Bauer of Washington, D.C.

Art Director: Derry Noyes of Washington, D.C.

Photographers: Guggenheim Museum, Glass House, Yale Art & Architecture, High Museum of Art and Hancock Center, all by Ezra Stoller (deceased), represented by Esto Photographics, Mamaroneck, New York; Chrysler Building, Margaret Bourke-White (deceased); Vanna Venturi House, Matt Wargo, Philadelphia, Pennsylvania; TWA Terminal, Georg Fischer, New York, New York; Walt Disney Concert Hall, Todd Eberle, New York, New York; 860-880 Lake Shore Drive, Guido Guidi, Venice, Italy; National Gallery of Art East Building, Ben Spiegel (deceased); Exeter Academy Library, Grant Mudford, Los Angeles, California.

Modeler: Joseph Sheeran of Ashton-Potter (USA) Ltd., Williamsville, New York

Stamp Manufacturing: Stamps printed by Ashton-Potter on a Mueller Martini A76 modified offset press. Stamps processed by Ashton-Potter.

Quantity Ordered: 60,000,000

Plate Number Detail: none

Paper Supplier: Paper Corporation of the United States/Glatfelter

Tagging: nonphosphored paper, block tagging over stamps

The Stamps

On May 19, the Postal Service issued a pane of 12 stamps, each bearing a photograph of a distinctive example of American architecture from the

On the liner paper behind each stamp is text that describes the building and credits the architect.

84

past 75 years. The stamps had their first day sale in Las Vegas, Nevada, at the annual convention of the American Institute of Architects.

The self-adhesive stamps are semijumbo in size, arranged vertically on a pane with wide selvage on the right bearing the words "Masterworks of Modern American Architecture." Text on the liner paper behind each stamp describes the building and credits the architect. Ashton-Potter (USA) Ltd. printed the stamps by the offset process.

The set had its origin some four years earlier when Terrence McCaffrey, manager of stamp development for USPS, issued a challenge to members of the Citizens' Stamp Advisory Committee and its art directors.

"I said to them, 'If you were stamp czar, what stamps would you issue?'" McCaffrey said. "Doug Lewis [C. Douglas Lewis, then curator of sculpture

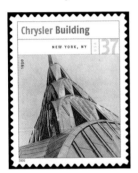

ture at the National Gallery of Art] made a presentation on architecture, which is one of his passions. He suggested an ongoing series of stamps, covering Indian burial mounds to modern-day architecture and everything in between."

CSAC thought the Lewis proposal was excessive, but decided that architecture was a worthwhile subject and that it was time to revisit it. A quarter of a century earlier, between 1979 and 1982, USPS had issued four blocks of four — 16 stamps in all — devoted to various periods of American architecture, from colonial days to the 20th century.

The committee asked art director Derry Noyes to explore the possibility of creating a prestige booklet containing stamps, text and pictures

This block of four 20¢ stamps of 1982, the last four stamps in the 16-stamp American Architecture series, also pictured outstanding examples of 20th-century architecture: Frank Lloyd Wright's Fallingwater, Ludwig Mies van der Rohe's Illinois Institute of Technology, Walter Gropius' Gropius House and Eero Saarinen's Dulles Airport (Scott 2019-2022).

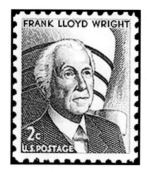

Two of the buildings shown on the Masterworks of Modern American Architecture pane had been previous U.S. stamp subjects. An exterior view of the Guggenheim Museum had appeared on the 2¢ Frank Lloyd Wright stamp of 1966, a part of the Prominent Americans definitive series (Scott 1280). Peter B. Kaplan's photograph of the Chrysler Building illustrated the 32¢ Art Deco Style stamp on the Celebrate the Century pane for the 1920s, issued in 1998 (Scott 3184j).

on outstanding architects and their work. Noyes enlisted designer Margaret Bauer for the project, while PhotoAssist, the Postal Service's research firm, asked Paul Goldberger, art critic for *The New Yorker* magazine, to serve as consultant.

In the end, Noyes and CSAC decided that the stamps should focus on buildings themselves rather than on their architects, and that they should be issued in pane form, to give them greater public exposure than they would receive in a prestige booklet.

Goldberger provided a list of 24 outstanding examples of American architecture, ranging chronologically from 1891 to 2002, for the consideration of CSAC and the design team. Ten of the buildings, plus two extras, were selected for stamps. Covering the period from 1930 to 2003, the 12 subjects are:

CHRYSLER BUILDING, New York City, 1930, designed by William Van Alen. The building previously was shown on a 32¢ stamp featuring the

Art Deco style on the Celebrate the Century pane for the 1920s, issued in 1998.

GLASS HOUSE, New Canaan, Connecticut, 1949, designed by Philip Johnson.

860-880 LAKE SHORE DRIVE, Chicago, Illinois, 1951, designed by Ludwig Mies van der Rohe.

TWA TERMINAL, New York City, 1962, designed by Eero Saarinen.

YALE ART & ARCHITECTURE BUILDING,

New Haven, Connecticut, 1963, designed by Paul Rudolph. It is "a hard building to love," said the *Yale Alumni Magazine*, "particularly for former art students who endured cramped working conditions, falling asbestos and multiple abrasions from the building's rough concrete walls." Two of those students were the stamps' designers, Derry Noyes (MFA '76) and Margaret Bauer ('86, MFA '91). The building "is admired as Rudolph's most elaborate attempt to reinvigorate modern architecture with weighty materials and complex flowing and

shifting spaces," the alumni magazine continued. "But Noyes says she didn't notice during her student days: 'I was so tired most of the time I didn't even think about it.' "

VANNA VENTURI HOUSE, Philadelphia, Pennsylvania, 1963, designed by Robert Venturi.

JOHN HANCOCK CENTER, Chicago, Illinois, 1970, a 100-story, X-braced tower designed by architect Bruce Graham and engineer Fazlur Khan of Skidmore, Owings & Merrill.

PHILIPS EXETER ACADEMY LIBRARY, Exeter, New Hampshire, 1971, designed by Louis I. Kahn.

NATIONAL GALLERY OF ART, EAST BUILDING, Washington, D.C., 1978, designed by I.M. Pei.

SOLOMON R. GUGGENHEIM MUSEUM, New York City, 1959, designed by Frank Lloyd Wright. This museum on Fifth Avenue, famed for its circular ramp topped by a glass dome, is shown on its stamp in an interior view; in 1966, an exterior view was depicted on the 2¢ Frank Lloyd Wright stamp of the Prominent Americans definitive series.

HIGH MUSEUM OF ART, Atlanta, Georgia, 1983, designed by Richard Meier. Besides being depicted on the stamp, the High Museum also is shown in an architect's line drawing that decorates the pane selvage.

WALT DISNEY CONCERT HALL, Los Angeles, California, 2003, designed by Frank Gehry. This building, home of the Los Angeles Philharmonic, also was not on Goldberger's list, but was added late in the process so the Western United States would be represented on the pane. It replaced a stamp depicting another Gehry work, the Weisman Museum in St. Paul, Minnesota, built in 1993. In early 2005, Gehry agreed to allow a mirror-pol-

ished stainless steel section of the concert hall to be sandblasted to match the brushed-steel appearance of the rest of the building because glare from the metal was blinding drivers and reflected heat was being felt by residents of nearby condos.

In all, the set featured two skyscrapers, three museums, a concert hall, an airport terminal, a college building, a library, an apartment building and two private houses. USPS described these structures as "some of the most recognizable and iconic architectural forms in the built environment."

In some cases, the availability of a striking photograph solidified a building's inclusion on the pane. This was the case with the Guggenheim Museum. It wasn't on Goldberger's list, but Ezra Stoller's interior shot, up through the coiling ramp to the glass dome, proved irresistible to Derry Noyes and Margaret Bauer.

Besides the Weisman Museum, Goldberger had offered these alternative choices:

Wainwright Building, St. Louis, Missouri, 1891, designed by Louis Sullivan. A stamp design was created showing the Wainwright, but was set aside after Paul Goldberger suggested, and CSAC agreed, that the buildings in the set should be limited to a more recent architectural period.

Unity Temple, Oak Park, Illinois, 1904, designed by Frank Lloyd Wright.

Nebraska State Capitol, Lincoln, Nebraska, 1932, designed by Bertram Goodhue.

Philadelphia Saving Fund Society Tower, Philadelphia, Pennsylvania, 1932, designed by Howe & Lescaze.

Fallingwater, Mill Run, Pennsylvania, 1937, designed by Frank Lloyd Wright. Fallingwater was shown on one of the stamps in the last block of four in the American Architecture series, issued in 1982.

S.C. Johnson Company complex, Racine, Wisconsin, 1939, designed by Frank Lloyd Wright.

Lever House, New York City, 1952, designed by Skidmore, Owings & Merrill.

Air Force Academy Chapel, Colorado Springs, Colorado, 1956, designed by Skidmore, Owings & Merrill. The chapel was pictured on a 37¢ stamp commemorating the 50th anniversary of the Air Force Academy in 2004.

Dulles Airport, Chantilly, Virginia, 1962, designed by Eero Saarinen. This work also appeared on one of the last four stamps in the American

Architecture series in 1982.

Ford Foundation, New York City, 1967, designed by Kevin Roche.

Kimball Art Museum, Fort Worth, Texas, 1972, designed by Louis Kahn.

Atheneum, New Harmony, Indiana, 1979, designed by Richard Meier.

Peter B. Lewis Building, Case Western Reserve University, Cleveland, Ohio, 2002, designed by Frank Gehry.

Three other buildings besides the Wainwright Building were considered for the set and reached the stamp-design stage but were dropped after it was decided to focus on the "modern" period beginning in 1930. They were the Allegheny County Courthouse in Pittsburgh, Pennsylvania, designed by Henry Hobson Richardson and built between 1883 and 1888; the Gamble House in Pasadena, California, designed by Charles and Henry Greene and completed in 1908; and McKim, Mead & White's Pennsylvania Station in New York City, built in 1910 and demolished in 1964.

While the stamps were in preparation, the American Institute of Architects asked that the Postal Service issue a series of architecture stamps beginning in 2007 to mark the AIA's 150th anniversary. In 1957, the U.S. Post Office Department had pro-

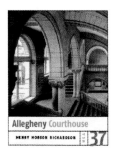

These four stamp designs were created but not used because the buildings were constructed before the "modern" architectural period beginning in 1930 that was arbitrarily chosen for the pane. Henry Hobson Richardson's Allegheny County Courthouse in Pittsburgh, Pennsylvania, was built between 1883 and 1888. (Note that the architect's name is erroneously given as "Henry Hudson Richardson.") The Wainwright Building in St. Louis, designed by Louis Sullivan, was built in 1891. The Gamble House in Pasadena, California, designed by Charles and Henry Greene, was completed in 1908, and McKim, Mead & White's Pennsylvania Station in New York City was built in 1910 and demolished in 1964.

In 1957, the Post Office Department issued this 3¢ red lilac stamp designed by Robert J. Schultz (Scott 1089) depicting a Corinthian capital and mushroom-type head and shaft to commemorate the 100th anniversary of the American Institute of Architects. When the AIA requested a series of stamps for its sesquicentennial in 2007, the Masterworks of Modern American Architecture pane was already in preparation.

duced a 3¢ stamp to commemorate the institute's centennial.

"They had seen our Nature of America stamps, and they suggested a series of panes using the same principle: a scene from which you could peel stamps showing different buildings," McCaffrey said. "I pointed out that all these distinguished buildings are not in the same place, so it would have to be a bogus city!

"We couldn't tell them at the time that we had already developed these 12 stamps, so we just thanked them very much for their suggestion. When we issued the stamps, we did so at the institute's annual convention, and Doug Lewis was one of the speakers.

"They have been very well received and have gotten a lot of play in the press."

The Designs

Derry Noyes' selection of Margaret Bauer of Washington, D.C., to design the stamps marked a reunion of prior collaborators. Under Noyes' direction, Bauer, a designer of books, exhibition catalogs and other museum publications at the National Gallery of Art, previously had designed the 32¢ Georgia O'Keeffe commemorative of 1996 and the four 37¢ Teddy Bears stamps of 2002.

Inspired by a photo spread in *Communication Arts*, a photography annual, Noyes decided early on to use black-and-white photos of the buildings and to crop them to create tight shots of interiors and exteriors rather than show whole buildings, as had been done with the American Architecture series of 1979-1981.

She and Bauer created a layout of 12 semijumbo stamps, vertically arranged, four stamps across by three down. Bauer placed the photographs of the buildings above the typography in the first and third vertical rows of stamps and below the typography in the second and fourth rows. "It was more visually dynamic than having the pictures all lining up," Noyes said.

For several of the photos, the camera is pointed upward, to show the concentric loops inside the Guggenheim, the sharp angles of the National Gallery of Art, the soaring towers of the Chrysler Building and the X-

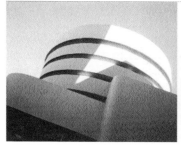

Masters of
American
Architecture

FRANK GEHRY
PHILIP JOHNSON
FRANK LLOYD WRIGHT
RICHARD MEIER
I.M. PEI
EERO SAARINEN
LOUIS SULLIVAN
MIES VAN DER ROHE

This could be a really great quote by this very famous architect.

Guggenheim Museum

Frank Lloyd Wright

New York, New York
1956 – 1959

This Arabic phrase, which means "blessed festival" or "May your religious holiday be blessed," is the happy greeting of Muslims during the two most important festivals—or eids—in the Islamic calendar: Eid al-Fitr and Eid al-Adha. The phrase Eid mubarak also appears on this stamp that commemorates these holidays and the blessings they bring. For American Muslims, this stamp is sure to add a colorful and festive touch to cards and letters. For non-Muslims, it represents an opportunity to learn more about the beliefs and traditions of their Muslim friends, neighbors, and coworkers. The first day of the Muslim lunar month of Shawwal. The first day of the Muslim lunar month of Shawwal, Eid al-Fitr signifies "The

Feast of Breaking the Fast" because it marks the end of Ramadan, the month of fasting. As prescribed in the Qur'an, the holy book of Islam, fasting during Ramadan begins from just before first light until sunset, when Muslims must abstain not only from food and drink, but also from evil thoughts, sexual activity, and smoking. Eid al-Fitr is observed by offering special alms with prayers, feasting, exchanging gifts, and visiting family and friends. The phrase Eid mubarak also appears on this stamp that commemorates these holidays and the blessings they bring. For American and coworkers. The first day of the Muslim lunar month.

Guaranty Building

Louis Sullivan

Cityhere, Statealso
1956 – 1959

This Arabic phrase, which means "blessed festival" or "May your religious holiday be blessed," is the happy greeting of Muslims during the two most important festivals—or eids—in the Islamic calendar: Eid al-Fitr and Eid al-Adha. The phrase Eid mubarak also appears on this stamp that commemorates these holidays and the blessings they bring. For American Muslims, this stamp is sure to add a colorful and festive touch to cards and letters. For non-Muslims, it represents an opportunity to learn more about the beliefs and traditions of their Muslim friends, neighbors, and coworkers. The first day of the Muslim lunar month of Shawwal. The first day of the Muslim lunar month of Shawwal, Eid al-Fitr signifies "The

Feast of Breaking the Fast" because it marks the end of Ramadan, the month of fasting. As prescribed in the Qur'an, the holy book of Islam, fasting during Ramadan begins from just before first light until sunset, when Muslims must abstain not only from food and drink, but also from evil thoughts, sexual activity, and smoking. Eid al-Fitr is observed by offering special alms with prayers, feasting, exchanging gifts, and visiting family and friends. The phrase Eid mubarak also appears on this stamp that commemorates these holidays and the blessings they bring. For American and coworkers. The first day of the Muslim lunar month.

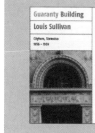

This could be a really great quote by this very famous architect.

This could be a really great quote from this very famous architect. Its possible that it could be several lines long maybe.

PHILIP JOHNSON

Glass House

Philip Johnson

New Canaan, Connecticut
1956 – 1959

This Arabic phrase, which means "blessed festival" or "May your religious holiday be blessed," is the happy greeting of Muslims during the two most important festivals—or eids—in the Islamic calendar: Eid al-Fitr and Eid al-Adha. The phrase Eid mubarak also appears on this stamp that commemorates these holidays and the blessings they bring. For American Muslims, this stamp is sure to add a colorful and festive touch to cards and letters. For non-Muslims, it represents an opportunity to learn more about the beliefs and traditions of their Muslim friends, neighbors, and coworkers. The first day of the Muslim lunar month of Shawwal. The first day of the Muslim lunar month of Shawwal, Eid al-Fitr signifies "The

Feast of Breaking the Fast" because it marks the end of Ramadan, the month of fasting. As prescribed in the Qur'an, the holy book of Islam, fasting during Ramadan begins from just before first light until sunset, when Muslims must abstain not only from food and drink, but also from evil thoughts, sexual activity, and smoking. Eid al-Fitr is observed by offering special alms with prayers, feasting, exchanging gifts, and visiting family and friends. The phrase Eid mubarak also appears on this stamp that commemorates these holidays and the blessings they bring. For American and coworkers. The first day of the Muslim lunar month.

These are layouts of covers and interior pages, with dummy type, made by Derry Noyes for a prestige booklet containing stamps, text and pictures featuring "Masters of American Architecture" and their works. In the end, Noyes and CSAC decided that the stamps should focus on buildings themselves rather than on their architects, and that they should be issued in pane form, to give them greater public exposure than they would receive in a prestige booklet.

braced Hancock Center, and the rough texture of the Yale Art & Architecture Building. "Sparkling glass facades, monumental swirls of concrete and shimmering waves of stainless steel make for a grand and muscular cityscape," commented Linda Hales in *The Washington Post*.

The designers chose the photos to be compatible but distinctive, Bauer told the Postal Service. "Like a family," she said. "And, like a family, they each had to have room. I couldn't have too many angles all together, or too many curves together. The details needed to be separated from each other, so that someone who looked at all the stamps together could tell that they were honoring buildings — whether we showed an interior or exterior shot — but each stamp needed to be able to stand on its own as well."

Five of the photographs were made by renowned architectural photographer Ezra Stoller, who died October 29, 2004, at age 89. They are the Guggenheim Museum, Yale Art & Architecture Building, High Museum of Art, Glass House and John Hancock Center. Stoller's images, wrote Joseph Giovannini in a tribute in *Architectural Record*, "often provide the lasting record of a building understood in the way the architect intended, revealed in a chiaroscuro of light and shade that explained its form, spatiality and sensibility."

The other photo credits are: Walt Disney Concert Hall, Todd Eberle, New York; 860-880 Lake Shore Drive, Guido Guidi, Venice, Italy; Chrysler Building, the late Margaret Bourke-White; Vanna Venturi House, Matt Wargo, Philadelphia; National Gallery of Art, East Building, the late Ben Spiegel; Exeter Academy Library, Grant Mudford, Los Angeles; TWA Terminal, Georg Fischer, Hamburg, Germany. Bourke-White's photo made at the Buchenwald concentration camp shortly after its liberation in 1945 was the basis for the illustration on one of the World War II commemorative stamps of 1995.

The typography, in a font called Fago bold, is enclosed in two horizontal strips, with the "USA" and "37" in small compartments within the second strip. The lines are meant to give an appropriate "structural feel" to the type, Noyes said. Bauer chose a palette of Pantone Matching System (PMS) colors — red, purple, dark orange, light orange, green and blue — for the names of the buildings and denominations that contrast with the

Late in the design process, CSAC decided to replace Frank Gehry's Weisman Museum in St. Paul, Minnesota, with another Gehry-designed structure, the Walt Disney Concert Hall in Los Angeles, California, so the Western United States would be represented in the set.

black and white of the photographs. The stamps in a vertical row have the same color combinations, "to provide consistency, so the colors aren't just jumping around at random," the art director explained.

Originally, the designers intended to place the names of the architects inside the second of the two typography strips in the designs. Postal officials vetoed the idea because several of the individuals were still living. Instead, the names were included in the text on the back of each stamp's liner paper, and in the vacated spot on the front was placed the name of the city where the building is located.

The line drawing on the selvage, by Richard Meier & Partners, is a three-dimensional view of the High Museum of Art, shown in lighter blue against a solid dark blue background. The image "is supposed to feel a little like a blueprint," Noyes said. "The blue came out a bit brighter than we had anticipated, but that's OK. It still worked."

Varieties

Panes of the Architecture stamps with the dark orange ink missing were purchased at post offices in the St. Louis, Missouri, area.

Brian Laschober told *Linn's Stamp News* he had bought a total of 34 color-missing panes. Savoy Horvath of Wisconsin informed *Linn's* that his daughter had purchased a pane at a postal facility "within sight of the Gateway Arch" in St. Louis and had used three of the stamps for postage, including one on a letter to him.

Six stamps on each pane are affected by the missing dark orange. The "USA 37" is absent on the Chrysler Building, 860-880 Lake Shore Drive and High Museum of Art stamps. The words "TWA," "Glass" and "Hancock" are missing on the TWA Terminal, Glass House and Hancock Center stamps, respectively.

Linn's reported that four color-missing panes were sold on eBay before August 1, 2005, for $191.38, $212.50, $215.50 and $261.51. An advertise-

Shown here are two stamps from a pane on which the dark orange ink is missing. The Chrysler Building stamp is without its "USA 37"; the TWA Terminal stamp has lost the initials "TWA."

ment in the August 8 issue of *Linn's* offered a pane for $1,850. Jacques C. Schiff Jr. included a pane in his auction held August 17-18, 2005, in New Jersey.

First-Day Facts

Anita Bizzotto, senior vice president and chief marketing officer for USPS, dedicated the stamps at an 8:15 a.m. ceremony at the AIA convention in the ballroom of the Mandalay Bay Resort and Casino in Las Vegas.

Speakers were Adrian Smith, consulting design partner with Skidmore, Owings & Merrill, designers of the John Hancock Center, and C. Douglas Lewis, chairman of CSAC, who made the proposal that led to the stamps' issuance. Douglas L. Steidl, president of the AIA, gave the welcome. Honored guests were Oscar B. Goodman, mayor of Las Vegas; Norman L. Koonce, AIA executive vice president and chief executive officer; and Kate L. Schwennsen, first vice president of the AIA.

For a limited time, Stamp Fulfillment Services offered first-day covers of a full pane with conventional black postmark for $6.94. First-day covers with digital color postmarks also were offered, at $1.50 for a random single and $18 for a full set of 12.

37¢ HENRY FONDA
LEGENDS OF HOLLYWOOD SERIES

Date of Issue: May 20, 2005

Catalog Number: Scott 3911

Colors: black, cyan, magenta, yellow, purple (PMS 536)

First-Day Cancel: Los Angeles, California

First-Day Cancellations: 76,753

Format: Pane of 20, vertical, 5 across, 4 down. Offset printing plates printing 180 stamps per revolution (12 across, 15 around). Also sold in uncut press sheets of 9 panes (3 across by 3 down).

Microprinting: "USPS" to the right of and below the knot of necktie

Gum Type: self-adhesive

Overall Stamp Size: 0.98 by 1.56 inches; 24.892 by 39.624 mm

Pane Size: 8.74 by 7.169 inches; 221.996 by 182.092 mm

Uncut Press Sheet Size: 26⅞ by 23 inches

Perforations: 11 by 10¾ (die-cut simulated perforations) (IDC custom two station die cutter)

Selvage Inscription: "LEGENDS OF HOLLYWOOD/HENRY FONDA (1905-1982) was noted/for his naturalness and sincerity in/stage roles and on the screen./Effective in comedic or dramatic roles,/he typically played thoughtful men of/integrity. In a career spanning nearly 50/years, he won many honors, including/a Tony Award in 1948 for his work in the/Broadway production of *Mister Roberts*/and the Academy Award for best actor/in 1982 for *On Golden Pond.*" "11th IN A SERIES." "*The Grapes of Wrath*™ & © 1940, 2004 Twentieth Century Fox Film Corporation./All rights reserved."

Selvage Markings: "© 2004 USPS." ".37 x 20 = $7.40." "PLATE/POSITION" and diagram.

Back Markings: Universal Product Code (UPC) "458600" in 4 locations on back of liner paper.

Illustrator: Drew Struzan of Pasadena, California

Designer, Art Director and Typographer: Derry Noyes of Washington, D.C.

Modeler: Joseph Sheeran of Ashton-Potter (USA) Ltd., Williamsville, New York

Stamp Manufacturing: Stamps printed by Ashton-Potter on a Mueller Martini A74 offset press. Stamps finished by Ashton-Potter.

Quantity Ordered: 65,000,000

Plate Number Detail: 1 set of 5 plate numbers preceded by the letter P in selvage beside each corner stamp

Plate Number Combination Reported: P11111

Paper Supplier: Paper Corporation of the United States/Glatfelter

Tagging: block tagging over stamps

The Stamp

On May 20, the Postal Service issued a stamp in Beverly Hills, California, honoring actor Henry Fonda, whose legacy of distinguished stage, screen and television performances spanned nearly 50 years. The date was four days after the 100th anniversary of his birth.

The stamp was the 11th in the annual Legends of Hollywood series, which was launched in 1995 with a commemorative depicting Marilyn Monroe. She was followed by James Dean, Humphrey Bogart, Alfred Hitchcock, James Cagney, Edward G. Robinson, Lucille Ball, Cary Grant, Audrey Hepburn and John Wayne.

Ashton-Potter (USA) Ltd. printed the Fonda stamp, a self-adhesive, by the offset process. It was the company's first Legends of Hollywood stamp and only the second, after Lucille Ball, to be offset-printed; the others were produced by the gravure process by Sennett Security Products or its predecessor, Stamp Venturers.

Like all the previous Legends of Hollywood stamps, the Fonda stamp is vertically arranged and was distributed in panes of 20, five across by four down, with a wide pictorial selvage on the right side. Also like the others, it was made available to collectors in uncut

96

press sheets at face value — in the case of the nine-pane Fonda sheet, $66.60.

The Fonda press sheet has a few unusual characteristics. Production markings that often are trimmed away on these collector-directed issues were left intact, creating a sheet that is surrounded by a border inscribed with an array of alternating color bars and dots, alignment and slice-point markings, and die-cut indicators.

Scott Publishing Company reported that each of three press sheets ordered by the firm included a dot-matrix line of text printed upside down in the margin directly above the upper left pane. The text reads "HENRY FONDA 22:22 09/09/05" followed by a multi-digit number. On the Scott examples, the numbers advance in sequence from 004589764 through 004589766.

The Scott *Specialized Catalogue of U.S. Stamps & Covers* lists four position pieces from the uncut sheet: a cross-gutter block of eight, a block of eight with vertical gutter, and horizontal and vertical pairs with gutters.

The pattern of the pane's die-cut simulated perfs is similar to that of conventional or die-cut perfs on the previous Legends of Hollywood stamps. A second row of die-cuts around the outer edges of the block of 20 stamps creates a narrow inner selvage, which is blank except for a set of plate numbers in each corner. Three of the horizontal rows of die cuts extend to the edge of the pane on the left side and penetrate the liner paper to enable postal clerks to detach and sell singles or blocks.

The Citizens' Stamp Advisory Committee had selected Fonda to be on a Legends of Hollywood stamp, but no one realized that 2005 would be his centennial year until postal officials met with the star's widow, Shirlee Fonda, at her home overlooking Los Angeles to show her the photograph on which they wanted to base the design. "We hadn't done our homework," said Terrence McCaffrey, manager of stamp development. "We were thinking about Fonda for a future stamp, but not necessarily locking him in to 2005. When we were reminded that May 16, 1905, was his birth date, we hustled back to Washington to get the committee's approval to make Fonda the 'Legend' for 2005."

Henry Fonda was born in Grand Island, Nebraska, and was still an infant when the family moved to Omaha, where his father opened a print shop. After high school, Fonda enrolled at the University of Minnesota as a journalism major, but later dropped out.

He made his amateur acting debut with the Omaha Community Playhouse under the direction of Dorothy Brando, whose son Marlon would become a distinguished actor himself. In 1928, Fonda moved East and joined the Cape Cod University Players group, where he met other future theatrical luminaries, including Joshua Logan, Mildred Natwick, James Stewart and Margaret Sullavan. Fonda and Stewart roomed together for a time and were firm friends throughout their lives.

In 1931, Fonda and Sullavan married, but the marriage lasted only a few months. In 1936, he married socialite Frances Seymour Brokaw, who bore him two children, Jane and Peter, both of whom also became actors. Fonda would marry three more times: His fifth wife, who survived him, was Shirlee May Adams, a flight attendant many years his junior.

By 1934, Fonda was on Broadway playing the lead role of the love-struck farmer in *The Farmer Takes a Wife*. When the play was made into a film in 1935, Fonda reprised the role opposite Janet Gaynor, and his movie career was under way.

The success of his film career accelerated with a series of movies made for 20th Century Fox beginning in 1939. In that year, he played the title role in *Young Mr. Lincoln*, directed by John Ford, and won praise from *The New York Times* for the "warmth and kindliness, the pleasant modesty, the courage, resolution, tenderness, shrewdness and wit" he brought to the role. Ford chose him to play the dispossessed farmer Tom Joad in *The Grapes of Wrath* (1940), for which he received an Academy Award nomination for best actor. He followed that somber turn by playing the deadpan straight man to Barbara Stanwyck and Charles Coburn in Preston Sturges' comedy *The Lady Eve* (1941). His last movie before his career was interrupted for Navy service in World War II was a Western, *The Ox-Bow Incident* (1943).

In 1942, at age 37, Fonda was considered too old for active duty, but he enlisted as a seaman over the objections of studio boss Darryl F. Zanuck. He rose through the ranks, won a Bronze Star, and was discharged as a lieutenant in 1946.

Two years later, Fonda returned to Broadway in the title role in *Mr. Roberts*, which he performed 1,077 consecutive times and for which he won a Tony Award. He later played the part on tour and in the 1955 film version, his final collaboration with director John Ford.

Through the postwar period and for three more decades, Fonda continued to make films, with an occasional hiatus for stage work: *My Darling Clementine* (1946); *Fort Apache*, with John Wayne (1948); *The Wrong Man*, directed by Alfred Hitchcock (1956); *War and Peace*, with Audrey Hepburn (1956); *Twelve Angry Men* (1957); *How the West Was Won* (1962); *The Longest Day* (1962); *Fail-Safe*, in which he played the president of the United States (1963); *In Harm's Way* (1965); *Yours, Mine and Ours* (1968); and *Once Upon a Time in the West*, directed by Sergio Leone (1968). His stage work included *Point of No Return* (1951), *The Caine Mutiny Court-Martial* (1953) and a one-man show as famed criminal lawyer Clarence Darrow (1973) that netted him a best-actor Tony nomination. The play was also shown on television.

His autobiography, *Fonda: My Life*, was published in 1981. In 1978, he won a Life Achievement award from the American Film Institute; in 1979, he received a special Tony award for his contributions to the theater; and in 1981, he was awarded an honorary Academy Award for lifetime achievement in film. The next year, Fonda finally won a best-actor Oscar for his performance as an irascible old professor in *On Golden Pond* (1981) with Katharine Hepburn, who also won an Oscar, and his daughter Jane, who was nominated for one. "As you watch him," wrote *New York Times* critic Vincent Canby, "you're seeing the intelligence, force and grace of a talent that has been maturing on screen for almost 50 years." At 76, Fonda was the oldest man ever to win an Academy Award for best actor.

Fonda's last film appearance was in the 1981 made-for-TV movie *Summer Solstice*. He died of pancreatic cancer and heart failure on August 12, 1982, in Los Angeles.

The Design

As her illustrator, art director Derry Noyes chose Drew Struzan, an entertainment artist whose numerous stamp credits include the Edward G. Robinson, Lucille Ball and John Wayne stamps in the Legends of Hollywood series, the 1999 Alfred Lunt and Lynn Fontanne commemorative, and the 15 Celebrate the Century stamps of 2000 that marked the decade of the 1990s.

"Finding a photograph for Drew to use as his model for the stamp was kind of tough," Noyes said. "There were very few photographs of Henry Fonda that were not studio shots, showing him in one of his roles."

The photo they chose was a black-and-white full-face portrait made by Frank Powolny in 1941, when Fonda was 36. Powolny, who was the chief

Drew Struzan based his stamp portrait of Henry Fonda on this black-and-white full-face photograph made by Frank Powolny in 1941, when the actor was 36. Shown with it is Struzan's preliminary pencil sketch for the stamp illustration.

This is the still from the 1940 film The Grapes of Wrath *on which Struzan based the pencil sketch of Fonda, as dispossessed farmer Tom Joad, in the pane selvage. Joad is partly reflected in an oval mirror that also reflects the faces of two other characters.*

portrait and still photographer for 20th Century Fox, later took some of the best-known shots of Marilyn Monroe, as well as the most famous GI pinup picture in history: the 1943 photo of Betty Grable, in swimsuit and pumps, peeking coyly over her shoulder.

"I liked the fact that he's looking straight at you," Noyes said of the Fonda photograph. In making his acrylic painting, Struzan emphasized the eye contact by making Fonda's eyes a penetrating blue. Blue is predominant elsewhere, in Fonda's dark jacket, the tint of his shirt, the highlights of his hair, and the unfinished background.

"The stamp came out much darker than Drew's painting," Noyes said. "In the original, he doesn't have that five o'clock shadow, and his eyes are a much brighter blue. It's OK, though. I think it's a strong portrait. It's still compelling. It gets your attention."

Noyes knew at the outset that she wanted the selvage image to depict Fonda in his role as Tom Joad in *The Grapes of Wrath*. When she saw Struzan's preliminary pencil sketch, based on a still from the film, she told him to take the artwork no further. "I liked seeing the strokes of the pencil," she said. "It had a spontaneity to it. It brought out the grittiness

100

The microprinted letters "USPS" are to the right of and below the knot of Fonda's necktie.

of the role, and contrasted nicely with the finished painting in the stamp portrait." In the sketch as Noyes cropped it, the image of Tom Joad fills the selvage frame, with the descriptive text superimposed on the bib of his overalls in dropout white.

"If we had chosen *On Golden Pond* or *Mr. Roberts* instead of *The Grapes of Wrath* for the selvage, it would have had a very different feel," Noyes said. "I wanted to do something slightly different from what we had done with all the other Legends of Hollywood selvages, by coming in close and tight, and making him bigger than life and looking into his face and sort of reading his mind, rather than just showing a studio portrait of a handsome man. I wanted to sort of get into the psychology of his role. To have backed off and shown a scene would have been more like everything else we do."

Noyes placed the name "Henry Fonda" in Frutiger type across the top of the design, and "USA 37" in the lower left corner. The typography is printed in a PMS purple color. Ashton-Potter used the four standard process colors for the stamp portrait and process black for the selvage image.

Because the stamp was offset-printed, microprinting was included in the design for security reasons. The letters "USPS" can be found to the right of and below the knot of Fonda's necktie.

First-Day Facts

John F. Walsh, a member of the USPS Board of Governors, dedicated the stamp in an evening ceremony at the Academy of Motion Picture Arts and Sciences' Samuel Goldwyn Theatre in Beverly Hills.

Speakers were Fonda's daughter Jane and his grandchildren, Vanessa Vadim and Troy Garity, who are Jane's two children, and Justin Fonda, son of Fonda's son Peter Fonda. Peter could not attend because he was working on a film in Australia.

The master of ceremonies was Robert Osborne, author, film critic and host of Turner Classic Movies. Osborne moderated a panel consisting of Mark Rydell, director of *On Golden Pond*, and actor Larry Hagman, who worked with Fonda in the films *Fail-Safe* and *In Harm's Way*. Rydell recalled that he had introduced Fonda to Katherine Hepburn before filming *On Golden Pond*; remarkably, the two Hollywood veterans never had met, let alone worked together.

A cinematic montage called *A Life in Film* was shown, with clips from such classics as *Young Mr. Lincoln*, *The Grapes of Wrath*, *Mister Roberts* and *Once Upon a Time in the West* (1968). Frank Pierson, president of the Academy of Motion Picture Arts and Sciences, gave the welcome. Honored guests included Fonda's widow, Shirlee Fonda; his son Peter's wife, Becky Fonda; Al Iniguez, vice president for Pacific Area operations, USPS; stamp artist Drew Struzan; and Koula Fuller, Beverly Hills postmaster.

After the ceremony, the 1946 film *My Darling Clementine* was shown. Most of the people in the large audience stayed to watch.

The earliest known pre-release use of a Henry Fonda stamp was on a cover that was machine-canceled May 17, three days before the date of issue, in Cincinnati, Ohio. The cover was sent to *Linn's Stamp News* by an Ohio reader, Gordon Milne.

For a limited time, Stamp Fulfillment Services offered uncacheted first-day covers for $1.50 (digital color cancellation) and 75¢ (conventional black cancellation). A full-pane first-day cover was sold for $9.90.

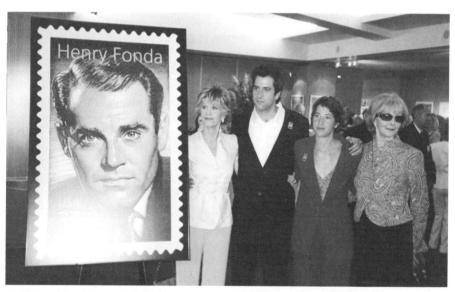

Actress Jane Fonda, left, her children Troy Garity and Vanessa Vadim, and Henry Fonda's wife Shirlee pose next to a blowup of the Fonda stamp design at the first-day ceremony in Beverly Hills.

37¢ THE ART OF DISNEY: CELEBRATION (4 DESIGNS)

Date of Issue: June 30, 2005

Catalog Numbers: Scott 3912-3915, stamps; 3915a, block or vertical strip of 4

Colors: red (PMS 704), black, cyan, magenta, yellow, gold

First-Day Cancel: Anaheim, California

First-Day Cancellations: 379,255 (includes picture postal cards)

Format: Pane of 20, vertical, 5 across, 4 down. Offset printing plates printing 180 stamps per revolution (15 across, 12 around).

Gum Type: self-adhesive

Stamp Size: 1.23 by 1.56 inches; 31.24 by 39.62 mm

Pane Size: 7.13 by 8 inches; 181.1 by 203.2 mm

Perforations: 10½ by 10¾ (die-cut simulated perforations) (Heidelberg rotary die cutter)

Selvage Inscription: "The Art of Disney/Celebration." "Disney Materials ©
  Disney."

Selvage Markings: "© 2005/USPS". ".37/x20/$7.40". "PLATE/POSITION" and
  diagram.

Back Markings: On selvage liner: "THE ART OF DISNEY: CELEBRATION"/
  "With this stamp pane, the U.S. Postal Service honors the art of celebration as imagined by Walt Disney and his studio animators./Now, with help
  from a few beloved Disney characters, it's easy to add some zest to your
  correspondence./This is the second stamp pane honoring the art of Disney to be issued by the U.S. Postal Service. The first, issued in 2004, was
  on the theme of friendship." Universal Product Code (UPC) "567200" in 4
  locations.

On stamp liners: "Mickey Mouse and Pluto/Anticipating a celebration/can be
  half the fun./Mickey Mouse and his/faithful dog Pluto are/experts when
  it comes to/sharing cake and having/good times. They're sure/to help
  get your party/started early!" "Alice and the Mad Hatter/A very merry tea
  party/hosted by the Mad/Hatter gives Alice a chance to catch up on all/the
  news in Wonderland./This cheerful stamp/makes it easy for you/and your
  friends to stay/in touch." "Ariel and Flounder/Wherever you are, just/being
  in touch with pals/can lead to merriment./Ariel, a little mermaid,/longs
  to enjoy life on land,/but that doesn't stop her/from enjoying music with/
  Flounder and her other/undersea friends." "Snow White and Dopey/When
  it's time to/celebrate, our best/advice is to follow the/lead of Snow White
  and/Dopey and dance! With/this festive stamp, you/can keep the 'silly/
  song' playing a little/bit longer."

Designer: David Pacheco of Burbank, California

Illustrator: Peter Emmerich of New York, New York

Art Director: Terrence McCaffrey, USPS

Modeler: Donald Woo of Sennett Security Products

Stamp Manufacturing: Stamps printed by Banknote Corporation of America/
  Sennett Security Products, Browns Summit, North Carolina, on Roland
  300 offset press. Stamps processed by Unique Binders, Fredericksburg,
  Virginia.

Quantity Ordered: 215,000,000

Plate Number Detail: 1 set of 6 plate numbers preceded by the letter S in
  selvage above or below each corner stamp

Plate Number Combination Reported: S111111

Paper Supplier: MACtac

Tagging: block tagging over stamps

The Stamps

On June 30, in Anaheim, California, the Postal Service issued the second block of four stamps in its Art of Disney series. The set, The Art of
Disney: Celebration, features characters from the films of the Walt Disney

Studios in festive settings.

The stamps had their first-day sale in Disneyland, which was observing its 50th anniversary in 2005. Disneyland also had been the dedication site for the first block of four in the series, The Art of Disney: Friendship, on June 23, 2004.

A block of four with the theme of Romance will be issued in 2006 to complete the series.

Like the 2004 set, the Celebration stamps were accompanied by a set of four 23¢ stamped picture postal cards (see separate chapter). However, this time there was no companion issue of stamped stationery. In 2004, USPS was strongly criticized in some quarters for issuing four letter sheets reproducing the Disney Friendship stamps that were sold in packets of 12 — three specimens of each variety — for $14.95, more than $10 above the total face value of $4.44.

Under the advance plan for the series worked out by USPS and the Disney Studios, each of the three sets would comprise one stamp starring Mickey Mouse, whom the company was attempting to re-establish as its signature character; two stamps depicting other characters that Disney describes as "classics"; and a fourth stamp showing characters "that are fairly contemporary but rapidly becoming classic," in the words of Terrence McCaffrey, manager of stamp development.

"We didn't want to feature films as such, but to feature the relationships between the characters," McCaffrey said. "The [Citizens' Stamp Advisory] Committee said explicitly that we weren't going to endorse movies. That's why we came up with our themes: friendship, romance and celebration."

The four Celebration stamps depict Mickey and his dog Pluto; the Mad Hatter and Alice from *Alice in Wonderland*, and Snow White and Dopey from *Snow White and the Seven Dwarfs*, two classic films; and Ariel and her best friend, Flounder, from *The Little Mermaid*, a more recent production. Each stamp illustrates a different way of celebrating, through food, drink, dance and music, respectively.

Like the stamps in the first set, the Celebrations are self-adhesive semi-jumbos printed by the offset process by Banknote Corporation of America/Sennett Security Products and distributed in panes of 20 with decorative selvage. The panes are laid out in four horizontal rows of five, with each horizontal row consisting of two alternating designs. Any block or vertical strip of four from the pane comprises all four varieties. Verso text on each stamp describes the characters shown on the front.

Plate numbers are found above or below each of the four corner stamps. On the first pane in the series, there are plate numbers only beneath the two corner stamps in the bottom row.

With the success of his short animated cartoon features in the early 1930s, Walt Disney began planning a feature-length animated motion picture. He chose for his story the Grimm brothers' fairy tale *Snow White and the Seven Dwarfs*. Under his supervision, the script, with its beautiful princess, handsome prince and evil queen, was developed; the dwarfs were

THE ART OF DISNEY: CELEBRATION

With this stamp pane, the U.S. Postal Service honors the art of celebration as imagined by Walt Disney and his studio animators.
Now, with help from a few beloved Disney characters, it's easy to add some zest to your correspondence.
This is the second stamp pane honoring the art of Disney to be issued by the U.S. Postal Service. The first, issued in 2004, was on the theme of friendship.

Mickey Mouse and Pluto
Anticipating a celebration can be half the fun. Mickey Mouse and his faithful dog Pluto are experts when it comes to sharing cake and having good times. They're sure to help get your party started early!

Alice and the Mad Hatter
A very merry tea party hosted by the Mad Hatter gives Alice a chance to catch up on all the news in Wonderland. This cheerful stamp makes it easy for you and your friends to stay in touch.

Ariel and Flounder
Wherever you are, just being in touch with pals can lead to merriment. Ariel, a little mermaid, longs to enjoy life on land, but that doesn't stop her from enjoying music with Flounder and her other undersea friends.

Snow White and Dopey
When it's time to celebrate, our best advice is to follow the lead of Snow White and Dopey and dance! With this festive stamp, you can keep the "silly song" playing a little bit longer.

To view a full variety of Disney-related philatelic products and collectibles, such as stationery and prints, visit The Postal Store at www.usps.com/shop or call 1 800 STAMP-24 to order a free catalog.

Text is printed on the backing paper behind the stamps and selvage.

named and given personalities and images; original music was created; dozens of technical problems were confronted and solved; and Disney artists prepared 240,000 separate drawings. The film was completed at a cost of $1.5 million, unprecedented for its day, and made its debut December 21, 1937. Reviewers were enthusiastic, audiences filled theaters to see the movie, Disney won a special Academy Award for his achievement, and Snow White went on to become a classic and a milestone in cinema making.

The 1951 film *Alice in Wonderland* was based on Lewis Carroll's classics, *Alice in Wonderland* and *Through the Looking-Glass*, which Carroll developed from stories he told to 12-year-old Alice Liddell, the daughter of a colleague. Critics found the Disney translation to be uneven, with some portions described as brilliant — including the Mad Tea Party, the event depicted on the stamp, in which veteran comics Ed Wynn and Jerry Colonna supplied the voices of the Mad Hatter and the March Hare — but other parts were deemed inferior, including elements that were pure Disney inventions. British critics, in particular, were dismayed at the liberties the studio had taken with the story. Alice was a box-office failure, losing an estimated $1 million.

On the other hand, *The Little Mermaid*, which was based on the Hans Christian Andersen tale but also strayed far from the original story line, drew strong critical acclaim. The 1989 feature-length film won two Academy Awards, two Golden Globes and two Grammy Awards for its music: best original score, by Alan Menken, and best song, "Under the Sea," by Menken and Howard Ashman. After a run of unsuccessful Disney animated productions, *The Little Mermaid* is credited with launching a renaissance in cartoon musicals for the studio. It led to an animated television series about Ariel.

Both Mickey Mouse and Snow White, as characters, were making their second U.S. stamp appearances. Mickey was shown on one of the 2004 Art of Disney: Friendship stamps (Scott 3865), and Snow White was depicted on a 32¢ stamp of the Celebrate the Century pane for the 1930s, issued in 1998 (Scott 3185h).

The Designs

The decorative selvage that surrounds the stamps has the same design that was used for the first pane, but is in gold instead of light blue. It is filled with what Terrence McCaffrey called "stars, swishes and pixie dust." The header, or top segment, depicts Tinker Bell, the fairy from the Disney film *Peter Pan*, with the words "The Art of Disney" in a combination of Stempel Garamond italic and the Disney logo. These are in dropout white. Below, in red uppercase and lowercase letters with a black dropped shadow, is the word "Celebration."

The stamps in the first pane in the series displayed tight close-ups of the characters, but the Celebration stamps show their characters full length, or nearly so. The only typography on the stamps is "37 usa" in an upper corner. The "37" is in the gold color of the selvage, and the lowercase "usa," in red, is in a studio font called Mickey's Wacky.

As before, the illustrators assigned by Disney were David Pacheco, creative director of Walt Disney Art Classics, and Peter Emmerich of New York City, a free-lance illustrator and former Disney animator. The Disney team worked closely with the Postal Service's McCaffrey, who served as art director and made certain the designs met the peculiar requirements of postage-stamp art.

Pacheco sketched out the designs in pencil, and based on these draw-

This sequence shows the evolution of the Mickey Mouse and Pluto design, from David Pacheco's first pencil sketches (note that the cake has candles in the original rough) to Peter Emmerich's initial drawing that he colored with a felt-tip pen to his finished acrylic-on-canvas painting.

ings, Emmerich created the finished art. Emmerich's acrylic-on-canvas paintings conveyed a "retro look, with a texture and three-dimensionality that was just what we were looking for," McCaffrey said.

The background color for the four stamps in the first block of four is tan; for this one, it is blue, a choice that was dictated by the fact that the Little Mermaid, in an undersea setting, was one of the subjects.

The Mickey Mouse and Pluto stamp shows Mickey holding aloft a frosted cake as Pluto watches, tongue lolling in anticipation. Bits and streamers of confetti fill the air to convey the spirit of celebration.

"This one was the easiest of the four to do," McCaffrey said. "Peter Emmerich is good at painting Mickey, especially the retro Mickey that we used on the stamp, which is one of the reasons he was chosen for the series.

"We had to create a scene for Mickey and another character, and we decided on Pluto. Originally the cake was a birthday cake, with candles, but we decided that was too limiting. Without the candles, it could still be a birthday cake, but it could also be a cake for celebrating at a picnic, or the Fourth of July. So we put a little cherry on top instead. The confetti was added later."

In the Ariel and Flounder stamp, the mermaid, her red hair swirling in the current and her blue-green tail curving down and up again, plays a golden lyre as her fish companion grins appreciatively. Between the first pencil sketch and the finished art, the image changed in subtle ways: the number of additional fish was reduced to two, and the lyre was placed in Ariel's outstretched hands, which at first were empty. "We all felt that one of the highlights of the movie was the great, bubbly music," McCaffrey explained.

The Mad Tea Party (described in the stamp's verso text as "a very merry tea party") shows the Mad Hatter seated cross-legged on the table, holding a stack of four cups and saucers and pouring tea into the top cup. Alice, her hands clasped in wonder, watches from her seat at the table.

The early sketches, and even Emmerich's finished color painting, depicted a third character, the March Hare. (There was a fourth partygoer, the Dormouse, but at this point in the book and film, he had been stuffed

The subtle changes in the Ariel and Flounder stamp can be seen in this progression from first pencil sketch to finished art. The number of additional fish was reduced to two, and a lyre was placed in Ariel's outstretched hands.

This sequence of sketches and color renderings for the Mad Tea Party scene shows three characters, Alice, the Mad Hatter and the March Hare, with Alice standing. In David Pacheco's second pencil sketch and Peter Emmerich's two color versions, the Hatter is pouring tea into the Hare's cup, first in a steady stream from the teapot, then with only a single drop showing. However, CSAC members felt that the picture would be too crowded at stamp size, so the March Hare was eliminated.

into a teapot by the Hatter and Hare and was out of sight.) "I took the art back to the committee, and everyone said, that's cool, but at stamp size it's really 'busy,' " McCaffrey said. "We decided we were going to have to eliminate a character. So we asked David to take out the March Hare.

"The folks at Disney groaned, but I said, 'We can't keep him; there just isn't room, and each of the other stamps has only two characters. We don't need three. So we had them rework the picture and stack the teacups. We felt it worked much better. It was a major change at the last minute, but they were accommodating."

The design team had the most difficulty with the design for the Snow White stamp, in which the title character is shown dancing with Dopey. The artists developed pencil and color renderings showing the pair in different positions and relationships, but each of them presented a problem. The design that actually was released to the public, in the foldout poster

David Pacheco's pencil sketch for the revised Mad Tea Party stamp shows the Mad Hatter seated cross-legged on the table pouring tea into the top cup of a stack of four cups and saucers while Alice, seated at her place at the table, looks on. Pacheco's notes on the sketch include these comments: "Precarious stack," "Be sure [Hatter's] arm connects to body," "smaller hands," "smaller pot," "watch tangents."

The design team made several attempts at developing a satisfactory Snow White-Dopey image.

On the left is the Snow White-Dopey design that originally was shown to the public. It ultimately was replaced by the painting on the right, which shows Dopey leaping in the air. Because the leap is concealed by the cropping, the dwarf looks taller on the stamp than he actually is.

depicting the commemorative stamps planned for 2005, showed Snow White with her left arm extended and her right hand holding her skirt, while Dopey cavorts on her right side. This picture "had too much empty space," McCaffrey said, and ultimately it was replaced with a more tightly cropped image in which the positions of Snow White and the dwarf are reversed. Dopey appears taller than he actually is because the cropping of the painting conceals the fact that he is leaping into the air. "I personally feel that the dwarf appears a little too big in the size relationship," McCaffrey said. "But it's a good, strong visual and fills the space well."

Varieties

Two error varieties of the Art of Disney: Celebrations pane were listed in the 2006 Scott *Catalogue of United States Stamps & Covers*: a pane with no die cutting (Scott 3915b) and a pane that is printed on the backing paper (Scott 3915c).

First-Day Facts

The first-day ceremony was held at Sleeping Beauty's Castle inside Disneyland. Patrick R. Donahoe, USPS deputy postmaster general and chief operating officer, dedicated the stamps. Also participating were Matt Ouimet, president of Disneyland Resorts, and Andrae Rivas, Disneyland Resort ambassador. Actors dressed as the characters shown on the stamps were on hand.

USPS sold a set of four uncacheted first-day covers with the conventional black postmark for $3. A random single stamp on first-day cover with a digital color postmark was offered for $1.50, and a set of four for $6.

37¢ AMERICAN ADVANCES IN AVIATION (10 DESIGNS)

Date of Issue: July 29, 2005

Catalog Number: Scott 3916-3925, stamps; 3925a, block of 10

Colors: black, cyan, magenta, yellow, yellow (PMS 127), cool gray 4 (PMS), orange (PMS 712)

First-Day Cancel: Vienna, Virginia, and Oshkosh, Wisconsin

First-Day Cancellations: 346,767

Format: Pane of 20, horizontal, 4 across, 5 down. Offset printing plates printing 180 stamps per revolution (15 across, 12 around).

Gum Type: self-adhesive

Overall Stamp Size: 1.56 by 1.225 inches; 39.624 by 31.115 mm

Pane Size: 7.24 by 7.85 inches; 183.896 by 199.39 mm)

Perforations: 10¾ by 10½ (die-cut simulated perforations) (IDC two-station die cutter)

Selvage Inscription: "American Advances in Aviation."

Selvage Markings: "© 2004/USPS." ".37/x 20/$7.40." "PLATE/POSITION" and diagram.

Back Markings: On header: "American Advances in Aviation/Building on the popular Classic American Aircraft collection issued in 1997, the planes chosen for this stamp pane illustrate American/innovations and technological contributions to military, commercial, and general aviation during the 1930s, '40s, and '50s." "Boeing's YB-52 Stratofortress was a 1952/prototype for the still-operational B-52 bomber." "Averaging 327.15 mph, the Hughes H-1 racer set a/new transcontinental speed record on January 19, 1937." On bottom selvage: "To view a variety of philatelic products and other collectibles/associated with these stamps, visit The Postal Store at www.usps.com/shop/or call 1-800-STAMP-24 to order a free catalog." On side selvage in 4 locations: Universal Product Code (UPC) "458700." On stamps: "B-29 Superfortress/The advanced armament, propulsion, and/avionics systems in Boeing's/B-29 Superfortress included remote-/controlled gun turrets and pressurized/crew compartments. The sophisticated/long-range bomber served in/both WWII and Korea." "P-80 Shooting Star/The laminar-flow wing of the Lockheed/P-80 Shooting Star streamlined airflow/and contributed to the speed and overall/performance of the first operational/U.S. jet fighter. A P-80 made history/in 1950 by winning the first/all-jet aerial combat." "YB-49 Flying Wing/Deemed futuristic in the late '40s, the/all-wing configuration of Northrop's/YB-49 Flying Wing jet-propelled bomber/had great potential but stability problems/shelved the project. Technology finally/caught up with vision in the/B-2 stealth bomber." "B-24 Liberator/Designed as a heavy bomber, the/Consolidated B-24 Liberator — with its/great range and payload/cargo capacity —/proved highly versatile during WWII./High-lift wing airfoils and retractable/'roller-type' bomb bay doors were/B-24 innovations." "P-47 Thunderbolt/Originally planned as a lightweight/interceptor, Republic's P-47 Thunderbolt/turned out to be an immense/multipurpose fighter. Fast and rugged,/it earned a reputation as both a high-/altitude escort fighter and a low-level/fighter-bomber during WWII." "35 Bonanza/The Beechcraft Bonanza has been/in continuous production since 1947,/although the 35 model was discontinued/in 1982. Its distinctive V tail was/designed to reduce weight and drag,/as well as buffeting from the/wing and canopy wakes." "247/The first modern commercial/airliner set new standards for speed,/safety, and comfort in 1933. With twin/engines, retractable landing gear, and an/insulated ten-passenger cabin, Boeing's/streamlined, all-metal Model 247 boasted/state-of-the-art technology." "F6F Hellcat/A WWII 'workhorse,' the/carrier-based Grumman F6F Hellcat/met with perfection the requirements that/had dictated its simple and straightforward/design. The robust and maneuverable/fighter was easy to mass/produce and maintain." "PBY Catalina/An internally braced cantilever wing/and retractable wingtip floats were/aerodynamic innovations of the reliable/and versatile Consolidated PBY Catalina/flying boat. First acquired by the/U.S. Navy in 1936, many still fly/in nonmilitary roles." "Ercoupe 415/Designed in the mid-1930s,/the Ercoupe 415 introduced safe,/practical technologies for general aviation./The linked control system made it/spin-proof; tricycle landing gear with/a steerable nose wheel simplified/landing and taxiing."

Illustrator: William S. Phillips of Ashland, Oregon

Designer, Art Director and Typographer: Phil Jordan of Falls Church, Virginia

Modeler: Joseph Sheeran of Ashton-Potter (USA) Ltd., Williamsville, New York

Stamp Manufacturing: Stamps printed by Ashton-Potter on Mueller Martini offset press. Stamps finished by Ashton-Potter.

Quantity Ordered: 110,000,000

Plate Number Detail: 1 set of 7 plate numbers preceded by the letter P in selvage beneath each lower corner stamp

Plate Number Combinations Reported: P1111111, P2222222

Paper Supplier: Paper Corporation/Glatfelter

Tagging: unphosphored paper, block tagging over stamps

The Stamps

On July 29, the Postal Service issued 10 stamps featuring aircraft that epitomize "American advances in aviation." The stamps comprise a pane of 20, two of each variety, with a header, or decorative top selvage, depicting two additional airplanes.

Two first-day ceremonies were held, at the Americover 2005 show in Vienna, Virginia, and at the AirVenture Oshkosh fly-in convention in Oshkosh, Wisconsin.

The stamps were designed by the same team that produced the 1997 set of 20 37¢ Classic American Aircraft stamps: Phil Jordan, a USPS art director, and William S. Phillips, one of the world's foremost aviation artists. Semijumbo in size and self-adhesive, the new stamps were produced by the offset process by Ashton-Potter (USA) Ltd. USPS ordered a printing of 110 million, about double the number of recent commemorative issues.

A paragraph of text is printed on the back of the liner paper behind each stamp, describing the plane depicted. Similar descriptive text for the two aircraft on the header is on the back of its liner, along with this explanation of the pane's theme:

"Building on the popular Classic American Aircraft collection issued in 1997, the planes chosen for this stamp pane illustrate American innovations and technological contributions to military, commercial, and general aviation during the 1930s, '40s, and '50s."

The stamps are arranged on the pane four across by five down, in such a way as to allow its separation into two vertical blocks of 10, each containing all 10 varieties. However, the layouts of the two blocks themselves are different.

When the 1997 stamps were in the planning stage, Phil Jordan proposed that the Postal Service issue not one but three panes of 20, each featuring different aviation eras or aircraft characteristics. The Citizens' Stamp Advisory Committee thought that would be too much of a good thing, and decided to issue one pane showing aircraft that originated in the first half-century of heavier-than-air flight, 1903 to 1953.

"The three panes that I had suggested originally turned out to be not really practical," Jordan said. "But CSAC felt after a while that there was a place in the program for a follow-on to the first group of stamps. We had had to exclude a number of aircraft when we made our final choices, and proponents of some of those planes raised an uproar about it."

The strongest "uproar" came from World War II veterans who had flown the B-29 Superfortress and B-24 Liberator bombers and the P-47 Thunderbolt fighter. One of the most persistent proponents was Major William E. (Bill) Hendrix Jr. of Wichita, Kansas, who, as a lieutenant with the Eighth Air Force in World War II, had flown a B-24 over Europe. Hendrix wrote numerous letters to CSAC and wrote to other officials as well, including First Lady Hillary Clinton, urging a stamp for the plane. The B-24 "outperformed all other heavy bombers in every category, but continues to be unknown and unrecognized," he told Mrs. Clinton.

"Bill ran into Walter Boyne [a special consultant to USPS on the 1997 stamps] at the Oshkosh show in 1998 or thereabouts, and Walter gave him my telephone number," Jordan said. "When he called me, I told him there were avenues to follow if he wanted to start a campaign for the B-24. He said he already had started one.

"We became pen pals and telephone buddies. I promised him I would raise the issue with CSAC. CSAC's reaction was that there already had been a B-24 stamp."

That stamp — one of 50 issued between 1990 and 1995 to mark the 50th anniversary of World War II — had depicted the high-casualty daylight raid by B-24s on the oil fields and refineries of Ploesti, Romania, in 1943. "The proponents didn't buy that reasoning for a minute," Jordan said. "The stamp commemorated Ploesti, not the B-24 specifically. But CSAC held on, and that was it.

"Bill Hendrix's continual campaign wasn't necessarily the reason the new pane was done, but it sort of kept us aware that we had missed some airplanes the first time and maybe we ought to have another issue at some point."

By early 2002, CSAC's Subject Subcommittee decided the time had come for another aviation issue. The group asked Jordan to start work on a new set of 20 stamps, with the caveat that it might ultimately limit the set to the 10 most worthy aircraft as part of the effort to limit the overall size of the commemorative stamp program.

Jordan returned to his files and came up with a list of 20 aircraft for CSAC's consideration. In a memo to David Eynon, chairman of the Subject Subcommittee, he explained that the new set couldn't simply pick up chronologically where the first set left off, in 1953, because that would exclude the World War II planes whose advocates had been so forceful and persistent. Instead, he offered this rationale:

"While the first sheet used cosmetic appeal and public recognition in addition to aviation importance as selection criteria, this sheet concentrates on aviation innovation and technological contributions exclusive of public awareness and cosmetic appeal."

CSAC accepted the concept, but capped the number of stamps at 10. Dan Hagedorn, archivist and adjunct curator at the National Air & Space Museum, was hired to be the chief consultant on the project, and with his help Jordan cut his list to the 10 planes that would end up on stamps and the two additional aircraft that would appear on the header. With Jordan's explanatory comments, they were:

Boeing 247 (1933). The first truly modern airliner, the 247 was all metal and streamlined, with twin engines, cantilevered wing, semi-retractable landing gear, autopilot and deicing equipment — all very advanced features for its day. The plane had the first cabin air conditioning. Seventy miles per hour faster than its competitors, it cut coast-to-coast time by 7½ hours. It was the first airliner that could climb with a full load and one engine out.

Consolidated PBY Catalina (1935). The PBY, the finest long-range patrol flying boat in the world and the first plane to carry radar, trans-

formed the ocean patrolling capability of the U.S. Navy and played a pivotal role in World War II. It had an almost cantilevered wing mounted on a pylon that housed the flight engineer above a broad, shallow hull. Its unique wingtip floats electrically retracted to reduce drag in flight. More than 100 PBYs were still flying in various capacities 67 years after the war.

Grumman F6F Hellcat (1942). Easy to fly, stable and controllable, the Hellcat was designed specifically for one kind of war: fighter to fighter. Its "kill ratio" of 19 to 1 was unmatched by any fighter plane in history. The plane's inclined single-hinge wings folded backward along the fuselage for storage on carriers. It had the largest wing area of any U.S. fighter in World War II.

Republic P-47 Thunderbolt (1941). The P-47 started out as a lightweight interceptor and evolved into the largest and heaviest single-seat fighter of World War II and, arguably, the most versatile. It was produced

in larger numbers than any other U.S. fighter plane. It had a unique turbosupercharger layout and a pioneering telescoping landing gear. All versions would exceed 400 mph and turn on a dime. Along with the similar Corsair, the P-47 was the best ground support aircraft of the war and a deadly high-altitude fighter-interceptor.

Engineering Research Corporation Ercoupe 415 (1939). Many of these little planes still are flying today. The Ercoupe had linked controls that made it non-stalling and impossible to spin. With the first castoring, controllable nose wheel, it introduced tricycle gear to general use. Its designer, Fred Weick, received the Fawcett aviation award for the greatest contribution to the advancement of private aviation.

Lockheed P-80 Shooting Star (1944). The P-80 was America's first operational jet fighter. It also was the first victor in aerial combat between jets when it shot down a MIG-15 in Korea. It was a very adaptable plane, used in many test programs, and later became the basis for the long-lived T-33 jet trainer and the F-94 fighter series. It had a radically different wing, never tested on propeller-driven planes. The Shooting Star was the first aircraft to exceed 500 mph in level flight.

Consolidated B-24 Liberator (1939). The Liberator's innovative wing airfoil gave it an advantage over the B-17 Flying Fortress, which it was designed to outperform. The Liberator could outrun a B-17 using only three engines and could fly farther and carry a larger bomb load. Its unique bomb bay doors retracted like the tops of old roll-top desks. Its many variations served in all World War II theaters.

Boeing B-29 Superfortress (1939). Truly a revolutionary airplane in multiple ways, the B-29 was the first mass-production aircraft of over 100,000 pounds gross weight. It had wings that would lift 90 times their own weight, with the largest flaps ever developed at that time. The Superfortress pioneered the use of remote-controlled gun turrets.

Beechcraft 35 Bonanza (first prototype flight in 1947). One of general aviation's most enduring success stories, the Bonanza was designed at the end of World War II and has been in production ever since. Its most distinctive characteristic is its "V" tail, the use of which reduces the number of parts and weight and gives control response equivalent to conventional tail surfaces 40 percent larger.

Northrop YB-49 Flying Wing (1947). This radical plane was the result

of many years of research and many functional examples of the flying-wing concept pursued by the gifted aeronautical engineer John K. "Jack" Northrop from 1923 to 1947. It was the immediate predecessor to the U.S. Air Force's present B-2 Stealth bomber. It was a unique concept, ahead of its time, waiting for advanced materials that wouldn't be developed for another 40 years.

On the header:

Boeing B-52 Stratofortress (1952). At 488,000 pounds the largest bomber ever built, the B-52 flew combat missions in Afghanistan, 50 years after its first flight. It underwent a vast range of improvements during its seven different configurations, with innovations in armaments, electronics and airframe construction.

Hughes H-1 (1935). This plane, designed for Howard Hughes by a team of gifted engineers, contained numerous innovations. It was the world's most aerodynamically refined and meticulously crafted plane of its time; even the flat screw heads had their slots aligned with the airflow. In the H-1, Hughes set the world speed record and the U.S. transcontinental speed record.

Three of the planes had previously appeared on U.S. stamps. A B-24 was shown on the 29¢ stamp of 1993 commemorating the Ploesti raid (Scott 2765d). On the 3¢ Army commemorative of 1945 (Scott 934), six B-29s in flight were added to a picture of a parade of U.S. troops through a Paris newly liberated from the Germans; it was a design inaccuracy, because B-29s operated only in the Pacific theater during World War II. And a B-52 Stratofortress was depicted on the 6¢ airmail stamp of 1957 commemorating the 50th anniversary of the U.S. Air Force (Scott C49).

The eight aircraft on Jordan's list that didn't make the final cut, with his comments, were:

Wright-Bellanca W.B.2 (1926), designed by Giuseppe Bellanca, an outstanding designer of the pioneer aviation period. The W.B.2 was Charles Lindbergh's first choice for his attempt to fly the Atlantic, but Lindbergh's bid to buy the plane was unsuccessful.

Douglas D-448-2 Skyrocket (1948), one of a series of six aircraft built to push the boundaries of aeronautical science and explore rocket-powered flight. In 1953, the Skyrocket set a world altitude record of 83,235 feet and became the first plane to fly at Mach 2, twice the speed of sound.

Curtiss Model HS Flying Boat (1914), the first twin-engine hydroplane. The Model H America was designed to be the first plane to fly the Atlantic, a project to which World War I put an end.

Northrop P-61 Black Widow (1942), the first plane designed solely as an all-weather night fighter. It had an extremely high-tech weapons system for the day, plus state-of-the-art radar.

Boeing 377 (C-97, KC-97) Stratocruiser, which was built as a military transport, based on the B-29 model. A large number were built to be aerial tankers. (With three Boeing-built planes already chosen for the pane, this aircraft was eliminated for the sake of a balanced selection.)

Lockheed Electra (1934), the plane used by Amelia Earhart in her ill-fated effort to fly around the world. Designed for swift, economical operation, the L-10 Electra, when introduced, was the fastest and least expensive airliner.

Luscombe Model 8 Silvaire (1937), the first commercially successful all-aluminum light aircraft. The Silvaire series revolutionized the personal aircraft industry with the introduction of all-metal design and innovative construction techniques.

North American F-100 Super Sabre (1953), the first jet plane to reach and sustain supersonic speed in level flight. It was the first production aircraft to use titanium extensively throughout its construction. It had a cockpit that was ergonomically designed, pressurized and air-conditioned, a rear-hinged canopy and the first autopilot designed for supersonic flight.

"After the project was approved," Jordan said, "I wanted to call Bill Hendrix and tell him that we were definitely going forward with a B-24 stamp, but I was instructed to wait until the stamps were announced publicly.

"I picked up the phone the first day I was authorized to do it, and Bill's wife answered and said, 'I'm sorry, but Bill died in April.' He had Parkinson's disease. I was crushed at the news."

The Designs

The popularity of the 1997 Classic American Aircraft stamps made the decision to reunite the design team, art director Jordan and painter Phillips, for the new project, an easy one.

Jordan operates his own design firm in Fairfax, Virginia, and is a former design director of *Air & Space/Smithsonian* magazine. He has designed scores of stamps since he became a Postal Service art director in 1991, but his specialty is aviation and space stamps. He is a licensed glider pilot and a member of the Skyline Soaring Club.

Phillips, of Ashland, Oregon, began sketching and painting while serving in the Air Force during the Vietnam War. His airplane and landscape paintings, which have a near-photographic quality, have been widely reproduced in books and limited-edition prints, and in 1987 the National Air and Space Museum presented a one-man show of his work that later toured the United States. Phillips' most recent book of aviation art, *Into the Sunlit Splendor*, was published by the Greenwich Workshop Press in the fall of 2005.

The artist made his paintings for the American Advances in Aviation stamps in oil on commercially prepared illustration board. For the fine detail work, such as the planes' identifying insignia and numbers, he used a triple-0 brush under a jeweler's loupe. He used commercially available scale models of the planes for reference, made by companies such as Revell/Monogram, Hasegawa Seisakusho Ltd. and AMT/ertl, then verified the pictorial details with historical photographs.

Many of the planes in the paintings bear markings and numbers that identify them as specific aircraft. None had a more stirring story than that of the B-24 Liberator.

One of Major William Hendrix's frequent notes to Phil Jordan was on a letter card made by the old pilot's grandson and illustrated with a side view of the B-24 Hendrix flew in World War II, the *Black Cat*. When the time came to design the B-24 stamp, Jordan said, "It seemed just right to reward Bill for his efforts [to obtain the stamp] by using his plane, since he had flown many combat missions in it and it was the epitome of the type.

"I discussed this with Bill Phillips, and he was all for it — he visualized the picture as 'a big aluminum machine over an English countryside, spar-

Jordan decided to show a specific bomber, the Black Cat, *on the stamp honoring the B-24, after he received a letter card from advocate William E. Hendrix Jr. made by Hendrix's grandson with this illustration of the plane Hendrix had flown during World War II. Not until after the stamps were printed did Jordan and others in USPS learn that the* Black Cat *had gone on to become the last U.S. bomber shot down over Europe before V-E Day.*

kling in a hazy sun.' " The plane, a late variant designated B-24J, is identifiable on the stamp by the name, "Black Cat," on the fuselage, along with the silhouette of a cat pouncing on its prey. Phillips copied these details in his stamp painting from the illustration on Hendrix's card.

What Jordan, Phillips and others at the Postal Service didn't know at the time was that after Hendrix had done his tour of duty in the *Black Cat*, the plane earned a unique and tragic place in the history of the war. Journalist Neely Tucker related the afterstory in *The Washington Post*:

> Howard Goodner plunged out of the *Black Cat*, the last American bomber shot down over Germany in World War II, early on the morning of April 21, 1945. The B-24 Liberator was hit at 22,000 feet and broke

*These are crew members of the **Black Cat**, the B-24 Liberator pictured on the stamp, which was the last U.S. bomber shot down over Germany in World War II. Kneeling, from left: Staff Sergeant Robert Peterson Sr., assistant radio operator and waist gunner; Staff Sergeant John "Jack" Brennan, assistant engineer and waist gunner; Technical Sergeant Jerome Barrett, engineer; Technical Sergeant Howard Goodner, radio operator; Staff Sergeant Al Seraydarian, tail gunner. Standing, from left: First Lieutenant John Murphy, radar operator; Second Lieutenant Jack Perella, first navigator; Second Lieutenant John "Jack" Regan, co-pilot; First Lieutenant Richard Farrington, pilot; First Lieutenant George Noe, second navigator; Second Lieutenant Christ Manners, bombardier. The photograph was made in March 1945, a month before the plane crashed, killing 10 of the 12 men aboard.*

into pieces.

Goodner, just 21, had no parachute. He came down in a free fall alongside bombs and oxygen tanks, spinning toward the Bavarian village of Scharmassing.

He landed in a field outside town, his body striking the earth so hard it left a crater nearly six inches deep.

Maria Wittig, then 19, saw him there. He was athletic looking, fair-skinned, handsome. Long fingers.

"I can see him before me," she told an interviewer, a half century later, so clear was her memory. Shown a picture of the entire crew, she picked out Goodner immediately. "That's him," she said, her voice breaking.

The story of Goodner, Wittig and the *Black Cat* is 60 years old. Other wars have come and gone, but the story has never really died, living on in the small shadows of the greatest generation.

Now the *Black Cat* was immortalized on a U.S. postage stamp, that diminutive marker of historical American moments large and small. Part of a series of 10 commemorative aviation stamps, this one shows the *Black Cat* still intact, still in flight, over the pastoral fields where it would crash. Nothing on the stamp denotes the plane's tragic end.

More than 60 million of the stamps have just gone on sale at post offices nationwide, but only a few customers know its story of heartbreak, and how it has continued to reverberate in the lives of a few for so long.

Two of the 12 crewmen on board survived. The other 10 died upon impact, none having lived to be 30.

Their families were informed of their loss on May 8, V-E Day, when the rest of the nation rejoiced.

"The plane being shot down at the very end of the war — it has haunted my family for so many years, and I finally went to Germany and found the crash site," says Thomas Childers, Goodner's nephew, whose 1995 book, *Wings of Morning*, chronicled the story of the plane and its crew. "This farmer started scratching around in the dirt, and he pulled out a 50-caliber machine gun bullet. I was speechless. Every year when they plow, parts of the plane come to the surface." ...

If not for Childers' curiosity, the *Black Cat*'s history would have almost certainly been lost. After the 1991 death of his grandmother in Cleveland, Tennessee, Childers went to clear out her house before it was sold.

He found a musty case of more than 300 letters that her son, Howard Goodner, had sent during the war. Childers was a historian of German culture and politics, and to find such a cache of original documents from World War II was striking.

He put down his academic research and took up the story of his uncle's flight crew: young men from Brooklyn, Peoria, Pittsburgh, St. Louis, a cross-section of mid-century America.

He discovered that the *Black Cat* was the last bomber shot down over Germany before peace was declared and that the crew wasn't originally scheduled to fly that day — bad weather should have forced them to cancel before takeoff. It lent the story its tragic footnote.

In Bavaria, he met Wittig. He did not tell her that Goodner was his uncle, only that he was researching the history of the plane. When she tapped Goodner's picture as the airman who came to earth in the field, he felt a tingle on the back of his neck.

The book's 1995 publication brought some critical acclaim but little in the way of sales. It may have reached its most widespread moment in pop culture in 2002, when best-selling historian Stephen Ambrose was found to have plagiarized a passage from the book in *The Wild Blue*, his history of B-24 bomber crews.

But the surviving members of the 466th Bomb Group, of which the *Black Cat* was a part, began petitioning the U.S. Postal Service to memorialize the *Black Cat* on a stamp. It was a long shot.

"We get 50,000 people a year who say, 'I've got the best idea ever for a stamp,' says David Failor, executive director of stamp services for the U.S. Postal Service. "We actually release about 25 or 30 subjects for commemorative stamps each year. You can figure the math."

Looking at the plane on the stamp — the sunlight warm on its silver wings, a river glinting in the green fields below — lends a bittersweet irony to one of Goodner's last letters home.

He was on a three-day break at a resort in Mundesley, on the British shore. There were dining rooms — not chow lines — soft beds, hot water, a golf course. He walked on the beach, played darts at a local pub. He loved it.

"Just hoping the war ends soon," he wrote to his family, "and we can all get home again."

The letter was dated April 8, 1945.

Howard Goodner had 13 days to live.

Goodner, a technical sergeant, was the plane's radio operator. His uncle, Thomas Childers, a professor of history at the University of Pennsylvania, spent four years in researching and writing the crew's story.

The 247 is owned by the Museum of Flight in Seattle, Washington. It was built in 1933 at the Boeing factory in Renton, Washington, and was returned there two years later to be upgraded to 247-D standards. The plane was a carrier for several airlines in the United States and South America, served in the Royal Canadian Air Force in World War II, and was used as a crop duster in Arizona and a cloud seeder in California. In 1966 it was christened *City of Renton* and began a long renovation involving tens of thousands of man-hours by willing volunteers. In 1995 it was restored to commercial flight status.

Phillips painted the 247 flying over Puget Sound. The waves below have been colored orange by a low-lying sun: "Sunrise or sunset, your choice," the artist laughed. The plane's colors were taken from photographs in the December 1966 *Wings* magazine.

United Air Lines gave its permission to show the words "United Air Lines" and "United" on the plane's side and wings. When it came to the stamp caption, however, the Boeing company insisted that only the number be used, 247, with no other wording. "It looks like another denomination figure," Phil Jordan complained.

The Catalina shown is a PBY-5, and its markings identify it as the 14-P-11, which was used by Patrol Squadron 14 from November 1941 to

These are William Phillips' early concept sketches of the 247 and the P-80 Shooting Star. He later refined the sketches into finished art with greater detail and identifying markings on the planes.

September 1942. The stamp's background, the sky with an elongated cloud in the distance, is purplish in tone.

"We had more trouble with the Catalina painting than any of the others," said Jordan. "We couldn't see the top area of the wing very well on our reference photos, and when Bill originally painted it, the lines across the wing were a little too far back and we had to put them forward. Bill has got the airplane headed into the light, and we couldn't work out some of the details on the front."

Clouds and a blue sky provide a background for the F6F Hellcat. The plane's markings identify it as the F6F-5 from the carrier *USS Intrepid*.

The P-47 Thunderbolt is shown in a climbing mode, also against a cloudy blue sky. The aircraft shown was named "Angie," assigned to the 512th Fighter Squadron, 406th Fighter Group, during the war, and is a variant designated P47D-28-RE.

For his painting of the Ercoupe 415, Phillips relied on pictures from the book *American Classics of the Air: Commercial and Private Airplanes From the 1920s to the 1960s* by Geoff Jones and Chuck Stewart, published in 2000 by Motorbooks International. The plane is flying over the Grand Canyon, which is shown looking to the east, toward the Cape Royal area of the national park, late in the afternoon. The artist based the landscape on photographs he had shot from Mather Point on the South Rim on one of many trips he has made to the Grand Canyon.

For the P-80A, Phillips and Jordan chose a plane with a Postal Service connection. The jet, PN-354, carried a sack of mail from LaGuardia Airport in New York City to Washington National Airport on May 15, 1948, to mark the 30th anniversary of the first regularly scheduled airmail flights between New York and Washington. The plane on the stamp bears the nose insignia of the 334th Fighter Squadron, a red rooster with boxing gloves on a yellow circle.

The B-29, shown flying against a background of cloudbanks in a golden evening sky, is a late version, dating to the Korean War. "We didn't want to get into the *Enola Gay* controversy," said Phil Jordan, referring to the B-29 that dropped the first atomic bomb on Hiroshima, Japan, in the final days of World War II. "So Bill deliberately selected a B-29 that didn't even fly during the Second World War."

The plane was part of the 93rd Bomb Squadron, 19th Bomb Group, which flew missions from Guam over North Korea. Its crew had named it *The Big Shmoo*. Shmoos, invented by cartoonist Al Capp in the 1940s for his comic strip *Li'l Abner,* were lovable creatures but too delicious for their own good. Phillips found pictorial reference materials for the fuselage art and colors in *Aircraft Nose Art* by C. Simonsen.

The artist based his painting of the Beechcraft Bonanza on pictures from *Private Pilot* magazine, May 2003, as well as the same Jones-Stewart book on which he relied for his illustration of the Ercoupe. He showed the Bonanza in flight over Monument Valley, using a series of photographs of

Phillips' original concept sketch of the Beechcraft Bonanza didn't show to advantage the plane's most visible feature, its V-shaped tail assembly. The problem would have been increased by reducing the image to stamp size. Phillips repainted the plane from a different angle.

the landscape as reference. Although the artist never had visited Monument Valley, which straddles the Arizona-Utah border, he considered the colors of its mountains and buttes "stunning." "You can't ask for anything better as a background for aircraft than either Monument Valley or the Grand Canyon, late in the afternoon," he said.

The artist originally showed the Bonanza in an attitude that didn't effectively display its unique empennage, or tail assembly, which is in a V shape. Reducing the painting to stamp size would have made it even harder to see the V. Accordingly, he repainted the aircraft from another angle. PhotoAssist then pointed out that the artist had neglected to paint the elevators red to match the trim and wingtip colors. Dodge Color, which does the Postal Service's prepress work, tried to fill in the missing red by computer, but the result was unsatisfactory, and the painting was returned to Phillips to make the correction the old-fashioned way — with his paintbrush.

His YB-49 Flying Wing is shown in flight against dramatic-looking clouds and a gray-violet sky.

Phillips' picture of the Boeing B-52 Stratofortress on the header was based on six photographs from the book *Boeing B-52 Stratofortress* by William G. Holder, Aero Series 24. Structural and color details for the Hughes H-1 came from photographs taken by Wayne Sagar for All Aviation Flightline Online (www.aafo.com) and reproduced in the Smithsonian's *Air & Space* magazine, May 2003.

Jordan placed the title "American Advances in Aviation" on the header, in a typeface called Odyssey. The aircraft names on the stamps are in Letter Gothic italic, and the "37" denominations are in a font called A.G. Stencil, to suggest the stenciled-on identification numbers on military and civilian planes. PhotoAssist provided the descriptive text on the back of the liner paper.

Ashton-Potter printed the pane in the four standard process colors — black, cyan, magenta and yellow — plus three PMS colors, yellow, cool gray and orange. It used the PMS yellow and cool gray for the stamp denominations and "USA," respectively, and the orange for the header letters.

"The whole thing turned out very well," Jordan said. "Dan Hagedorn made many suggestions that improved the pane, and we made fewer mistakes this time because we were better researched than we were with the first set. We knew a lot more about where we were going, and where to get the information. Also, the accessibility of information on the Web has increased tremendously in 10 years.

"Everything Bill [Phillips] did, the committee liked. We never got a negative word; it just flowed right through. We did very little changing."

"I enjoyed this one even more than the first sheet," Phillips said. "The airplanes were really exciting. I don't know if I was nervous during the first project, but I was more relaxed on this one, and I enjoyed the painting process more.

"Some of the aircraft that were used are ones that I've flown in. I've piloted the Ercoupe. That's one of my favorite airplanes — the last plane I flew, in fact, was an Ercoupe. Real classics. I grew up during some of the eras that are displayed on those stamps, and so the airplanes are near and dear to my heart. And the Flying Wing — what a design! I was really excited to see that one included."

First-Day Facts

Lynn Malcolm, USPS vice president, controller, dedicated the stamps at the Americover show, held at the Sheraton Premier in Vienna, Virginia. The speaker was Thomas Childers, nephew of the *Black Cat*'s radio operator and the author of the history of the plane and its crew.

"The issuance of this stamp is a fitting memorial for all the brave young airmen who flew the B-24 in the Second World War," said Childers, "but especially for the men of the *Black Cat* who died 60 years ago. I know

This style of postmark was applied to first-day covers from Oshkosh. The postmark was 3½ inches wide by 1½ inches high.

I speak for the families of those men when I say we are grateful — and humbled — to see their memory honored in this way."

Tom Foust, president of the American First Day Cover Society, gave the welcome at the ceremony.

Linda Kingsley, USPS vice president for strategic planning, was the dedicating official for the stamps at 2005 EAA AirVenture Oshkosh, the annual air show and fly-in convention of the Experimental Aircraft Association.

Guest speaker at the event at the show's Aero Shell Square were Colonel Hal Shook, USAF retired, a recipient of the Distinguished Flying Cross in World War II, and Tom Poberezny, president of the EAA. Shook, at 23, commanded a squadron of P-47 Thunderbolts and flew 105 missions between D-Day and V-E Day. Although his plane was hit six times, he credited his survival to training, teamwork and "the beloved 'jug,' " his rugged plane. He also served in the Korean and Vietnam conflicts. His book, *Fighter Pilot Jazz*, describes his wartime experiences.

Among the guests recognized at the event were relatives of the *Black Cat*'s crew who contributed their loved ones' letters to Thomas Childers' research.

Admission to the AirVenture show cost $30 per person, but USPS obtained a limited number of free passes for collectors who wished to attend the first-day ceremony. Passes were obtained by calling the Oshkosh postmaster and were issued on a first-come, first-served basis.

Planes that were scheduled to be on display at Oshkosh were a B-24 Liberator, B-29 Superfortress, F6F Hellcat, P-80 Shooting Star, 35 Bonanza and Ercoupe 415.

For a limited time, the Postal Service offered a set of 10 uncacheted first-day covers from Oshkosh with conventional black postmarks for $7.50. USPS also offered covers with digital color postmarks from Oshkosh or Vienna at $15 for a set and $1.50 for a random single. The postmarks were designed by Phil Jordan.

37¢ NEW MEXICO RIO GRANDE BLANKETS (4 DESIGNS) DOUBLE-SIDED CONVERTIBLE BOOKLET OF 20 AMERICAN TREASURES SERIES

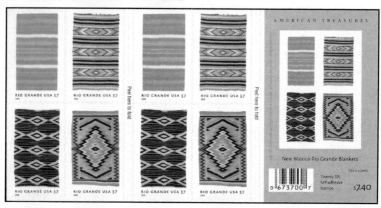

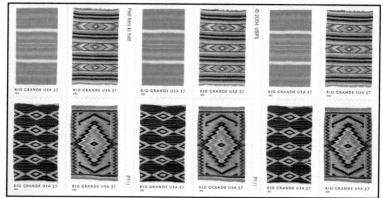

Date of Issue: July 30, 2005

Catalog Numbers: Scott 3926-3929, stamps; 3929a, block of 4; 3929b, convertible booklet of 20

Colors: black, cyan, magenta, yellow

First-Day Cancel: Santa Fe, New Mexico

First-Day Cancellations: 171,101

Format: Convertible booklet pane of 20, vertical, arranged vertically. Stamps on both sides, 8 (2 across by 4 down) plus label (booklet cover) on one side, 12 (2 across by 6 down) on other side, with horizontal peel-off strips between blocks of 4 on each side. Offset printing plates printing 640 stamps per revolution (cover side, 16 across, 16 around; all-stamp side, 24 across, 16 around).

Gum Type: self-adhesive

Overall Stamp Size: 0.98 by 1.56 inches; 39.624 by 24.892 mm

Pane Size: 3.12 by 6.18 inches; 79.248 by 156.972 mm

Perforations: 10¾ (die-cut simulated perforations) (IDC custom rotary die-cutter). Backing paper rouletted behind peel-off strips.

Selvage Markings: "© 2004 USPS" and plate numbers on one peel-off strip and "Peel here to fold" and plate numbers on another peel-off strip, both on all-stamp side. "Peel here to fold" on both peel-off strips on label side.

Back Markings: "AMERICAN TREASURES/New Mexico Rio Grande Blankets/Fifth in a series/Twenty 37¢/Self-adhesive/Stamps/$7.40." "top left: Colorado Springs Fine Arts Center; all others; Museum of New Mexico." Universal Product Code (UPC) "0 673700 7," all on booklet cover

Designer, Art Director and Typographer: Derry Noyes of Washington, D.C.

Modeler: Joseph Sheeran of Ashton-Potter (USA) Ltd., Williamsville, New York

Stamp Manufacturing: Stamps printed by Ashton-Potter on Mueller Martini A 74 offset press. Stamps finished by Ashton-Potter.

Quantity Ordered: 420,000,000 stamps

Plate Number Detail: 1 set of 4 plate numbers preceded by the letter P on 2 peel-off strips

Plate Number Combination Reported: P1111

Paper Supplier: Flexcon/Glatfelter

Tagging: phosphored paper

The Stamps

On July 30, the Postal Service issued four stamps bearing photographs of 19th-century woven New Mexico Rio Grande blankets. The self-adhesive, commemorative-size stamps were distributed in double-sided convertible booklets of 20, 12 on one side and eight on the other.

The first-day ceremony was held on the Santa Fe, New Mexico, Plaza Community Stage during the 54th annual Traditional Spanish Market, the oldest and largest exhibition and sale of traditional Spanish colonial art in the United States.

The stamps were the fifth entry in a series called American Treasures, which Terrence McCaffrey, manager of stamp development for USPS, promised at the outset would feature "existing art masterpieces [in] a series of attractive, colorful images that people would be prone to use on their mail."

However, the first two American Treasures issues, four Amish Quilts (2001) and a John James Audubon single (2002), were issued in panes of 20 and saw no greater use than had been the case with other commemoratives. USPS then decided to produce American Treasures in the convertible booklet format, which is popular with postal patrons and convenient for clerks to stock. The third entry, a block of four stamps depicting paintings by Mary Cassatt (2003), and the fourth, a single reproducing Martin Johnson Heade's painting *Giant Magnolias on a Blue Velvet Cloth* (2004), were printed in large quantities and were seen frequently on mail.

USPS ordered 420 million Rio Grande Blankets stamps, compared to 794 million Martin Johnson Heades and 778.8 million Mary Cassatts. Ashton-Potter (USA) Ltd. printed them by the offset process.

The choice of Rio Grande Blankets was consistent with the Postal Service's recent efforts to increase its use of Hispanic culture and personalities as stamp subjects. Originally, Derry Noyes, the art director for the American Treasures series, envisioned a set that would feature not only blankets but furniture and other artifacts of the Hispanic Southwest. Ultimately, the decision was made to show only blankets.

Collectors of used stamps found the Rio Grande Blankets to be particularly difficult to remove from their envelopes. "The stamps would not separate easily from envelope paper after an overnight soak," *Linn's Stamp News* reported. "Peeling the stamp off by hand greatly thinned the entire back of the stamp."

Linn's later gave further details. One Rio Grande Blankets stamp the newspaper tested separated cleanly from its clipping after soaking for several minutes. During the drying process, however, it was discovered that the entire adhesive layer, which typically remains on the paper clipping after a self-adhesive stamp is removed, remained on the back of the stamp.

Such a stamp cannot be hinged to an album page or placed within a stamp mount without sticking to the page or to the inside of the mount. Either scenario is unacceptable to a collector.

In contrast, another Rio Grande Blankets stamp tested by *Linn's* left its adhesive layer on the envelope paper — along with part of the stamp itself. Removing the stamp from the clipping caused severe thinning.

Linn's questioned USPS spokesman Mark Saunders about the problem and got an explanation that was, at best, unclear.

"The stamps were printed to specification," Saunders said. "While the ability to remove stamps by soaking envelopes may be diminished, our primary concern is producing high-quality stamps that will adhere to the mailpiece from deposit to delivery."

Linn's asked whether USPS required the stamp printer, Ashton-Potter, to provide soakability — a specification that has been in place for suppliers since the first modern U.S. self-adhesive stamps were issued in 1989.

"Yes, water removability is one of our current battery of tests for stamps," Saunders replied. "The testing is optional, as this element is not required for the ultimate performance of a stamp in meeting our needs for mail processing and revenue protection."

According to *Linn's*, Saunders confirmed that "water removability" was one of the factors tested for the Rio Grande Blankets stamps. However, he said, the stamps were given what he called an "exception" for ease of soaking "because the quality of the stamp image coupled with the need to remain affixed to the mailpiece from deposit to delivery supersedes the requirement to soak a stamp for removal from the mailpiece."

The spokesman didn't explain why an "exception" was needed for the Rio Grande Blankets, in view of the fact that most U.S. self-adhesive stamps are soakable with no apparent compromising of "the quality of the stamp image."

The paper for the Rio Grande Blankets was supplied to Avery Dennison by Glatfelter and converted by Flexcon.

According to a Postal Service news release, woven textiles have a long history in the American Southwest, and many regional styles developed over time. The textiles produced in Spanish settlements in the northern Rio Grande Valley were influenced by Spanish, Mexican, Pueblo and Navajo designs. Often worn, Rio Grande blankets, as these textiles came to be known, also functioned as rugs, bedding and sacking.

The indigenous Pueblo Indians already had achieved a sophisticated textile tradition of their own by the time Spanish immigrants began colonizing the Rio Grande Valley in 1598. The first settlers brought with them the churro sheep, whose long, straight, lustrous, low-grease wool was ideal for weaving. Later immigrants brought the horizontal treadle loom. Some families set up looms in their own homes, while others established formally organized weaving workshops using Spanish and Indian labor.

Early Rio Grande blankets were striped, a simple pattern derived from Pueblo designs, and weavers were limited to the black, brown, tan, gray and white colors of the churro fleece and indigo, a natural blue dye imported from Mexico. Natural red dyes made from cochineal insects or madder roots were in use, although sparingly, by the 1770s. The horizontal treadle looms were narrow, so a more functional width was achieved in one of two ways: either by weaving a folded blanket using two sets of warps or by sewing two pieces together, leaving a lengthwise ridge or seam down the center of each blanket.

Between 1807 and 1809, two master weavers sent from Mexico by the Spanish government taught weavers in Santa Fe how to create the intricate designs of the finely woven Mexican Saltillo serape, distinguished by a large, central serrate diamond set against a complex vertical background. In addition to this new design, weavers continued to produce the classic Rio Grande band and stripe pattern and also created a third style by combining bands and stripes with isolated Saltillo elements such as small serrate diamonds and stepped chevrons.

After synthetic dies became available, the three basic patterns of Rio Grande textiles became even more complex as the use of these vivid colors increased. Around the same time, a fourth pattern called the Vallero star was created. The star motif may have been derived from American quilt designs.

The demand for Rio Grande blankets began to wane in the 1880s, as the market became flooded with machine-woven cloth and commercially produced yarns brought in by rail. By the turn of the 20th century, only

small Spanish communities in northern New Mexico and the San Luis Valley in Colorado continued the Rio Grande weaving tradition.

Derry Noyes selected these blanket designs for the four New Mexico Rio Grande Blankets stamps:

Upper left: Handspun wool, synthetic-dyed red, orange, yellow and white, with a highly traditional symmetrical five-band pattern, circa 1895. The blanket is in the Taylor Museum, Colorado Springs Fine Arts Center, Colorado Springs, Colorado.

Upper right: Handspun wool, natural undyed light and dark, synthetic-dyed pink, red, orange and yellow, with three bands of serrate chevrons with tiny hourglass figures separated by zones of wide colored stripes, circa 1880. The blanket was the gift of Florence Dibell Bartlett to the Museum of New Mexico Collection at the Museum of International Folk Art in Santa Fe, New Mexico.

Lower left: Handspun wool, natural undyed light and dark, indigo dye, originally with six bands of stepped chevrons forming diamonds at the center seam, separated by zones of blue and brown stripes, in a design related to the Navajo "chief blanket," pre-1865. The item was given by Mrs. Edgar L. Rossin to the Museum of New Mexico Collection at the Museum of International Folk Art in Santa Fe.

Lower right: Handspun wool, natural undyed light and dark, synthetic-dyed red and blue-green, with a complex central Saltillo-style serrate diamond extending into side borders containing serrate zigzag columns, circa 1890s. The blanket is in the Museum of New Mexico Collection at the Museum of Indian Arts & Culture/Laboratory of Anthropology in Santa Fe.

Native American weaving from the Southwest was not new to U.S. stamps, nor to art director Noyes. In 1986, she designed a block of four 22¢ commemoratives in the Folk Art series depicting Navajo Art, specifically four red, black and white patterned blankets (Scott 2235-2238) owned by the Lowe Art Museum and the Museum of the American Indian. One of the 10 37¢ Art of the American Indian stamps of 2004, designed by Richard Sheaff, depicted a tapestry in the Navajo tradition woven in the 1940s by the late Daisy Taugelchee (Scott 3873h). Taugelchee was widely known as a creator of finely woven Navajo textiles.

Derry Noyes, art director and designer of the Rio Grande Blankets stamps, also designed these four Navajo Art stamps of 1986 depicting blankets that were part of the Folk Art series (Scott 2235-2238).

The Designs

Early in the design process, before officials decided to change the format for the American Treasures series from panes to convertible booklets, Derry Noyes made several layouts for stamps featuring the culture of the Hispanic Southwest as panes of 20, with numerous varieties included in each pane. She included furniture and other artifacts as well as blankets among her design subjects.

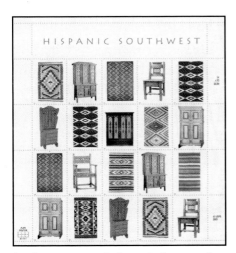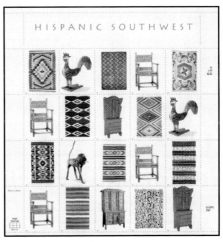

In these two early layouts in pane format, the set featured a broad range of the culture of the "Hispanic Southwest," including blankets, furniture and artifacts.

135

After the subject was narrowed to Rio Grande blankets and the convertible-booklet format was chosen, it was necessary to limit the number of design varieties to four. "I just tried to find four that represented the different types of weavings but weren't too dissimilar from each other. They had to work together as stamp designs," she said.

She made her selection from photographs in a book titled *Rio Grande Textiles: A New Edition of Spanish Textile Tradition of New Mexico and Colorado*, published by the Museum of New Mexico Press (1994). The two museums that own the blankets furnished color transparencies to USPS for reproduction on the stamps.

The only typography on the vertically arranged stamps is a single line of black capitals across the bottom: "RIO GRANDE USA 37." On the label/booklet cover is a reproduction of a block of the four stamps in reduced size and the series logo, "AMERICAN TREASURES," in black Minion type against a tan background.

First-Day Facts

Mary Anne Gibbons, senior vice president and general counsel for USPS, dedicated the stamps in a ceremony at the Traditional Spanish Market in Santa Fe.

Speakers were C. Douglas Lewis, chairman of CSAC; Cathy Wright, director and chief curator of the Taylor Museum at the Colorado Springs, Colorado, Fine Arts Center, where one of the blankets is housed; U.S. Senator Jeff Bingaman, Democrat of New Mexico; and Stuart Ashman, secretary of the New Mexico Department of Cultural Affairs.

Santa Fe Postmaster Ruben Romero was master of ceremonies. Honored guests were representatives of the two Santa Fe museums that own blankets shown on the stamps, plus a third: Joyce Ice, director of the Museum of International Folk Art; David E. McNeece of the Museum of Indian Arts & Culture; and Bud Redding, director of Spanish Market operations for the Museum of Spanish Colonial Art.

Stamp Fulfillment Services offered uncacheted first-day covers with conventional black postmarks for $3 for a set of four. Digital color postmarks also were available for $6 for a set and $1.50 for a random single.

FIRST DAY OF ISSUE

RIO GRANDE BLANKETS

JULY 30, 2005 SANTA FE, NM 87501

This pictorial first-day cancellation from Santa Fe bears a design suggestive of a Rio Grande blanket pattern.

37¢ PRESIDENTIAL LIBRARIES

Date of Issue: August 4, 2005

Catalog Number: Scott 3930

Colors: ivory, reflex blue, red (PMS 202)

First-Day Cancel: Abilene, Kansas; Ann Arbor, Michigan; Atlanta, Georgia; Austin, Texas; Boston, Massachusetts; College Station, Texas; Grand Rapids, Michigan; Hyde Park, New York; Independence, Missouri; Little Rock, Arkansas; Simi Valley, California; West Branch, Iowa; Yorba Linda, California

First-Day Cancellations: 150,804

Format: Pane of 20, vertical, 5 across, 4 down. Offset printing plates printing 180 stamps per revolution (15 across, 12 around). Also sold in uncut press sheets of 9 panes (3 across by 3 down).

Microprinting: "USPS" beneath the bottom right leaf on the olive branch in the eagle's right talon

Gum Type: self-adhesive

Stamp Size: 0.98 by 1.56 inches; 24.89 by 39.62 mm

Pane Size: 5.9 by 7.26 inches; 149.86 by 184.4 mm

Uncut Press Sheet Size: 17½ inches by 21¾ inches

Perforations: 10¾ (die-cut simulated perforations) (Goebel Optiforma 26 rotary die-cutter)

Selvage Markings: plate numbers only

Back Markings: "PRESIDENTIAL LIBRARIES: AN AMERICAN ARCHIVE/ Acknowledging the critical/importance to a democracy/of an open government and/an informed public, the U.S. Postal/Service issues this 2005 commemo-/rative stamp celebrating the 50th/anniversary of the Presidential/ Libraries Act of 1955. There are/currently 11 libraries in the Presi-/dential Library system; they house/the materials generated during the/administrations of Presidents Her-/bert Hoover, Franklin Roosevelt,/Harry Truman, Dwight Eisenhower,/John Kennedy, Lyndon Johnson,/Gerald Ford, Jimmy Carter, Ronald/Reagan, George H.W. Bush, and/Bill Clinton. In late 2005, a 12th/library will be added when the/Richard M. Nixon Presidential/Library in Yorba Linda, California,/is scheduled to become part of the/Presidential Library system./Presidential Libraries have/been established in the home state/of each President after he has left/office. In addition to being an/accessible archive, each library/features a museum and offers an/ongoing series of public programs/on a variety of cultural and histori-/cal topics. Only one museum is/located apart from its associated/library: The Gerald R. Ford Library/is in Ann Arbor, Michigan; the/museum is in Grand Rapids." With inset map and location numbers. "PRESIDENTIAL LIBRARIES SPAN/THE UNITED STATES/(1) Herbert Hoover/Presidential Library/and Museum/West Branch, IA 52358-0488/(2) Franklin D. Roosevelt/Presidential Library/and Museum/Hyde Park, NY 12536-1999/(3) Harry S. Truman/Presidential Library/& Museum/Independence, MO 64050-1798/(4) Dwight D. Eisenhower/Presidential Library/& Museum/Abilene, KS 67410-2900/(5) John F. Kennedy/Presidential Library/& Museum/Boston, MA 02125-3398/(6) Lyndon Baines Johnson/Library and Museum/Austin, TX 78705-5702/(7) Richard M. Nixon/Presidential Library/Yorba Linda, CA 92886-3903/(8) Gerald R. Ford Library/Ann Arbor, MI 48109-2114/(9) Gerald R. Ford Museum/Grand Rapids, MI 49504-5353/(10) Carter Presidential/Library & Museum/Atlanta, GA 30307-1498/(11) Ronald Reagan/Presidential Library/and Museum/Simi Valley, CA 93065-0600/(12) George Bush/Presidential Library/and Museum/College Station, TX 77845-3906/(13) William J. Clinton/Presidential Library/& Museum/Little Rock, AR 72201-1213/To contact the libraries online, go to www.archives.gov and click on the link for each library." Universal Product Code (UPC) "458200." "© 2005 USPS." "PLATE/POSITION" and diagram. ".37 x 20 = $7.40."

Designer and Art Director: Howard Paine of Delaplane, Virginia

Calligrapher and Typographer: Julian Waters of Gaithersburg, Maryland

Modeler: Donald Woo of Sennett Security Products, Chantilly, Virginia

Stamp Manufacturing: Stamps printed by Banknote Corporation of America/Sennett Security Products, Browns Summit, North Carolina, on Goebel Optiforma 26 offset press. Stamps processed by Unique Binders, Fredericksburg, Virginia.

Quantity Ordered: 40,000,000

Plate Number Detail: 1 set of 3 plate numbers preceded by the letter S in selvage above or below each corner stamp

Plate Number Combination Reported: S111

Paper Supplier: Mactac

Tagging: phosphored paper

The Stamp

On August 4, the Postal Service issued a commemorative stamp to mark the 50th anniversary of the act of Congress that established the presidential library system. The act, signed by President Dwight D. Eisenhower August 12, 1955, authorized presidents leaving office to donate their material to the government for preservation and public access at special libraries, which would be constructed at private expense.

The stamp had its first-day ceremonies at the 11 presidential libraries and one presidential museum that are under the direction of the National Archives and Records Administration (NARA). They were: the Herbert Hoover Presidential Library and Museum in West Branch, Iowa; the Franklin D. Roosevelt Presidential Library and Museum in Hyde Park, New York; the Harry S. Truman Presidential Library & Museum in Independence, Missouri; the Dwight D. Eisenhower Presidential Library & Museum in Abilene, Kansas; the John F. Kennedy Presidential Library and Museum in Boston, Massachusetts; the Lyndon Baines Johnson Library and Museum in Austin, Texas; the Gerald R. Ford Library in Ann Arbor, Michigan; the Gerald R. Ford Museum in Grand Rapids, Michigan; the Carter Presidential Library & Museum in Atlanta, Georgia; the Ronald Reagan Presidential Library and Museum in Simi Valley, California; the George Bush Presidential Library and Museum in College Station, Texas; and the William J. Clinton Presidential Library & Museum in Little Rock, Arkansas. The Ford museum is the only museum located apart from its associated library.

Additional first-day ceremonies took place at the Richard M. Nixon Presidential Library in Yorba Linda, California — which was not part of the federal system at the time, but has since been taken into the fold — and at the American Philatelic Society Stampshow in Grand Rapids, Michigan.

The campaign for a stamp for the anniversary of the Presidential Libraries Act began at the nation's newest presidential library and before it opened its doors November 18, 2004.

Skip Rutherford, president of the William J. Clinton Presidential Foundation, said officials at the Clinton library wanted the stamp, but not just for the new facility. "We thought it would be good for all the libraries," Rutherford told *Linn's Stamp News*.

Rutherford said he contacted postal officials with the idea for a Presidential Libraries stamp, and the idea was endorsed by John W. Caslin, head of NARA. It had a strong advocate within the Citizens' Stamp Advisory Committee in Ron Robinson, the retired chairman of a Little Rock marketing agency, who was a fund-raiser for the Clinton library. (In 2005, Robinson would become chairman of CSAC.)

The self-adhesive stamp was printed by Banknote Corporation of America for Sennett Security Products by the offset process and distributed in panes of 20. Stamp Fulfillment Services also offered uncut press sheets of nine panes for $66.60.

Printed on the back of the pane's liner release paper is a short history of the presidential library system, a locator map of the United States and a numbered list of the libraries keyed to the map. Also on the reverse is the printed information that normally is found in the selvage on the front of a pane: copyright, full-pane price and plate-position diagram. The only selvage printing on the front of the Presidential Libraries pane is a plate number in each of the four corners.

Presidential libraries have been described by *The Washington Post Magazine* as "history and hagiography, archival mother lodes and gift shops pushing star-spangled dish towels and 'Gippergear.'" Each one is a working archive of presidential papers, accompanied by a museum that offers public programs on topics ranging from Caroline Kennedy's doll collection to World War II.

When a president leaves office, NARA establishes a presidential project to house and index the documents until a new library is built and transferred to the federal government. Libraries and museums exist for

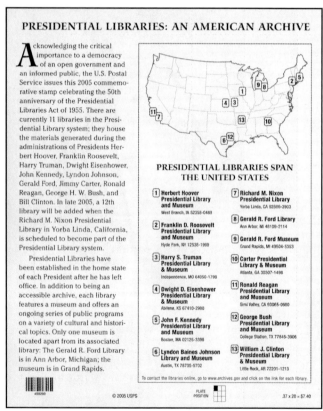

A short history of the presidential library system, a locator map, and the names and addresses of the 12 presidential libraries and one presidential museum are printed on the liner release paper of the stamp pane.

140

presidents before Hoover, but they are run by state governments or other agencies outside the NARA system. These include the Calvin Coolidge, Rutherford B. Hayes, Abraham Lincoln and Woodrow Wilson libraries.

Although the Richard M. Nixon Library and Birthplace was not part of the presidential library system when the stamp was issued, the process of transferring the facility to the national system had been under way since January 2004, when Congress approved the necessary legislation. The verso text of the stamp pane stated that the process of transfer was scheduled to be complete in late 2005, but this didn't happen until the following year. On April 10, 2006, U.S. Archivist Allen Weinstein appointed Cold War historian Timothy Naftali to be the first federal director of the Nixon library, effective October 16, 2006.

The presidential library system had its beginnings in 1939, when President Franklin D. Roosevelt donated his personal and presidential papers to the U.S. government and pledged part of his estate at Hyde Park, New York, to be the site of a library and museum building. A safe, accessible archive for the materials of each administration was needed, Roosevelt said, to "bring together the records of the past and to house them in buildings where they will be preserved for the use of men and women in the future." A non-profit corporation was founded to build the facility, and the president asked the National Archives to take custody of his papers and other historical materials and to administer his library.

In 1950, President Harry S. Truman decided that he, too, would build a library to house his presidential papers. Five years later, Congress passed the Presidential Libraries Act. Each presidential library established since then has been built with private funds and, after completion, turned over to NARA for administering.

The 1955 law didn't require presidents to surrender their records to the federal government. However, the Presidential Records Act of 1978 went further and defined as the property of the United States all statutory, constitutional and ceremonial papers generated during a president's completed term in office, and placed the records in the custody of the archivist of the United States. The 1978 act also established that the presidential library system should continue to be the repository for subsequent presidential records.

Every American president since Hoover is or has chosen to be buried at his presidential library, with the exception of John F. Kennedy and Lyndon B. Johnson. Kennedy is buried in Arlington National Cemetery; Johnson is buried at his ranch in the Texas hill country, west of Austin.

The presidential library system, as an asset to the nation, "has a quiet ally: time," wrote *The Washington Post Magazine*'s Paula Span.

"The passage of decades improves presidential libraries, eventually leaching away the political and financial pressures, the tendency toward idolatry," she wrote. "The presidents and their undersecretaries die; the partisan fires subside; the documents once stamped 'CONFIDENTIAL' no longer contain secrets worth hiding. Even the museums become more balanced.

"History takes over and slowly works its will, and the records of a political era are there, collected, a trove waiting to yield its information. If you're willing to wade through it, says [Lyndon Johnson biographer] Robert Caro, who's spent years doing just that, it's astonishing what you can find."

The Design

In 2003, when Postal Service art director Howard Paine volunteered to design the stamp, he didn't suspect that the task would be long, complex and difficult. It turned out to be all of the above.

Paine was initially drawn to the idea of showing the faces of the deceased presidents whose libraries were part of the federally run system in tall, narrow frames arranged side by side like library books on a shelf. At the time, six presidents fit that description: Hoover, Roosevelt, Truman, Eisenhower, Kennedy and Johnson.

Aided by typographer John Boyd, Paine developed the design and experimented with it, altering the spacing of the portraits and tipping the Truman portrait slightly to make the resemblance to the spines of books more obvious. The visual effect — especially on a full pane of 20 stamps — was of a crowded library bookcase.

Then USPS learned that preparations were under way to admit the Nixon library to the system. "So my six books on the shelf became seven," Paine said. "With the addition of Nixon, all the portraits had to be narrowed and tightened. I suggested that the stamp be made long and skinny, like one of the Submarine stamps of 2000, but Terry [Terrence McCaffrey, manager of stamp development] wanted to keep it commemorative size."

Paine also proposed an added feature that he optimistically predicted collectors would "love": the creation of seven different varieties of the basic stamp by removing a different portrait from each one, leaving a gap as if the book had been checked out. "I thought collectors would have fun spotting whether their stamp was missing a Truman, or a Johnson, or whoever," Paine said. But the prospect of artificially boosting the count of varieties found no supporters.

The final blow to the shelf-of-books concept came when Ronald Reagan died June 5, 2004. "I squeezed yet another book onto the shelf, and I cut all the heads a little narrower, and it was getting really tight," Paine said. "They decided that this wasn't working and I should come up with something else."

"There was another problem, as well," McCaffrey said. "We could put only dead presidents on a stamp, but how were we to explain that to people who would say, 'Where's Clinton? He has a library. Where's Ford? Where's Bush?' It was just too problematic, and we had to rethink the whole thing."

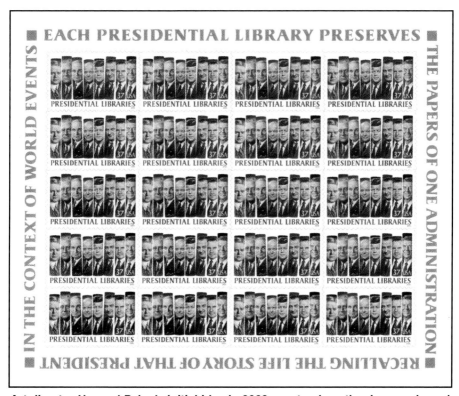

Art director Howard Paine's initial idea in 2003 was to show the deceased presidents whose libraries were part of the federal system in narrow vertical frames suggestive of books on a shelf. At the time six presidents fit that description: Herbert Hoover, Franklin D. Roosevelt, Harry S. Truman, Dwight D. Eisenhower, John F. Kennedy and Lyndon B. Johnson. However, in January 2004 Congress approved the necessary legislation to transfer Richard M. Nixon's library to the federal system, and it was necessary to add a seventh book depicting Nixon. Five months later, in June, Ronald Reagan died, and his portrait had to be squeezed into the lineup, making eight in all. The impression of a crowded bookcase is particularly effective on a full pane of 20 stamps, as shown here. Nevertheless, Paine said, "They decided that this wasn't working and I should come up with something else."

Paine returned with a handful of alternative designs. One was a montage of items that would be found in a presidential library: tape reels, punch cards, stationery. CSAC's design subcommittee turned it down. "We don't want to show audiotape," McCaffrey told him. "It would make people think of the 18½ minute gap in the Nixon tapes."

Another consisted of a photograph of a bookcase full of red bound books, rolled back to reveal a photo of the White House. McCaffrey was unenthusiastic, pointing out that the image was reminiscent of previous White House stamps.

John Boyd created a sequence of pictures set at an angle, showing a presidential inauguration, with the faces blurred for anonymity; the American flag; the White House; a file folder; and an archival scene that would bleed across the die cuts into the abutting stamp. Eric Kriemelmeyer of Dodge Color, which does the Postal Service's prepress work, developed a design showing a hand holding a quill pen in front of the presidential seal and the quotation from President Roosevelt describing the purpose of the presidential library system. These, too, failed to excite anyone.

At Paine's invitation, artist Michael Cronan, who had designed the Prostate Cancer Awareness and NATO commemoratives of 1999, submitted sketches showing stylized icons meant to represent the contents of a presidential library, and other sketches showing hands holding an open book. Paine himself turned down these offerings. The book image looked too much like a stamp promoting literacy and reading, he said, and the icons were "childish," hard to decipher at stamp size and failing to convey the idea of presidential libraries.

After the shelf-of-books design concept was abandoned, Paine returned to CSAC with these alternatives: angled photos, a bookcase and the White House, and a montage of items that would be found in presidential libraries. The latter was turned down because of the prominence of the audiotape reel, which officials thought would evoke the memory of the 18½-minute gap in the Nixon tapes.

Eric Kriemelmeyer of Dodge Color developed this design showing a hand holding a quill pen in front of the presidential seal and a Franklin D. Roosevelt quotation describing the purpose of the presidential library system. The presidential seal itself would become the sole graphic element in the final design.

At one point, Paine found a painting of a political nominating convention in the portfolio of Mark Stutzman, a sometime stamp illustrator, and his wife Laura, and made a square stamp of it, surrounding the image with a running sentence about the stamp subject. "I thought it could show a colorful, exuberant aspect of presidential libraries," Paine said. "It never went anywhere."

In the meantime, however, he and Boyd had been developing a backup approach. A friend had showed Paine a White House invitation bearing the presidential seal, embossed on heavy cream stationery. The presidential seal consists of the familiar Great Seal of the United States — an eagle with shield, holding an olive branch and arrows in its claws — surrounded by 50 white stars, all inside a ring bearing the words "Seal of the President of the United States." The invitation had gravitas, it symbolized the presidency, and "it made you feel important just to hold it," Paine said.

Remembering this experience, he said, he concluded that the solution lay in a design featuring the presidential seal, accompanied by distinctive-looking typography that would announce the linkage to presidential libraries. The seal had not been shown previously on a stamp, although it

Michael Cronan offered these sketches showing stylized icons meant to represent the contents of a presidential library and hands holding an open book.

had been considered for use in 1989 on the 22¢ stamp commemorating the 200th anniversary of the executive branch of the U.S. government.

The design team created numerous vertical treatments of the seal, some in full color, others in a single color, with and without the outer ring of words. Paine called on calligrapher Julian Waters, who had assisted in the designing of several previous stamp issues, to custom-letter the words "Presidential Libraries." For the final version, the seal was modified to remove the outer ring of words and the background, and a script version of the wording with elaborate loops and flourishes was used.

Because the White House is vigilant in preventing unauthorized use of the seal, the Postal Service had to obtain official permission from the Executive Office of the President to modify the device and display it on a stamp. This task took Postal Service attorney Layne Owens several weeks to accomplish; it wasn't until the spring of 2005, as the time drew near for the stamp to go to the printer, that the White House came through.

Shown here are two preliminary versions of the presidential seal design, with calligraphy by Julian Waters. In these sketches, the entire seal with its ring of letters is shown. For the final design, the seal was modified to remove the lettering and open up the background, and Waters' script version of "Presidential Libraries" was used, in a somewhat heavier weight.

146

More complications ensued, however.

The colors of the stamp, when issued, were reflex blue for the seal, calligraphy and "37 USA," and red (PMS 202) for the phrase "FIFTY YEARS" and the year date, all on an ivory background. These were not the colors in the original stamp image that USPS had made public January 21, 2005.

In that image, the vignette and typography were in metallic gold against a light cream background. This striking combination was widely reproduced, most prominently in an enlargement that dominated the cover of the July 2005 *American Philatelist* magazine as part of a promotion for the American Philatelic Society's forthcoming Stampshow in Grand Rapids.

Both Paine and Terrence McCaffrey had wanted the stamp to be engraved and printed in metallic gold. "It would be formal, it would be archival, it would be 'presidential,' " Paine said. But when the decision was made to use less expensive offset printing, the plan broke down. The printer, Sennett/Banknote Corporation of America, was unable to hold the fine lines of the presidential seal in the metallic ink.

"Sennett said, 'If we remove every other line of the seal, and we do this and we do that, we can print it in metallic gold,' " said McCaffrey. "I said, 'I don't think so. We had enough trouble getting the White House to approve the use of the seal. If they see that we simplified it, they'll kill us. But we have to do something.' "

After metallic gold was abandoned, Paine asked for a gold color that would match that of two long-ago commemoratives, the 3¢ Gold Star Mothers stamp of 1948 (Scott 969) and the 3¢ California Statehood Centennial stamp of 1950 (Scott 997). But he was disappointed.

"Sennett came back with a number of trial runs using different inks that could simulate gold. They looked like dirty, muddy bathwater," McCaffrey said. Added Paine: "The gold turned out to look like olive drab, and olive drab on ivory looked terrible."

The microprinted letters "USPS" can be found beneath the bottom right leaf on the olive branch in the eagle's right talon.

Ultimately, the blue and red color combination was proposed and approved. Even so, the final result was not quite what postal officials had wanted. Paine had specified that the PMS red be used for the entire bottom line of type — "FIFTY YEARS 37 USA" — but the printer used it only for the "FIFTY YEARS."

Because the stamp was printed by offset, microprinting is included in the design. The letters "USPS" can be found beneath the bottom right leaf on the olive branch in the eagle's right talon.

In Paine's early design layouts, he included in the pane selvage a map of the United States with the presidential libraries located, numbered and keyed to an accompanying list. In time, he conceded that it would be more practical to move the map to the back of the liner paper, which is where it ended up.

First-Day Facts

Following is a summary of the ceremonies at each of the first-day sites:

GEORGE H.W. BUSH. Carolyn Lewis Gallagher, a member of the USPS Board of Governors, dedicated the stamp. The principal speaker was Warren Finch, director of the library and museum. Mike Wright, vice president and general manager of KBTX-TV, was master of ceremonies.

JIMMY CARTER. William J. Brown, USPS vice president for Southeast Area operations, was the dedicating official. The principal speaker was President Carter's grandson, Jason Carter, an attorney. Dr. Jay Hakes, director of the Carter library and museum, gave the welcome, and Anderson Hodges Jr., Atlanta District manager for USPS, was master of ceremonies. Honored guests were members of the Carter family; former U.S. Senator Max Cleland, Democrat of Georgia; and Bert Lance, Carter campaign advisor and former director of the Office of Management and Budget.

BILL CLINTON. Alan C. Kessler, vice chairman of the USPS Board of Governors, dedicated the stamp. The principal speaker was Dr. Allen Weinstein, archivist of the United States. U.S. Senator Mark Pryor, Democrat of Arkansas, attended.

DWIGHT D. EISENHOWER. The dedicating official was Joleen Baxa, manager of the USPS Central Plains District. Mary Eisenhower, chief executive officer of People to People International and a granddaughter of President Eisenhower, and Dan Holt, director of the library and museum, were the speakers. Abilene Mayor Diane Miller gave the welcome. Daniel M. Taylor, manager of post office operations for the Central Plains District, was master of ceremonies.

GERALD R. FORD. George A. Omas, chairman of the Postal Rate Commission, dedicated the stamp at the library in Ann Arbor. The speakers were U.S. Representative John Dingell, Democrat of Michigan; Representative Thaddeus McCotter, Republican of Michigan; William

Gosling, curator of the children's literature collection for the University of Michigan Libraries; and Gloria Tyson, Detroit District manager for USPS. Elaine Didier, director of the library, was master of ceremonies. U.S. Representative Vernon J. Ehlers took part in the ceremony at the Ford Museum in Grand Rapids.

HERBERT HOOVER. Participants in the ceremony included Iowa U.S. Representatives Jim Leach, Republican, and Leonard Boswell, Democrat. Among those attending were President Hoover's grandson, Andy Hoover, Andy's wife Jean, his daughter Margaret and his son Alexander.

LYNDON B. JOHNSON. Susan Plonkey, vice president for customer service of USPS, dedicated the stamp. Lynda Johnson Robb, one of President Johnson's two daughters, was a speaker. Also participating were Betty Sue Flowers, the library's director, and Neal Spelce of USPS.

JOHN F. KENNEDY. John F. Walsh of the USPS Board of Governors dedicated the stamp. Participating in the ceremony were Thomas Putnam, deputy director of the Kennedy library; Megan Brennan, USPS vice president, Northeast Area; Charles Lynch, USPS Boston District manager; Marsha Cannon, Boston postmaster, and John Lespasio, senior plant manager for the Boston Mail Processing Center.

RICHARD M. NIXON. The dedicating official was William Johnstone, secretary of the USPS Board of Governors. Speakers were John H. Taylor, executive director, Nixon Library and Birthplace Foundation, and Eduardo Ruiz Jr., the Postal Service's Santa Ana District manager. U.S. Representative Gary Miller, Republican of California, and Michael D. Duvall, mayor pro tem of Yorba Linda, also participated.

RONALD REAGAN. James C. Miller 3d, chairman of the USPS Board of Governors, dedicated the stamp. Also participating was Duke Blackwood, executive director of the library. Earlier in 2005, the Reagan Library had been the site of a dedication ceremony for the Ronald Reagan memorial stamp.

FRANKLIN D. ROOSEVELT. David L. Solomon, vice president of USPS for the New York Metropolitan Area, dedicated the stamp. Participating in the ceremony were David Roosevelt, the president's grandson; Cynthia Koch, director of the library; U.S. Representative John Sweeney, Democrat of New York; and Nicholas Barrance of USPS.

HARRY S. TRUMAN. Ormer Rogers Jr., Mid-America District manager for USPS, was the dedicating official. Former U.S. Senator Thomas F. Eagleton, president emeritus of the Harry S. Truman Library Institute, and Thomas Washington Daniel, a software engineer for IDX Systems Corporation and a grandson of President Truman, were the speakers. Ron Stewart, mayor of Independence, gave the welcome. Dr. Michael Devine, director of the Truman museum and library, was master of ceremonies. An honored guest was U.S. Representative Ike Skelton, Democrat of Missouri.

STAMPSHOW 2005. Participating in the first-day ceremony were

Each of the first-day postmarks for the Presidential Libraries stamp features a presidential signature. The specific city and state appeared in the circular date-stamp of each postmark in place of "CITY, ST STATION." This example was used at the August 4 ceremony at the Gerald R. Ford Library in Ann Arbor, Michigan.

Charles Howe, Greater Michigan District manager for USPS; U.S. Representative Vernon Ehlers of Michigan; John Hotchner, CSAC member; Dave Failor, executive director, stamp services for USPS; Janet Klug, president of the American Philatelic Society; and Grand Rapids Postmaster Nancy Rettinhouse.

Each first-day cancellation from a presidential library and/or museum bore a replica of that president's signature.

For a limited time, Stamp Fulfillment Services offered a set of 13 uncacheted first-day covers, one from each presidential library and/or museum, for $9.75. Random single first-day covers were sold for 75¢.

37¢ AMERICA ON THE MOVE: 50S SPORTY CARS (5 DESIGNS)
DOUBLE-SIDED CONVERTIBLE BOOKLET OF 20

Date of Issue: August 20, 2005

Catalog Numbers: Scott 3931-3935, stamps; 3931a, vertical strip of 5; 3931b, convertible booklet of 20

Colors: black, cyan, magenta, yellow

First-Day Cancel: Detroit, Michigan

First-Day Cancellations: 337,512 (includes picture postal cards)

Format: Convertible booklet pane of 20, horizontal, arranged vertically. Stamps on both sides, 8 (2 across by 4 down) plus label (booklet cover) on one side, 12 (2 across by 6 down) on other side, with horizontal peel-off strips between blocks of 4 on each side. Offset printing plates printing 640 stamps per revolution: 256 on label side (16 around, 16 across) and 384 on all-stamp side (24 around, 16 across).

Gum Type: self-adhesive

Overall Stamp Size: 1.56 by 0.98 inches; 39.624 by 24.892 mm

Pane Size: 3.12 by 6.18 inches; 79.248 by 156.972 mm

Perforations: 10¾ (die-cut simulated perforations) (IDC custom rotary die-cutter). Backing paper rouletted behind peel-off strips.

Selvage Markings: "© 2004 USPS" and plate numbers on one peel-off strip and "Ford & Thunderbird™ Ford Motor Company" on another peel-off strip, both on all-stamp side. "General Motors Corvette Trademarks used under license to the USPS" on one peel-off strip on label side.

Back Markings: "AMERICA ON THE MOVE/50s/Sporty Cars/$7.40/Twenty 37¢ Self-adhesive Stamps • Five Separate Designs" and Universal Product Code (UPC) "0 673800 6" on booklet cover

Artist and Designer: Art M. Fitzpatrick of Carlsbad, California

Art Director and Typographer: Carl Herrman of Carlsbad, California

Modeler: Joseph Sheeran, Ashton-Potter (USA) Ltd., Williamsville, New York

Stamp Manufacturing: Stamps printed by Ashton-Potter on Mueller Martini offset press. Stamps finished by Ashton-Potter.

Quantity Ordered: 640,000,000 stamps

Plate Number Detail: 1 set of 4 plate numbers preceded by the letter P on 1 peel-off strip

Plate Number Combination Reported: P1111

Paper Supplier: Flexcon/Glatfelter

Tagging: phosphored paper with phosphor blocker on cover

The Stamps

On August 20, the Postal Service issued five stamps depicting what it called "sporty cars" from the 1950s. The first-day ceremony was held at the Michigan State Fair in Detroit, Michigan, the city at the heart of the U.S. automobile industry.

At the same time, USPS placed on sale a companion set of five 23¢ picture postal cards bearing the same designs on their imprinted stamps (see separate chapter).

To encourage wide use of the stamps by automobile-loving Americans, the Postal Service issued them in the convenient double-sided convertible booklet format and ordered a printing of 640 million, an unusually large number for a commemorative issue. Ashton-Potter (USA) Ltd. was the printer, using offset lithography.

"My guess is that it is going to be the first of a series" of post-World War II automobile stamps, said Terrence McCaffrey, manager of stamp development for USPS.

In fact, Sporty Cars itself could be called the third segment of a long-running series. Two previous U.S. five-stamp sets also had featured American cars from specific periods in the past. In 1988, USPS issued a booklet of stamps illustrating Classic Cars of the 1920s and 1930s, and followed it in 1995 with a pane showing Antique Automobiles from the 1890s and 1900s.

Two earlier five-stamp sets also pictured U.S. automobiles from specific periods: the Classic Cars booklet of 1988 and the Antique Automobiles pane of 1995. Ken Dallison illustrated both sets.

The Sporty Cars project was launched in 2002 with the support of two car enthusiasts on the Citizens' Stamp Advisory Committee, Michael Brock, then chairman of the CSAC design subcommittee, and the late Phil Meggs. Both considered the 1950s to have been a decade of singular distinction and futuristic concepts in U.S. automobile design.

"The problem we encountered up front was that there were just too many different cars to think about," recalled Carl Herrman, the stamps' art director. "We finally redefined the subject to be 'sports cars,' but then we discovered that the official definition of a sports car by the American Sports Car Association is so precise that cars like the Chevrolet Corvette aren't included.

"We decided to call it 'Sporty Cars' so we could make our own list and wouldn't have the experts questioning whether we knew what a sports car was."

PhotoAssist, the Postal Service's research firm, engaged Michael Lamm, a writer on automobiles and automotive history, to help select the subjects for the set. He recommended 10 cars for consideration, including all the ones that ultimately were chosen except for one, the 1953 Studebaker Starliner. The remaining cars on his list were the Cunningham (1951-1953), the Crosley Hot Shot/Super Sport (1949-1952), the Chrysler C300 (1955) and the Studebaker Golden Hawk (1957). If the period were stretched to include the early 1960s, Lamm wrote, he would add the AC Shelby (Ford) Cobra (1962-1968) and the Studebaker Avanti (1963-1964).

In e-mail conversations among Meggs, Brock, Herrman and PhotoAssist's Louis Plummer, Lamm's list and other makes and models were discussed and questions raised. Should they include the Chrysler C300 so that the third of Detroit's "Big Three" automakers (with Ford and General Motors) would be represented? They decided it wasn't necessary. Was the Crosley Hot Shot primarily a "street car," made for public consumption, or a race car? Herrman confirmed that it was a street car; he had a neighbor who owned one. How about the 1951 Studebaker Super Aero, a bullet-nosed car designed by Raymond Loewy? How about Preston Tucker's Tucker Torpedo, a commercial failure but a triumph of innovation?

The five cars that made the final cut were:

1952 NASH HEALEY. A little sports car noted for its hybridized styling, it was the product of the creative skills of three countries. The Nash six-cylinder engine was created in the United States, the Donald Healey-engineered chassis was developed in England, and Pinin Farina's sports-car body came from Italy. The car finished first in its class in the 1952 LeMans sports car race in France, and third overall. Industry historians say that with only 150 made, it priced itself out of the market.

1953 STUDEBAKER STARLINER. Considered by some to be "the first American sports car," the Loewy-designed 1953 Starliner was developed to appeal to younger drivers. Low-slung, long and wide, and light on the chrome, it had a sophisticated European look. The Museum of Modern Art in New York City proclaimed the car "a work of art" and featured it as the lone American representative in an auto exhibition in 1953.

1953 CHEVROLET CORVETTE. At the GM Motorama in New York City in January 1953, the new fiberglass-bodied, two-seater Corvette was unveiled and quickly captured the public's imagination, while setting the bar for the competition. Only 300 models were produced that year, all hand-built and white with a red interior and black convertible top, in a marked departure for GM. Its sporty appearance promised speed and high performance. In 1955, Chevrolet added a V8 engine.

1954 KAISER DARRIN. Henry J. Kaiser, a sand and gravel entrepreneur, teamed up with master designer Howard "Dutch" Darrin, formerly of Packard, to develop this fiberglass model. A two-seater, it featured retractable doors that slid forward into the front fenders; a unique pointed, compact grille; long, sloping lines; and a three-position Landau top. A total of 435 were made in 1954, but the car could not compete with the Corvette, which offered more horsepower for slightly less cost. Darrin himself bought 100 of the leftover cars

and refitted them for sale with powerful Cadillac V8 engines.

1955 FORD THUNDERBIRD. This "sports car with luxury," as Ford dubbed it, was designed to compete with the Corvette, and its road performances were virtually identical to the Chevrolet's. It featured a steel body, interchangeable hard and soft tops, an over-head-valve V8 engine and roll-up windows. More than 16,000 cars were produced in 1955. The styling remained the same until 1958, when Ford added a back seat, after which sales quadrupled.

Bob Stevens, editor-at-large of *Cars & Parts* magazine, told *Linn's Stamp News* that the selection of the 1953 Corvette and 1955 Thunderbird for the stamps made sense in that they represented the first production years of two cars that still are very popular among automotive enthusiasts.

Interest in restored 1953 Corvette roadsters was boosted by the car's 50th anniversary in 2003, and the cars now command $125,000 to $150,000 and sell very quickly when they are placed on the market, Stevens said. The Thunderbird "appealed to more than just sports-car buyers and is credited with launching a new generation of sporty, personal cars," he said. "Authentically restored examples currently fetch from $30,000 to $60,000, depending on equipment. Supercharged 1957 Thunderbirds grab the top money."

Of the five manufacturers represented on the stamps, only Chevrolet and Ford still make automobiles.

The stamp designs were unveiled August 15, 2004, at the 54th Pebble Beach Concours D'Elegance international classic car show in Pebble Beach, California.

Automobiles have been frequent U.S. stamp subjects. The first of these, a battery-powered taxi in front of the U.S. Capitol, was pictured on the 4¢ Pan-American Exposition commemorative of 1901. The same stamp, with center inverted, was reproduced on a souvenir pane issued in 2001 to mark the Pan-American stamps' centennial. In 1913, a post office automobile was depicted on the 15¢ value of the parcel post set.

Stamps in the Celebrate the Century series of 1998-2000 showed a Model T Ford, a limousine resembling a Duesenberg, the tailfins of a 1957 Chevrolet Bel Air, a 1964 Ford Mustang, a generic sport utility vehicle of the 1990s and a 1950s stock-car race. The long-running Transportation series of definitive stamps included among its subjects a 1900s fire engine, a 1909 Stanley Steamer, a 1910s star route truck, a 1911 racing car, a 1917 electric auto, a 1920s school bus, a 1920s tow truck, a 1930s tractor trailer and a 1933 Stutz Bearcat. Other definitive stamps have depicted the front end of a generic car, a tailfin resembling that of a 1959 Cadillac El Dorado and a 1941 Ford "woody" station wagon.

The Designs

At the outset, Terrence McCaffrey asked two of his art directors, Carl Herrman and Richard Sheaff, to prepare concept sketches "to give us a feel for what we wanted to do with the project," McCaffrey said.

Sheaff adapted a group of existing photos and advertising art from the 1950s to create designs that showed not only entire cars but also tight close-ups of wheels, mirrors and other portions of the specified makes and models.

Herrman, for his part, hired two well-known automotive illustrators to

At the beginning of the project, when CSAC was searching for the right design approach for the stamps, two well-known automobile illustrators prepared these pencil sketches and color compositions for art director Carl Herrman. They included cars that didn't make it into the stamp set, such as the Chrysler 300C.

Art director Richard Sheaff used existing photographs and illustrations to create these stamp designs in which he focused on details rather than entire cars.

prepare some comps, or visual compositions. At the request of Michael Brock, one of the CSAC originators of the project, he also contacted Art M. "Fitz" Fitzpatrick, a fellow townsman in Carlsbad, California.

Fitzpatrick, who turned 87 in November 2005, has had a distinguished career designing automobiles and painting sleek, dramatic portraits of cars to illustrate advertisements and magazine articles. His original paintings and limited-edition prints command high prices from collectors, and he frequently lectures as part of exhibitions of his work.

"Fitz is the Michelangelo of car artists," Herrman said. "I tracked him down at the Newport Beach [California] Concours, selling his advertising art from the '50s and '60s, and he said he would do some comps for me. I brought them back to the committee, and they just blew everyone away. The members were delighted with the idea of evoking the look of 1950s automobile advertising on the stamps."

The result was that Fitzpatrick agreed to take on his first-ever stamp assignment.

The artist had been only 20 when he designed the Darrin Packard four-door convertible and hardtop sedans before World War II. At 22, he was a consulting designer to General Electric. While working for noted car designers and coach builders John Tjaarda (Briggs Body), Werner Gubitz

(Packard) and Howard "Dutch" Darrin, the young man custom-built cars for such notables as Clark Gable, Errol Flynn and Al Jolson.

After serving as a naval officer in the war, Fitzpatrick turned to advertising art. With a partner, the late Van Kaufman, providing the backgrounds, Fitzpatrick created romantic, evocative automobile paintings for ads for General Motors, Lincoln/Mercury, Nash, Chrysler, Dodge, DeSoto, Plymouth, Kaiser, Studebaker and Buick. In 1953, Buick signed him to an exclusive contract, beginning what would be a 21-year association with General Motors' Buick, Pontiac and Opel automobiles. In addition to his work for GM, Fitzpatrick created art, graphic and product design for General Electric, Texaco, Quaker State and Chris-Craft and editorial illustrations for *Life*, *Look*, *Esquire* and *Automobile Quarterly*.

Fitzpatrick "painted" the Sporty Cars illustrations on his computer, starting with scanned-in photographs that he converted to simple line art with the Adobe Illustrator program. A copy of each line drawing was sent to the owner and consultant for that particular car, who returned it with annotated corrections and comments. The artist then used Photoshop software to airbrush in color and backgrounds. All the stamp illustrations were done in this manner except for the Studebaker Starliner, which Fitzpatrick painted the old-fashioned way, with brush and acrylics, "just for the exercise," Herrman said. "However, he did use the computer afterward to smooth out the brushstrokes."

CSAC had asked that the five different vehicles on the stamps be depicted from a variety of angles and heights. With this direction in mind, and with the help of Louis Plummer of PhotoAssist, Herrman and Fitzpatrick began the search for specimens they could photograph. Fortuitously, they found four of the cars in their own state of California.

1952 NASH HEALEY. The only non-California car to "pose" for Fitzpatrick was the Nash Healey. The silver-gray convertible was owned by Leonard McGrady of Aberdeen, Maryland, a prominent collector of the make and model. "I had to attend a CSAC meeting in Washington, D.C., so Louis [Plummer] and I drove to Aberdeen to meet Mr. McGrady," Herrman said. "He had a barn with two levels, and it

This silver-gray 1952 Nash Healey that "posed" for the stamp illustration was one of several owned by Leonard McGrady of Aberdeen, Maryland. The car was missing a dashboard rear mirror, which Art Fitzpatrick added on his computer.

was wall-to-wall Nash Healeys. They were basically unrestored — not wrecks, but not all in great shape either. He had Donald Healey's original racing cars; he had Walt Disney's car with Mickey Mouse ears on the rear-view mirror. If anyone who was anyone ever had a Nash Healey, it seemed as though he ended up with it.

"He had no trouble pulling out a nice one for us that I was able to photograph with my Nikon Cool-Pick camera, standing on the roof of his old beat-up pickup truck."

The car's dashboard mirror was missing. Fitzpatrick inserted the mirror into his artwork electronically, working from a pencil tracing of the authentic accessory provided by McGrady. The artist painted the car, its top down, driving along a coastal highway, while four yachts ride at anchor in the background. A man is at the wheel; a woman is in the passenger seat. The setting is from a photo taken by Fitzpatrick in the Virgin Islands. The couple are models, also photographed by the artist.

1953 STUDEBAKER STARLINER. The red-and-white car shown on the stamp was owned by Ron Wakefield of Point Loma in San Diego, a former editor of *Road & Track* magazine. The model the design team

wanted to depict had no center post between the front and rear windows and looked like a hardtop convertible when the windows were rolled down. However, Wakefield's car had the center post. Again using digital sleight-of-hand, Fitzpatrick removed it from the image. The change "made it look more elegant," Herrman explained. Fred K. Fox, a Studebaker and automotive historian, served as consultant for this stamp.

The red-and-white 1953 Studebaker Starliner shown here was the property of Ron Wakefield of Point Loma, San Diego, California. Fitzpatrick electronically removed the center posts between the front and rear windows to convert the vehicle to the model he and Carl Herrman wanted to depict on the stamp.

Fitzpatrick painted the Starliner on the road with a man at the wheel and a woman in the front seat beside him. In the background are snowy mountains that the artist based on a photograph of the Cascades he had taken for the purpose near Bend, Oregon.

1953 CHEVROLET CORVETTE. The white Corvette shown on the stamp was owned by Noland Adams of El Dorado, California, the author of several books about early Corvettes. The car is No. 284 of the 300 Corvettes that were sold in the 1953 model year. USPS also credited Adams as a technical adviser on the Corvette stamp. *Corvette* magazine called Adams "the guy who pioneered the field of Corvette detective work that has led to the exhaustive store of factory-correct info we have today."

The photo of Noland Adams' restored white 1953 Chevrolet Corvette provided the principal visual reference for Fitzpatrick's computer illustration.

The car had an active history. After Adams wrecked his first Corvette, a used 1954, he replaced it with a car that was advertised as a '54, but turned out to be a '53. In 1961, after the birth of his daughter Kimberly, Adams traded the Corvette for a 1947 Chevrolet sedan. Eight years later, he tracked down his 1953 Corvette, which the new owner's teen-age son had taken apart for a "restoration" that he had abandoned.

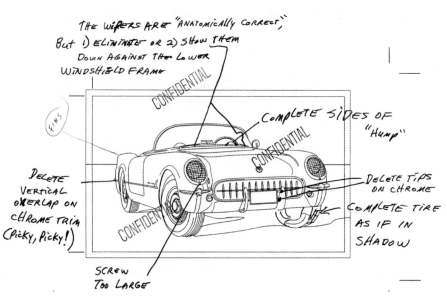

The Postal Service's passion for design accuracy down to the last detail is reflected in these annotations by consultant Noland Adams on Fitzpatrick's computer-generated outline drawing of the 1953 Chevrolet Corvette. Adams wrote to PhotoAssist's Louis Plummer: "Now, I know that most of the little picky stuff will get too small to see when the drawing is reduced to its final size, but why take a chance?"

This initial concept sketch by Fitzpatrick shows a driverless Corvette in a head-on view against a starry backdrop.

Adams bought the parts for $700 and took them home. Through an acquaintance who held a management position at GM, he was given access to previously restricted company files on the Corvette, which guided him in reassembling his vehicle and in writing his first how-to book on Corvette restoration.

Fitzpatrick based his painting on an existing photograph of the car, parked in a driveway, made by automotive photographer Ron Kimball. In his illustration, the car is moving along a highway with a man at the wheel. After trying other backgrounds, the artist painted a coastal scene with the sun setting, based on a photograph he made in his hometown of Carlsbad. "It had just the kind of sky he wanted," Herrman said.

Fitzpatrick painted the Corvette in two desert settings before settling on the California coastal scene. In one of these alternatives, his driver wears sunglasses.

1954 KAISER DARRIN. The pine-green Kaiser Darrin on the stamp was found in Spring Valley, California. Its owner is Rudy Phillips. Dave Antram of Somerset, Pennsylvania, who keeps a registry of Darrin owners, served as consultant. In Fitzpatrick's illustration, the car, with a smiling man at the wheel, has just emerged from a short tunnel in a hilly landscape. The artist based the background on a photograph he had taken in the Italian lake district.

The pine-green 1954 Kaiser Darrin in this reference photograph was owned by Rudy Phillips of Spring Valley, California.

1955 FORD THUNDERBIRD. The black Thunderbird on the stamp was owned by Tom Peluso of Rancho Santa Margarita, California. In Fitzpatrick's illustration, the car is stopped as the woman at the wheel chats with a man who stands outside, arms resting casually on the sill of the open window. In the background is a walled garden rich with blossoms. The background is based on the artist's photo of the gardens behind the Marriot Hotel in Long Beach, California. The man and woman are the same models that Fitzpatrick had used for his Nash Healey painting.

Peluso's car had some very unauthentic accessories, including fuzzy dice hanging from the mirror and a set of aftermarket hubcaps. The design team's solution was to photograph the car as it was and restore its authenticity by manipulating the image on Fitzpatrick's computer.

The 1955 Ford Thunderbird on the stamp was based on this photograph by Carl Herrman of a car owned by Tom Peluso. Fitzpatrick scanned the photo into his computer and in the process electronically removed the fuzzy dice from the mirror, changed the aftermarket hubcaps to the kind that originally came with the car, and made other revisions to ensure authenticity.

Gil Baumgartner of California, a restorer of Thunderbirds, was the consultant for the stamp. In reviewing Fitzpatrick's line drawing, Baumgartner pointed out several

162

details to correct, including a half-circle horn ring that was visible above the dashboard. "The horn ring wouldn't show on a '55 with the wheels straight forward," he wrote. "It may partially show with the wheels turned." The artist eliminated the horn ring in his finished illustration, which was authentic down to the six rows of square holes that characterized the 1955 and 1956 Thunderbird grills, the crossed flags on the hood just above them, and the Ford crest behind the side window that appears only on the 1955 hardtop.

In designing the stamps, Herrman placed black typography in a white band beneath each vignette. The name and model year of the car, in a typeface called Myriad, are on the left and "USA 37" is on the right. Herrman tucked the "2005" in the lower left corner of the illustration itself rather than beneath the vignette on the left, the customary location of the year date.

The art director designed alternative booklet covers using the Corvette and Thunderbird images. The Corvette was the final choice. "Of all these cars, the Corvette is probably the best known and most recognizable," Herrman explained. "Also, using that picture gave me an empty upper right corner to put the words '50s Sporty Cars.' The Thunderbird picture didn't have that convenient space."

Late in its review and approval process, CSAC decided to add the tagline "America on the Move" to the cover of the booklet.

"It was good to have the stamps out there in booklet form where they would be used on letters, and not just a sheet that only collectors would buy," said Herrman. "Unfortunately, the booklet format took away our ability to put verso text on the stamps, which would have allowed us to tell some fascinating little stories about the cars."

Carl Herrman designed this alternative booklet cover using Fitzpatrick's Ford Thunderbird stamp illustration. The Corvette illustration was his final choice.

A first-day cancellation ties a Chevrolet Corvette stamp to the dashboard of Noland Adams' 1953 Corvette, which was the model for the stamp's design.

First-Day Facts

Patrick Donahoe, deputy postmaster general and chief operating officer for USPS, dedicated the stamps at the Michigan State Fair. Gloria Tyson, Detroit district manager for customer service and sales for USPS, was master of ceremonies. Speakers were U.S. Senator Carl Levin, Democrat of Michigan, and Noland Adams, the Postal Service's technical adviser for the 1953 Corvette stamp and owner of the car that was the model for it. The Adams car was on display at the ceremony, along with two 1955 Ford Thunderbirds and two 1954 Kaiser Darrins.

These are the two different postmarks used on Sporty Cars first-day covers. They were obtained August 20 at the first-day ceremony in Detroit, Michigan. At left is the digital color postmark, available only on covers sold by Stamp Fulfillment Services. The inscription "50s Sporty Cars" and the car body are printed in red. At right is the black-and-white postmark used on conventional covers and the ceremony programs.

Afterward, Donahoe applied a first-day cancellation to a pane of stamps on each vehicle. Adams requested that a postmark be applied directly to the Corvette, and at some point a Corvette stamp from the pane used for the first canceling on the car was affixed to the dashboard and tied by the first-day postmark.

For a limited time, Stamp Fulfillment Services offered first-day covers with two different postmarks: a conventional black postmark and a digital color postmark featuring a red car and inscription "50s Sporty Cars." Covers with black postmarks were sold at $3.75 for a set of five, and the color-postmark covers were priced at $1.50 for a random single and $7.50 for all five.

37¢ ARTHUR ASHE

Date of Issue: August 27, 2005

Catalog Number: Scott 3936

Colors: black, cyan, magenta, yellow, brown (PMS 1605C)

First-Day Cancel: Flushing, New York

First-Day Cancellations: 65,893

Format: Panes of 20, vertical, 5 across, 4 down. Offset printing plates printing 240 stamps per revolution (12 across, 20 around).

Gum Type: self-adhesive

Microprinting: "USPS" on edge of tennis racket where it meets left border of design

Overall Stamp Size: 0.98 by 1.56 inches; 24.892 by 39.624 mm

Pane Size: 5.95 by 7.24 inches; 151.13 by 183.896 mm

Perforations: 10¾ (die-cut simulated perforations) (IDC custom two-station die cutter)

Selvage Inscription: "Arthur Ashe™ c/o CMG Worldwide, Indianapolis, IN"

Selvage Markings: "© 2004/USPS" ".37/x20/$7.40" "PLATE/POSITION" and diagram.

Back Markings: On selvage: "Discover the universal language of stamps!/ Visit the Washington 2006 World Philatelic Exhibition May 27-June 3, 2006, in Washington, D.C." Universal Product Code (UPC) "457400" in 4 locations. On stamps: "Arthur Ashe/(1943-1993)/takes his place among the/finest tennis players of the/20th century. The first/African-American man to/win Grand Slam tennis/tournaments, Ashe became/well known for his humani-/tarian commitments to/the underprivileged and/to victims of AIDS."

Designer, Art Director and Typographer: Carl Herrman of Carlsbad, California

Photographer: Michael O'Neill of New York, New York

Modeler: Joseph Sheeran of Ashton-Potter (USA) Ltd., Williamsville, New York

Stamp Manufacturing: Stamps printed by Ashton-Potter on a Mueller Martini A74 offset press. Stamps finished by Ashton-Potter.

Quantity Ordered: 75,000,000

Plate Number Detail: 1 set of 5 plate numbers preceded by the letter P in selvage above or below each corner stamp

Plate Number Combination Reported: P11111

Paper Supplier: Paper Corporation of the United States/Glatfelter

Tagging: phosphored paper, block tagging over stamps

The Stamp

Arthur Ashe, the first black American male tennis player to win a singles title in a Grand Slam event, won not one but three of them: the U.S. and Australian Opens and Wimbledon. On August 27, the Postal Service issued a commemorative stamp in his honor.

USPS held the first-day ceremony during Arthur Ashe Kids' Day, which annually kicks off the U.S. Open in Flushing Meadows, Flushing, New York. The stamp's design had been unveiled at the same event a year earlier, August 28, 2004, by Henry A. Pankey, USPS vice president for emergency preparedness.

Jeanne Moutoussamy-Ashe, Arthur Ashe's wife, and the couple's 17-year-old daughter Camera pose with USPS vice president Henry Pankey at the unveiling of the Ashe stamp design in the stadium named for him August 28, 2004. (USPS photo)

167

The Citizens' Stamp Advisory Committee chose Ashe as a stamp subject as part of an effort to depict contemporary black American notables on stamps other than those of the annual Black Heritage series. Ashe became eligible to appear on a stamp in 2003, 10 years after his death, and his commemorative would have been part of the 2004 program but for the fact that a 23¢ definitive picturing track star Wilma Rudolph was scheduled to appear in 2004.

"[The committee] said, 'We've got two African-American athletes who aren't in Black Heritage; why are we issuing both stamps in the same year?'" recalled Terrence McCaffrey, manager of stamp development. "We decided to stick with Rudolph, because we also want to honor more women on stamps, and move Ashe to another year."

The Ashe stamp, a self-adhesive, was printed by Ashton-Potter (USA) Ltd. by the offset process and distributed in panes of 20. A paragraph of text about Ashe appears on the liner paper behind each stamp.

Arthur Ashe was born in Richmond, Virginia, July 10, 1943. His father was a policeman in the city's recreation department, and the family lived next door to the segregated city's largest playground for black children.

Arthur's mother, Mattie Cordell (Cunningham) Ashe, died when he was 6 years old, leaving his father to raise him and his younger brother, Johnnie. His father later married Lorene Kimbrough, and Arthur became close to his stepmother and enjoyed a stable, loving home life.

Ashe showed an early aptitude for tennis, an unusual sport for a black child in the mid-century South. When he was 10, tennis coach Ronald Charity arranged for the boy to spend a summer in Lynchburg, Virginia, at the home of Dr. Walter Johnson. Johnson had been the coach of Althea Gibson, who became the first black woman ever to win a major tennis singles title. He taught his protégés to play with abandon but always to keep their emotions in check, and Ashe's cool demeanor on the court would become a trademark. "I envied players who could sling a racket and get away with it," he once recalled.

Unable to compete locally because of segregation, Ashe traveled hundreds of miles to play in tournaments. His first big victory came in 1957 when he capitalized on his extraordinary reflexes and his excellent backhand to win the boys' singles state championship in Maryland.

For his senior year in high school, Ashe moved into the home of another coach, Richard Hudlin, in St. Louis, Missouri, which enabled him to compete in tournaments without having to commute long distances. After graduation, he received a tennis scholarship to attend the University of California at Los Angeles, where he would graduate with a degree in business administration.

Ashe won the U.S. hard-court singles tennis title in 1963, and that year became the first black man ever to be a member of the U.S. Davis Cup team. He would go on to play in 32 Davis Cup matches in his career, winning 27. In 1965, he won the NCAA men's singles championship and led UCLA to the team championship.

His game now augmented by a big serve, Ashe won his historic grand slam singles title in 1968 when he defeated Tom Okker of the Netherlands 14-12, 5-7, 6-3, 3-6, 6-3 in the finals of the U.S. Open. Not only was he the first black American to win it; he was the first American of any color to wear the crown since 1955. In 1970, he added the Australian Open to his victory list.

In 1975, Ashe defeated Jimmy Connors in four sets to win the men's singles title at Wimbledon, the world's most prestigious tennis tournament. He was ranked the world's No. 1 male tennis player that year. Two years later, he married Jeanne Moutoussamy, a professional photographer. Their daughter Camera was born in 1986.

Ashe was a leader in the fight for social justice and equal opportunity, at home and abroad. Among the many organizations for which he raised money was the United Negro College Fund. He established the Safe Passage Foundation, which operates tennis centers in inner cities, and the Athlete-Career Connection, which aimed at improving the graduation rates of minority athletes.

After visiting South Africa and seeing apartheid at close range, Ashe successfully campaigned for the expulsion of South Africa from the International Lawn Tennis Federation and from Davis Cup competition. He participated in many peaceful demonstrations against apartheid. When South Africa released Nelson Mandela from prison after 27 years, Mandela expressed a desire to meet Ashe, and the two held conversations in both South Africa and the United States.

In 1979, at age 36, Ashe suffered a heart attack. It forced him to have bypass surgery and ended a competitive tennis career in which he won 818 matches and 51 titles. Within a year, Ashe was serving as national campaign chairman of the American Heart Association.

In retirement, Ashe coached the U.S. Davis Cup team for five years, leading the team to victory in 1981 and 1982. He also did color commentary for HBO and ABC Sports, and wrote columns for *The Washington Post* and *Tennis* magazine. A voracious reader and self-described "information freak," he discovered that there was no comprehensive study of black American athletes, and over the next half-decade he researched and wrote *A Hard Road to Glory* (1988), a three-volume history that corrected the omission. He won an Emmy for co-writing the television adaptation.

During a second bypass operation, in 1983, Ashe received HIV-contaminated blood, from which he contracted AIDS. In 1992 he publicly disclosed his condition, and became a champion and spokesman for AIDS treatment and research. Courageous and stoically philosophical about his condition, he said, "If I were to say, 'God, why me?' about the bad things, then I should have said, 'God, why me?' about the good things that happened in my life."

Ashe was inducted into the Tennis Hall of Fame in 1985. In December 1992, *Sports Illustrated* named him Sportsman of the Year with the saluta-

The city of Richmond installed this monument to its native son in 1996 on what would have been Ashe's 53rd birthday.

tion: "Arthur Ashe epitomizes good works, devotion to family and unwavering grace under pressure." In the accompanying article, Kenny Moore wrote: "Ashe looks hale, eats like a horse, climbs stairs two steps at a time and has a steady blood count." The optimism proved sadly misplaced. A little more than a month later, on February 6, 1993, Ashe died of AIDS-related pneumonia. He was just 49.

On what would have been his 53rd birthday, a statue of Ashe was installed on Monument Avenue in Richmond, where the tennis star took his place in the unlikely company of such other heroes of Virginia as Robert E. Lee, Stonewall Jackson, J.E.B. Stuart and Jefferson Davis.

In 1997, the U.S. Tennis Association named its new 23,000-seat U.S. Open tennis facility the Arthur Ashe Stadium and Commemorative Garden. Like other former sports stars like (Mel) Ott and (Bobby) Orr, Ashe also lives on in crossword puzzles because of the brevity and simplicity of his last name.

Ashe is the first male tennis player to be honored as such on a U.S. postage stamp, although at least two women tennis players previously appeared on U.S. stamps. Mildred "Babe" Didrikson Zaharias was pictured on an 18¢ stamp in 1981 (Scott 1932). Although more famous for her golfing career, Zaharias, who has been called "the greatest woman athlete of the 20th century," also was a successful professional tennis player. In 1990, USPS issued a 25¢ stamp for Hazel Wightman (Scott 2498), a U.S. tennis gold medalist in the 1924 Olympic Games, as part of its U.S. Olympians strip of five.

A 32¢ stamp commemorating recreational tennis (Scott 2964) was issued in 1995.

Michael Cassidy made this pencil sketch at the request of art director Carl Herrman.

The Design

Carl Herrman, assigned by Terrence McCaffrey to design the Ashe stamp, first called on Michael Cassidy of Leucadia, California, near Herrman's hometown of Carlsbad, to provide an illustration. Herrman was developing designs for the Duke Kahanamoku stamp of 2002 when he met Cassidy, an artist with an affinity for surfing and other sports subjects, and he liked what he called the artist's "very fresh, spontaneous, plain-air painting style."

Cassidy submitted a sketch showing a full-face portrait of Ashe and a smaller figure of the tennis player stroking a backhand. "It was a very nice image, and I was all set to take it to CSAC, when I happened into a sports photo gallery in La Jolla [California]," Herrman said. "What did I see there but a magnificent black-and-white photograph of Arthur Ashe. I immediately bought it and showed it to the committee at its next meeting, along with Michael Cassidy's sketch. The committee agreed with me that [the photo] would make a classy stamp."

The photograph was a close-up, three-quarters portrait of a pensive Ashe, wearing his familiar aviator glasses, holding a tennis racket next to his

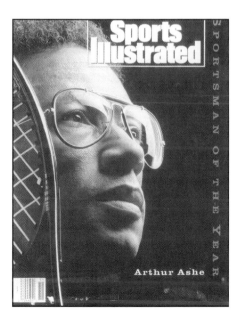

Michael O'Neill's photograph of Ashe for the December 21, 1992, "Sportsman of the Year" edition of Sports Illustrated *struck Carl Herrman and CSAC as the ideal stamp portrait.*

At the request of Ashe's wife, Herrman developed this alternative design from another photograph. He was relieved when she gave her approval to use the O'Neill photo from **Sports Illustrated.**

cheek. It turned out to be a flopped (reversed) version of a color photo by Michael O'Neill of New York City that had appeared on the cover of *Sports Illustrated*'s "Sportsman of the Year" edition dated December 21, 1992. PhotoAssist, the Postal Service's research firm, obtained rights to use the picture, and Herrman turned it into a vertically arranged, commemorative-size stamp.

At the request of Jeanne Moutoussamy-Ashe, Herrman also worked up a design using another photo portrait, but he considered it much less compelling than the O'Neill photo, and it lacked any element to suggest that Ashe was a tennis player. To Herrman's relief, Ashe's wife approved the design that he wanted to use.

The predominant tones of the stamp are the same as those of the magazine cover: browns, tans and oranges against a rich black-brown background. To print it, Ashton-Potter used the four standard process colors plus a reddish brown self-color. "USA 37" is in dropout white capitals in the upper right corner and "Arthur Ashe," in the reddish-brown, is in the lower right. The typeface is Futura medium condensed.

Because the stamp was offset-printed, microprinting is included in the design. The letters "USPS" are on the edge of the tennis racket near the point where it meets the left frameline.

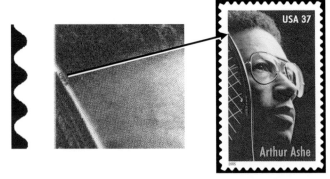

A microprinted "USPS" can be found on the edge of the tennis racket where it meets the left border of the design.

FLUSHING, N.Y.
11355
AUGUST 27,
2005

This is the first-day postmark for the Arthur Ashe stamp.

First-Day Facts

Henry Pankey, USPS vice president for emergency preparedness, dedicated the stamp in a brief ceremony at the South Plaza on the grounds of the U.S. Tennis Association National Tennis Center in Flushing's Corona Park. Pankey was the only speaker, although the ceremony program indicated that additional speakers had been scheduled.

On hand for the ceremony were Franklin R. Johnson, chairman of the board and president of USTA; Jeanne Moutoussamy-Ashe, the late tennis star's wife; their daughter, Camera; Billie Jean King, a member of the International Tennis Hall of Fame and founder of World TeamTennis, and former New York City Mayor David Dinkins. The dedication ceremony was free and open to the public.

Arthur Ashe Kids' Day, the day's principal event, is presented each year by Amerada Hess and produced by the U.S. Tennis Association. It continues Ashe's mission of using tennis as a means to instill in young people the values of humanitarianism, leadership and academic excellence.

For a limited time, Stamp Fulfillment Services sold uncacheted first-day covers of the Ashe stamp with the conventional black postmark for 75¢ and with a digital color postmark for $1.50.

37¢ TO FORM A MORE PERFECT UNION
(10 DESIGNS)

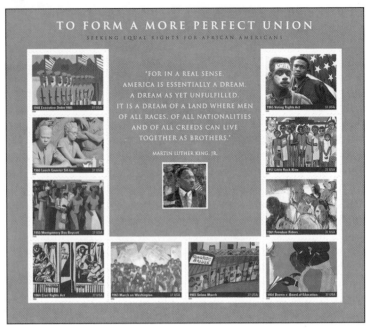

Date of Issue: August 30, 1005

Catalog Numbers: Scott 3937, pane of 10; 3937a-3937j, single stamps

Colors: black, cyan, magenta, yellow, blue (PMS 297), gray (PMS 535)

First-Day Cancel: Greensboro, North Carolina; Jackson, Mississippi; Little Rock, Arkansas; Memphis, Tennessee; Montgomery, Alabama; Selma, Alabama; Topeka, Kansas; Washington, D.C., and nationwide

First-Day Cancellations: 425,297

Format: Pane of 10, horizontal, 4 down each side, 4 across at bottom. Offset printing plates printing 120 stamps (12 panes) per revolution.

Gum Type: self-adhesive

Stamp Size: 1.56 by 1.225 inches; 39.624 by 31.115 mm

Pane Size: 7.25 by 6.25 inches; 184.15 by 158.75 mm

Perforations: 10¾ by 10½ (die-cut simulated perforations) (IDC two-station die cutter)

Selvage Inscription: "TO FORM A MORE PERFECT UNION/SEEKING EQUAL RIGHTS FOR AFRICAN AMERICANS/'FOR IN A REAL SENSE,/ AMERICA IS ESSENTIALLY A DREAM,/A DREAM AS YET UNFUL-FILLED./IT IS A DREAM OF A LAND WHERE MEN/OF ALL RACES, OF ALL NATIONALITIES/AND OF ALL CREEDS CAN LIVE/TOGETHER AS BROTHERS.'/MARTIN LUTHER KING, JR."

Selvage Markings: none

Back Markings: On selvage liner: "Our nation's founders created the Constitution/'in order to form a more perfect union.'/The U.S. Postal Service recognizes the courage and/achievement of the men and women who, during the years/of the civil rights movement, struggled to bring the/vision of the founders closer to reality./Each stamp on this sheet presents a detail from/a contemporary artwork commenting on historical events./From Selma to Montgomery/Louis Delsarte/(detail)." "© 2004 USPS." ".37 x 10 = $3.70." "The name, likeness, and copyrighted words of Dr. Martin Luther King, Jr., are used by permission of/Intellectual Properties Management, Atlanta, Georgia, as exclusive licenser of the King estate." Universal Product Code (UPC) "567100." On stamp liners: "1965 Voting Rights Act/After this bill was signed into law, African Americans who had been/kept from voting could finally have/an impact on local, state, and/federal elections./*Youths on the Selma March, 1965*/Bruce Davidson." "1957 The Little Rock Nine/In the face of steadfast opposition,/nine courageous African-American/students in Little Rock, Arkansas,/were the first to integrate the city's/Central High School./*America Cares*/George Hunt." "1961 Freedom Riders/Biracial groups of courageous men/and women challenged discrimination/by taking interstate bus trips through/the South and using the 'wrong'/facilities at stops./*Freedom Riders*/May Stevens." "1954 Brown v. Board of Education/Racial segregation was the standard/in American public schools until the/U.S. Supreme Court unanimously/declared that separate educational/facilities are inherently unequal./*The Lamp*, 1984/© Romare Bearden Foundation." "1965 Selma March/In the spring of 1965, demonstrators/demanding an end to discrimination/gathered in Selma, Alabama, to/march to the state capital,/Montgomery, fifty miles away./*Selma March*/Bernice Sims." "1963 March on Washington/In August 1963, more than 250,000/people gathered in Washington,/D.C., to demand racial justice;/Martin Luther King, Jr. gave his/'I Have a Dream' speech./*March on Washington*/Alma Thomas." "1948 Executive Order 9981/On July 26, 1948, President/Harry S. Truman issued an executive/order, implemented over several/ensuing years, abolishing segregation/in the United States armed forces./*Training for War*/William H. Johnson." "1960 Lunch Counter Sit-Ins/When four African-American college students/placed an order at a 'whites only' lunch/counter in Greensboro, North Carolina, in/1960, they sparked acts of civil disobedience/in many other cities./National Civil Rights Museum exhibit/StudioEIS." "1955 Montgomery Bus Boycott/After Rosa Parks was arrested in 1955 for/refusing to let a white passenger take her/seat on a bus in Montgomery, Alabama,/African Americans began a prolonged/boycott of the bus company./*Walking*/Charles Alston." "1964 Civil Rights Act/This bill designed to outlaw discrimination/in public accommodations — initiated by/President John F. Kennedy in 1963 — was/signed into law by President Lyndon B./Johnson on July 2, 1964./*Dixie Cafe*/Jacob Lawrence."

Designer and Art Director: Ethel Kessler of Bethesda, Maryland

Typographer: Greg Berger of Bethesda, Maryland

Modeler: Joseph Sheeran of Ashton-Potter (USA) Ltd., Williamsville, New York

Stamp Manufacturing: Stamps printed by Ashton-Potter on Mueller Martini A74 offset press. Stamps processed by Ashton-Potter.

Quantity Ordered: 50,000,000 stamps

Plate Number Detail: none

Paper Supplier: Paper Corporation/Glatfelter

Tagging: block tagging over stamps

The Stamps

On August 30, the Postal Service issued a pane of 10 stamps marking milestones in the civil rights movement for black Americans. USPS called the pane a souvenir sheet and titled it "To Form a More Perfect Union," a phrase borrowed from the preamble to the U.S. Constitution.

The stamps collectively commemorated the 50th anniversary of the movement, although the individual events marked by the stamps occurred during a period from 1948 (57 years in the past) to 1965 (40 years).

In concept, the pane is similar to the five panes issued by USPS from 1991 to 1995, each of which bears 10 different stamps recalling major events and developments of one of the World War II years half a century earlier. However, the World War II stamps displayed new illustrations created specifically for the purpose, while To Form a More Perfect Union makes use of existing works of art.

The Citizens' Stamp Advisory Committee, in considering anniversaries of historic events coming up, had noted that there would be a number of 50th anniversaries related to civil rights. "PhotoAssist [the Postal Service's research firm] put together a list of the major events and the years in which they happened, and the CSAC subject subcommittee found it a bit daunting," said Terrence McCaffrey, manager of stamp development.

"We asked ourselves, did we want to honor each one with a separate stamp on its anniversary? Did we really want a bunch of single stamps every year, in some years more than one stamp, eating into the commemorative stamp program?

"The committee decided to find a way to honor the seminal events of the civil rights movement on one sheet. Narrowing the list down to 10 was a challenge, but they did it; they picked the 10 that seemed most significant."

To help CSAC make this choice, PhotoAssist, the Postal Service's research firm, hired three consultants: Johanna Miller Lewis, professor and chair of history at the University of Arkansas at Little Rock; Charles Payne, professor and director of African and African-American Studies at Duke University;

1948 Executive Order 9981   37 USA

and David Lewis, professor of history at New York University and a biographer of W.E.B. DuBois.

PhotoAssist prepared a list of 23 events, ranging chronologically from Marian Anderson's vocal concert at the Lincoln Memorial in 1939 (see chapter on the Anderson Black Heritage stamp) to the assassination of Martin Luther King Jr. in 1968. The consultants reviewed the list and made recommendations, after which CSAC selected these 10 subjects:

• Executive Order 9981, integrating the armed forces, signed by President Harry S. Truman in 1948. Consultant Payne noted that "Truman did this largely because of threats of civil disobedience from A. Philip Randolph," head of the Brotherhood of Sleeping Car Porters, and suggested that the stamp honor Randolph as well. Because the set was intended to commemorate events rather than individuals, this wasn't done.

• The 1954 decision of the U.S. Supreme Court in *Brown vs. Board of Education of Topeka* forbidding legalized segregation of public schools.

• The Montgomery, Alabama, bus boycott of 1955 that ended segregation in the city's public transportation. Payne and David Lewis suggested that Rosa Parks, whose arrest for sitting in a bus seat reserved for whites was the catalyst for the boycott, and other key women involved in the event be honored, but Parks still was living at the time and thus was ineligible for stamp honors under CSAC rules. She died October 24, 2005, less than two months after the stamps were issued.

• The integration of Little Rock, Arkansas, public schools by nine black American students protected by the National Guard in 1957.

• The sit-ins at whites-only lunch counters initiated by four black college students, who staged their peaceful demonstration at a Woolworth's counter in Greensboro, North Carolina, February 1, 1960.

• The Freedom Riders' bus trips through the South in 1961, organized by the Congress of Racial Equality (CORE), to challenge Jim Crow laws.

• The March on Washington, D.C., in 1963, at which Martin Luther King Jr. delivered his "I have a dream" speech. (Consultant Payne demurred, saying this topic was "overdone.")

• The passage of the federal Civil Rights Act of 1964 barring discrimination in hiring and public accommodations.

• The 1965 march from Selma to Montgomery, Alabama, by demonstrators demanding an end to segregation.

• The enactment of the federal Voting Rights Act of 1965.

Other events on the larger list that were endorsed by the consultants but had to be omitted included the founding of the Student Non-Violent Coordinating Committee (SNCC) at Shaw University in Raleigh, North Carolina, in 1960, and the integration of the University of Mississippi with the admission of James Meredith, supported by federal troops, in 1961.

The stamps were placed on sale nationwide on the first day of issue, but there were eight designated first-day cities: Greensboro, North Carolina; Jackson, Mississippi; Little Rock, Arkansas; Memphis, Tennessee; Montgomery, Alabama; Selma, Alabama; Topeka, Kansas; and Washington, D.C. However, the Jackson and Memphis ceremonies were canceled because of Hurricane Katrina.

The self-adhesive, semi-jumbo stamps were printed by the offset process by Ashton-Potter (USA) Ltd. They are arranged in a U shape on the pane, with two vertical rows of four stamps each down the sides connected by two side-by-side stamps at the bottom. Postal clerks were instructed not

The pane bears descriptive text on the liner paper.

178

1961 Freedom Riders   37 USA

to sell individual stamps from a pane.

On the selvage, below the headlines "To Form a More Perfect Union" and "Seeking Equal Rights for African Americans," is a square-framed portrait of Martin Luther King Jr., the civil rights movement's most famous leader, and this King quotation: "For in a real sense, America is essentially a dream, a dream as yet unfulfilled. It is a dream of a land where men of all races, of all nationalities and of all creeds can live together as brothers."

On the back of the liner paper behind each stamp is a paragraph of text describing the event the stamp commemorates and giving the title of the artwork used in the design and the name of the artist. A Postal Service statement about the Civil Rights movement is on the backing paper of the central selvage.

1964 Civil Rights Act   37 USA

CSAC and USPS staffers were pleased with the solution of combining stamps for the major events on one pane, McCaffrey said. The title, To Form a More Perfect Union (which the planners shortened to "TFAMPU" in conversations and memos) came out of brainstorming sessions among postal officials and PhotoAssist staffers.

After the pane was designed, McCaffrey and Mike Owens of PhotoAssist showed the stamp illustrations to Dorothy Height, the 90-plus-year-old civil rights activist and Presidential Medal of Freedom recipient who is past president of the National Council of Negro Women. Height, who participated in many of the major events commemorated on the pane, was credited by USPS as a consultant on the stamp project.

"She's an incredible woman," McCaffrey said. "When we were ushered into her office, she was all dressed up, wearing a hat, sitting at her big desk. We explained what we were doing and showed her the artwork. She loved it.

1963 March on Washington   37 USA

"We asked whether she was offended by anything on it, or felt that we had misinterpreted anything. The only stamp she had any concerns about was the Brown vs. Board of Education painting by Romare Bearden, which shows two black children reading by lamplight. She felt the stamp should show a white child and a black child, to illustrate school integration." Just such a scene had been shown on the 33¢ Celebrate the Century stamp for the decade of the 1950s that commemorated the desegregation of public schools.

"We went back and searched and there was no [existing] art that we found that we could substitute and would work as a stamp," McCaffrey continued. "In researching the Bearden artwork, we found that it had been created to honor the Brown decision. We sent Height a letter and said, 'We tried but we can't find a better piece of art, and we hope you're not upset, but we're going to stay with this one.' She told us it wasn't a problem and she was happy to endorse the entire pane of stamps.

"We were happy to have the blessings of one of the pillars of the civil rights movement."

The Postal Service announced the stamps at a meeting with philatelic journalists August 12, 2004. The design of the stamps and pane was unveiled October 16, 2004, as part of the American Association of Retired Persons' National Event and Expo at the Sands Expo and Convention Center in Las Vegas, Nevada.

Sylvester Black, vice president for USPS western area operations, unveiled the design. Joining him were Dorothy Height; actor Danny Glover; Jose Maldonado, AARP board member; Raul Yzaguirre, president and chief executive officer, National Council of La Raza; Dolores Huerta, co-founder and first vice president emeritus of the United Farm Workers of America; and Juan Williams, National Public Radio senior correspondent and author.

Another unveiling took place June 23, 2005, at the Lincoln Theater in Washington. Dorothy Height took part in this ceremony as well, along with Delores J. Killette, Washington's postmaster, and Wade Henderson, executive director of the Leadership Conference on Civil Rights. It was followed by the opening of a musical play, *If This Hat Could Talk*, based on Height's memoirs.

Martin Luther King Jr. has been pictured on two U.S. commemoratives: a 15¢ Black Heritage stamp in 1979, and a 33¢ stamp in the 1960s Celebrate the Century set, issued in 1999, that commemorated his "I have a dream" speech.

The Designs

When the project was launched in 2003, Ethel Kessler was assigned to be its art director. "We knew at the beginning that there would be different possible visual directions for these stamps," she said.

One of those directions, suggested by a colleague, was to reproduce news photographs of the events being commemorated accompanied by newspaper-style headlines. Kessler was uncomfortable with this approach.

"It upset me emotionally," she said. "Having to look at the photographs of those actual events was, to me, not a way to celebrate how far we've come.

"To show the 10 pivotal events in civil rights and African-American history with photos would mean we would show people spraying other people with fire hoses, and setting dogs on them, and carrying enraging signs, because those were the news photos at the time."

Serendipitously, at about this time the Smithsonian Institution was presenting an exhibition of visual arts celebrating the life and power of the movement's premier leader. "In the Spirit of Martin: The Living Legacy of Dr. Martin Luther King Jr." ran from May through July 2003 and featured

 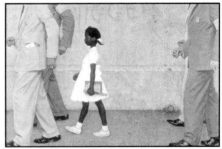

Shown here are four pieces of art that Ethel Kessler developed as stamp designs but later replaced with other paintings. Two are by Jacob Lawrence: Bus, *depicting the segregation in public transportation that the Montgomery bus boycott helped to end, and* Confrontation at the Bridge, *showing a police dog menacing participants in the Selma-to-Montgomery March.* Dream Big, *a poster celebrating Martin Luther King's speech at the march on Washington, was created by Malaika Favorite in paper and oil on tin. Norman Rockwell's well-known painting,* The Problem We All Live With, *shows a young girl in the company of U.S. marshals braving threats from bigots to exercise her right to an equal education established in* Brown vs. Board of Education.

Walking, *this Charles Alston oil on canvas, honors the men, women and children who made the 1955 Montgomery bus boycott a success. It illustrates the stamp on that subject.*

paintings, drawings, lithographs and photographs inspired by King and the struggle for equal rights.

"I went to see the exhibit," Kessler said. "I knew that most of the items wouldn't make a stamp. We weren't doing a pane of stamps about Martin Luther King, and many of the works in that exhibit were about him, showing him in some way.

"But there were a lot of promising things. I tried to identify works that I thought would relate to the master list of pivotal events. I loved the idea that by using artists' interpretations such as these, I would not be an art director commissioning art from someone who might or might not have been old enough to remember these moments in history, but rather I would be using art from artists who had felt compelled on their own to make their own statements.

"In many cases, these were African-American artists who were not really unknown, but at least were names that were unfamiliar to me."

Ultimately, Kessler developed five of her 10 stamp designs from art in the exhibition and in the lavishly illustrated book that was based on the show and bore its title. They were:

• "1955 Montgomery Bus Boycott." After considering a 1941 painting by Jacob Lawrence showing a segregated bus, Kessler decided on *Walking*, an oil-on-canvas painting done by Charles Alston in 1958 to honor the men, women and children of Montgomery who made the boycott effective. The painting is from the collection of Sydney Smith Gordon of Chicago, Illinois. Kessler had to crop it only slightly to fit it onto the stamp.

• "1965 Selma March," which depicts a 1991 acrylic-on-canvas paint-

Selma March, *a painting by Bernice Sims, shows the marchers on Selma's Edmund Pettus Bridge at the start of their walk to Montgomery, Alabama. To fit the scene on the stamp, Kessler cropped out the menacing white police officers on the bridge at the left and in the police boat below the span. The bridge is misspelled "Pettis" in the painting.*

To illustrate the Voting Rights Act stamp, Kessler extracted a detail from the upper left corner of this Bruce Davidson photograph, Three Youths on the Selma to Montgomery March. *For the stamp design, Davidson electronically erased the young man on the left and another young man whose head can be seen between the two youths facing the camera.*

ing, *Selma March*, by Bernice Sims of Brewton, Alabama. It shows marchers on Selma's Edmund Pettus Bridge (misspelled "Pettis" in the painting
and on the stamp), where they were attacked by armed police. Cropped
out of the stamp image are two white police officers on the bridge at the
left and a third below in a boat with the identifying words "Selma P.D."
The artwork is from the collection of the law office of Micki Beth Stiller
of Montgomery, Alabama. Kessler earlier had considered a more shock-
ing picture, called *Confrontation at the Bridge*, a screen print on paper by
Jacob Lawrence that showed a police dog menacing the marchers.

• "1965 Voting Rights Act," which presents a detail from a photograph,
Three Youths on the Selma to Montgomery March, March 21-25, 1965,
by Bruce Davidson of New York City. Two young black American men
are in the foreground; the face of the nearer of the two is daubed with a
white substance on which the word "VOTE" has been traced. Between
their faces, the head of a third youth, turned in the opposite direction, can
be seen. The starry field of a billowing American flag fills the right side
of the picture. At Ethel Kessler's request, Davidson himself electronically
erased the third youth and another young man, standing at the left, from
the stamp image.

• "1963 March on Washington." Kessler chose an oil-on-canvas painting, predominantly in blue, by the late Alma Thomas, cropping it at the
left, top and bottom to fit it onto the stamp. It shows a crowd of misty

Shown here is Alma Thomas' oil-on-canvas painting The March on Washington.
*It was cropped at the left, top and bottom for use on the stamp commemorating
that event.*

184

The stamp honoring the 1961 Freedom Riders displays this gouache-on-paper painting by May Stevens in shades of blue and gray.

figures holding posters aloft. A study for the painting was included in the Smithsonian exhibit, while the original is in the Columbus, Georgia, Museum of Art. Louis Plummer of PhotoAssist had suggested *Dream Big* by Malaika Favorite, a composite work featuring the words "I have a dream" from Martin Luther King Jr.'s speech at the march, and Kessler created a stamp design from it, but decided late in the design process to use the Thomas work instead.

• "1961 Freedom Riders." This stamp image is from a 1963 gouache-on-paper painting by May Stevens of Santa Fe, New Mexico. In shades of blue and gray, it shows the heads of a group of demonstrators seated aboard an interstate bus as it makes its way across the segregated South. The painting is in a private collection in New York City.

The art director then addressed the question of how to illustrate the remaining five events. For assistance, she called on Plummer, as well as Sylvia Harris, a CSAC member and Yale University design critic. Harris, in turn, directed her to Richard Powell, chairman of the Duke University art and art history department and author of a major reference book on 20th-century black American art. Following their recommendations, she reviewed hundreds of magazines, artists' portfolios and other resources.

For the stamp for "Brown vs. Board of Education," Plummer recommended two alternatives: Romare Bearden's *The Lamp* and Norman Rockwell's *The Problem We All Live With*. Rockwell's well-known painting, which was included in the "In the Spirit of Martin" exhibition, shows a small black American girl walking to school between two pairs of U.S. marshals. On the wall behind the child is the evidence of bigots' bitter resistance: a spattered tomato and the scrawled word "nigger."

185

Romare Bearden's The Lamp *was chosen by the NAACP Legal Defense and Education Fund for its 1984 poster marking the 30th anniversary of the* Brown vs. Board of Education *decision. Kessler chose it for the stamp celebrating the decision's 50th anniversary.*

The Rockwell painting is a simple and powerful statement, Kessler said, and she would have chosen it except for her concern that some people might resent the use of an illustration that displayed the racial epithet, even if she cropped it from the stamp design.

Instead, she used the Bearden silkscreen; it was the picture of two black children at their studies that Dorothy Height had initially considered an

This three-dimensional exhibit commemorating the 1960 lunch-counter sit-ins that began in Greensboro, North Carolina, was made by StudioEIS for the National Civil Rights Museum. The exhibit shows four plaster-and-resin figures of students seated at a whites-only lunch counter, while two young white men stand behind them in an intimidating manner. A video of the sit-ins is shown on the screen at the rear and is part of the exhibit. To fit the photograph on the stamp, Kessler cropped out the student shown here on the left and a fourth student (not shown), and cropped the faces of the white youths just above their chins.

186

unsuitable image to represent school desegregation. However, the art had been chosen by the NAACP Legal Defense and Education Fund in 1984 to appear on its poster celebrating the 30th anniversary of the Brown decision, and Kessler thought it would be appropriate to use it on a stamp marking the 50th anniversary. "It was very nice symmetry," she said.

"1960 Lunch Counter Sit-Ins" shows a color photograph of a portion of an exhibit made by StudioEIS of Brooklyn, New York, for the National Civil Rights Museum in Memphis, Tennessee. It comprises the plaster-and-resin sculptured figures of four college students, two males and two females, sitting at a lunch counter that is complete with ketchup and mustard containers, while two young white men stand behind them in an intimidating manner. To fit the photo on the stamp, Kessler omitted two of the students and cropped the faces of the white men just above their chins.

For "1964 Civil Rights Act," Kessler considered using a photograph of President Lyndon B. Johnson signing the bill into law, but decided to stay with artists' interpretations. She chose a brush-and-ink-on-paper illustration, *Dixie Cafe*, by the late Jacob Lawrence that vividly depicts the segregation in public accommodations that existed before 1964. Two lunch counters with their segregated clientele are shown, one counter marked "Colored," the other "White," separated by what appears to be a doorway with the restaurant name, "The Dixie Belle." The work is in the collection

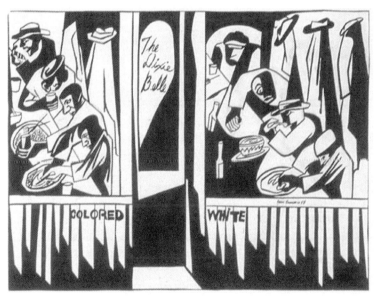

This Jacob Lawrence brush-and-ink-on-paper work showing segregated lunch counters that Kessler selected to illustrate the Civil Rights Act of 1964 was almost a perfect fit for the horizontal semijumbo stamp format. She had to crop it only slightly at the sides and bottom.

George Hunt's painting Little Rock Nine, *in acrylic and collage on canvas, once hung in the conference room of First Lady Hillary Clinton's White House office. Kessler cropped the picture at the bottom, just above the children's feet, to make it fit the stamp.*

of Margaret and Michael Asch of Victoria, British Columbia, Canada. It was almost a perfect fit for the horizontal semijumbo stamp format and required only slight cropping on the sides and at the bottom.

"Little Rock Nine" depicts an acrylic-and-collage-on-canvas work by George Hunt of Memphis, Tennessee, titled *America Cares*, depicting the nine black American students who integrated Little Rock Central High School. An adult woman stands on one side and a helmeted National Guardsman on the other, protecting the children.

The painting, 52 inches wide by 63½ inches high, was commissioned by the Central High Museum Inc. for the 40th anniversary of the school's integration in 1997. President Bill Clinton and First Lady Hillary Clinton attended the dedication of a new National Park Service visitors' center at Central High that year, and Mrs. Clinton asked whether she could borrow the painting, which was too large to be effectively displayed at the center, for the conference room of her office in the White House. After the Clintons left Washington, the painting was stored at the Arkansas Art Center in Little Rock, awaiting the completion of a larger visitors' center that will be dedicated on the 50th anniversary of the integration of Central High in 2007. Ethel Kessler cropped the picture at the bottom, just above the children's feet, to make it fit the stamp.

"1948 Executive Order 9981" depicts a black American unit of 11 soldiers lined up at order arms in a training camp. A barracks and American flags are seen, and in the distance is a blue mountain range. Chosen at the suggestion of consultant Richard Powell, the oil-on-paperboard painting, some 28 inches wide by 24 inches high, is part of a 1942-1944 series on the Army by William H. Johnson done in what the artist called a "primitive" style, using bright and contrasting colors and two-dimensional figures and objects.

"It was difficult to find works that responded to, or commented on, Executive Order 9981," Kessler said. "The painting we selected, *Soldiers Training*, doesn't show the effect of President Truman's decision to integrate the military, but it speaks powerfully about the segregation that existed." To make the image fit the stamp, Kessler cropped it at the top, right and bottom. The cropping eliminated all but the left arm of a squad leader standing on the right side, as well as two barracks and other objects.

CSAC's plan to use a portrait and quotation of Martin Luther King Jr. in the center of the pane couldn't be completed until permission was received from the Atlanta, Georgia, company that handles licensing rights for the King estate. At one point, Kessler and postal officials decided they would have to abandon the plan, and Kessler created an alternative pane design with a quotation from the late Thurgood Marshall, the first black justice of the U.S. Supreme Court. However, the company gave its go-ahead to use

William H. Johnson's oil-on-paperboard painting Soliders Training, *done in primitive style, was cropped at the top, right and bottom to fit on the stamp commemorating the integration of the armed forces. The cropping eliminated the squad leader and the barracks and bench on the right side of the picture.*

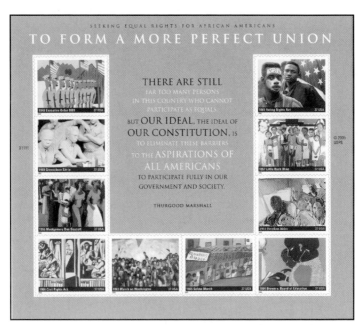

As late as August 2004, with all the stamp designs completed, the Postal Service had not received confirmation from the company that licenses the name, image and works of Martin Luther King Jr. that it could use his portrait and quotations on the pane. Accordingly, Ethel Kessler prepared this alternative pane with a quotation from the late Thurgood Marshall, the first black justice of the U.S. Supreme Court. Soon afterward, permission came to use the King material.

The small portrait of King shown in the center of the pane was taken from this acrylic and mixed-media work by Louis Delsarte, From Selma to Montgomery.

Shown here is an early 2004 version of the pane, incorporating some stamp designs that later were replaced. In this version, the central portion is filled with James H. Karales' photograph of the Selma to Montgomery march of 1963. The line beneath each stamp identifies the artist or photograph; on the finished pane, this information is in the verso text.

King's image and words just in time.

The King portrait is a detail from a 2000 acrylic and mixed-media work, *From Selma to Montgomery*, by Louis Delsarte of Atlanta. It is in the collection of Herbert and Darlene Charles in Atlanta. Kessler found the quotation in the book *In the Spirit of Martin* that accompanied the Smithsonian's exhibition.

On the pane, the stamps and the King portrait are set on white backgrounds. The rest of the pane selvage is blue-gray. The pane's headline, "TO FORM A MORE PERFECT UNION," and the King quotation are in white Trajan Bold capitals, dropped out of the background. Beneath the headline is a subhead in black Trajan capitals, "SEEKING EQUAL RIGHTS FOR AFRICAN AMERICANS."

The typography on each stamp is Frutiger and is dropped out of a narrow black band across the bottom. When it was suggested to Kessler that she had reduced the size of the "37 USA" to close to the limit of visibility, she said with a laugh, "My colleagues are all over me about that, but I pointed out that other art directors have made the denominations small, too. I tried putting the '37' inside those busy images, and it was very distracting. It didn't make any sense to put it there."

First-Day Facts

Postmaster General John E. Potter dedicated the stamps at the Washington, D.C., ceremony. Dorothy Height was the featured speaker. Also participating were Brent Glass, director of the Behring Center of the Smithsonian National Museum of American History, and the Rev. Walter Fauntroy, pastor of the New Bethel Baptist Church.

Fred Gray spoke at the Montgomery ceremony. At the age of 24, less than a year out of law school, Gray represented Rosa Parks when she was arrested for refusing to move to the back of the segregated city bus. He also represented Martin Luther King Jr. on legal issues related to civil rights. The Postal Service quoted him as saying, "As I look over the 10 events these stamps represent, I realize I've been involved with nearly all of them in one way or another."

Others taking part at Montgomery were Earl Artis, public affairs and communications manager for the Postal Service's Southeast Area, who dedicated the stamps; Lucy Baxley, lieutenant governor of Alabama; Bobby Bright, mayor of Montgomery; Georgette Norman, director of the Rosa Parks Library; attorney Micki Beth Stillar; Johnnie Carr, president of the Montgomery Improvement Association; and Tonya Terry, anchor for WSFA-TV.

At Greensboro, Franklin McCain, a member of the "Greensboro Four," described his role planning the 1960 lunch counter sit-in. The stamps were dedicated by Henry Pankey, Postal Service vice president for emergency preparedness.

At Little Rock, all nine members of the "Little Rock Nine," who integrated Central High School under military escort, were present for the

Dorothy Height, CEO and chair emerita of the National Council of Negro Women and a civil rights pioneer, autographs program covers at the Washington, D.C., first-day ceremony. (USPS photograph)

192

All the members of the Little Rock Nine, who integrated Central High School in 1957 under military escort, are joined by other participants in Little Rock's first-day ceremony with an enlargement of the stamp depicting George Hunt's painting of the group, America Cares. *(USPS photograph)*

dedication. Among the speakers was Melba Pattillo Beals, one of the nine. Flanked by members of the group, USPS finance manager Angelo Wilder dedicated the stamps.

At Selma's Walton Theater, U.S. Representative John Lewis, Democrat of Georgia, told of being beaten by club-wielding troopers as he attempted to lead more than 600 marchers across the Pettus Bridge in 1965. USPS Vice President DeWitt Harris dedicated the stamps, and other participants were Alston Fitts, a Selma historian, and Don Murphy, deputy director of the National Park Service.

Cheryl Brown Henderson, president and chief executive officer of the Brown Foundation for Educational Equity, Excellence and Research, spoke at Topeka's Brown vs. Board of Education National Historic Site about the role of her father, Oliver L. Brown, as the plaintiff in the landmark school segregation case. Roy Betts, the Postal Service's manager of specialty communications, was the dedicating official. Other participants were Dennis Vasquez, superintendent of the Brown vs. Board of Education National Historic Site; U.S. Senator Sam Brownback, Republican of Kansas; and Joleen Baxa, manager of the USPS Central Plains District.

The Memphis event was canceled when local schools were closed because of Hurricane Katrina. The scheduled speaker at Memphis had been the Rev. Samuel Billy Kyles, who was with Martin Luther King Jr. during the last hour of his life. The hurricane also forced cancellation of the Jackson ceremony. However, the Postal Service provided first-day cancellations for the two cities.

For a limited time, Stamp Fulfillment Services offered an uncacheted first-day cover with full pane of 10 for $6.20. Collectors could also buy a first-day cover of a random single from the pane with a digital color postmark for $1.50.

The earliest known pre-release use of a stamp from the To Form a More Perfect Union pane was an Executive Order 9981 stamp on an envelope with a machine postmark from Industry, California, dated August 26, four days before the official first day of issue.

TO FORM A MORE PERFECT UNION

First Day of Issue ★ Washington, DC 20066
August 30, 2005

This is the first-day postmark used in eight cities — in this case, Washington, D.C. — for the To Form a More Perfect Union stamps.

37¢ CHILD HEALTH

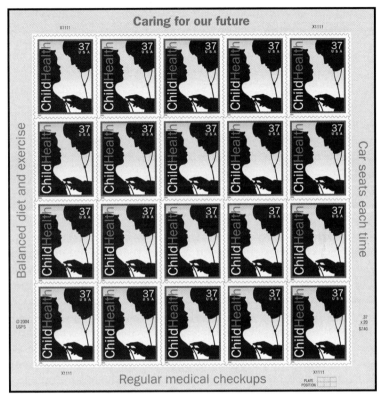

Date of Issue: September 7, 2005

Catalog Number: Scott 3938

Colors: yellow (PMS 116), red (PMS 485), blue (PMS 285), black

First-Day Cancel: Philadelphia, Pennsylvania

First-Day Cancellations: 58,500

Format: Pane of 20, vertical, 5 across, 4 down. Gravure printing cylinders printing 200 stamps per revolution (2 panes across, 5 panes around).

Gum Type: self-adhesive

Stamp Size: 1.225 by 1.56 inches; 31.115 by 39.624 mm

Pane Size: 7.125 by 7.25 inches; 180.795 by 184.15 mm

Perforations: 10½ by 11 (die-cut simulated perforations) (Comco Commander rotary die cutter)

Selvage Inscription: "Caring for our future" "Car seats each time" "Regular medical checkups" "Balanced diet and exercise."

Selvage Markings: "© 2004/USPS." ".37/x20/$7.40". "PLATE/POSITION" and diagram.

Back Markings: Universal Product Code (UPC) "458500" in 4 locations.

Illustrator, Designer and Typographer: Craig Frazier of Mill Valley, California

Art Director: Carl Herrman of Carlsbad, California

Stamp Manufacturing: Stamps printed by Avery-Dennison Security Printing Division, Clinton, South Carolina, on a Dia Nippon Kiko gravure press. Stamps processed by Avery-Dennison.

Quantity Ordered: 65,000,000

Cylinder Number Detail: 1 set of 4 cylinder numbers preceded by the letter V in selvage above or below each corner stamp

Cylinder Number Combination Reported: V1111

Paper Supplier: Fasson Division of Avery Dennison

Tagging: block tagging over stamps

The Stamp

On September 7, the Postal Service placed a stamp on sale nationwide to raise awareness of the need for early childhood health care, screening and immunization to prevent disease, and parental action to prevent injury to their children.

Its prime sponsor was Ron Robinson, a Little Rock, Arkansas, advertising executive and head of the Citizens' Stamp Advisory Committee's subject subcommittee. Robinson proposed that the stamp be issued in 2005 to coincide with the 150th anniversary of the opening of the Children's Hospital of Philadelphia, the nation's first hospital dedicated exclusively to caring for children. CSAC concurred, and the hospital was the site of the first-day ceremony.

The stamp's timing also coincided with the designation of 2005 as "The Year of the Healthy Child" by the U.S. surgeon general, and the observance of Child Health Month in October by the American Academy of Pediatrics.

The Child Health stamp, a self-adhesive in semijumbo size, was printed by the gravure process by Avery Dennison Security Printing Division and distributed in panes of 20, five across by four down.

Each of the pane's four selvage strips contains a message related to the theme of child health. "Caring for our future" is on the header at the top, "Balanced diet and exercise" is on the left, "Car seats each time" is on the right and "Regular medical checkups" is at the bottom.

The Postal Service explained the inscriptions this way:

"Diseases of adulthood such as diabetes and hypertension often start in childhood. Keeping chil-

These U.S. stamps related to health care also have children in their designs. A 3¢ stamp of 1957 (Scott 1087) is inscribed "Honoring Those Who Helped Fight Polio." A 33¢ stamp in the 1950s pane in the Celebrate the Century series (Scott 3187a), issued in 1999, shows a doctor gently administering a polio shot to a little girl. A smiling girl and two children playing are featured on a 1959 4¢ commemorative promoting dental health (Scott 1135), while a 37¢ stamp of 2004 (Scott 3877) urges parents to "Test Early for Sickle Cell."

dren well now means caring for the future.

"A balanced diet and exercise maximizes the likelihood of a child growing up healthy and strong. Meals should be shared as a family. Children should eat three nutritious meals daily, which includes fruits and vegetables. They should be supplemented with two healthy snacks a day. Foods and drinks high in sugar or caffeine should be avoided. Encourage at least an hour of physical activity every day, like taking a walk around the block or playing organized or pickup sports with other families and children. Limit television, video and computer time.

"Always use a car safety seat. Motor vehicle accidents are the leading cause of death among children ages 5 to 9. Children should always ride in an age-, weight- and height-appropriate child safety seat or booster seat, correctly installed in a vehicle's back seat. Many local fire and police departments will help answer questions about how to install them.

"Regular medical checkups are key to prevention and a healthy childhood. Parents need to make sure children have a primary health-care provider, such as a pediatrician or family practitioner, who will monitor an illness, injury or developmental delay that requires professional attention."

The 430-bed Children's Hospital of Philadelphia, the nation's first pediatric hospital, was founded in 1855. Its pediatric research program is among the largest in the country, ranking second in National Institutes of Health funding.

The Child Health stamp is the latest of several of what USPS calls social awareness stamps that have focused on childhood illnesses.

Two stamps related to the fight against polio have children in their designs. One, a 3¢ stamp of 1957 (Scott 1087), is inscribed "Honoring Those Who Helped Fight Polio." A 33¢ stamp in the 1950s pane in the Celebrate the Century series (Scott 3187a), issued in 1999, commemorated the discovery of an effective vaccine against the disease, and shows a doctor gently administering a polio shot to a little girl. (Illustrator Dean Ellis had to make several preliminary paintings before he depicted the act in what CSAC felt to be an appropriately benign fashion.)

Children also are pictured on a 1959 4¢ commemorative promoting dental health and marking the 100th anniversary of the American Dental Association (Scott 1135), and on a 37¢ stamp of 2004 (Scott 3877) urging parents to "Test Early for Sickle Cell," an inherited condition that affects one in 12 African Americans.

The Design

The Child Health stamp is an example of pure graphic design. In it, a health-care professional listens to a child's heartbeat through a stethoscope. Both figures are in silhouette, a solution that finesses the issue of race and gender. Bold primary colors are used: black for the silhouettes, a graduated yellow for the background and dropout white and red for the words "Child Health," which are in large uppercase and lowercase Helvetica letters up the left side. "37 USA" is also in dropout white, in the upper right corner. A narrow blue frame surrounds the vignette.

The selvage is solid yellow, with red inscriptions. These, too, are Helvetica, with the header inscription, "Caring for our future," in boldface.

The color combination makes the stamp "almost like a stop sign," said art director Carl Herrman. "It's very arresting. It's almost too much on an entire pane, but a single stamp on an envelope is really strong, like a poster."

The art and typography were the work of Craig Frazier, an illustrator and graphic designer from Mill Valley, California. "He's a very exciting artist," Herrman said. "He's at the top of his line, about as hot as anyone is right now. Pick up any of the leading graphics magazines, or the Society of Illustrators annual, and he's all over it.

"Craig is good at solving problems, putting ideas into his subjects. He doesn't do literal illustrations. He likes to take as much away as he can, keep it simple, and still carry the message."

In Frazier's own book, *The Illustrated Voice*, the artist says of design in general: "The type of thinking that makes design work well is the same type that makes an illustration work well. They share a common goal: to produce clean and memorable content while employing ample doses of simplicity, wit and intelligence."

For the Child Health stamp, Frazier sent Herrman a half-dozen computer-generated concept designs, some incorporating such familiar health symbols as a plus-sign cross, a heart and an apple. One design showed a silhouetted doctor examining a patient, as in the finished stamp, but wielding a tongue depressor rather than a stethoscope. When CSAC settled on the stethoscope image, the artist turned it out in a dozen different color combinations, including black against a background of yellow, blue, red or green, black against a four-color checkerboard, white against a rainbow, multicolor against white, blue against yellow, and red against yellow and white.

Black on yellow was CSAC's choice. "The committee thought some of the other combinations looked too gloomy, like the black on blue," Herrman said.

In devising the selvage inscriptions, the mandate was to "keep it simple," Herrman said. PhotoAssist, the Postal Service's research firm, consulted experts on child health for help in finding the right wording. In the end, the only change made was in the header inscription, which originally read "Health care for every child," and was revised to read "Caring for our future."

Shown here are five of Craig Frazier's computer-generated concept designs for the Child Health stamp. CSAC chose a sixth image, depicting a health-care professional listening to a child's heart with a stethoscope.

First-Day Facts

Alan C. Kessler, vice chairman of the USPS Board of Governors, dedicated the stamp at the Children's Hospital of Philadelphia.

Billy Gilman, country music artist and 2005 national youth chairman for the Muscular Dystrophy Association, spoke and offered a musical tribute. Gilman, now 17, was the youngest soloist ever to appear on *Billboard*'s Country charts, doing so two days before his 12th birthday with his debut single *One Voice*.

Steven M. Altschuler M.D., president and chief executive officer of the hospital, was master of ceremonies. Honored guests, all from USPS, were Frank Neri, Philadelphia Metro District manager; Joseph M. Leonti, senior plant manager for the Philadelphia Metro District; and Philadelphia Postmaster Judith L. Martin.

For a limited time, Stamp Fulfillment Services sold uncacheted first-day covers of the Child Health stamp for 75¢. No digital color postmarks were offered.

The earliest known pre-release use of a Child Health stamp is on a cover with a Los Angeles/Hollywood, California, machine postmark dated September 3, four days before the official issue date.

This is the first-day postmark for the Child Health stamp.

37¢ LET'S DANCE/BAILEMOS (4 DESIGNS)

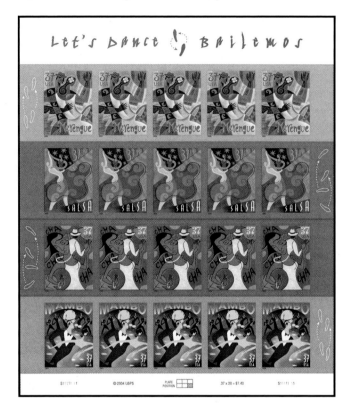

Date of Issue: September 17, 2005

Catalog Numbers: Scott 3939-3942, stamps; 3942a, vertical strip of 4

Colors: red (PMS 187), golden brown (PMS 1245), greenish brown (PMS 126), purple (PMS 667), magenta, yellow, cyan, black

First-Day Cancel: Miami, Florida; New York, New York, and nationwide.

First-Day Cancellations: 192,337 (both locations) (includes Let's Dance/Bailemos picture postal cards)

Format: Pane of 20, vertical, 5 across, 4 down. Gravure printing cylinders printing 360 stamps per revolution (30 across, 12 around) manufactured by Armotek Industries.

Gum Type: self-adhesive

Overall Stamp Size: 1.225 by 1.56 inches; 31.115 by 39.624 mm

Pane Size: 7.12 by 8.3 inches; 180.975 by 210.82 mm

Perforations: 10¾ (die-cut simulated perforations) (Comco custom rotary die cutter)

Selvage Inscription: "Let's Dance Bailemos" and dance steps diagrams

Selvage Markings: "© 2004 USPS." "37 x 20 = $7.40." "PLATE/POSITION" and diagram.

Back Markings: On selvage liner: "Let's Dance Bailemos" "After gaining broad popularity in the Latin dance clubs of New York City, mambo, salsa,/ *cha-cha-cha*, and merengue are now common fare in salsa clubs around the world. With/these stamp designs, Latino artists present their personal interpretations of the dances./Tras volverse muy populares en los clubes nocturnos latinos de Nueva York, ahora es/muy común bailar mambo, salsa, cha-cha-chá y merengue en los clubes de todo el mundo./En estas estampillas, artistas latinos ofrecen su interpretación personal de estos ritmos." "To view a variety of philatelic products and other collectibles associated with these stamps,/visit The Postal Store at www.usps.com/ shop or call 1-800 STAMP -24 to order a free catalog." Universal Product Code (UPC) "457700" in four locations. Dance steps diagrams. On stamps: "A blend of European and/African-derived styles,/merengue, with its/cross-class appeal, is/the national dance of the/Dominican Republic." "El merengue, co su/combinación de estilos/europeos y africanos y/su encanto para todas/las clases sociales, es el/baile nacional de la/República Dominicana." "Popularized in the 1960s/by New York Puerto/Rican musicians, salsa/integrates rhythm and/blues and jazz into/Afro-Cuban rhythms." "El ritmo salsa, que/musicos puertorriqueños/hicieron popular en/Nueva York en los años/60, combina la música/de jazz y blues con/ritmos afrocubanos." "Derived from Cuba's/*danzón* and taking its/name from the last three/beats in its 1-2, 1-2-3/rhythm, *cha-cha-cha*/became a dance craze/in the 1950s." "A partir del danzón/cubano y adoptando su/nombre del sonido de los/tres tiempos seguidos/del ritmo 1-2, 1-2-3, el/cha-cha-chá hizo furor/en los años 50." "An elaboration of the/lively rhythms added to/the Cuban son and/danzon, mambo became/an international dance/ craze in the 1950s." "El mambo es un ritmo/musical derivado del son/y danzón cubanos que/se convirtió en un baile/de moda en los años 50/a nivel internacional."

Artist-Typographers: Edel Rodriguez of Mount Tabor, New Jersey; Sergio Baradat of New York, New York; Rafael López of San Diego, California; José Ortega of Toronto, Ontario, Canada

Designer and Art Director: Ethel Kessler of Bethesda, Maryland

Modeler: Donald H. Woo of Sennett Security Products, Chantilly, Virginia

Stamp Manufacturing: Stamps printed for Sennett Security Products by American Packaging Corporation, Columbus, Wisconsin, on Cerutti 950 gravure press. Stamps finished by Unique Binders of Fredericksburg, Virginia.

Quantity Ordered: 70,000,000

Cylinder Number Detail: 1 set of 8 cylinder numbers preceded by the letter S in selvage below each lower corner stamp

Cylinder Number Combination Reported: S11111111

Paper Supplier: Mactac

Tagging: unphosphored paper, block tagging over stamps and side selvage

The Stamps

On September 17, the Postal Service issued four colorful stamps featuring dances that trace their origins to the islands of the Caribbean: merengue, salsa, cha-cha-cha and mambo. They comprise a pane of 20 in which each horizontal row of five consists of stamps of the same design.

The stamps were placed on sale nationwide, with official dedication ceremonies in New York, New York, and Miami, Florida. Also issued was a companion set of picture postal cards, reproducing the stamp designs in their imprinted stamps and the illustrations on the picture sides (see separate chapter).

Their issuance coincided with the start of National Hispanic Heritage Month, and represented a newly inspired effort by the Postal Service to recognize Latin American culture in the stamp program.

Research on stamp retention has shown that Hispanic-American stamp collectors now outnumber black American collectors, according to Terrence McCaffrey, manager of stamp development. In the spring of 2004, the Citizens' Stamp Advisory Committee was briefed by an expert on marketing to the Latin American community, who specifically suggested a set of stamps illustrating Latin dances.

"At the same time, we had been hearing that Hispanics have become the largest minority group in the United States," McCaffrey said. "We felt we needed to communicate with this audience and do stamps that relate to them."

At its June 2004 meeting, CSAC agreed on dances as a stamp topic, chose the four to be featured — and ordered full speed ahead. The committee wanted the stamps issued the following year, meaning that the announcement would be made at the official rollout of the 2005 program in August 2004. "We gave Ethel [art director Ethel Kessler] the assignment and told her we wanted to see designs at the July meeting," McCaffrey said.

Kessler, who had volunteered — "I love Latin dancing," she explained — met the demanding schedule. She commissioned four artists, all Latino, to illustrate the four dances, and the stamps were duly announced in August, under the bilingual title "Let's Dance" and "Bailemos," its Spanish equivalent.

American Packaging Corporation printed the stamps for Sennett Security Products by the gravure process. They are self-adhesives and semijumbo in size. On the reverse of each stamp's liner paper is a brief description, alternately in English and Spanish, of the dance that is depicted. The use of a foreign-language text — a first for USPS — led to an error that turned out to be extremely expensive.

In August 2005, it was disclosed that USPS had destroyed the entire print

Let's Dance ✦ **Bailemos**

After gaining broad popularity in the Latin dance clubs of New York City, mambo, salsa, cha-cha-cha, and merengue are now common fare in salsa clubs around the world. With these stamp designs, Latino artists present their personal interpretations of the dances.

Tras volverse muy populares en los clubes nocturnos latinos de Nueva York, ahora es muy común bailar mambo, salsa, cha-cha-chá y merengue en los clubes de todo el mundo. En estas estampillas, artistas latinos ofrecen su interpretación personal de estos ritmos.

A blend of European and African-derived styles, merengue, with its cross-class appeal, is the national dance of the Dominican Republic.

El merengue, con su combinación de estilos europeos y africanos y su encanto para todas las clases sociales, es el baile nacional de la República Dominicana.

Popularized in the 1960s by New York Puerto Rican musicians, salsa integrates rhythm and blues and jazz into Afro-Cuban rhythms.

El ritmo salsa, que músicos puertorriqueños hicieron popular en Nueva York en los años 60, combina la música de jazz y blues con ritmos afrocubanos.

Derived from Cuba's danzón and taking its name from the last three beats in its 1-2, 1-2-3 rhythm, cha-cha-cha became a dance craze in the 1950s.

A partir del danzón cubano y adoptando su nombre del sonido de los tres tiempos seguidos del ritmo 1-2, 1-2-3, el cha-cha-chá hizo furor en los años 50.

An elaboration of the lively rhythms added to the Cuban son and danzón, mambo became an international dance craze in the 1950s.

El mambo es un ritmo musical derivado del son y danzón cubanos que se convirtió en un baile de moda en los años 50 a nivel internacional.

To view a variety of philatelic products and other collectibles associated with these stamps, visit The Postal Store at www.usps.com/shop or call 1 800 STAMP-24 to order a free catalog.

Each stamp's liner paper contains a brief description, alternately in English and Spanish, of the dance that is depicted.

runs of 70 million Let's Dance stamps and 48,700 books of picture postal cards (974,000 cards) because of mistakes in the text on the backs of the stamp liners and on the cards. "Ay caramba!" was *The Washington Post*'s lament as it reported that the cost to the Postal Service was $172,000.

David Failor, executive director of Stamp Services, said only that the errors were in accent marks in the Spanish text on the back of the liner. *Linn's Stamp News* quoted Failor as saying: "We wanted to get it right, so we reprinted."

Part of the erroneous printings of both stamps and cards was sent to some stamp distribution offices on the West Coast, *Linn's* said. The offices were notified, and the stamps were recalled.

According to Terrence McCaffrey, the errors stemmed from bad communication between computers at Dodge Color, which does the Postal Service's prepress work, and American Packaging Corporation, the printer, and weren't caught by Postal Service proofreaders because the text was in Spanish. "There were a few accent marks in the wrong places and a few misspelled words here and there," McCaffrey said. To the suggestion that the Postal Service needed bilingual proofreaders, he said, "Either that, or we're not going to do foreign languages on stamps any more. We've learned our lesson."

Some collectors reported problems removing used Let's Dance stamps from their envelopes by soaking. The author of *The Yearbook* tackled a batch of stamps on a Priority Mail envelope and found that no less than 48 hours' immersion in room-temperature water was required for them to float clear. Attempts to peel specimens from the envelope before this time resulted in thinning.

PhotoAssist, the Postal Service's research firm, provided these descriptions of the four dances on the stamps:

SALSA. Literally translated it means "sauce," but in Latino music the word refers to the feeling and energy with which the musicians perform — spicy, hot and tasty. At especially heightened musical moments, musicians often shout out "salsa."

The term became a commercial tag and gained widespread currency beginning in the late 1960s, when it was applied to the style of music played by New York musicians — primarily Puerto Rican, but other Latinos and black Americans and European Americans as well. The music was based on a variety of mainly Cuban-based music and dance styles — son, mambo, danzón, cha-cha-cha — that were redefined and reinterpreted by New York musicians whose musical influences included rhythm and blues, rock 'n' roll and jazz. Latin-American countries such as Colombia and Venezuela created styles of salsa based on the New York model, but with their own national flavor. Salsa also has gained international popularity as bands, as well as industries and a fan base, have sprung up in Asia, Europe and Africa.

MAMBO. Although rooted in Cuban popular and traditional music and dance, it was in the hands of New York Latino musicians that mambo became a national and international dance craze at the start of the 1950s and into the 1960s, morphing into cha-cha-cha, while continuing to maintain its own integrity and popularity.

In Cuba, mambo became a style in its own right in the mid- to late 1930s, when musicians extracted from and elaborated upon the rhythmic sections of two other forms (son and danzón). In the late 1940s, New York mambo was adapted to the Latin big bands, which were modeled on the Swing big bands; it was this format that became so wildly popular as to inspire mainstream pop crooners to make cover versions and songs with "mambo" in the title despite having no musical relationship to mambo.

CHA-CHA-CHA. As with mambo, cha-cha-cha's roots are in Cuba, but its international popularity was based on the New York interpretation. The

dance got its name from the sound of dancers' feet shuffling across the floor to the 1-2, 1-2-3 rhythm.

Its popularity followed much the same course as that of mambo. Cha-cha-cha emerged from the Cuban danzón and was played in orchestras called charangas, modeled after European salon ensembles and featuring violins and flutes. In Cuba, cha-cha-cha was performed by charangas, while in New York it became popular first through the mambo big bands, with charangas not becoming popular in New York and beyond until the early 1960s.

MERENGUE. The national music and dance of the Dominican Republic, merengue has become an integral part of the New York Latin music scene and has, like and along with salsa, gained international popularity.

Laymen often include merengue under the rubric "salsa," but scholars and musicians do not. This differentiation does not exclude merengue from the Latin music scene in which it plays a critical role. Salsa bands all include merengue in their repertoire, and dance clubs present salsa and merengue bands on the same bill.

Merengue emerged in the mid-19th century as an elite European-derived dance music that shortly became tinged with Afro-Caribbean music and dance elements. This factor led to its ultimate rejection by urban elite society. Country folk, however, adopted it, adapted it to local instru-

mentation and aesthetics and infused it with even more African-rooted elements in both the music and dance. Political and social factors in the first half of the 20th century resulted in the emergence of a more national style and its acceptance by all levels of society.

Currently, merengue continues to be performed in this style as well as in a more commercial style in larger ensembles. Both, however, use the tambora (double-headed drum held horizontally on the lap) and button accordion.

American dance first was postally commemorated in 1978 with a block of four diamond-shaped 13¢ stamps featuring four forms of dancing: ballet, theater, folk and modern (Scott 1749-1752). In 1998, American ballet was singled out on a single 32¢ stamp (Scott 3237) and a 20¢ picture postal card (Scott UX297). Another quartet of stamps, issued in 1994 with 37¢ denominations, honored great choreographers: Alvin Ailey, George Balanchine, Agnes de Mille and Martha Graham (Scott 3840-3843).

The Designs

With four dances of different origin as the subjects, art director Ethel Kessler knew that she wanted different artists to illustrate them.

"Their styles would have to be compatible but not the same," she said. "Each one should be fresh, bringing a distinctive technique, but they couldn't be wildly different, because the four stamps have to live together."

Her first telephone call was to Ecuador native José Ortega, with whom she had worked on non-stamp projects. Ortega told her that he now owns a salsa club in his home city of Toronto, Ontario, Canada, and the serendipity of it bolstered her confidence. "It was like, 'OK, we're going to be fine here,'" she said. Ortega agreed to illustrate the salsa stamp.

At his suggestion, Kessler then called Rafael López, a free-lance illustrator and dance aficionado who was born in Mexico and lives in San Diego, California. "I asked him what his favorite dance was," she said. "He said, merengue. I said, 'OK, it's yours!'"

Ortega also recommended a call to Sergio Baradat, who left Cuba with his parents when he was a child and came to the United States, where he grew up in Miami and New York. "I looked at Sergio's work, and it seemed perfect," Kessler said. Baradat agreed to illustrate the mambo, a dance he remembered watching his parents dance in their living room.

For the cha-cha-cha, Kessler contacted an artist whom both she and fellow art director Howard Paine had considered for another stamp project,

When art director Ethel Kessler saw this Edel Rodriguez cover of Communication Arts *magazine shortly after she had spoken with Rodriguez about illustrating the cha-cha-cha stamp, she knew she had made a good choice.*

Edel Rodriguez. Rodriguez, like Baradat a Cuban who came to America with his parents as a child, now lives in Mount Tabor, New Jersey. It wasn't until after Kessler discussed the project with him, however, that she saw an illustration of a band and a woman singer that he had done for the cover of *Communication Arts* magazine's July 2004 issue. "I hadn't seen any of his work until then that would cement the feeling that he was perfect for the job," Kessler said. "Then this magazine cover came along, and I knew I had chosen well."

Kessler allowed each artist to make his own choice of colors, hoping that the results would be compatible. She invited them to integrate the name of the dance and the "37 USA" into their illustrations, with the understanding that she would modify the typography if necessary.

"Each has a different way of working, and I didn't really know what I was going to get until their color studies and pencil sketches began coming in," she said. "They all used the same color palette, but differently. It was magical."

What Kessler ultimately received from her illustrators were images that expressed each man's personal interpretation of his dance, using vivid col-

Rafael López made these pencil sketches and a color study before settling on the right mix of dancers, instruments and background for the merengue stamp.

ors and sinuous shapes to convey the energy generated by dancers moving to the beat of the music.

MERENGUE. Rafael López did his preliminary artwork on his computer, but his finished picture is in acrylic on wood. His dancers, poised in characteristic attitude, engage in short sideways movements typical of this dance. Tension shows in their bodies as they move in tight embrace, their shoulders shifting left while their hips shift right. Their heads face away from their shoulders, and their hands are clasped. A tambora drum, hallmark of merengue, can be seen at the lower right, while palm leaves show on the left. The stylized figures suggest a kind of muralist art typical of the 1930s.

"The first thing that came to my mind was the closeness of the partners — closer than in any other Latin dance except lambada," López said in an e-mail to Kessler. "So the central figures needed to portray the closeness as the most important characteristic. I also wanted to give the picture an African feeling, since the origin of the dance is strongly tied to the history of the first African slaves who arrived in the Caribbean.

"The male figure needed to be shown as very strong, since it is the male who leads during the dance. However, the focal point of the dance is to emphasize the beauty of the movements of the woman and her feminine qualities."

López used a warm palette of colors, from red and orange to yellow and lime green, to suggest the tropical sunlight and vegetation of the Caribbean islands.

SALSA. To convey a sense of old-style dance-hall elegance, José Ortega used art deco motifs in his computer-generated illustration. Against a background of abstract shapes and stars, a couple is shown in one of the many pauses that anticipate the defining steps of their dance. They are momentarily apart, arms poised and bodies ready to reverse direction or execute a spin.

Although most salseros dress in tight-fitting clothes, Ortega gave his female billowing skirts that swirl around her partner to better evoke a sense of movement and musical energy. The stars emphasize that salsa is a nighttime pursuit, to be danced when the day's work is over.

Shown here is an alternative illustration for the salsa stamp by José Ortega.

In these three proposed illustrations by Rodriguez for the cha-cha-cha stamp, the band members are featured. Ethel Kessler and CSAC felt that the focus of the images should be on the dancers.

CHA-CHA-CHA. Edel Rodriguez says that he recalls the family gatherings and special occasions that meant music and dancing, and remembers that his father and sister were particularly adept at the shuffling 1-2, 1-2-3 beat of the cha-cha-cha.

In his illustration, the suntanned dancers turn away from each other, against a background of two shades of blue. They wear white, including a white hat on the man and a pearl bracelet and necklace on the woman that swing with her movement. Rodriguez made his original picture using pastels, acrylic and colored inks on paper that gave a textured appearance to the woman's dress and the man's jacket and hat. He then scanned the image and modified it electronically.

MAMBO. Sergio Baradat's computer artwork evokes the dance's heyday in the 1950s, when Latin big bands performed for patrons in elegant clubs. Baradat said he drew on his parents' memories of starlight and moonlight filtering through the glass ceiling of a nightclub and onto its

Sergio Baradat's alternative mambo illustrations depict different versions of the same sinuous couple who are featured in the artwork on the finished stamp.

210

polished dance floor, with the splintered beams bouncing around the room and off the spinning dancers.

Shown against a gold and purple background, two long-limbed stylized figures dance in the foreground, she in a red dress and he in a tuxedo, while five band members in the background are silhouetted against a chartreuse, drum-shaped moon. The word "MAMBO," its letters outlined in tiny lights, curves across the top of the design.

Kessler strengthened the "37" in Baradat's illustration to make it more legible, and in the process she placed a strike mark across the 7 — unusual for a denomination on a U.S. stamp — to match the 7 that Rafael López had painted for the merengue stamp. The 7s on the other two stamps are conventional.

As the artists were submitting their concepts, Kessler and a long-time design associate, Greg Berger, were planning the layout of the stamps on the pane. Rather than arrange them in blocks of four, they decided to create four horizontal rows, each with stamps of the same design, to suggest multiple couples on a dance floor.

To enhance that impression, Kessler and Berger duplicated the dominant color of each stamp in the stamp's border. This created four horizontal strips of different colors, each strip surrounding its own five stamps. "The bands of red and purple and gold helped draw your eye across the pane and let you feel the motion of the dance a little more," Kessler explained.

Colored borders posed a printing problem, however. It would be impossible to register the colors so precisely that they wouldn't bleed across the die-cut simulated perforations into a stamp of a different color. Kessler solved it by inserting a fraction of an inch of additional space between the horizontal rows of stamps so that abutting strips of color could meet in a clean line outside the die cuts. "This let us make sure that when a stamp was peeled off the pane and put on an envelope, it would have a consistent border all the way around it," she said.

The header, or top selvage, contains the titles "Let's Dance" and "Bailemos" in red and purple, respectively. The unusual font chosen by Kessler is Fancy Writing Mega.

Also on the header, as well as on the side selvage on the left or right end of each horizontal row of stamps, are sets of footprints linked by dotted lines that recall the way dance instructors illustrate the steps for beginners. The same step patterns also appear on the back of the pane.

"They aren't true dance steps, so don't try to dance to them," said Terrence McCaffrey. "You'll look like Elaine" — a reference to the contorted dancing style displayed by the Elaine Benes character in a *Seinfeld* episode on television.

American Packaging Corporation used eight colors in the printing: the four standard process colors, magenta, yellow, cyan and black, for the stamps, and four self-colors, red, golden brown, greenish brown and purple, for the borders.

"When I presented the illustrations to the design subcommittee, I brought my laptop and put on salsa music so the members would all be in the mood," Kessler laughed.

First-Day Facts

The Postal Service originally announced that the Let's Dance stamps would have their first-day sale in Miami. Later, it said the ceremony had been moved to New York City because New York "has a higher concentration of Hispanics inclusive of Cubans, Puerto Ricans and Dominicans." The final decision was to hold a ceremony in each city.

David L. Solomon, vice president of USPS for the New York Metropolitan Area, was the dedicating official at New York's Copacabana. Speakers were Maria Elena Girone, president and chief executive officer of the Puerto Rican Family Institute, and musical artist Willie Colon. Maria Lourdes Pell, USPS manager for events and specialty marketing, was master of ceremonies. Song and dance were provided by Vonzell Solomon, a finalist on the televised show *American Idol*, and by the Copacabana Dancers. Stamp illustrators Edel Rodriguez and José Ortega were on hand to autograph covers and programs.

At Miami's Coconut Grove Convention Center, Anita Bizzotto, USPS chief marketing officer and executive vice president, was the dedicating official. Also participating were Miami Mayor Manny Diaz and Lissette Gonzalez, singer, actress, television host and former Miss Florida. Stamp illustrators Sergio Baradat and Rafael López took part, and singer-entertainer Albita and her Latin band performed.

For a limited time, Stamp Fulfillment Services sold uncacheted first-day covers with conventional black cancellations for $3 for a set of four. Covers with digital color postmarks were priced at $6 for a set of four and $1.50 for a random single.

37¢ GRETA GARBO
JOINT ISSUE WITH SWEDEN

Date of Issue: September 23, 2005

Catalog Number: Scott 3912

Color: black

First-Day Cancel: New York, New York

First-Day Cancellations: 76,770

Format: Pane of 20, vertical, 5 across, 4 down. Intaglio printing plates printing 120 stamps per revolution (15 across, 8 around).

Gum Type: self-adhesive

Stamp Size: 1.225 by 1.56 inches; 31.12 by 39.62 mm

Pane Size: 7.12 by 7.24 inches; 180.85 by 183.9 mm

Perforations: 10¾ (die-cut simulated perforations) (Arpeco 068-407-92 rotary die-cutter)

Selvage Markings: "© 2004/USPS." ".37/x20/$7.40." "PLATE/POSITION" and diagram.

Back Markings: On selvage liner: "Garbo™ 2005 Harriett Brown & Company, Inc. Licensed by Global Icons. All Rights Reserved./*As You Desire Me* © 1932 Turner Entertainment Co. A Warner Bros. Entertainment Company. All Rights Reserved." Universal Product Code (UPC) "458400" in 4 locations. On stamp liner: "Greta Garbo/(1905-1990)/was born in Sweden and/ became one of the greatest/stars of the silver screen./Transitioning from silent/films to the sound movies of/Hollywood, Garbo captivated/audiences with her seductive/voice, which enhanced the/acting style and beauty that/made her a legend."

Designer, Typographer and Art Director: Carl Herrman of Carlsbad, California

Engraver: Piotr Naszarkowski of Sweden

Modeler: Donald Woo of Sennett Security Products

Stamp Manufacturing: Stamps printed by Banknote Corporation of America/ Sennett Security Products, Browns Summit, North Carolina, on Cellini Epikos intaglio press. Verso text printed on Goebel Optiform FFR 670 offset press. Stamps processed by BCA/Sennett Security Products at Browns Summit.

Quantity Ordered: 40,000,000

Plate Number Detail: 1 plate number preceded by the letter S in selvage above or below each corner stamp

Plate Number Reported: S1

Paper Supplier: Mactac

Tagging: phosphored paper

The Stamp

On September 23, the Postal Service issued a 37¢ stamp to commemorate the 100th anniversary of the birth in Sweden of film star Greta Garbo. On the same day, Sweden Post issued a 10-krona stamp with the same design. First-day ceremonies for the two stamps were held in New York, New York, and Stockholm, Sweden.

The Citizens' Stamp Advisory Committee had approved Garbo as a potential joint-issue subject even before she became eligible for stamp honors in 2000, 10 years after her death. "As her 100th birthday got closer, I said, 'We've got to start thinking about this,' " said Terrence McCaffrey, manager of stamp development.

However, it was Hans Nyman, Sweden Post's sales director, who formally proposed the joint issue, in a communication to McCaffrey. "Hans was very pleased to hear that we wanted to do it," McCaffrey said.

The joint issue was the fifth for the United States and Sweden. In 1983, they issued single stamps to mark the 200th anniversary of the Treaty of Amity and Commerce between the two countries. In 1986, each country issued four stamps in booklet form celebrating stamp collecting.

A third country, Finland, joined the two nations in 1988 to commemorate the 350th anniversary of the settlement of New Sweden in what is now Delaware, southern New Jersey and southeastern Pennsylvania. And, in 1991, the United States and Sweden postally marked the centennial of the Nobel Prizes, which were endowed by Swedish inventor and philanthropist Alfred Nobel.

The U.S. Garbo stamp, a self-adhesive, was printed by the intaglio process by Banknote Corporation of America/Sennett Security Products and distributed in panes of 20. With its glamorous portrait of Garbo, semijumbo size, masterful engraving by Piotr Naszarkowski of Sweden and black color, the stamp is visually striking. The back of the liner paper contains a brief biographical paragraph.

Sweden issued a second variety along with its joint-issue stamp. Printed in black and violet, it features a caricature profile portrait of Garbo by

Sweden linked its joint-issue Garbo stamp with another design, showing a caricature profile portrait of the actress by Einar Nerman, in a se-tenant booklet pane of four.

Einar Nerman. Both varieties are engraved, as are most of Sweden Post's stamps. Two specimens of each stamp are contained in a se-tenant booklet pane. Stamp Fulfillment Services of USPS offered the booklet to U.S. collectors for $6.

Sweden also produced the joint-issue stamp in a souvenir sheet of four,

This is Sweden's Greta Garbo souvenir sheet of four 10-krona stamps. The selvage photograph of Garbo shows her as she appeared in the 1937 film Conquest. *The English translation of the selvage inscription, "Garbo DEN GUDOMLIGA," is "Garbo, the divine."*

When art director Derry Noyes was designing the 20 Masters of American Photography stamps of 2002, she wanted to use this 1928 photograph of Greta Garbo on the stamp honoring Edward Steichen. However, Steichen's widow refused to allow the use of any of her husband's celebrity photos, and Noyes used a floral still life on Steichen's stamp instead.

Edward Steichen 1879-1973

with a limited printing (30,000 sheets) that sold out in less than four weeks and was not stocked by Stamp Fulfillment Services. In March 2006, souvenir sheets were selling on eBay for $32 to $50.

A photograph of Garbo would have appeared on a U.S. stamp three years earlier if officials had been able to get the necessary permission. When the 20 Masters of American Photography stamps of 2002 were in the planning stage, Derry Noyes, the stamps' designer, and Professor Peter C. Bunnell of Princeton University, the project consultant, wanted to honor Edward Steichen by using the evocative photo of Garbo he had made in 1928 for *Vanity Fair* magazine. However, Joanna Steichen, the photographer's widow, refused to allow the use of any of his celebrity photos, and Noyes and Bunnell settled for a floral still life for the Steichen stamp.

Garbo was born Greta Lovisa Gustafsson in Stockholm on September 18, 1905, to Karl and Anna Gustafsson. Her father died when Garbo was 14, and she went to work to help support her family.

As an employee of a department store, she modeled hats and made her first motion-picture appearance in a short promotional film for the store. In 1922, she won a scholarship to the Royal Dramatic Theater Academy and began appearing in short films. In 1924, at age 19, she was cast in the feature movie *The Saga of Gosta Berling*, directed by Mauritz Stiller.

Stiller gave Garbo her stage name and adopted her as his protégé and acting property. In 1925, she accompanied him to Hollywood, where Louis B. Mayer, head of MGM Studios, cast her in *The Torrent* (1926). The movie was a hit and so was Garbo.

Garbo made 10 silent feature films for MGM from 1926 to 1929. She became romantically involved with John Gilbert, her co-star in the 1926 *Flesh and the Devil*, but rejected his pleas that she marry him. Her later romantic interests included director Rouben Mamoulian, actors George Brent and Gilbert Roland, conductor Leopold Stokowski, photographer Cecil Beaton, and George Schlee, husband of fashion designer Valentina.

Garbo was a legendary beauty (although Cole Porter mocked her foot size in this line from his 1941 song, *Let's Not Talk About Love*: "If you know Garbo, then tell me this news, is it a fact the Navy's launched all her old shoes?") The camera seemed to enhance her loveliness. She was aware of this and insisted on always filming on closed sets. "When people are watching," she said, "I'm just a woman making faces for the camera. It destroys the illusion."

Shy by nature, Garbo granted no interviews, signed no autographs, made no publicity tours and answered no fan mail. This reticence only increased her mystique and allure.

Her smoky, accented voice was first heard in theaters in a screen adaptation of Eugene O'Neill's *Anna Christie* (1930) that MGM promoted with the catch phrase, "Garbo talks!" She was nominated for an Academy Award for best actress twice in 1930, for *Anna Christie* and *Romance*, but lost to Norma Shearer. In 1931, she starred in a German version of *Anna Christie*.

Garbo went on to make 14 other feature films. She played the title roles of the ill-fated spy Mata Hari (1931) and Sweden's Queen Christina (1933). She also starred in *As You Desire Me* (1932), *Anna Karenina* (1935), and *Camille* (1936), her personal favorite of all her films. She received her third Oscar nomination for *Camille*, but lost to Luise Rainer.

One of Garbo's most memorable roles was as the fragile Russian ballerina Grusinskaya in *Grand Hotel* (1932), in which she uttered the famous line, "I want to be alone." In 1939, she made the romantic comedy *Ninotchka*, which MGM promoted with the tagline "Garbo laughs!" For the fourth time, Garbo was nominated for an Oscar, but Vivien Leigh won it for *Gone With the Wind*.

Garbo's last film was a little-remembered farce called *Two-Faced Woman* (1941). Afterward, she quit the business. "I was tired of Hollywood," she told author Sven Broman. "I did not like my work … I did not get any good scripts or any good ideas for films." Other movie projects were proposed after that, but none came to fruition.

During World War II, Garbo aided the Allies by carrying messages to neutral Sweden for British intelligence and by identifying Nazi sympathizers in Sweden. In 1951, she became a U.S. citizen. Three years later, she was awarded an honorary Academy Award, but didn't attend the ceremony.

In her later years, she stayed out of the limelight, living in her apartment on New York's Upper East Side and traveling to Switzerland and the French Riviera with jet-set companions like Aristotle Onassis. Regarding her reclusive lifestyle, Garbo said, "I never said 'I want to be alone.' I only said, 'I want to be left alone.' There is a whole world of difference."

Audiences never saw her grow old on screen. "I think we are dealing here with the Marilyn [Monroe] factor," said Jan-Chris Horak, curator of the Hollywood Entertainment Museum. "It is as if she died young." Her actual death, of pneumonia, occurred April 15, 1990, 49 years after she made her final movie. She was 84. Nine years later, her ashes were taken to her native Stockholm for burial.

Before the 2005 joint stamp issue, Garbo had been pictured on a Swedish 1.65-krona stamp of 1981 (Scott 1386c) that was part of a souvenir sheet of five stamps commemorating Swedish films. She also had appeared on stamps of Grenada-Grenadines, Germany and Romania.

The Design

Carl Herrman, a USPS art director, is Swedish on his father's side and corresponds regularly with a cousin, Ingrid, in Sweden. He requested and got the assignment of designing the Garbo stamp.

With the help of PhotoAssist, the Postal Service's research firm, Herrman reviewed dozens of photographs of the actress. "There was a banquet to choose from," he said. "Not a bad photo among them. I could have just thrown them up in the air and picked the first one to land."

He developed commemorative-size stamp designs from several of the photos. He even made one of the designs into a pane in the Legends of Hollywood format, complete with a wide decorative side selvage showing Garbo, in the film *Queen Christina*, seated in the prow of a ship in a final scene well known to film buffs. However, CSAC wasn't interested in making the stamp part of the Legends series. "It would have eliminated the joint issue," Herrman said.

The art director particularly liked a photo showing Garbo with a languid expression, wearing a suit, white blouse and beret. "It sort of conveyed 'the Garbo look,'" he said. "I was enthralled with this photo, but the committee turned out not to be." One CSAC member quipped, "Why, she looks like a drunken airline stewardess!" "That remark killed that photo," Herrman laughed.

The portrait that Herrman and CSAC chose showed Garbo with her hair over her right eye in a peekaboo style. It was made by Clarence Sinclair Bull, MGM's staff photographer, during the filming of *As You Desire Me*

Art director Carl Herrman was particularly fond of this photograph of Garbo, but its chances disappeared when a CSAC member quipped: "Why, she looks like a drunken airline stewardess!"

218

These four Garbo portraits are among several that Herrman developed as stamp designs in commemorative size, arranged vertically.

in 1932, when the actress was 27. Bull was quoted as saying that Garbo's face was "the most inspirational I ever photographed."

Although USPS officials knew that Sweden's stamp would be engraved, Herrman initially opposed the idea of using an engraving for the U.S. version. "I felt an engraving couldn't capture the tonality and the warmth of a photo," he said. He persuaded McCaffrey and CSAC to plan for a joint issue in which the two countries' stamps would feature the same image reproduced by two different processes.

In the summer of 2003, McCaffrey and Bill Gicker, USPS creative director for stamp design, traveled to Sweden to meet their Sweden Post counterparts and discuss the design process. At the first meeting, on an

Herrman also created a design treatment of a Garbo stamp to be part of the Legends of Hollywood series, with the image on the side selvage showing Garbo as Queen Christina in the final scene of the 1933 film of that name. Making the stamp part of the Legends series would have eliminated the joint issue with Sweden, and CSAC turned down the idea.

unusually hot summer day, were Sweden Post's Hans Nyman and Stephan Fransius, chief designer. Also present was legendary stamp engraver Czeslaw Slania, who had engraved the dies for more than 1,000 stamps for Sweden and other countries, including the United States. Among his U.S. stamps were two of the earlier joint issues with Sweden, the Treaty of Amity and Commerce and the Nobel Prizes.

"We explained to Mr. Slania our premise of photo vs. engraving," McCaffrey said. "His response was: 'Tsk, tsk, you will be so sorry!'

"We had just gotten off the plane three or four hours earlier. We were suffering

This is the full photograph of Greta Garbo made by MGM staff photographer Clarence Sinclair Bull that Carl Herrman cropped for the U.S. and Swedish stamp designs.

220

USA
37

2005

GRETA GARBO

This is the preliminary design of the Garbo stamp released by USPS in mid-December 2004, showing the actress' portrait as a photograph rather than an engraving, as officials originally intended it to be. After they saw Piotr Naszarkowski's engraving of the portrait for Sweden Post, however, they made a swift decision to ask Naszarkoswki to engrave the U.S. stamp as well.

from severe jet lag. It was a warm day, and there was no air conditioning in the room because they normally don't need it. Bill and I were tired and hot, and we were trying to be diplomatic with this 82-year-old man who was chastising us and telling us we would not be happy with what we were proposing to do. 'You will be embarrassed by your work when you put mine next to it!' he said. 'OK,' we said, 'we'll leave it open for discussion, but this is our approach right now.'

"The Sweden Post folks loved the photo we had chosen, and accepted it for the stamps. But they had a problem with our vertical commemorative-size layout. They suggested the stamps be done in their semijumbo size, which is very close to ours."

Carl Herrman reworked the portrait as a semijumbo and tried out an assortment of type treatments. CSAC chose a font called Skia. In mid-December 2004, USPS made public a design in which the portrait was a photograph, with the actress' name in black capitals on a white panel across the bottom.

Meanwhile, however, at McCaffrey's invitation, Britt-Inger Hahne, managing director of Sweden Post Stamps, and Stephan Fransius had scheduled a visit to Washington, D.C., in October 2004 to attend a meeting of CSAC and observe its procedures. When they arrived, they had with them the engraved die for their stamp, along with a proof. But the engraving wasn't by Slania; the master engraver had become gravely ill, and would die a few months later (see Year in Review). Instead, it was by Piotr Naszarkowski, a Slania protégé.

"Everyone, including me, was amazed at how beautiful the engraving was," said Carl Herrman. "On the spot, we made up our minds in front of them that we would go with the engraving, too."

Naszarkowski was commissioned to make a separate engraving for USPS with "USA 37" instead of "10 KR," and with the name in white dropout capitals inside the vignette. USPS released the design of the engraved stamp in late January 2005.

No color other than black was considered for the stamp. "Black connotes style and sophistication. Think of tuxedos," Herrman said. Sweden Post also used black for its stamp, but added a brownish tone. "I kind of liked it," Herrman said. "Everybody had their own opinion as to whether the added color softened the image or made it look sexier. I thought it gave the stamp a little more warmth. I like both the Swedish stamp color and our color equally well."

Herrman bought a large number of Garbo stamps for his personal use, although he had to add 2¢ in postage to each envelope after the January 8, 2006, rate change. "I love the way they look on envelopes," he said.

First-Day Facts

The U.S. first-day ceremony was held at Scandinavia House, The Nordic Center in America, at 58 Park Avenue in New York, New York. The dedicating official was David L. Solomon, USPS vice president for New York Metro Area operations.

Speakers were Kjell Anneling, ambassador and consul general of Sweden in New York; Ingemar Persson, deputy chief executive officer of Sweden Post; and Derek R. Reisfield, Garbo's great-nephew. Also present were Derek's mother, Gray G. Reisfield, who is Garbo's niece and only heir, and his father, Donald R. Reisfield. David E. Failor, executive director of Stamp Services for USPS, was master of ceremonies, and Edward P. Gallagher, president of the American-Scandinavian Foundation, gave the welcome.

The Swedish ceremony was held at the Postmuseum in the Old City area of Stockholm. Britt-Inger Hahne, director of Sweden Post Stamps, welcomed the audience. Representing USPS was Michael Regan, its director of international postal affairs, and Teel Bivins, U.S. ambassador to Sweden. Regan dedicated the U.S. stamp and joined Hahne in unveiling enlarged images of the two Swedish designs. Piotr Naszarkowski, the stamps' engraver, autographed covers and other items for collectors. The event included the showing on a large flat-screen television of part of Garbo's first film, *The Saga of Gosta Berling*.

For a limited time, Stamp Fulfillment Services offered uncacheted first-day covers of the U.S. Garbo stamp for 75¢ (conventional cancellation) or $1.50 (digital color postmark). Collectors also could buy a first-day joint cover bearing the U.S. stamp and the Swedish stamp with the same design for $2.25.

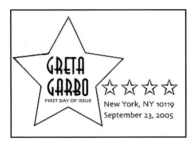 

Shown here are the postmarks used by the United States and Sweden for first-day covers of the two countries' Greta Garbo stamps.

37¢ JIM HENSON, THE MAN BEHIND THE MUPPETS (11 DESIGNS)

Date of Issue: September 28, 2005

Catalog Numbers: 3944, pane of 11; 3944a-3944k, stamps

Colors: yellow, magenta, cyan, black, cool gray 9, green (PMS 355)

First-Day Cancel: North Hollywood, California

First-Day Cancellations: 272,160

Format: Pane of 11 stamps, 10 stamps square in a block 2 across and 5 down, 1 stamp vertical and free-standing. Gravure printing cylinders printing 10 panes per revolution (2 across, 5 around) manufactured by Keating Gravure.

Gum Type: self-adhesive

Stamp Size: square stamps, 1.225 by 1.225 inches; 31.115 by 31.115 mm. Vertical stamp, 1.225 by 1.56 inches; 31.115 by 39.624 mm

Pane Size: 5.5 by 6.6 inches; 139.7 by 167.64 mm

Perforations: 10½ (Muppet stamps), 10½ by 10¾ (Henson stamp) (die-cut simulated perforations) (Comco Commander rotary die-cutter)

Selvage Inscription: "Jim Henson/the man behind the Muppets/'When I was young, my ambition was to be/one of the people who made a difference in/this world. My hope is to leave the world a/little better for my having been there.'/Jim Henson."

Selvage Markings: none

Back Markings: On selvage: "Jim Henson/As a performer, a television pioneer, and an/innovator in puppetry, technology, and the/visual arts, Jim Henson (1936-1990) created/vivid new worlds populated by unforgettable/characters. From his involvement in the/groundbreaking educational television series/*Sesame Street* to the international success of/*The Muppet Show* and a series of movies/starring Kermit, Miss Piggy, and the whole/Muppet gang, Henson had a profound/influence on entertainment, education, and/culture. His ability to bring together a strong/team of performers, artists, and collaborators/who shared his creative vision has ensured/the continuation of his greatest hope:/to make the world a better place by inspiring/people to celebrate life./Muppet Characters © Muppets Holding Company, LL.C.,/a subsidiary of The Walt Disney Company./The JIM HENSON image, trademark and signature are used/with permission from Henson Family Properties LL.C./© 2004 USPS/11 x .37 = $4.07." Universal Product Code (UPC) "458800." On stamps: "Hiya! Now you can send your/letter via bear mail! Ahh-AAH!/And remember: if you stick to/something, you can get/anywhere…especially when/you're a stamp! Wocka wocka!/Hoo-boy, tough mailbox./Fozzie Bear" "Hi ho! Kermit the Frog here!/I've gone from the swamp to a/stamp — one sticky situation after/another. Time to get out your/lily pad and write a letter!/Amphibiously yours,/Kermit the Frog" "Moi is thrilled…for all those lucky/people who will get your letter with/moi's gorgeous face on the/envelope. Don't even think of/canceling moi, sweetie!/Kissy kissy!/Miss Piggy/XX" "I am humbled and honored to be/on a stamp issued by this great/nation. Out of respect for the U.S./Postal Service and yours truly,/please do not put me on a letter/with any of these other weirdoes./Patriotically yours,/SAM the/EAGLE" "Neider rüun, nor snee, nor de/düskee-dusk will støopin de/mailee, yøø betcha!/Børk! Børk!/SWEDISH/CHEF" "S: I'm glad the Muppets are on/stamps./W: Why is that?/S: 'Cause now all you have to do to/get them cancelled is to take 'em to/the post office!/Hohohohoho!/Statler/Waldorf" "Oh Beakie, what a great day for/Muppet Labs! We've made/ourselves completely flat and/pasted ourselves to an envelope./Isn't science nifty!?/Meep! Meep! Meep!/DR. BUNSEN HONEYDEW PHD ESQ./BEAKER" "Mail me!/Mail me!/Thankew!!!/ANIMAL" "Good news! All mail bearing my likeness will be/shot out of a cannon in the general/direction of the person you're/sending this letter to!/Cool!/The Great Gonzo!/CAMILLA" "Dear Postal Carrier,/On behalf of dogs everywhere, sorry about that./Rowlf"

Designer and Typographer: Edward Eyth of Carmel, California

Photographers: Jay David Buchsbaum of Los Angeles, California; Norman Seeff of Burbank, California

Art Director: Terrence McCaffrey, USPS

Stamp Manufacturing: Stamps printed by Avery Dennison Security Printing

Division, Clinton, South Carolina, on 8-color Dia Nippon Kiko webfed gravure press. Stamps processed by Avery Dennison.

Quantity Ordered: 231,000,000

Cylinder Number Detail: none

Paper Supplier: Fasson Division of Avery Dennison

Tagging: unphosphored paper, block tagging over stamps

The Stamps

On September 28, the Postal Service issued 10 stamps bearing photographs of the television and motion-picture puppets known as the Muppets, and an 11th stamp with a portrait of their creator, Jim Henson. The date coincided with the 50th birthday of Henson's best-known Muppet, Kermit the Frog.

The Muppets, 13 in all, were characters on *The Muppet Show*, which ran from 1976 to 1981 and was the most popular first-run syndicated series in TV history. "Jim Henson, the Man Behind the Muppets," as the stamp set was officially called, was another in a sequence of U.S. stamps in recent years that have featured fantasy characters from the comics, television or movies.

The self-adhesive stamps are grouped in a novel format in which the Muppets comprise a block of 10 on the left side of a pane and the Henson stamp is isolated in a wide selvage on the right. The selvage also contains text and a black-and-white photograph of Henson in conversation with Kermit.

On the liner paper behind each stamp is a whimsical "quotation and signature" by the Muppet character or characters shown on the front.

225

From the literally hundreds of Muppet characters available, these were chosen for stamp honors: Kermit the Frog; Fozzie Bear; Sam the Eagle; Miss Piggy; Statler and Waldorf; Swedish Chef; Animal; Dr. Bunsen Honeydew and his assistant, Beaker; Rowlf the Dog; and Great Gonzo and Camilla the Chicken.

On the liner paper behind each stamp is a whimsical "quotation and signature" by the character or characters shown on the front. The quotations encourage the use of letters for communicating, or refer to mail in general. For example, Rowlf apologizes to letter carriers for an unspecified canine offense.

The stamps were printed by the gravure process by Avery Dennison Security Printing Division. A total of 231 million panes — 21 million of each stamp variety — was ordered.

Although USPS originally announced that a set of matching stamped postal cards would accompany the stamps, no such cards were issued. However, postcards without imprinted stamps were sold as part of a $16.95 "Mailing the Muppets Keep in Touch Kit" that included 10 jumbo cards, letter-writing stationery and a

Ten jumbo postcards such as this one, without imprinted stamps, were sold in a kit that included Muppets stamps and writing stationery.

pane of stamps. There was no card equivalent for the Jim Henson stamp.

The project dated to 1999, when Terrence McCaffrey, manager of stamp development for USPS, and Kelly Spinks, a USPS lawyer in charge of obtaining licensing rights, met with officials of The Jim Henson Company to explore stamp possibilities.

"We were trying to come up with stamps that were contemporary, that would appeal to kids and young adults and send a message," said McCaffrey. "Our idea was to do something related to the environment. We sat down with the Henson people, a wild, wacky creative team, and tried to come up with an idea.

"We just couldn't work out anything that clicked. After a year and a half, the project just died on the vine, and it bothered me, because I love the Muppets.

"Some time later, the [Citizens' Stamp Advisory] Committee decided to revisit the idea of the Muppets, but to do it by honoring Jim Henson as a creative artist. At the time, we were developing the [2004] Dr. Seuss stamp, and the CSAC members said, 'Maybe you could do a Henson stamp with some of the Muppets sitting around him.' I said, 'I don't want to repeat the Dr. Seuss solution; let me try something else.' They said, 'Fine, have at it.' "

McCaffrey returned to Hollywood with William Gicker, creative director of stamp design for USPS, and Derry Noyes, a USPS art director, to meet again with the group from the Henson company. "I told them we wanted to do Muppets stamps and a Henson stamp, and to have fun with the Muppets and show a number of them, three, four, five or more," McCaffrey said. The company officials agreed, and a team headed by Edward Eyth, the company's director of creative services, set to work on the design.

Jim Henson was born September 24, 1936, in Greenville, Mississippi. In 1954, as a high school student in Maryland, he began his TV career with performing puppets on a Washington, D.C., Saturday morning program. The following year, as a freshman at the University of Maryland, he was given his own twice-daily, five-minute show, *Sam and Friends*, on the local NBC affiliate, WRC-TV.

This show, which won a local Emmy award in 1958 and ran until 1961, featured a large cast of characters called Muppets, a word Henson coined to describe his combination of marionette and foam-rubber hand puppets. Included in the cast was a green Muppet named Kermit who later would become the famous Kermit the Frog.

Henson introduced several enduring Muppet

features on the show — music, offbeat humor and innovative technical tricks. He was assisted by a fellow student and his future wife, Jane Nebel, and two employees who would make a major contribution to his success: Frank Oz, whom Henson once called "the greatest puppeteer in the world," and Jerry Juhl, who had a hand in writing nearly every Muppet production for 35 years. (Juhl died at 67 September 27, 2005, less than a month after the stamps were issued.)

In the 1960s, Henson helped support his young company by using his puppets in television commercials. Rowlf the Dog, a character created for these ads, helped him gain nationwide attention by appearing in regular comedy bits on *The Jimmy Dean Show*. Henson also produced experimental films, including the Academy Award-nominated *Time Piece* (1965), that expanded his knowledge of the medium and inspired his later innovations.

Joan Ganz Cooney and the Children's Television Workshop asked Henson to create characters for the educational children's television show *Sesame Street*, which made its debut on public television in 1969. Many of the show's Muppets, including Cookie Monster, Bert and Ernie, Grover and Oscar the Grouch, became icons of American popular culture. More than 35 years after its inception, *Sesame Street* continues to entertain and inform children around the world.

In England, Henson produced the television comedy hit *The Muppet Show*. Hosted by Kermit, the syndicated program featured a new cast of Muppet characters, as well as celebrity guest stars. It received four Emmy awards and was nominated for 17 others, and its success led to six feature films, three of which were nominated for Academy Awards.

Henson's creations for television also included *Fraggle Rock* (1983-1988) and the Emmy-winning animated series *Muppet Babies* (1984-1992), which placed his characters back in time to their early childhood in a nursery. With the help of fantasy illustrator Brian Froud, Henson developed a Tolkien-like world for the film *The Dark Crystal*, populated by extremely detailed, realistic-looking puppets. Based on what he and his team learned from work on *The Dark Crystal*, he founded the Creature

Shop to create three-dimensional characters with advanced movement abilities for his films and outside productions.

Henson was elected to the Hall of Fame of the Academy of the Television Arts & Sciences in 1987. Three years later, on May 16, 1990, in New York City, he died of pneumonia brought on by an infection by an aggressive strain of Group A streptococcus bacteria. *Time* magazine honored him in 1998 as one of the most influential artists and entertainers of the 20th century.

His legacy continues through The Jim Henson Company, which entertains family audiences worldwide through a wide range of film and television projects. In 2004, the firm sold the Muppet characters and the Muppet film and television library to The Walt Disney Company.

The sale to Disney took place while the stamp-production process was under way, and meant that the Postal Service had to renegotiate its rights to show the Muppets with the new controlling entity, called Muppets Holding Company, LL.C. A separate deal had to be made with another company, Henson Family Properties LL.C., for rights to use Henson's picture, name and signature. Although the negotiations weren't difficult, they were time-consuming, and the Disney affiliate didn't sign off until after the stamps were printed and only a few weeks before they were scheduled to be issued.

A brief biography of each Muppet on the stamp pane follows, from the Kermitage.com Web site and other sources:

KERMIT THE FROG. Kermit — the first Muppet — hosted *The Muppet Show*, sometimes sang and danced, and kept things going smoothly backstage. In his original appearances on *Sam and Friends* in 1955, he was a jazzy, abstract character with feet instead of flippers and no collar. Later he evolved into a frog, and on *Sesame Street* he appeared in various Streetscenes, as well as *Sesame Street* News Flash skits. His signature song, *It's Not Easy Being Green*, was written for *Sesame Street*. Jim Henson himself played the character.

FOZZIE BEAR. An insecure comedian with bad acts, Fozzie, played by Frank Oz, performed monologues and played the lead in "Bear on Patrol," a regular police sketch.

SAM THE EAGLE. Patriotic Sam (Oz) wanted to make sure the show was decent and morally upright. "Of course, he never succeeded," Kermitage.com noted dryly.

MISS PIGGY. *The Muppet Show*'s self-perceived superstar, Miss Piggy (Oz) performed in the regular sketches, flirted with the male guest stars and tried to get Kermit to love her. She dealt with people who got in her way with a yell and a karate chop.

STATLER AND WALDORF. Statler (Richard Hunt) and Waldorf (Henson) were two grumpy men who heckled the rest of the cast from their balcony seats. Along with Waldorf's wife Astoria, they were

229

named for old New York City hotels.

SWEDISH CHEF. The Swedish Chef (Henson) spoke mock Swedish and possessed very unusual cooking talents.

ANIMAL. Animal (Oz) was the wild man drummer for The Electric Mayhem and The Orchestra.

DR. BUNSEN HONEYDEW AND HIS ASSISTANT, BEAKER. Dr. Honeydew (Dave Goelz) was an inventor who worked at Muppet Labs and invented things like a gorilla detector, an automatic wastebasket, a pet converter and an electronic nose warmer. Beaker (Hunt) was his nervous assistant and consistent victim of Bunsen's inventions. Beaker had a squeaky way of talking that only Bunsen seemed to understand.

ROWLF THE DOG. A scruffy brown dog of indeterminate breed with a rounded black nose and big floppy ears, Rowlf (Henson) was the first Muppet to be featured on national TV through his *Jimmy Dean Show* appearances. He was a master of upstaging while playing the piano in the background.

GREAT GONZO AND CAMILLA THE CHICKEN. Gonzo (Goelz), a blue "whatever" with a question-mark nose and a love for the weird and unknown, was a daredevil and stuntman. Camilla, Gonzo's girlfriend, usually was performed by Jerry Nelson.

None of these Muppets had appeared on U.S. stamps before. However, in 1999, one of their *Sesame Street* colleagues, Big Bird, was shown on a 33¢ stamp in the Celebrate the Century series for the 1970s that commemorated the groundbreaking children's TV show (Scott 3189c).

The first puppet to appear on U.S. postage was Charlie McCarthy, who shared an Al Hirschfeld caricature with his ventriloquist partner Edgar Bergen on a 29¢ Comedians booklet stamp in 1991 (Scott 2563).

The Designs

The first pane layout created by Edward Eyth and his associates contained 20 stamps in 11 varieties. Nine of them displayed existing photographs of Muppets — including Pepe the Prawn, who starred in the TV series *Muppets Tonight!* — and their simulated signatures. A tenth variety

A photograph of Big Bird was shown on this 1999 stamp from the Celebrate the Century series for the 1970s (Scott 3189c).

This is the original design for a pane of stamps developed by designers of The Jim Henson Company. Each shows a photograph of a Muppet or Muppets under a lighted proscenium arch that recalls the set of The Muppets Show. There are 11 stamp varieties, including one showing Henson himself and another depicting the little-known Jim Henson Muppet. The Norman Seeff photo of Henson on the side selvage later was used on the stand-alone stamp on the issued pane.

bore a photo of Henson, and the 11th showed the little-known Henson Muppet, who was a banjo player with the Country Trio in the first season of *The Muppet Show* and made occasional appearances in later seasons.

Each character was shown under a proscenium arch that recalled *The Muppet Show*.

In the wide selvage on the right, the layout displayed a full-face photograph of Henson, made in New York City by photographer Norman Seeff in 1986, with a quotation from Henson: "When I was young my ambition was to be one of the people who made a difference in this world. ... My hope still is to leave the world a bit better for having been here."

"The arch they placed on each stamp, with the lights, made the layout very busy," Terrence McCaffrey said. "We told them, 'We need something more exciting.' It turned out that they had done a book with a cover picture of Kermit bursting through a piece of paper. We said, 'That's it. Can we do that with each Muppet?'"

The designers came back to USPS with a layout in which each of the Muppets was shown breaking out of a plain white background. Again,

existing photographs were used. This time, only one Henson stamp was included; it stood alone on the right side of the pane, and bore the Norman Seeff portrait of Henson that had been enlarged on the selvage of the first layout. Below it, on the selvage of the new pane, was a photograph showing Henson in profile silhouette, seated in a window with Kermit the Frog. Its origin is unknown. The selvage also contained the quotation from the earlier layout, with some minor variations.

The designers settled on a layout that included a block of 10 stamps on which the Muppet characters appeared to be bursting out of white paper. The photographs used in the layout shown here were existing pictures; for the finished pane, new pictures were taken, and Fozzie Bear replaced Pepe the Prawn on the stamp at top right.

After CSAC approved the design, the Henson company team insisted on rephotographing each Muppet especially for its stamp.

"They wanted shots that were made exclusively for the stamps," McCaffrey said. "They couldn't get space in their studios or the Disney studios — everything was booked up for months — so they rented a studio for a day in the summer of 2004, paid for by Disney, and brought in the Muppets. Bill Gicker and I flew to Los Angeles to watch the process."

The photo shoot was directed by *Rolling Stone* cameraman and Muppet photographer Jay David Buchsbaum. "Ed [Eyth] and the Henson Creature Shop crew built the set, and we posed the characters in the opening," Buchsbaum told the Postal Service. "We had a stylist who had worked with the puppets for years and it still took about an hour to get each one into position. The Muppets are different sizes, so they didn't all fit inside the paper burst."

To ensure that the photographs would work at stamp size, Buchsbaum created an acetate overlay that could be positioned over the viewfinder to show what the final composition would look like, including the Muppet's location relative to the 37¢ denomination. Working with Muppets could be as challenging as a shoot with live subjects, he said, although in this case it was for stamp-related reasons.

Miss Piggy and Kermit hold a pane of stamps at the first-day ceremony at the Academy of Television Arts and Sciences.

233

"We'd get the puppet all set up, and then we'd run back to the camera and find out that we'd covered the 37¢ sign," he said. "It took us all day to get it right."

McCaffrey confirmed that report. "They worked for hours just on Fozzie Bear," he said. "They couldn't get the lighting the way they wanted it. They had their stylist doing his curls. They were doing this, they were doing that. And they still had nine more photographs to go!"

Once a satisfactory photo of a Muppet or pair of Muppets was obtained, it was merged with a separate photo of torn paper, and the combination was digitally enhanced to produce highlights and shadows.

Avery Dennison printed the stamps in the four standard process colors, plus cool gray 9 (for the "USA 37" on the Muppets stamps) and PMS 355 green (for the name "Jim Henson" on his stamp). The typeface is called ITC American Typewriter medium.

First-Day Facts

Anita Bizzotto, USPS executive vice president, dedicated the pane in a ceremony in the Leonard H. Goldenson Theater at the Academy of Televi-

Before the first-day ceremony, a bronze sculpture commemorating Jim Henson's induction into the Academy of the Television Arts and Sciences Hall of Fame was unveiled in the academy's Hall of Fame Plaza. Shown here, left to right, are Phil Wayne, sculpture committee chairman; Dick Stiles, Hall of Fame sculptor; Lisa Henson, daughter of Jim Henson; and Dick Askin, chairman of the academy. The sculpture, showing Henson surrounded by a few of his most famous creations, was more than seven feet high and weighed 1,200 pounds.

sion Arts and Sciences in North Hollywood, California.

Also participating were the academy's chairman and chief executive officer, Dick Askin; Lisa and Brian Henson, children of Jim Henson and co-chief executive officers of The Jim Henson Company; and Kermit the Frog and Miss Piggy. Kermit thanked USPS "on behalf of sticky, long-tongued people like me for inventing self-adhesive stamps — saves the tongue."

Prior to the first-day ceremony, Askin and Lisa Henson helped unveil a 1,200-pound bronze sculpture on the academy's Hall of Fame Plaza commemorating Jim Henson's induction into the Hall of Fame in 1987. The sculpture showed Henson surrounded by a few of his most famous creations.

For a limited time, Stamp Fulfillment Services offered uncacheted first-day covers of a full pane of stamps for $6.57. First-day covers with digital color postmarks were sold for $1.50 for a random single stamp and $16.50 for a set of 11.

CONSTELLATIONS (4 DESIGNS)

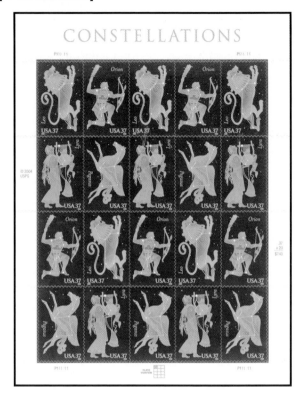

Date of Issue: October 3, 2005

Catalog Numbers: Scott 3945-3948, single stamps; 3948a, block or vertical strip of 4

Colors: black, cyan, magenta, yellow, gold (PMS 871), silver (PMS 877)

First-Day Cancel: Bloomfield Hills, Michigan

First-Day Cancellations: 163,821

Format: Pane of 20, vertical and horizontal, 5 across, 4 down. Offset printing plates printing 240 stamps per revolution (12 across, 20 around).

Gum Type: self-adhesive

Stamp Size: 0.98 by 1.56 inches; 25.892 by 39.625 mm

Pane Size: 5.92 by 7.769 inches; 150.368 by 197.332 mm

Perforations: 10¾ (die-cut simulated perforations) (IDC two-station die cutter)

Selvage Inscription: "CONSTELLATIONS"

Selvage Markings: "© 2004/USPS." ".37/x20/$7.40." "PLATE/POSITION" and diagram.

236

Back Markings: On selvage: UPC (Universal Product Code) "457500" in 4 locations.

Designer and Artist: McRay Magleby of Provo, Utah

Art Director and Typographer: Carl Herrman of Carlsbad, California

Modeler: Joseph Sheeran of Ashton-Potter (USA) Ltd., Williamsville, New York

Stamp Manufacturing: Stamps printed by Ashton-Potter on a Mueller Martini A76 modified offset press. Stamps processed by Ashton-Potter.

Quantity Ordered: 70,000,000

Plate Number Detail: 1 set of 6 plate numbers preceded by the letter P in selvage above or below each corner stamp

Plate Number Combination: P111111

Paper Supplier: Flexcon/Glatfelter

Tagging: nonphosphored paper, block tagging over stamps

The Stamps

For thousands of years, humans have traced among the stars the outlines of familiar things, living and inanimate. These patterns in the night sky are constellations, from the Latin for "together" and "stars." Over the ages, constellations not only have stirred the imagination but have guided travelers, told farmers when to plant and to harvest, and enabled astronomers to map the heavens and track the wandering planets.

Historians believe the names of many of the animal constellations, such as the Bull, Ram and Lion, first were bestowed some seven millennia ago by the Sumerian shepherds and farmers of Mesopotamia. Later, the Greeks adopted the old Sumerian names and named other constellations for their gods, heroes and creatures of their mythology. The Romans translated the names into the Latin words that still apply.

About 150 A.D., Ptolemy listed 48 constellations known to him. In later years, astronomers added new ones to the list, and in 1929 the International Astronomical Union created official boundaries for the 88 constellations that are recognized today.

On October 3, 2005, at the Cranbrook Institute of Science in Bloomfield Hills, Michigan, the Postal Service issued a block of four se-tenant stamps illustrating four constellations familiar to viewers in the Northern Hemisphere: Orion, Leo, Lyra and Pegasus. Each stamp shows its constellation's major stars, connected by lines to form an outlined shape that, in turn, is surrounded by artist McRay Magleby's conception of the full figure.

The stamps helped launch National Stamp Collecting Month, which USPS sponsors annually. Its theme for 2005 was "Be a Stargazer: Let the Stars Guide You Into Stamp Collecting!" Another kind of celestial phenomena, clouds, had been featured on the commemoratives for the 2004 National Stamp Collecting Month.

The designing of the stamps began in 1999 and essentially was completed in 2001, four years before the issue date. Constellations as a topic originated in the Citizens' Stamp Advisory Committee's subject subcommittee, which believes that stamps relating to space and astronomy have a special appeal for young people. However, no one CSAC member or art director appears to have been its particular advocate. After briefly considering making the set part of a prestige booklet on constellations and stars, CSAC decided to issue only the stamps.

PhotoAssist, the Postal Service's research firm, hired four experts for the project: Dr. Lincoln J. Greenhill of the Harvard-Smithsonian Center for Astrophysics; Dr. David Theison of the University of Maryland's Department of Astronomy; Dr. William L. Hansen, chairman of the Department of Classical Studies and Department of Mythology Studies at the University of Indiana; and Dr. Wallace Bennett Ragan, holder of the Hurlbut Chair of Classics at St. Albans, the National Cathedral School for Boys, in Washington, D.C.

Ashton-Potter (USA) Ltd. printed the self-adhesive stamps by the offset process and distributed them in panes of 20, five across by four down, with a header containing the single word "CONSTELLATIONS." In the first and third horizontal rows, the Leo and Orion designs alternate; the Lyra and Pegasus designs are in the second and fourth horizontal rows. Each stamp has a solid black background that bleeds across the four edges into the adjacent ones.

USPS announced that the bottom selvage of the pane would contain a promotion for the following year's Washington 2006 World Philatelic Exhibition, and released a picture that included the selvage text. However, there was no text on the actual pane. Questioned by *Linn's Stamp News*, Postal Service spokesman Mark Saunders described the omission as an oversight by the printer that wasn't caught when officials signed off on the final proof.

USPS announced that the bottom selvage of the pane would contain a promotion for the Washington 2006 World Philatelic Exhibition, and released a picture of the pane, here graphically cropped to show the selvage text. However, the actual pane didn't carry it. A USPS spokesman said the omission was an oversight.

This 37¢ Pegasus stamp lost part of its design when a collector in Minnesota attempted to soak it from its envelope.

The Constellations stamps, like several others produced by the Postal Service's private printers in recent years, presented collectors of used stamps with a major soaking problem. In this case, the stamps were highly vulnerable to damage from the water that is used to remove them from their envelope corners.

A Minnesota collector complained to *Linn's* that the printing inks, which cover the entire surface of the stamps, tend to flake off the paper during drying (see illustration). The writer of *The Yearbook* found that the Constellations required an overnight soak in room-temperature water before they would come off the envelopes, after which they curled tightly and required careful smoothing before being pressed dry between sheets of cardboard. When dry, they showed tiny cracks across the printed surface and evidence of minor flaking at the tips of the simulated perfs.

A similar problem had attended the 37¢ Summer Olympics commemorative of 2004, which also featured complete coverage of the paper with ink. The common denominator for the Summer Olympics and Constellations stamps is that both were produced by Ashton-Potter (USA) Ltd. using Glatfelter paper. In both cases, collectors of used stamps should consider making an exception and saving mint specimens instead.

Each of the four constellations depicted on the stamps is prominent during a different season of the year.

Leo, Latin for "lion," can be found in the southern sky in the spring. A constellation of the Zodiac, it contains the bright star Regulus at the joint of the lion's right foreleg. Pliny wrote that the Egyptians worshiped the stars of Leo because the rise of the Nile was coincident with the sun's entry into the constellation. It also was a time when the lions left their accustomed haunts for the cooler banks of the great river. In Greek mythology, Leo was identified as the Nemean lion that was killed by Hercules as one of his 12 labors and subsequently put into the sky.

The consultants offered the designers a choice of summer constellations between Lyra and Cygnus, the swan, which contains the easy-to-spot "Northern Cross." They chose the small constellation Lyra, which includes Vega, the fifth brightest star in the heavens.

Lyra's stars define the lyre of Orpheus, who tried to free his wife from the realm of Hades by charming the god of the underworld with his music.

During the autumn, the winged horse Pegasus flies upside down in the heavens to the south. Four bright stars in the shape of a square outline the horse's body. Pegasus was an alternative choice for the consultants, who originally proposed that the autumn constellation be Cassiopeia, the wife of King Cepheus and mother of Andromeda. Cassiopeia has stars of high magnitude, the astronomers pointed out, while the mythology experts liked its "uncomplicated story with an easily understood moral, namely, vanity is punished by the gods."

When winter comes, the mythological Greek hunterhero Orion stands high overhead. Nearby are his two hunting dogs, the constellations Canis Major, which contains Sirius, the brightest star, and Canis Minor, with Procyon, the eighth brightest. The two major stars of Orion are Betelgeuse, a red star on his right shoulder, and Rigel, a blue-white star on his left foot. The most familiar part of the figure are the three stars of his belt, which are known to some as the "three kings" and, in South America, as the "three Marys" of the New Testament: Mary of Nazareth, Mary Magdalene and Mary of Bethany. The constellation Orion is mentioned in Virgil's *Aeneid*, Horace's *Odes*, Homer's *Iliad* and *Odyssey*, Milton's *Paradise Lost*, Tennyson's *Locksley Hall*, and in the Old Testament in Job 9:9, Job 38:31 and Amos 5:8.

Postal officials announced the Constellations stamps

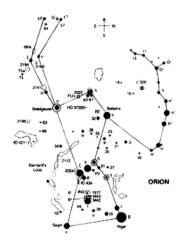

This is a star chart from 1835 that shows the constellation Orion.

240

at a meeting with the philatelic press in August 2004. At that time, David Failor, executive director of Stamp Services, said USPS wasn't planning to issue stamps for additional constellations. "There are no other stamps in the works," he said.

Constellations have made rare appearances on U.S. stamps in the past. The Big Dipper, a part of Ursa Major, and Polaris, the North Star, were shown on the 7¢ Alaska Statehood airmail stamp of 1959 (Scott C53) and again on the flag of Alaska in the 50 State Flags pane of 1976 (Scott 1681).

The Designs

To illustrate the stamps, art director Carl Herrman chose McRay Magleby of Provo, Utah, a long-time friend and associate. Magleby, who is creative director for Brigham Young University and a professor of graphic design at the University of Utah, previously had provided the artwork for the Utah Centennial commemorative of 1996 and the First Flight stamp of 2003.

In his computer-generated illustrations for the Constellations stamps, the figure represented by each constellation surrounds its principal stars, which are connected by white lines. In the case of Lyra, Magleby added the figure of Orpheus, the lyre player, which is not part of the constellation itself.

Among the sources on which the artist based his patterns were star maps made by Wil Tirion of The Netherlands, who has been called "this generation's foremost celestial cartographer." Magleby also referred to

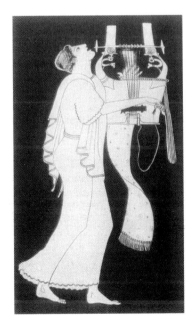

Among the reference material used by stamp illustrator McRay Magleby was this detail from a Greek amphora showing a lyre player.

The Mapping of the Heavens, by Peter Whitfield (1995), *Star Myths of the Greeks and Romans: A Sourcebook*, translated by Theony Condos (1997), and other books.

Magleby and Herrman also discovered a useful resource called *The Box of Stars*, by Catherine Tennant, which includes 32 aquatint cards first developed in London in the 19th century to teach recognition of the constellations. Each card is pierced along the pattern of the constellation with holes of varying sizes that glitter when held up to the light.

"It gave me the idea to have laser holes drilled through the pane for light to shine through," Herrman said. "But the production people told us it would be too complicated, and it would have ruled out self-adhesive stamps. So we decided not to do it and [to] print the stars in white instead."

Although the stamps are vertical, two of the figures, Leo and Pegasus, and their titles are shown sideways, to conform to the way the constellations appear in the sky during their respective seasons. One consultant had suggested that the two animals be shown leaping upward or rearing back on their hind legs, but Magleby demurred on grounds that such poses would make the animals look unnatural.

In a preliminary sketch, Magleby depicted Orion as a helmeted fighter, holding a club aloft in his right hand and a shield on his right arm. After the consultants pointed out that Orion was known in Greek and Roman mythology as a hunter, not a warrior, the artist changed the helmet to a cap and the shield to a hunting bow and two arrows.

Another consultant recommended that the artist give the lyre a more rounded shape typical of Greek art, and forwarded photocopies of images on classical vases and friezes to illustrate what he meant. Magleby made the appropriate change. The expert also pointed out that the curls in Leo's mane were more typical of Mesopotamian art than Greek. The artist chose to leave the mane unaltered.

The consultants' original advice was to show all the visible stars in and around each constellation. "We had Lyra with so many dots that it looked

The consultants' original advice was to show all the visible stars in and around each constellation. As these examples demonstrate, such an abundance of stars would have compromised the clarity of the images. "We had Lyra with so many dots that it looked as if we had let loose with a Gatling gun," Carl Herrman commented.

McRay Magleby's picture of Leo was enlarged and reproduced on the cover of the Winter 2005 issue of USA Philatelic, *shown here. In the cover illustration, the stars making up the constellation, and the lines connecting them, are printed in glow-in-the-dark ink.*

as if we had let loose with a Gatling gun," Herrman said. "We finally got the scientists to let us limit the stars to the essential ones, which eliminated most of those that were too tiny to reproduce at stamp size."

On each stamp, the constellation's name is in italic, in a typeface called Mrs. Eaves, and "USA 37" is in Trajan capitals. The fine linework of the figures and the word "CONSTELLATIONS" in the header are printed in metallic gold ink, while the "USA 37" and the 2005 year date are in metallic silver. The blues, plums, browns and red-oranges inside the figures are blended from the four standard process colors.

"We were dealing with delicate lines against backgrounds of solid black and process colors, and I was worried about how well the stamps would reproduce," Herrman said. "I don't often say this, but the printer did a magnificent job. I was thrilled by the result."

Magleby's picture of Leo was enlarged and reproduced on the cover of the Winter 2005 issue of *USA Philatelic*, the official catalog of Stamp Fulfillment Services, above the caption "Stars shine brighter in the dark." As a novel touch, the stars making up the constellation on the cover and the lines that connect them are printed in a white ink that glows in the dark after being exposed to light.

Varieties

Three imperforate panes of Constellation stamps were purchased in Olympia, Washington, and auctioned on eBay in January and February 2006. The panes sold for $432.97, $427.97 and $332.87. Two were purchased by Joseph Dombek of Missouri, who sent one to *Linn's Stamp News* to examine and the other to the American Philatelic Society to be expertized.

Linn's reported that the pane its editors examined has normal die-cuts on the back, in the liner paper. These cuts are applied during the finishing process so users can remove individual stamps and their liners from the pane. According to Dombek, the pane that he sent to the APS has no die cuts on either side.

Scott catalog editor James Kloetzel said the variety would be listed as a major error in the 2007 Scott *Specialized Catalogue of United States Stamps & Covers*.

First-Day Facts

Kelly L. Sigmon, senior plant manager of the USPS Southeast Michigan Cluster, dedicated the stamps at the Cranbrook Institute of Science. The Institute is Michigan's leading natural history museum, featuring interactive exhibits, astronomy and laser shows, the Digistar planetarium, dinosaurs and a collection of more than 200,000 items.

Speakers were U.S. Representative Joseph Knollenberg, Republican of Michigan's Ninth District; Rick Nahm, president of the Cranbrook Educational Community; and David S. Brose, director of the Cranbook Institute of Science.

David E. Failor, executive director of Stamp Services for USPS, gave opening and closing remarks. Michael J. Narlock, head of astronomy and the planetarium for the Cranbook Institute of Science, was an honored guest.

For a limited time, Stamp Fulfillment Services sold uncacheted first-day covers of the Constellations stamps for $3 for a set of four with the conventional black postmark. Covers with digital color postmarks were sold for $6 per set and $1.50 for a random single.

The earliest known pre-release use was a Pegasus stamp found on an envelope with a machine cancellation from the East Texas P&DC (processing and distribution center) dated September 28, five days before the official first day of issue.

This is the first-day postmark for the Constellations stamps. It measures 2 inches by 1¼ inches.

37¢ DISTINGUISHED MARINES (4 DESIGNS)

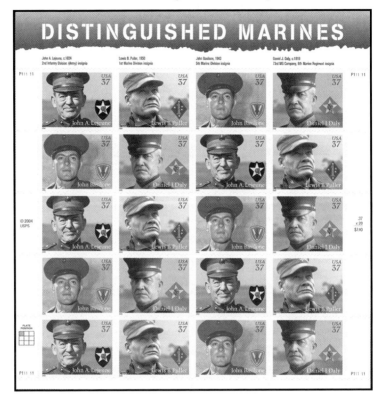

Date of Issue: November 10, 2005

Catalog Numbers: Scott 3961-3964, stamps; 3964a, block or horizontal strip of 4

Colors: black, cyan, magenta, yellow, green (PMS 349), purple (PMS 2735)

First-Day Cancel: Washington, D.C. and Oceanside, California. Stamps sold nationwide the first day.

First-Day Cancellations: 279,931

Format: Pane of 20, horizontal, 4 across, 5 down. Offset printing plates of 180 stamps (15 across, 12 around).

Gum Type: self-adhesive

Stamp Size: 1.56 by 1.225 inches; 39.624 by 31.115 mm

Pane Size: 7.24 by 7.5 inches; 183.896 by 190.5 mm

Perforations: 11 by 10½ (die-cut simulated perforations) (IDC two-station die cutter)

Selvage Inscription: "DISTINGUISHED MARINES/John A. Lejeune, c.1924/ 2nd Infantry Division (Army) insignia/Lewis B. Puller, 1950/1st Marine

Division insignia/John Basilone, 1943/5th Marine Division insignia/Daniel J. Daly, c.1919/73rd MG Company, 6th Marine Regiment insignia."

Selvage Markings: "© 2004/USPS." ".37/x 20/$7.40." "PLATE/POSITION" and diagram.

Back Markings: Universal Product Code (UPC) "458900" in 4 locations on back of liner paper.

Designer and Art Director: Phil Jordan of Falls Church, Virginia

Typographer: John Boyd of New York, New York

Modeler: Joseph Sheeran of Ashton-Potter (USA) Ltd., Williamsville, New York

Stamp Manufacturing: Stamps printed by Ashton-Potter on a Mueller Martini A74 modified offset press. Stamps processed by Ashton-Potter.

Quantity Ordered: 60,000,000

Plate Number Detail: 1 group of 6 plate numbers preceded by the letter P in selvage beside each corner stamp

Plate Number Combination Reported: P111111

Paper Supplier: Paper Corporation of the United States/Glatfelter

Tagging: unphosphored paper, block tagging over stamps

The Stamps

On November 10, the Postal Service issued a block of four stamps bearing photo portraits of U.S. Marine Corps heroes of World Wars I and II. The stamps were placed on sale nationwide, with first-day ceremonies at the Marine Barracks in Washington, D.C., and at the Marines' Camp Pendleton, California.

They were the last commemoratives of 2005 and covered the first-class postal rate for less than two months. On January 8, 2006, the rate rose from 37¢ to 39¢, and mailers using Distinguished Marines stamps were required to add 2¢ extra postage.

The Marines honored are Lieutenant General John A. Lejeune, Lieutenant General Lewis B. "Chesty" Puller, Gunnery Sergeant John Basilone and Sergeant Major Daniel J. Daly.

Ashton-Potter (USA) Ltd. printed the semijumbo, self-adhesive stamps by the offset process and distributed them in panes of 20, five of each variety, so arranged that any block or horizontal strip of four contains all varieties. A header, or top selvage, bears the inscription "Distinguished Marines."

The stamps were successors to the four Distinguished Soldiers stamps of 2000, and are similar to them in appearance and format. Like that issue, they feature an officer and an enlisted man from each of the two global wars of the 20th century. And, as in 2000, they afforded the Postal Service an opportunity to satisfy large and persistent groups of advocates for two of the heroes who were depicted.

In the case of the Distinguished Soldiers, the subjects with the most vigorous cheering sections were infantryman Audie Murphy, the most decorated U.S. soldier in World War II, and Sergeant Alvin C. York, considered the greatest U.S. hero of World War I. The Marines who inspired fervent advocacy were John Basilone, the only serviceman ever to receive both the Congressional Medal of Honor and the Navy Cross, and General Puller, a five-time Navy Cross winner.

The campaign for a stamp for Basilone was centered in his home state of New Jersey. Here, public officials, ex-Marines, the National Italian American Foundation and others had long touted Basilone's bravery and devotion to duty. U.S. Senator Jon Corzine and Representative William Pascrell Jr., New Jersey Democrats, sponsored bills in Congress calling for postal commemoration for Basilone, and petitioners using a special Web site collected some 150,000 signatures.

The Puller stamp campaign was led by Jacques Loraine of Richmond, Virginia, a former Marine and stamp collector, and his wife, also an ex-Marine. By the mid-1990s, they had collected nearly 98,000 signatures on petitions, had won the backing of the Virginia legislature and were promoting their campaign on four Internet sites.

"Once we did Distinguished Soldiers, we knew the other services wouldn't allow us to get away with stopping there," said Terrence McCaffrey, manager of stamp development. Distinguished Marines was a logical next step, he said, because of the pent-up public demand for stamps for Basilone and Puller.

"Just as we did with Audie Murphy and Alvin York — adding two more soldiers to make a block — we decided to add two other Marines to the two we started with," McCaffrey said. The next step was to determine who those additional subjects should be.

The research assignment went to Louis Plummer of PhotoAssist and Phil Jordan, who had served as art director for Distinguished Soldiers and was assigned to the same role for Distinguished Marines. Jordan began with a working knowledge of Marine history; the son of a Seabee who had been attached to the 1st Marine Air Wing during World War II, he had grown up near Marine bases. Now, he and Plummer reviewed biographies and photographs at the U.S. Marine Corps Museum at Quantico, Virginia.

"We had a lot of candidates to pick from," Jordan said. "There were a lot of really super people who had done some pretty impressive things. We could very easily have done three different blocks of four.

"We finally came up with Lejeune and Daly to go with Basilone and Puller. The Marine Corps people we consulted told us that we had nailed it — that these were the four guys whom they absolutely had to have. So we felt pretty good about it."

McCaffrey conceded that "Distinguished Sailors" and "Distinguished Airmen" stamps inevitably would be coming, but as of mid-2005 neither project had been started. "We're spacing these out," he said, noting that

Earlier in 2005, the U.S. Mint issued this commemorative silver dollar marking the 230th anniversary of the U.S. Marine Corps. The obverse reproduces Associated Press photographer Joe Rosenthal's photo of Marines raising the U.S. flag atop Mount Suribachi on Iwo Jima, an image that has appeared on two U.S. commemorative stamps. On the reverse is the Marine Corps symbol, the eagle, globe and anchor, with the Marine motto, "Semper Fidelis," always faithful.

five years had elapsed between Distinguished Soldiers and Distinguished Marines.

Although the fact was unrelated to the stamp issue, the year 2005 was the 230th anniversary year of the Marine Corps. In August, the U.S. Mint issued a commemorative silver dollar for the occasion. The obverse reproduces Associated Press photographer Joe Rosenthal's photograph of Marines raising the U.S. flag atop Mount Suribachi on Iwo Jima (an image that has appeared on two U.S. commemorative stamps). The reverse is an engraving of the Marine Corps symbol, the eagle, globe and anchor, with the Marine motto, "Semper Fidelis," always faithful.

LEJEUNE. Chronologically the first of the four Marines in the stamp set was Lieutenant General John A. Lejeune, whom admirers have called "the greatest of all leathernecks."

Born January 10, 1867, in Pointe Coupee Parish, Louisiana, Lejeune attended Louisiana State University and the U.S. Naval Academy. After a required two-year cruise as a midshipman, he was commissioned a Marine second lieutenant in 1890. He saw duty in Panama, the Philippines, Cuba and Mexico.

In July 1918, in the closing months of World War I, he was promoted to major general and became the first Marine to command an Army division. He led the Army's 2nd Infantry Division, which included the 4th Marine Brigade, in the St. Mihiel and Meuse-Argonne offensives, which helped end the war. Lejeune was awarded the Distinguished Service Medal by both the Army and Navy, the French Legion of Honor and the Croix de Guerre with Palm.

From 1920 to 1929, while commanding the Corps, Lejeune is credited with saving the Marines from budget cuts and consolidations. Foreseeing the need for specialized amphibious assault capabilities, he put in place training and policies that prepared the Marines for the island invasions that would help defeat Japan in World War II.

From his retirement from the Corps in 1929 until 1937, Lejeune was superintendent of the Virginia Military Institute. In February 1942 he was promoted to lieutenant general on the retired list. He died nine months later, on November 20, 1942, and is buried in Arlington National Cemetery.

The Marine training base near Jacksonville, North Carolina, was named Camp Lejeune in his honor. In keeping with an order he issued in 1921, an annual message summarizing the history, mission and traditions of the Marine Corps is published each November during the Corps' birthday celebration.

DALY. Sergeant Major Daniel J. Daly was one of only two Marines to receive two Congressional Medals of Honor for separate acts of heroism. General Lejeune once called him "the outstanding Marine of all time," and the *Historical Dictionary of the United States Marine Corps* says that "his record as a fighting man remains unequaled in the annals of Marine Corps history." Daly's warrior qualities came in a small package: He stood only 5 feet, 6 inches tall and weighed 132 pounds.

He was born in Glen Cove, New York, on November 11, 1873, a date that people of the next century would call Armistice Day. He enlisted in the Marines in 1899, and the following year he was sent to China, where the Boxer Rebellion had erupted. Here he earned his first Medal of Honor for defending an embattled bastion and fighting off attackers until reinforcements arrived.

He later was stationed in Puerto Rico, Cuba and Mexico. In 1915, he was dispatched with Marines to Haiti to protect American lives after an anti-government uprising. He earned his second Medal of Honor for his heroism as part of a small patrol of Marines that battled and routed an estimated 400 Cacos rebels.

During World War I, Daly served as a Marine with the 73rd Machine Gun Company in the 6th Regiment, 2nd Infantry Division (Army). His numerous heroic acts included extinguishing an ammunition-dump blaze, single-handedly capturing an enemy machine-gun emplacement with only hand grenades and a pistol, and bringing in wounded under fire. He won the Navy Cross at Belleau Wood, where words he uttered became legendary. Ordering an attack against overwhelming German forces, he shouted to his tired men as he leaped forward: "Come on, you sons of bitches, do you want to live forever?"

Daly retired as a sergeant major in 1929, and died April 28, 1937. He is buried in Cypress Hills, New York. The Navy later named a destroyer in his honor.

PULLER. Nicknamed "Chesty" for his physique and his aggressiveness, Lieutenant General Lewis B. Puller was renowned for his leadership during major battles in World War II and the Korean War.

Born June 26, 1898, in West Point, Virginia, Puller attended the Virginia Military Institute in 1917 and enlisted in the Marine Corps the following year. As a second lieutenant, he was placed on the inactive list during cutbacks after World War I. He re-enlisted in the Marines and distinguished himself in fighting against rebels in Haiti from 1919 to 1924, when he again became a second lieutenant.

Between 1928 and 1933, Puller served in Nicaragua, where he earned his first two Navy Crosses. He then was assigned to the American legation in China, where his duties included command of the famous Horse Marines.

In 1942, after training the 1st Marine Battalion, 7th Marine Regiment, 1st Marine Division, Puller led his troops through fierce combat at Guadalcanal, where their defense of the airstrip at Henderson Field earned him his third Navy Cross. In January 1944, while serving as executive officer of the 7th Marines, Puller won his fourth Navy Cross at Cape Gloucester, New Britain. Later, he led the 1st Marines in bloody fighting on Peleliu.

During the Korean War, Puller again commanded the 1st Marines, who were key participants in the amphibious landing at Inchon in 1950 that cut off the North Korean forces in the south. In December, after Chinese troops entered the war in force and sent the outnumbered Americans on a long retreat, Puller's 1st Marines held the village of Koto-ri, allowing the 5th and 7th Marines to withdraw from the Chosin Reservoir area. Puller won his fifth Navy Cross and a promotion to brigadier general.

He retired as a lieutenant general in 1955. Eleven years later, with the United States engaged in Vietnam, Puller offered to serve his country once more, but his age, 68, kept him from one final tour of duty. He died October 11, 1971.

BASILONE. John Basilone was the only member of the quartet shown on the stamps to be killed in action. He was born November 4, 1916, in Buffalo, New York, one of 10 children, and grew up in Raritan, New Jersey. His initial enlistment, in 1934 at age 18, was in the Army.

After service in the Philippines, Basilone was honorably discharged in 1937. In 1940, he enlisted in the Marines, and two years later he found himself a member of General Puller's 1st Battalion, 7th Marine Regiment, 1st Marine Division on Guadalcanal, in charge of two sections of heavy machine guns during a fierce Japanese assault.

One gun crew was put out of action, leaving only two men able to carry on. Moving an extra gun into position, Basilone repaired and manned another until help arrived. A little later, with ammunition running low and the supply lines cut off, he fought his way through enemy lines to bring shells to his gunners. His Medal of Honor citation for the action said Basilone contributed "in large measure to the virtual annihilation of a Japanese regiment."

Sent home to sell war bonds, Basilone was pictured on the cover of *Life* magazine, but all he wanted was to return to his unit to "be with my boys." The Marines granted his wish.

As a gunnery sergeant, he took part in the landing on Iwo Jima with the 1st Battalion, 7th Marine Regiment, 5th Marine Division. He demonstrated his characteristic heroism on the beach on invasion day, February 19, 1945, single-handedly destroying an enemy blockhouse and helping guide a friendly tank out of a minefield. Then an exploding enemy shell killed him. He was posthumously awarded the Navy Cross. After the war, his remains were reinterred at Arlington.

In July 1949 a destroyer was named for Basilone. Today, a statue of him stands in Raritan, where a parade has been held in his honor every September since 1981.

Phil Jordan's research led him to these other Marines who could well have been included in the set:

• General Roy S. Geiger, a flyer and winner of the Navy Cross with Gold Star. He became the first Marine to lead a numbered Army when he took command of the 10th Army in Okinawa after the death of its commanding general and led it in World War II's final campaign.

• Major General Smedley D. Butler, the other Marine, with Daniel Daly, to win two Medals of Honor. The first was awarded in 1914 following action at Vera Cruz, Mexico, where Butler commanded the force that landed and occupied the city. He won the second the following year for bravery and leadership as commanding officer of detachments of Marines and seamen in repulsing Caco rebel resistance in Haiti.

• Brigadier General Herman H. Hannekan. Hannekan won the Medal of Honor in Haiti in 1919 for personally killing the notorious bandit Charlemagne Peralte during a raid on Peralte's camp, and won the first of two Navy Crosses for dispatching his successor in another raid five months later. In World War II, while commanding the 7th Marines on Guadalcanal, he won the Silver Star for gallantry in action.

• Sergeant Major John H. Quick, who won the Medal of Honor during fighting in Cuba in the Spanish-American War. When a U.S. Navy ship mistakenly shelled Quick's detachment, he volunteered to use a signal flag to alert the ship to stop shooting, an action that exposed him to heavy rifle fire from the Spanish. Two decades later, at Belleau Wood during World War I, his gallantry earned him the Distinguished Service Cross and the Navy Cross.

The Designs

Like the Distinguished Soldiers stamps, the Marines stamps show their subjects in photographs, close-up and tightly cropped, with appropriate unit shoulder patches in a lower corner. The predominant color of the portraits is Marine green, while the patches are printed in full color.

At first, Phil Jordan experimented with making the stamps commemorative size, vertically arranged. However, Virginia Noelke, chairman of CSAC, urged that they be horizontal semijumbos like the first set. Noelke had not been enthusiastic about either set of military stamps, but her intercession preserved the consistency of the series. "She made the Marine Corps pane much better than it would have been," Jordan said.

The photograph of John A. Lejeune, circa 1924, shows the general standing in front of a railway car. The car was removed electronically from the picture and a new background, an out-of-focus horizon, inserted.

Daniel Daly's photo, circa 1919, shows the stern-faced Marine in winter dress uniform, his gunnery sergeant's chevrons on his sleeve. He wears his two Medals of Honor around his neck and his Navy Cross pinned to his breast. These are cropped from the stamp image so that only the tops of the Medal of Honor ribbons can be seen.

Shown here are stamps for Lejeune, Daly and Basilone in the vertical commemorative-size format with which Phil Jordan worked originally. The photos are different from those shown on the finished stamps. Here, Daly is shown in winter dress uniform, his two Medals of Honor around his neck and his Navy Cross on his chest. The unidentified out-of-focus shape on the horizon of the Basilone photograph ended up being transplanted to the final design of the Puller stamp.

General John A. Lejeune is standing in front of a railroad car in this circa 1924 photo that was cropped for the stamp.

"Chesty" Puller is shown wearing fatigues, with colonel's eagles on his collar and cap. His toughness and determination can be seen in his expression, which is that of an unamused bulldog. The photograph was taken in Korea in 1950. For the stamp background, an unidentified shape was taken from the actual background of an unused John Basilone photograph.

Basilone's stamp photo, made in 1943, shows the sergeant seated in front of a pair of acetate-covered maps of the Pacific Ocean. Two photos

This is the circa 1919 photo of Daniel J. Daly that was cropped for the stamp portrait. Again, Daly is shown in winter dress uniform with his Medals of Honor and his Navy Cross. His gunnery sergeant chevrons are on his sleeve.

John Basilone's portrait was cropped from this photograph of the sergeant in front of acetate-covered wall maps. A map from another photo taken on the same occasion was substituted for the background to provide more suitable shadows and highlights.

from the same shoot were electronically manipulated so the preferred portrait could be combined with a background with less distracting shadows and reflections.

The patches shown on the stamps were chosen by Jordan and Louis Plummer after extensive research and discussion.

Lejeune's insignia, an Indian head on a star on a shield, is that of the U.S. Army's 2nd Infantry Division, which he commanded during World War I. As Jordan pointed out, there were no Marine divisions at the time.

Daly's patch was decided upon with the aid of Marine Corps historian Mark Henry, who confirmed that Daly had been a gunnery sergeant with the 73rd Machine Gun Company of the 6th Regiment of Lejeune's 2nd Infantry Division. The patch shows the same Indian head and star as the division insignia, but on a purple diamond. "So — General Lejeune gets the 2nd Division patch and Sergeant Daly gets the Machine Gun [Company] patch," Jordan wrote to Plummer.

On Guadalcanal in World War II, Puller was Basilone's commanding officer in the 1st Battalion, 7th Regiment, 1st Marine Division, when Basilone won his Medal of Honor on Puller's recommendation. "Much of Puller's legendary service was in the 1st Division, so that's the patch we use for General Puller," Jordan wrote. "We don't want to use the same patch for both." The patch is a blue diamond with a red "1" bearing the word "Guadalcanal" surrounded by five stars.

The patch on Basilone's stamp, a blue arrowhead on a yellow V on a red shield, is that of the 5th Marine Division, in which he served when he returned to duty after his war-bond tour.

Jordan used a variety of typefaces for the stamps and selvage. On the header, the title "DISTINGUISHED MARINES" is in AG Book Stencil, while the small two-line identifications of each man and his insignia are in Akzidenz Grotesk. The Marines' names on the stamps are in Trump Mediaeval; the "USA" is in Trump Mediaeval Italic, and the "37" is in Cochin Bold. The torn-paper effect on the header is a clone of the same feature on the Distinguished Soldiers pane and was created with computer software called Page Edges.

First-Day Facts

Postmaster General John E. Potter dedicated the stamps at the Marine Barracks in Washington with the assistance of General Michael W. Hagee, commandant of the U.S. Marine Corps. Martha Puller Downs, one of General Puller's two daughters, was among those on hand.

At Camp Pendleton, outside the Paige Fieldhouse, John E. Platt, manager of the Postal Service's San Diego District, was the dedicating official. He was joined by Major General Michael Lehnert, commanding general, Marine Corps Installations West, and Major General Richard Natonski, commanding general of the 1st Marine Division.

First-day covers from Camp Pendleton bore an Oceanside, California, postmark. For a limited time, Stamp Fulfillment Services offered uncacheted covers of the Distinguished Marines stamps in sets of four from the two first-day sites at $3 per set.

Postmaster General John E. Potter shakes hands with General Michael W. Hagee, commandant of the Marine Corps, during the dedication of the four Distinguished Marines stamps at the Marine Barracks in Washington, D.C. (USPS photo)

37¢ LOVE BOUQUET
CONVERTIBLE BOOKLET OF 20

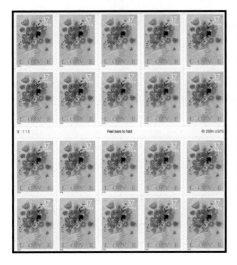

Date of Issue: February 18, 2005

Catalog Number: Scott 3898, single stamp; 3898a or BC206, convertible booklet of 20

Colors: yellow, magenta, cyan, black, stamps; yellow, magenta, cyan, black, blue (PMS 543), cover

First-Day Cancel: Atlanta, Georgia

First-Day Cancellations: 70,116

Format: Convertible booklet of 20, vertical, 5 across, 4 down, with horizontal peel-off strip between horizontal rows 2 and 3. Gravure printing cylinders printing 420 stamps per revolution (3 panes across, 7 panes around) manufactured by Southern Graphics Systems.

Gum Type: self-adhesive

Overall Stamp Size: 0.91 by 1.19 inches; 23.114 by 30.226 mm

Pane Size: 4.55 by 5 inches; 115.57 by 127 mm

Perforations: 10¾ by 11 (die-cut simulated perforations) (Comco Commander rotary die cutter). Backing paper rouletted behind peel-off strip.

Selvage Markings: Cylinder numbers and "• Peel here to fold • © 2004 USPS."

Back Markings: "Love/BOUQUET/Twenty 37¢/Self-adhesive/Stamps/$7.40" on front cover. Promotion for The Postal Store web site, USPS logo, Universal Product Code (UPC) "0 673600 8" on back cover.

Illustrator: Vivienne Flesher of San Francisco, California

Designer, Art Director and Typographer: Derry Noyes of Washington, D.C.

Stamp Manufacturing: Stamps printed by Avery Dennison Security Printing Division, Clinton, South Carolina, on Dia Nippon Kiko gravure press. Stamps finished by Avery Dennison.

Quantity Ordered: 1,500,000,000

Cylinder Number Detail: 1 set of 4 cylinder numbers preceded by the letter V on peel-off strip

Cylinder Number Combinations Reported: V1111, V1112

Paper Supplier: Fasson Division of Avery Dennison

Tagging: phosphored paper

The Stamp

On February 18, the Postal Service issued a Love stamp depicting a hand extending a bouquet of colorful spring flowers, which USPS described as "symbolic of the warmth, hope and happiness of love and friendship." The first-day ceremony was held at the American Philatelic Society's Ameri-Stamp Expo at the Cobb Galleria Center in Atlanta, Georgia.

The self-adhesive stamp was printed by the gravure process by Avery Dennison Security Products and issued in a convertible booklet of 20. All the stamps on the pane have one or two straight edges except for the six in the center. The stamp is in the special size used for the Love and Holiday Celebrations series. USPS ordered a total of 1.5 billion, twice the initial printing of the 2004 Candy Hearts Love stamp.

The first Love stamp, bearing an 8¢ denomination, was issued in 1973. In recent years, USPS issued Love stamps every other year, in pairs covering the one-ounce and two-ounce first-class rates. The two-ounce-rate stamp, with a design similar to its companion but not identical, was intended primarily for use in mailing wedding invitations or announcements that are accompanied by RSVP cards and return envelopes.

However, brides and their mothers were dissatisfied with some of the designs, considering them too whimsical or graphic to be appropriate for wedding invitations. To meet their needs, the Citizens' Stamp Advisory Committee changed its approach. Beginning in 2004, the one-ounce and two-ounce special stamps that are issued in alternate years would be designed with weddings in mind, CSAC decided, and a separate Love stamp at the one-ounce rate would be issued every year. The 37¢ Candy Hearts stamp was the first in the latter category, and the 37¢ Bouquet Love stamp was the second.

To those who wondered why USPS issued its 2005 Love stamp four days after Valentine's Day, the answer was that there remained plenty of Candy Hearts Love stamps available.

"The decision to issue the [Bouquet] Love stamp after Valentine's Day has always been a part of the overall inventory management plan," David Failor, director of stamp services, wrote in the February 11, 2005, issue of *The Direct Link*, a regional newsletter for postal employees in Northeast Indiana.

"We still have an adequate supply of the 2004 Candy Hearts stamps in stock, and by featuring them this Valentine's Day, we expect to dramatically drive down the number recalled.

"The stamps sold extremely well during last year's Valentine's Day celebration. This year should be no different.

"Post offices can help by making sure they have lots of Candy Hearts [stamps] in stock and ready for customers' valentines. As for the 2005 Love stamp, it will be out in plenty of time for Mother's Day and summertime wedding invitations. This year — there's lots of love to meet everyone's needs!"

The Design

Art director Derry Noyes asked Vivienne Flesher, a San Francisco, California, artist who works in pastels, to provide an illustration. Flesher has illustrated children's books and created artwork for numerous clients, including Starbucks and *Rolling Stone* magazine.

Although the Bouquet Love stamp is Flesher's first completed stamp assignment, she had produced three pictures of a mother and child for Noyes when the design for the 33¢ Adoption Awareness commemorative of 2000 was under development. The stamp ultimately was illustrated by Greg Berger, with Ethel Kessler as the art director.

"I asked her to do different bouquets of flowers in that blues pastel style of hers, keeping it loose and fresh," Noyes said. "I was thinking along the lines of a Picasso drawing or painting. Other Love stamps have been tight

Shown here are three of Vivienne Flesher's alternative pastel illustrations for the Bouquet Love stamp. The two bouquets on the left are shown against light blue backgrounds, while the third has a background of green.

and precise, like the Victorian flowers, and I wanted something more spontaneous, as if someone was handing you a bunch of flowers.

"It's hard to push the design envelope with the Love stamp. We don't want the stamp to look too Hallmarky. We've done stamps that really kowtowed to a public that likes schmaltzy stuff; the swans with the necks that turned into a heart shape was probably the all-time favorite of those folks.

"Vivienne's artwork is probably a little too loose and too spontaneous for many people, but I thought it was a fresh, new approach."

Flesher created an assortment of illustrations of hands holding bouquets of flowers of varied shapes and colors, against backgrounds of yellow-orange, light blue and green. The Citizens' Stamp Advisory Committee chose the bouquet with the yellow-orange background after deciding that the blue was "a little too somber," said Terrence McCaffrey, manager of stamp development. "We have the blue one in our design bank," McCaffrey said. "I don't know that we would ever issue it."

Originally, Noyes placed the word "Love" in white script across the bottom, but changed the typeface to Minion capitals and the color to red. "I decided just to keep the typography low-key and let the art dominate," she said. The "37 USA" is in dropout white in the upper right corner.

An enlarged image of the stamp appears on the back of the liner paper that serves as the cover of the convertible booklet.

First-Day Facts

Anderson Hodges Jr., manager of the Atlanta District for USPS, dedicated the stamp at the Cobb Galleria Center. Speakers were Janet Klug, president of the American Philatelic Society; Chris Calle, who has illustrated numerous U.S. stamps; and David Failor, director of stamp services for USPS. Marjorie M. Brown, Atlanta postmaster, was master of ceremonies and gave the welcome.

For a limited time, Stamp Fulfillment Services offered uncacheted first-day covers with a digital color postmark designed by Derry Noyes for $1.50. Covers with standard black first day postmarks were available for 75¢.

The earliest known pre-release use of a Bouquet Love stamp was on a cover bearing a machine cancellation from the Kilmer, New Jersey, processing and distribution center dated February 16, two days before the official date of issue.

37¢ HOLIDAY COOKIES (4 DESIGNS)
PANE OF 20

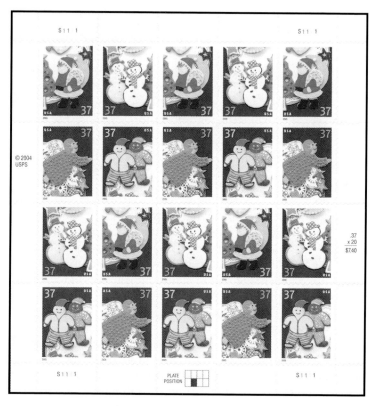

Date of Issue: October 20, 2005

Catalog Numbers: Scott 3949-3952, stamps; 3952a, block or vertical strip of 4

Colors: cyan, magenta, yellow, blue (PMS 2728), stamps; black, back markings

First-Day Cancel: Minneapolis, Minnesota, and New York, New York

First-Day Cancellations: 199,357 (includes all formats)

Format: Pane of 20, vertical, 5 across, 4 down. Offset printing plates printing 160 stamps per repeat (8 across, 20 around).

Gum Type: self-adhesive

Overall Stamp Size: 0.91 by 1.19 inches; 23.11 by 30.22 mm

Pane Size: 5.425 by 5.635 inches; 137.795 by 143.13 mm

Perforations: 10¾ by 11 (die-cut simulated perforations) (Heidelberg 102 Speedmaster rotary die cutter)

Selvage Markings: "© 2004/USPS." ".37/x 20/$7.40." "PLATE/POSITION" and diagram.

Back Markings: On selvage: "To view a variety of philatelic products and other collectibles associated with these stamps,/visit The Postal Store at www. usps.com/shop or call 1-800 STAMP-24 to order a free catalog." Universal Product Code (UPC) "567500" in 4 locations on back of liner paper.

Photographer: Sally Andersen-Bruce of New Milford, Connecticut

Designer, Art Director and Photographer: Derry Noyes of Washington, D.C.

Modeler: Donald H. Woo, Sennett Security Products

Stamp Manufacturing: Stamps printed for Sennett Security Products by Banknote Corporation of America, Browns Summit, North Carolina, on MAN Roland 300 offset press. Stamps finished by BCA.

Quantity Ordered: 200,000,000 stamps

Plate Number Detail: 1 set of 4 plate numbers preceded by the letter S in selvage above or below each corner stamp

Plate Number Combination Reported: S1111

Paper Supplier: Mactac

Tagging: phosphored paper

37¢ HOLIDAY COOKIES (4 DESIGNS)
DOUBLE-SIDED CONVERTIBLE BOOKLET OF 20

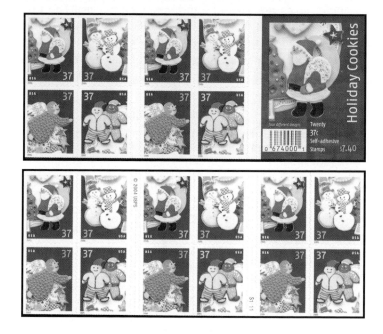

Date of Issue: October 20, 2005

Catalog Numbers: Scott 3953-3956, stamps; 3956a, block of 4; 3956b, convertible booklet of 20

Colors: magenta, yellow, cyan, blue (PMS 2728)

First-Day Cancel: Minneapolis, Minnesota, and New York, New York

First-Day Cancellations: 199,357 (includes all formats)

Format: Convertible booklet pane of 20, vertical, arranged horizontally. Stamps on both sides, 8 (4 across by 2 down) plus label (booklet cover) on one side, 12 (6 across by 2 down) on other side, with horizontal peel-off strips between blocks of 4 on each side. Gravure printing cylinders printing 288 stamps per repeat (12 across, 24 around), all-stamp side; 192 stamps per repeat (8 across, 24 around), cover side, manufactured by Southern Graphics Systems.

Gum Type: self-adhesive

Overall Stamp Size: 0.91 by 1.19 inches; 23.11 by 30.22 mm

Pane Size: 7.5 by 1.823 inches; 190.5 by 46.3 mm

Perforations: 10¾ by 11 (die-cut simulated perforations) (Comco custom rotary die-cutter). Backing paper rouletted behind or through peel-off strips.

Selvage Markings: "© 2004 USPS" on one peel-off strip on all-stamp side, cylinder numbers on the other peel-off strip on all-stamp side

Back Markings: "Holiday Cookies/four different designs/Twenty/37¢/Self-adhesive/Stamps $7.40" and Universal Product Code (UPC) "0 674000 1" on booklet cover

Photographer: Sally Andersen-Bruce of New Milford, Connecticut

Designer, Art Director and Typographer: Derry Noyes of Washington, D.C.

Modeler: Donald H. Woo, Sennett Security Products

Stamp Manufacturing: Stamps printed for Sennett Security Products by American Packaging Corporation, Columbus, Wisconsin, on Rotomec 5 3000 gravure press. Stamps finished by Unique Binders of Fredericksburg, Virginia.

Quantity Ordered: 800,000,000 stamps

Cylinder Number Detail: 1 set of 4 cylinder numbers preceded by the letter S on 1 peel-off strip

Cylinder Number Combination Reported: S1111

Paper Supplier: Mactac

Tagging: phosphored paper with phosphor blocker on cover

37¢ HOLIDAY COOKIES (4 DESIGNS)
VENDING BOOKLET OF 20

Date of Issue: October 20, 2005

Catalog Numbers: Scott 3957-3960, stamps; 3960a, block of 4; 3960b, booklet pane of 4; 3960c, booklet pane of 6, 1 each 3959 and 3960, 2 each 3957 and 3958; 3960d, booklet pane of 6, 1 each 3957 and 3958, 2 each 3959 and 3960; BK299, complete booklet

Colors: magenta, yellow, cyan, blue (PMS 2728)

First-Day Cancel: Minneapolis, Minnesota, and New York, New York

First-Day Cancellations: 199,357 (includes all formats)

Format: Vending booklet of 20, vertical, arranged vertically, 2 across by 10 down, in 2 4-stamp segments (2 by 2) and 2 6-stamp segments (2 by 3). Gravure printing cylinders printing 480 stamps per repeat (20 across, 24 around) manufactured by Southern Graphics Systems.

Gum Type: self-adhesive

Overall Stamp Size: 0.8698 by 0.982 inches; 22.09 by 24.94 mm

Pane Size: 1.7396 by 10.375 inches; 44.18 by 263.52 mm

Perforations: 10½ by 10¾ (die-cut simulated perforations) (Comco custom rotary die cutter). Cover scored for folding.

Selvage Markings: none

Back Markings: "Holiday/Cookies/four different designs/Twenty 37¢/Self-adhesive/Stamps/$7.40" on front of cover. Promotion for Postal Store web site, USPS logo, "© 2004 USPS," cylinder numbers and Universal Product Code (UPC) "0 674100 0" on back cover and inside flaps.

Photographer: Sally Andersen-Bruce of New Milford, Connecticut

Designer, Art Director and Typographer: Derry Noyes of Washington, D.C.

Modeler: Donald H. Woo, Sennett Security Products

Stamp Manufacturing: Stamps printed for Sennett Security Products by American Packaging Corporation, Columbus, Wisconsin, on Rotomec 5 3000 gravure press. Stamps finished by Unique Binders of Fredericksburg, Virginia.

Quantity Ordered: 100,000,000 stamps

Cylinder Number Detail: 1 set of 4 cylinder numbers preceded by the letter S on inside flap

Cylinder Number Combination Reported: S1111

Paper Supplier: Mactac

Tagging: phosphored paper

The Stamps

On October 20, the Postal Service issued a block of four contemporary Christmas stamps, each featuring a photograph of a frosted Christmas cookie or cookies on a portion of a plate: a Santa Claus, two snowmen, an angel and two elves. In keeping with the Postal Service's concern for diversity, each of the pairs, snowmen and elves, consists of one sugar cookie and one gingerbread.

Dedication ceremonies were held for the stamps at the Mega-Event Stamp Show in New York City and the Minneapolis, Minnesota, international headquarters of General Mills, parent company of Pillsbury, a leading producer of cookie ingredients. Minneapolis was added as a first-day city in early August.

Sennett Security Products produced the self-adhesive stamps in three formats, using two printers, to create a total of 12 varieties. They are:

• A pane of 20, five across by four down (Scott 3949-3952). The same two designs alternate in every other horizontal row, so that any block or vertical strip of four contains all four designs. The stamps are in what USPS calls its special size, which is slightly larger than the definitive size and is used principally for Holiday and Love stamps. The pane has selvage at top, bottom and sides, and the stamps have die-cut simulated perforations all around, gauging 10¾ by 11. Banknote Corporation of America did the printing for Sennett Security Products, using the offset process. A total of 200 million stamps were ordered.

• A double-sided convertible booklet of 20, with 12 stamps on one side and eight stamps plus a non-stamp label that doubles as a booklet cover on the other side (Scott 3953-3956). The stamps are grouped in blocks of

four separated by vertical pull-off strips, and those on one side of the booklet are inverted relative to those on the other side. Like the stamps on the pane of 20, they are special size with die-cuts gauging 10¾ by 11, but they have straight edges at the top or bottom and six have straight edges on the left or right as well. American Packaging Corporation printed 800 million stamps for Sennett Security Products by the gravure process.

• A vending booklet of 20, with the stamps grouped in two blocks of four and two blocks of six separated by narrow spaces

where horizontal pull-off strips were removed during processing (Scott 3957-3960). The arrangement of varieties on the blocks of four is the same as on the convertible-booklet blocks. The stamps are definitive size. The design of each stamp has been altered somewhat from its larger counterpart on the pane or convertible booklet to fit the differently pro-portioned design area. The gauge of the simulated perfs is 10½ by 10¾. All 20 stamps have at least one straight edge. Again, American Packaging produced the stamps for Sennett on a gravure press. USPS ordered 100 million stamps.

As an ancillary product, Stamp Fulfillment Services offered a "personal holiday planner" consisting of a pane of 20 stamps, four oversized post-cards bearing images of the stamps and cookie recipes, a gift/to-do list booklet, gift tags and a kids' coloring ornament with ribbon, for $14.95.

Although the U.S. Post Office Department issued the first U.S. Christ-mas stamp in 1962, and one or more new stamps have appeared each Christmas season since then, the 2005 stamps are the first in the series to feature food. The 8¢ Christmas Tree in Needlepoint stamp of 1973 includes a gingerbread man on the tree (Scott 1508), but it is unclear whether it is a Christmas ornament or a large cookie.

The first Christmas cookies probably originated in the Middle Ages in Europe, although sweet baked goods, including cookies, were prepared for various celebrations in ancient times. The English word "cookie" is derived from the Dutch word "koekje," meaning "small cake." The Dutch are credited with introducing cookies to the United States.

The familiar Christmas cookie shapes became popular in the 1930s when cutters made of tin became less expensive.

The Designs

The project reunited photographer Sally Andersen-Bruce of New Mil-ford, Connecticut, and USPS art director Derry Noyes, a team that had been responsible for numerous stamp designs, most recently the four Holi-day Ornaments of 2004.

The subject was Noyes' idea — "Cookies seemed a natural when you're thinking of holidays," she said — but her original plan for the layout was lost in the execution. She had wanted a full photographed plate of cookies to be reproduced on each block of four, so that each stamp in the block would show a different quadrant of the plate. This would have worked even though the stamps were separated by white borders or the removable strips

267

Shown here is one of many varied plates of cookies shot by Sally Andersen-Bruce. None of these cookies was chosen for stamp honors.

that are used in booklets, because the eye would connect the plate across the borders. However, the printers failed to line up the stamps appropriately in any of the formats, including the pane of 20.

"You get the bottom half of the plate working on the pane, but the top half is shifted over, so it never makes the full circle to look like a plate of cookies, as I intended," Noyes said. "It ended up a hodgepodge.

"Once you separate the stamps and put them on envelopes, they're fine, though. Each shows its section of the plate. So it was successful, I guess."

As is her custom, Sally Andersen-Bruce did extensive research before taking her first photograph. "I consulted ladies' magazines, and I wrote to my mom and all the women I know in their 70s and 80s to ask what they considered a classic 1940s and 1950s Christmas cookie," she said.

From the varied inventory of Tommy Simpson of Washington, Connecticut, a well-known artist and decorative craftsman, Andersen-Bruce chose an angel cookie cutter. Using her grandmother's recipe for sugar cookies, she baked a batch of angels, which she and Simpson decorated, and photographed them for Derry Noyes' approval. She then commissioned Simpson to create cookie cutters in the Santa, snowman and elf shapes.

Using the four cutters, plus some others of a holiday nature, Andersen-Bruce embarked on a marathon of cookie baking and decorating, assisted by Simpson and two other experts whom she enlisted: Emily Diffrient-Crumpton of Austin, Texas, a caterer, and Rebecca Vermilyea of Bethlehem, Connecticut, a pastry chef who had majored in fine arts at college.

The quartet baked and decorated with glossy royal icing nearly one thousand cookies in an effort to get the look just right. When *New York Times* writer Stephen Sawicki visited Andersen-Bruce's home in 2002 to

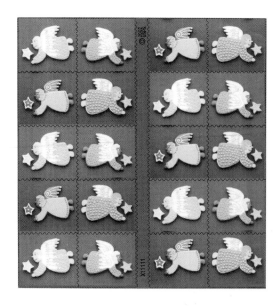

During design development, art director Derry Noyes created this alternative layout for a convertible booklet of 20 stamps featuring four different angel cookies flying solo.

interview her for an article about her previous stamp photographs, she had to keep him outside, she said, because "The stamp project was still confidential, and every surface of my house was covered with cookies."

Vermilyea told *The Times* of Litchfield County, Connecticut: "Sally had discussed with me that she wanted to get away from the typical Christmas colors, so I used traditional Christmas colors, but altered them just a few shades in either direction."

Three of the four stamp illustrations were cropped from this photograph of a plate of cookies. The angel at the upper right wasn't used, but was replaced by another angel with a different doily beneath her. A corner of the unused angel's robe can be seen on the Santa Claus stamp above Santa's head.

On the chance that USPS officials would want to issue picture postal cards to accompany the Christmas Cookies stamps, Sally Andersen-Bruce created this whimsical photo of a snack that had been set out for Santa Claus: a plate of cookies, a glass of milk and a child's note. One of the cookies is broken beside the plate, as if Santa had sampled it.

The decorated cookies were treated with a matte finish so they would hold up under the bright lights in Andersen-Bruce's studio. Using her view camera and shooting down from a six-foot stepladder, she photographed a wide variety of combinations of cookies, doily patterns and plate colors.

In the end, Derry Noyes extracted three of the stamp designs from one photographed plate. These were:

• The elves on the upper left quadrant of the plate. The sugar-cookie elf was baked and decorated by Emily Diffrient-Crumpton; the gingerbread elf by Tommy Simpson.

• The snowmen and partial Christmas tree on the lower left quadrant. The sugar-cookie snowman is credited to Simpson and the gingerbread, with buttons fashioned from the tops of cloves, to Rebecca Vermilyea. Vermilyea also made the tree.

• The Santa on the lower right quadrant, made by Diffrient-Crumpton.

The fourth design, the angel, came from the upper right quadrant of another plateful of cookies, with a different doily pattern beneath it. Baked by Vermilyea, the figure wears a turquoise robe decorated with little silver balls that bakers call dragees (pronounced drah-jays). Dragees of silver, red and blue also adorn the Christmas tree cookie, while gold ones form the buttons of the sugar-cookie elf.

In the past, USPS sometimes issued a set of picture postal cards to accompany its contemporary Christmas stamps. It wasn't done this time, but on the chance that officials would want to do so, Andersen-Bruce created a whimsical photo of a snack set out for Santa Claus: a plate of cookies, a glass of milk and a note beginning, "Dear Santa, I have been very good this year." One of the cookies is on the table, broken, as if Santa had sampled it.

The photographer saved the original stamp cookies on their plates and doilies — "I never threw them out in case there was a slight concept change and they needed to be re-shot," she said — and eventually turned the aging pastry over to the Postal Service. Its fate is unknown. For the first-day ceremony in Minneapolis, Rebecca Vermilyea baked and decorated five sets of duplicates. "They were on the morning TV talk shows there," Andersen-Bruce said. "The anchorwoman would take a bite and say, 'Mmm, these are delicious.'"

Stamps from the pane of 20 and from the convertible booklet of 20 can be told apart by the presence of straight edges in the latter format. There are other differences, as well, leading the Scott Publishing Company to assign different major catalog numbers to stamps from the two formats.

The offset-printed stamps from the pane are noticeably darker and clearer than the gravure-printed convertible-booklet stamps. The "2005" year date on the pane stamps is slightly smaller than on stamps from the convertible booklet. In addition, the cropping of photographs was detectably different, which allowed more of certain cookies to be visible on stamps from the convertible booklet than on stamps from the pane.

Stamps from the vending booklet are distinguishable at a glance from stamps from the other two formats by their smaller, definitive size. Because the relative proportions of a definitive stamp differ from those of a special stamp, Derry Noyes had to crop the photographs more tightly at the top and bottom for the vending booklet to show the cookies in their entirety, and place the "USA" vertically instead of horizontally, as it is on the larger stamps.

The typography is a font called Fago. The "37" on each stamp duplicates a color used prominently in one of the cookies shown on it.

First-Day Facts

Anita Bizzotto, chief marketing officer and executive vice president of USPS, dedicated the stamps at a ceremony under a large open-air tent on the north lawn of General Mills headquarters.

Peter Robinson, president of General Mills' Pillsbury USA Division, welcomed the audience. Belinda Jensen, a meteorologist at KARE-11 TV, was master of ceremonies. Honored guests included Sally Andersen-Bruce, the stamp photographer, and cookie makers Rebecca Vermilyea and Emily Diffrient-Crumpton. Vonzell Solomon, a former letter carrier and a 2005 finalist on the *American Idol* television program, sang Mariah

Carey's *All I Want for Christmas is You*. The well-known Pillsbury Dough-boy was a participant, as well.

William T. Johnstone, secretary of the USPS Board of Governors, was the dedicating official at the Mega-Event Stamp Show in the Expo Center of New York's Madison Square Garden. Also taking part were the American Stamp Dealers Association's Eric Jackson, president, and Joseph B. Savarese, executive vice president, and Janet Klug, president of the American Philatelic Society.

For a limited time, Stamp Fulfillment Services offered uncacheted first-day covers of stamps from the pane of 20 and the convertible booklet of 20. Covers with conventional black cancellations featuring a line drawing of the angel cookie were sold for $1.50 per set of four from Minneapolis or New York. Covers with digital color cancellations were priced at $1.50 for a random single and $6 for a set of four from either first-day city.

37¢ FLAG COIL, 2005 YEAR DATE

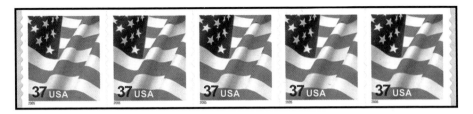

Date of Issue: June 2005

Catalog Number: Scott 3633B

Colors: black, cyan, magenta, yellow

First-Day Cancel: none

Format: Coil of 100, vertical. Offset printing plates printing 744 stamps per revolution (24 across by 31 around).

Gum Type: self-adhesive

Microprinting: "USA" at bottom of top red stripe on flag

Overall Stamp Size: 0.87096 by 0.98 inches; 22.1223 by 24.892 mm

Perforations: 9½ (die-cut simulated perforations)

Designer, Art Director and Typographer: Terrence McCaffrey, USPS

Photograph: from Pictor International

Modeler: Joseph Sheeran of Ashton-Potter (USA) Ltd., Williamsville, New York

Stamp Manufacturing: Stamps printed by Ashton-Potter on Mueller Martini A76 17-inch offset press. Stamps processed by Ashton-Potter.

Quantity Ordered: 500,000,000 stamps

Plate Number Detail: 1 set of 4 plate numbers preceded by the letter P on every 31st stamp

Plate Number Combination Reported: P1111

Paper Supplier: Paper Corporation of the United States/Glatfelter

Tagging: phosphored paper

The Stamps

Sometime in June 2005, the Postal Service issued its 21st and final stamp or format variety using the familiar American Flag design that made its debut in 2002. It is the only variety to bear a 2005 year date. All 21 stamps have a postage value of 37¢, although the first seven were printed without denominations.

The stamp — placed on sale without announcement or first-day cancellations — is self-adhesive and was distributed in coils of 100. Produced by the offset process by Ashton-Potter (USA) Ltd., it was the first Flag coil to be printed by that company, which previously had made Flag stamps in booklet and pane formats.

Ashton-Potter printed 500 million stamps for USPS, not 5 million, which was the quantity announced by the Postal Service and reported in the philatelic press. The error was due to a misreading of "5 million coils" on the Design and Production Sheet provided by the company. Ashton-Potter confirmed for *The Yearbook* that the correct total was 500 million.

The Design

In the design common to all varieties of the Flag stamp, the frame is filled by a portion of a waving American flag, from an unattributed photograph. A corner of the starry blue field occupies the upper-left quadrant, and seven red-and-white stripes, crossed diagonally by two dramatic ripples, occupy the rest of the space. The typography — "37," in black, and "USA," in dropout white — is at the bottom.

The stamp can be distinguished from other denominated Flag coil stamps by the 2005 year date and the presence of microprinting, which is used on offset-printed stamps as a security feature. The letters "USA," in black, can be found near the bottom of the topmost red stripe on the flag.

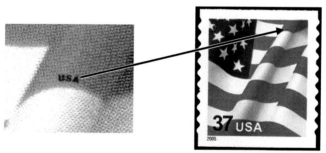

The microprinting on the 2005 Flag coil variety consists of the letters "USA" at the bottom of the topmost red stripe on the flag.

First-Day Facts

The Postal Service held no first-day ceremony and provided no first-day cancellation for the stamp, and Stamp Fulfillment Services offered no prepared first-day covers. In 2003, writer-dealer Stephen G. Esrati quoted David Failor, director of Stamp Services for USPS, as saying: "If there is a change in the design, the denomination or the format [of a stamp], there will be a first-day-of-issue cancellation and possibly a ceremony. If it is simply a reprint with a different printer, there will not be a first-day ceremony or postmark." In this case, USPS did not consider a change in the year date to be a design change.

5¢ SILVER COFFEEPOT COIL
AMERICAN DESIGN SERIES

Date of Issue: September 16, 2005

Catalog Number: Scott 3759

Colors: light maroon (PMS 194), silver (PMS 877), black, dark maroon (PMS 195)

First-Day Cancel: Milwaukee, Wisconsin

First-Day Cancellations: 10,848

Format: coil of 10,000, vertical, gravure printing cylinders of 616 (22 across by 28 around) manufactured by Southern Graphics systems

Gum Type: water-activated

Overall Stamp Size: 0.87 by 0.96 inches; 22.09 by 24.38 mm

Perforations: 9¾ (APS rotary perforator)

Illustrator: Tania Lee of Washington, D.C.

Designer, Art Director and Typographer: Derry Noyes of Washington, D.C.

Modeler: Donald Woo of Sennett Security Products, Chantilly, Virginia

Stamp Manufacturing: Stamps printed for Sennett Security Products by American Packaging Corporation, Columbus, Wisconsin, on Rotomec 3000 gravure press. Stamps processed by Unique Binders, Fredericksburg, Virginia.

Quantity Ordered: 210,000,000

Cylinder Number Detail: 1 4-digit cylinder number preceded by the letter S on every 14th stamp

Cylinder Number Combination Reported: S1111

Counting Number Detail: 1 5-digit counting number in magenta on back of every 10th stamp

Paper Supplier: Tullis Russell

Tagging: untagged

The Stamp

On September 16, at the MILCOPEX Stamp Show in Milwaukee, Wisconsin, the Postal Service issued a 3¢ coil stamp in the American Design definitive series depicting an 18th-century American silver coffeepot with a carved wood handle.

The stamp has water-activated gum and conventional perforations. It was printed by the gravure process by American Packaging Corporation for Sennett Security Products and distributed in rolls of 10,000.

The American Design series ranges in denomination from 1¢ to 10¢ and features distinguished examples of the utilitarian art of the United States in tightly cropped images. It was inaugurated in 2002 with a 5¢ coil stamp picturing a toleware coffeepot.

The Silver Coffeepot stamp was the sixth face-different stamp in the series and the seventh overall. The first five, all featuring antique artifacts, were illustrated with paintings done in the early 1990s by veteran stamp artist Lou Nolan of McLean, Virginia. Because Nolan no longer was available for stamp work, Derry Noyes, who conceived the series and is its art director, used a painting by artist Tania Lee of Washington, D.C., for the new stamp.

The idea behind American Design was "to get up into more modern designs," Noyes said, "but we're still stuck in history. The series has to last long enough, and contain more issues, for anyone to see where it's heading."

The problem with limiting the series to low-value stamps, she continued, is that "you plunk them next to something else, and they never connect. You use a Navajo Necklace [a 2¢ stamp American Design stamp issued in 2004] next to a Christmas Cookie [a 37¢ stamp of 2005] to make up the first-class rate, and you wonder, what are they doing together?"

Consequently, she said, the Citizens' Stamp Advisory Committee "is trying to figure out how to design these low-denomination stamps so they look as if they always belong with something. We're rethinking what we're doing here.

"Originally, the American Design series wasn't supposed to be low-denomination. They just got slotted into playing that role because the Postal Service had a need. I [originally] thought they would all be first-class-rate stamps."

The 3¢ Silver Coffeepot was meant to replace the 3¢ Star coil (Scott 3615) that was issued in 2002 as a makeup-rate stamp when the first-class rate rose from 34¢ to 37¢. Since the most recent rate increase of January 8, 2006, the Star has been available to make up the 3¢ difference between the old two-ounce first-class rate of 60¢ and the new one of 63¢.

The coffeepot shown on the stamp was made by Philadelphia silversmiths Joseph Richardson Jr. (1752-1831) and Nathaniel Richardson (1754-1827), two brothers who came from a long line of noted silversmiths and worked as partners from 1777 to 1790. It may have been presented to

Margaret Rawle on the occasion of her marriage to Isaac Wharton in 1786, a marriage that linked two prominent Philadelphia families. Margaret Rawle's initials are engraved on the body of the coffeepot but don't appear in the simplified painting on the stamp. The Philadelphia Museum of Art acquired the coffeepot in 1986.

"The elaboration of social life and the enormous popularity of tea, coffee and chocolate in the late 17th and 18th centuries contributed to the demand for household silver," the Postal Service said. "Each major American city boasted its own famous silversmiths who crafted made-to-order household utensils that were beautiful as well as useful, proudly proclaimed the wealth and social status of the owners, and served also as a means of storing savings in the days before banks."

The Design

Tania Lee is a free-lance illustrator whose projects include art for books and advertising as well as individual private commissions, including creating hand-painted invitations. Her corporate clients have included the American Red Cross, Bergdorf Goodman, Hearst Books and Thornwillow Press.

In an interview with Jay Bigalke of *Linn's Stamp News*, Lee recounted how Derry Noyes approached her to illustrate an American Design stamp in the style of Lou Nolan. "She reviewed my portfolio and asked me to choose an area of American design, historic or contemporary, that inspired me," Lee said. "I chose early American silver …

"What was serendipitous about this stamp commission was that I was trained as an art historian, with a focus on 18th- and 19th-century American art and decorative arts. This project brought me back around to a field I've loved, but in which I hadn't worked in some time.

"The research involved in finding just the right object to depict was like a treasure hunt … The challenge was not in selecting an object that would fit within the guidelines of the series — there are plenty of fine pieces of early American silver out there. Rather, it took a great deal of research to find the piece with proportions that would work best within the confines of the definitive postage stamp dimensions.

"Early on, Noyes and I realized that a coffeepot, which is tall and pear-shaped, would work better than a teapot, which is typically round and apple-shaped. Then it was a matter of finding the best example of its kind without much extraneous detail. This piece … is arguably that: an elegant vessel of exquisite craftsmanship and clean, classical lines, whose form is clearly readable even when cropped down to just a fraction of its whole."

Lee made extensive preliminary sketches of the coffeepot at the Philadelphia Museum of Art. The actual painting, she said, was "a good technical challenge, making a complex reflective object from black and white pigments." When she began that phase of the job, with watercolor and gouache on slightly textured paper, she used a small silver pitcher as a model to better understand how the reflections worked.

"The first painting I submitted was deemed too detailed to reproduce well at stamp size," she said. "So, back at the drawing board, I simplified the highlights and shadows significantly and eliminated certain details, such as the coffeepot's elaborately engraved monogram. The final painting is far bolder and stands out much better in its tiny format."

Lee painted the coffeepot against a pink background that Noyes converted to maroon. The border of the stamp is a darker shade of maroon. Black ink was used to print the coffeepot itself, with its reflections created by dot patterns of various sizes. As is standard with the American Design series, the descriptive words, in this case "Silver Coffeepot," are in Garamond type and run up the left side. "USA" and "3c" are in the upper left corner. The denomination is printed in metallic silver ink.

The artist also submitted a painting of an altogether different type of artifact, a highboy (a tall chest of drawers with a legged base). "It's in the bank for future use if the series carries on," Noyes said.

First-Day Facts

David E. Failor of USPS, executive director, Stamp Services, dedicated the stamps in a ceremony at the Four Points Sheraton in Milwaukee.

Robert J. Mather, MILCOPEX show chairman, was a speaker. Tania Lee gave a slide lecture on the process of illustrating the stamp, and Joan Houlehen, art consultant and partner of A. Houberbocken Inc., showed a selection of her antique silver coffeepots. Kimberly J. Peters, postmaster of Milwaukee, was master of ceremonies. David F. Martin, USPS district manager for the Lakeland Performance Cluster, was an honored guest.

For the occasion, the Sheraton ballroom was turned into what the Postal Service called "an upscale coffee house," with guests seated at cafe tables draped in white linen while waiters in black-tie attire served gourmet coffee in silver coffeepots. Musical selections included, appropriately, *Black Coffee* and *Java Jive*.

Stamp Fulfillment Services offered uncacheted first-day covers bearing the Silver Coffeepot stamp along with first-class postage for 78¢.

2¢ NAVAJO JEWELRY (SENNETT)
AMERICAN DESIGN SERIES

Date of Issue: December 8, 2005

Catalog Number: Scott 3749A

Colors: magenta, yellow, cyan, black, light blue (PMS 636), dark blue (PMS 309)

First-Day Cancel: Washington, D.C.

First-Day Cancellations: 52,035 (includes Ashton-Potter version of Navajo jewelry stamp and all versions of nondenominated Lady Liberty and Flag stamps).

Format: pane of 20, vertical, 5 across, 4 down. Gravure printing cylinders printing 240 stamps per revolution (15 across, 16 around) manufactured by Southern Graphics Systems.

Gum Type: self-adhesive

Overall Stamp Size: 0.87 by 0.98 inches; 22.09 by 24.89 mm

Pane Size: 5.38 by 4.969 inches; 136.65 by 126.21 mm

Perforations: 11¼ by 11½ (die-cut simulated perforations) (APS custom rotary die cutter)

Selvage Markings: "©2004/USPS." ".02/x20/$0.40." "PLATE/POSITION" and diagram.

Back Markings: Universal Product Code (UPC) "107200" in 4 locations on back of liner paper

Illustrator: Lou Nolan of McLean, Virginia

Designer, Art Director and Typographer: Derry Noyes of Washington, D.C.

Modeler: Donald Woo of Sennett Security Products, Chantilly, Virginia

Stamp Manufacturing: Stamps printed by American Packaging Corporation, Columbus, Wisconsin, for Sennett Security Products on Champlain 853 gravure press. Stamps processed by Unique Binders, Fredericksburg, Virginia.

Quantity Ordered: 750,000,000 stamps

Cylinder Number Detail: 1 set of 6 cylinder numbers preceded by the letter S in selvage above or below each corner stamp.

Cylinder Number Combination Reported: S111111

Paper Supplier: Mactac

Tagging: untagged

2¢ NAVAJO JEWELRY (ASHTON-POTTER)
AMERICAN DESIGN SERIES

Date of Issue: December 8, 2005

Catalog Number: Scott 3749B

Colors: black, cyan, magenta, yellow, blue (PMS 636)

First-Day Cancel: Washington, D.C.

First-Day Cancellations: 52,035 (includes Sennett version of Navajo jewelry stamp and all versions of nondenominated Lady Liberty and Flag stamps).

Format: pane of 20, vertical, 5 across, 4 down. Offset printing plates printing 240 stamps per revolution (15 across, 16 around).

Microprinting: "USPS" on top silver appendage next to and below the middle turquoise stone on right side of necklace

Gum Type: self-adhesive

Overall Stamp Size: 0.87 by 0.98 inches; 22.098 by 24.892 mm

Pane Size: 5.35 by 4.93 inches; 135.89 by 125.222 mm

Perforations: 11¼ by 11 (die-cut simulated perforations) (IDC two-station die cutter)

Selvage Markings: "©2004/USPS." ".02/x20/$0.40." "PLATE/POSITION" and diagram.

Back Markings: Universal Product Code (UPC) "107200" in 4 locations on back of liner paper

Illustrator: Lou Nolan of McLean, Virginia

Designer, Art Director and Typographer: Derry Noyes of Washington, D.C.

Modeler: Joseph Sheeran of Ashton-Potter (USA) Ltd., Williamsville, New York

Stamp Manufacturing: Stamps printed by Ashton-Potter on Stevens Variable Size Security offset press. Stamps processed by Ashton-Potter.

Quantity Ordered: 750,000,000 stamps

Plate Number Detail: 1 set of 5 plate numbers preceded by the letter P in selvage above or below each corner stamp.

Plate Number Combination Reported: P11111

Paper Supplier: Paper Corporation of the United States/Spinnaker Coatings

Tagging: untagged

The Stamps

In December 2005, the Postal Service issued two new varieties of the 2¢ Navajo Jewelry definitive stamp in the American Design series. The stamps were created by two different printers and were ordered in anticipation of postal customers' need for 2¢ stamps after January 8, 2006, when the first-class rate would rise from 37¢ to 39¢.

No first-day ceremony was held. Belatedly, the Postal Service assigned the stamps a date of issue of December 8, the same issue date for several varieties of nondenominated (39¢) Lady Liberty definitive stamps. First-day postmarks dated December 8 from Washington, D.C., were provided for the Navajo Jewelry stamps (see below).

In the past, nondenominated makeup-rate stamps have been issued prior to increases in the first-class rate to enable customers to make use of their existing supplies of first-class stamps. USPS didn't do that this time, preferring to order additional quantities of the low-value American Design definitives. Officials said they had enough of these stamps in place to avoid problems.

When the rate change took place, however, spot shortages occurred in post offices in New Jersey, Rhode Island, Ohio, New Mexico and Pennsylvania, according to newspaper reports.

"From what I've learned, many customers asked to buy a few dollars' worth of the 2¢ stamps," USPS spokesman Mark R. Saunders told *Linn's Stamp News*. "As the 2¢ stamps come in sheets of 20, that's 40¢ a sheet, so a $3 purchase equates to more than seven sheets. It was kind of like the hurricane syndrome. People see a storm coming and stock up."

The original Navajo Jewelry variety (Scott 3749) was issued August 20, 2004. A self-adhesive, it was printed by the gravure process by Avery Dennison Security Printing Division and distributed in panes of 20. It bears a 2004 year date.

The two new varieties, also self-adhesives in panes of 20, were printed by American Packaging Corporation for Sennett Security Products (Scott 3748A) and Ashton-Potter (USA) Ltd. (Scott 3749B). Curiously, both carry a 2006 year date. The Sennett stamp was gravure-printed, while the Ashton-Potter stamp was produced by offset lithography. USPS ordered 750 million stamps from each printer.

The Sennett stamp exists with two kinds of die-cut simulated perforation teeth. On one, the die cuts at the top of the stamp start with a peak and end with a valley; on the other, the die cuts start with a valley and end

282

Two die-cut variations exist on the Sennett version of the 2¢ Navajo Necklace stamp. The stamp on the left has peak/valley die cuts at the top; the one on the right has valley/peak die cuts.

with a peak (see illustration). Because the gauge is the same on both, the Scott catalog numbers are the same.

The Design

The new varieties of the Navajo Jewelry stamp display the same design as the 2004 prototype. It is based on artist Lou Nolan's painting of the naja pendant of a Navajo necklace and 14 silver squash blossom beads set with polished blue turquoise nuggets. Derry Noyes, who conceived the American Design series and is its art director, cropped the illustration to focus on the pendant and three beads on each side.

The two new stamps can be distinguished from the original by their 2006 year dates. They are visually distinguishable from each other in three ways.

The Sennett version bears a large year date, dropped out of the dark blue border, and has no microprinting. The Ashton-Potter stamp has a smaller year date and, because it was printed by offset, which the Postal Service considers a less secure method than gravure or intaglio, its design includes microprinting as a security measure. The letters "USPS," in black, can be found on the top silver appendage next to and below the middle turquoise stone on the right side of the necklace.

The six turquoise stones on the Ashton-Potter stamp are outlined in black. Black outlines are not present on the Sennett stamp.

First-Day Facts

Although no first-day ceremony was held for the two new Navajo Necklace stamps, Washington, D.C., postmarks dated December 8 were provided for them.

The announcement that the postmarks would be available followed a period of some confusion. The December 8, 2005, *Postal Bulletin*, the internal publication of USPS, indicated that collectors could mail in

Shown here are the two new 2¢ Navajo Necklace stamps, with close-ups of their differences. The Sennett version (Scott 3749A), with its larger 2006 year date, is shown at left, and the Ashton-Potter stamp (Scott 3749B), with its microprinted letters "USPS" on the top silver appendage, is at right. The turquoise stones on the Ashton-Potter stamp are outlined in black.

requests for first-day postmarks for the new stamps. However, *Linn's Stamp News* made a follow-up call to USPS December 8 and was told that covers wouldn't receive the first-day postmarks. The *Postal Bulletin* for January 5, 2006, carried a correction stating: "The section How to Order First Day Covers does not apply to this stamp issue."

A correction to the correction was published in the February 2, 2006, *Postal Bulletin*, stating that collectors could order uncacheted first-day covers from USPS, but it gave no item numbers and didn't indicate whether an extension would be granted for covers mailed in.

Meanwhile, on January 27, Stamp Fulfillment Services sent an e-mail to philatelic journalists announcing that the two Navajo Necklace stamps would receive December 8, 2005, first-day postmarks and that collectors would have a 90-day grace period, until March 8, 2006, to send their covers or cards to the Washington postmaster for the cancellations.

Stamp Fulfillment Services sold uncacheted first-day covers bearing one of the stamps plus additional postage to cover the first-class rate for 79¢.

Linn's asked USPS for a clarification of what stamps would receive first-day postmarks. This response was received:

"We have a first-day postmark for reprints [new stamps] under the following conditions:

"1. A change to the image (that is, a holiday stamp with new denomination);

"2. A change in the format (that is, we had been printing a stamp in booklet form, now we add a coil version);

"3. We use a different printer (that is, these new Navajo necklace stamps).

"We have been trying to stay consistent with this policy for the past three years."

Linn's made this comment:

"In the past, the third condition had not been a factor when assigning a first-day postmark. If this criterion for a first-day postmark is being followed, then the Ashton-Potter version of the 37¢ Flag stamp in a coil of 100 and the Sennett Security Products 60¢ Acadia stamp, both with '2005' year dates, should have received first-day postmarks. They did not."

NONDENOMINATED (39¢) LADY LIBERTY AND FLAG PANE OF 100, WATER-ACTIVATED GUM

Date of Issue: December 8, 2005

Catalog Number: Scott 3965

Colors: black, cyan, magenta, yellow

First-Day Cancel: Washington, D.C.

First-Day Cancellations: 52,035 (includes all rate-change items issued December 8)

Format: Pane of 100 stamps, vertical, 10 across, 10 down. Offset printing plates printing 400 subjects per revolution (20 across, 20 around).

Microprinting: "USPS" at top of top red stripe of flag

Gum Type: water-activated

Overall Stamp Size: 0.84 by 0.99 inches; 21.336 by 25.146 mm

Pane Size: 9 by 10.18 inches; 228.6 by 258.57 mm

Perforations: 11¼

Selvage Markings: "©2005 USPS." "PLATE/POSITION" and diagram. Universal Product Code (UPC) "108500."

Designer, Art Director and Typographer: Terrence McCaffrey, USPS

Photographers: Carl and Ann Purcell of Alexandria, Virginia

Modeler: Joseph Sheeran of Ashton-Potter (USA) Ltd., Williamsville, New York

Stamp Manufacturing: Stamps printed by Sterling Sommer Inc., Tonawanda, New York, for Ashton-Potter on Heidelberg 840 offset press. Stamps processed by Ashton-Potter.

Quantity Ordered: 35,000,000

Plate Number Detail: 1 set of 4 plate numbers preceded by the letter P in selvage next to 1 corner stamp

Plate Number Combination Reported: P1111

Paper Supplier: Tullis Russell

Tagging: nonphosphored paper, overall tagging

NONDENOMINATED (39¢) LADY LIBERTY AND FLAG PANE OF 20, SELF-ADHESIVE

Date of Issue: December 8, 2005

Catalog Number: Scott 3966

Colors: black, cyan, magenta, yellow

First-Day Cancel: Washington, D.C.

First-Day Cancellations: 52,035 (includes all rate-change items issued December 8)

Format: Pane of 20 stamps, vertical, 5 across, 4 down. Offset printing plates printing 240 subjects per revolution (15 across, 16 around).

Microprinting: "USPS" at top of top red stripe of flag

Gum Type: self-adhesive

Overall Stamp Size: 0.87 by 0.98 inches; 22.098 by 24.892 mm

Pane Size: 4.93 by 5.35 inches; 125.222 by 135.89 mm

Perforations: 11¼ by 11 (die-cut simulated perforations) (IDC 22-inch two-station die cutter)

Selvage Markings: "© 2005/USPS". "PLATE/POSITION" and diagram.

Back Markings: Universal Product Code (UPC) "567700" in 4 locations

Designer, Art Director and Typographer: Terrence McCaffrey, USPS

Photographers: Carl and Ann Purcell of Alexandria, Virginia

Modeler: Joseph Sheeran of Ashton-Potter (USA) Ltd., Williamsville, New York

Stamp Manufacturing: Stamps printed by Ashton-Potter on Stevens Vari-size Security offset press. Stamps processed by Ashton-Potter.

Quantity Ordered: 400,000,000

Plate Number Detail: 1 set of 4 plate numbers preceded by the letter P in selvage above or below each corner stamp

Plate Number Combination Reported: P1111

Paper Supplier: Paper Corporation of the United States/Glatfelter

Tagging: phosphored paper

NONDENOMINATED (39¢) LADY LIBERTY AND FLAG COIL OF 3,000, WATER-ACTIVATED GUM

Date of Issue: December 8, 2005

Catalog Number: Scott 3967

Colors: magenta, yellow, cyan, black

First-Day Cancel: Washington, D.C.

First-Day Cancellations: 52,035 (includes all rate-change items issued December 8)

Format: Coil of 3,000, vertical. Gravure printing cylinders printing 308 subjects per revolution (11 across, 28 around), manufactured by Southern Graphics Systems.

Gum Type: self-adhesive

Overall Stamp Size: 0.87 by 0.96 inches; 22.09 by 24.38 mm

Perforations: 9¾ (die-cut simulated perforations) (APS rotary die cutter)

Designer, Art Director and Typographer: Terrence McCaffrey, USPS

Photographers: Carl and Ann Purcell of Alexandria, Virginia

Modeler: Donald H. Woo of Sennett Security Products, Chantilly, Virginia

Stamp Manufacturing: Stamps printed by American Packaging Corporation, Columbus, Wisconsin, for Sennett Security Products on Cerutti 950 gravure press. Stamps processed by Unique Binders, Fredericksburg, Virginia.

Quantity Ordered: 300,000,000

Cylinder Number Detail: 1 set of 4 cylinder numbers preceded by the letter S on every 14th stamp

Cylinder Number Combination Reported: S1111

Counting Number Detail: 4-digit magenta counting number on back of every 10th stamp

Paper Supplier: Tullis Russell

Tagging: phosphored paper

NONDENOMINATED (39¢) LADY LIBERTY AND FLAG COIL OF 100, SELF-ADHESIVE, AVERY-DENNISON

Date of Issue: December 8, 2005

Catalog Number: Scott 3968

Colors: yellow, magenta, cyan, black

First-Day Cancel: Washington, D.C.

First-Day Cancellations: 52,035 (includes all rate-change items issued December 8)

Format: Coil of 100, vertical. Gravure printing cylinders printing 396 subjects per revolution (12 across, 33 around), manufactured by WRE/ColorTech.

Gum Type: self-adhesive

Overall Stamp Size: 0.87 by 0.982 inches; 22.098 by 24.9428 mm

Perforations: 8½ (die-cut simulated perforations) (Comco Commander rotary die cutter)

Designer, Art Director and Typographer: Terrence McCaffrey, USPS

Photographers: Carl and Ann Purcell of Alexandria, Virginia

Stamp Manufacturing: Stamps printed by Avery Dennison Security Products Division, Clinton, South Carolina, on Dia Nippon Kiko 8-station gravure press. Stamps processed by Avery Dennison.

Quantity Ordered: 1,500,000,000

Cylinder Number Detail: 1 set of 4 cylinder numbers preceded by the letter V on every 11th stamp

Cylinder Number Combination Reported: V1111

Paper Supplier: Fasson Division of Avery Dennison

Tagging: phosphored paper

NONDENOMINATED (39¢) LADY LIBERTY AND FLAG COIL OF 100, SELF-ADHESIVE, SENNETT

Date of Issue: December 8, 2005

Catalog Number: Scott 3969

Colors: magenta, yellow, cyan, black

First-Day Cancel: Washington, D.C.

First-Day Cancellations: 52,035 (includes all rate-change items issued December 8)

Format: Coil of 100, vertical. Gravure printing cylinders printing 1,092 subjects per revolution (39 across, 28 around), manufactured by Southern Graphics Systems.

Gum Type: self-adhesive

Overall Stamp Size: 0.87 by 0.96 inches; 22.10 by 24.38 mm

Perforations: 10¼ (die-cut simulated perforations) (Comco custom rotary die cutter)

Designer, Art Director and Typographer: Terrence McCaffrey, USPS

Photographers: Carl and Ann Purcell of Alexandria, Virginia

Modeler: Donald H. Woo of Sennett Security Products, Chantilly, Virginia

Stamp Manufacturing: Stamps printed by American Packaging Corporation, Columbus, Wisconsin, for Sennett Security Products on Cerutti 950 gravure press. Stamps processed by Unique Binders, Fredericksburg, Virginia.

Quantity Ordered: 1,500,000,000

Cylinder Number Detail: 1 set of 4 cylinder numbers preceded by the letter S on every 14th stamp

Cylinder Number Combination Reported: S1111

Paper Supplier: Mactac

Tagging: phosphored paper

NONDENOMINATED (39¢) LADY LIBERTY AND FLAG COIL OF 100, SELF-ADHESIVE, ASHTON-POTTER

Date of Issue: December 8, 2005

Catalog Number: Scott 3970

Colors: black, cyan, magenta, yellow

First-Day Cancel: Washington, D.C.

First-Day Cancellations: 52,035 (includes all rate-change items issued December 8)

Format: Coil of 100, vertical. Offset printing plates printing 744 subjects per revolution (24 across, 31 around).

Microprinting: "USPS" at top of top red stripe of flag

Gum Type: self-adhesive

Overall Stamp Size: 0.87096 by 0.98 inches; 22.1223 by 24.892 mm

Perforations: 9½ (die-cut simulated perforations) (Ashton-Potter die cutter)

Designer, Art Director and Typographer: Terrence McCaffrey, USPS

Photographers: Carl and Ann Purcell of Alexandria, Virginia

Modeler: Joseph Sheeran of Ashton-Potter (USA) Ltd., Williamsville, New York

Stamp Manufacturing: Stamps printed by Ashton-Potter on Mueller Martini A76 27-inch offset press. Stamps finished by Ashton-Potter.

Quantity Ordered: 500,000,000

Plate Number Detail: 1 set of 4 plate numbers preceded by the letter P on every 31st stamp

Plate Number Combinations Reported: P1111, P2222

Paper Supplier: Paper Corporation of the United States/Glatfelter

Tagging: phosphored paper

NONDENOMINATED (39¢) LADY LIBERTY AND FLAG CONVERTIBLE BOOKLET OF 20, ASHTON-POTTER

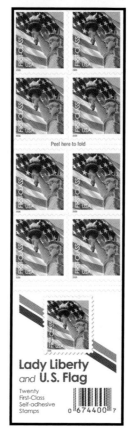

Date of Issue: December 8, 2005

Catalog Number: Scott 3966, single stamp; 3966a, convertible booklet of 20

Colors: black, cyan, magenta, yellow

First-Day Cancel: Washington, D.C.

First-Day Cancellations: 52,035 (includes all rate-change items issued December 8)

Format: Convertible booklet of 20, vertical. Stamps on both sides, arranged vertically, 8 (2 across by 4 down) plus label (booklet cover) on one side, 12 (2 across by 6 down) on other side, with horizontal peel-off strips between blocks of 4 on each side. Stamps on one side are upside down relative to stamps on the other side. Offset printing plates printing 1,200 subjects per revolution.

Microprinting: "USPS" at top of top red stripe of flag

Gum Type: self-adhesive

Overall Stamp Size: 0.87 by 0.98 inches; 22.098 by 24.892 mm

Booklet Size: 1.74 by 6.18 inches; 44.196 by 156.972 mm.

Perforations: 11¼ by 11 (die-cut simulated perforations) (IDC custom rotary die cutter)

Selvage Markings: on peel-off strips: "© 2005 USPS" "Peel here to fold" and plate numbers

Cover Markings: "Lady Liberty/and U.S. Flag/Twenty/First-Class/Self-adhesive/Stamps." Universal Product Code (UPC) "0 674400 7."

Designer, Art Director and Typographer: Terrence McCaffrey, USPS

Photographers: Carl and Ann Purcell of Alexandria, Virginia

Modeler: Joseph Sheeran of Ashton-Potter (USA) Ltd., Williamsville, New York

Stamp Manufacturing: Stamps printed by Ashton-Potter on Mueller Martini A76 offset press. Stamps finished by Ashton-Potter.

Quantity Ordered: 1,500,000,000 stamps

Plate Number Detail: 1 set of 4 plate numbers preceded by the letter P on 1 peel-off strip

Plate Number Combination Reported: P1111

Paper Supplier: Flexcon/Glatfelter

Tagging: phosphored paper

NONDENOMINATED (39¢) LADY LIBERTY AND FLAG CONVERTIBLE BOOKLET OF 20, AVERY-DENNISON

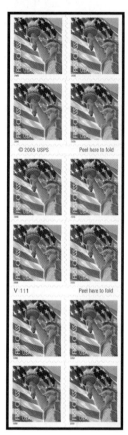

Date of Issue: December 8, 2005

Catalog Number: Scott 3972, single stamp; 3972a, convertible booklet of 20

Colors: yellow, magenta, cyan, black, stamps; same plus blue (PMS 294), label

First-Day Cancel: Washington, D.C.

First-Day Cancellations: 52,035 (includes all rate-change items issued December 8)

Format: Convertible booklet of 20, vertical. Stamps on both sides, arranged vertically, 8 (2 across by 4 down) plus label (booklet cover) on one side, 12 (2 across by 6 down) on other side, with horizontal peel-off strips between blocks of 4 on each side. Gravure printing cylinders printing 40 booklets in each press sheet (8 booklets across, 5 booklets around).

Gum Type: self-adhesive

Overall Stamp Size: 0.87 by 0.98 inches; 22.098 by 24.892 mm

Booklet Size: 1.74 by 6.167 inches; 44.196 by 156.642 mm

Perforations: 11¼ by 10¾ (die-cut simulated perforations) (Comco Commander rotary die cutter)

Selvage Markings: on peel-off strips: "© 2005 USPS" "Peel here to fold" and cylinder numbers

Cover Markings: "Lady Liberty/and U.S. Flag/Twenty/First-Class/Self-adhesive/Stamps." Universal Product Code (UPC) "0 674400 7."

Designer, Art Director and Typographer: Terrence McCaffrey, USPS

Photographers: Carl and Ann Purcell of Alexandria, Virginia

Stamp Manufacturing: Stamps printed by Avery Dennison Security Printing Division on Dia Nippon Kiko 8-station gravure press. Stamps finished by Avery Dennison.

Quantity Ordered: 1,500,000,000 stamps

Cylinder Number Detail: 1 set of 4 cylinder numbers preceded by the letter V on 1 peel-off strip

Cylinder Number Combination Reported: V1111

Paper Supplier: Fasson Division of Avery Dennison

Tagging: phosphored paper

NONDENOMINATED (39¢) LADY LIBERTY AND FLAG CONVERTIBLE BOOKLET OF 20, SENNETT

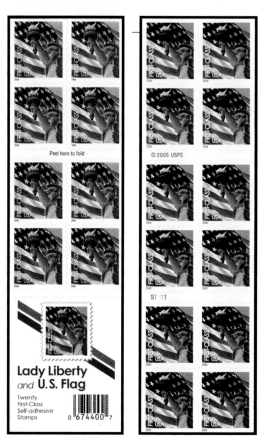

Date of Issue: December 8, 2005. Stamps were not distributed by USPS until January 2006.

Catalog Number: Scott 3973, single stamp; 3973a, convertible booklet of 20

Colors: magenta, yellow, cyan, black

First-Day Cancel: Washington, D.C.

First-Day Cancellations: 52,035 (includes all rate-change items issued December 8)

Format: Convertible booklet of 20, vertical. Stamps on both sides, arranged vertically, 8 (2 across by 4 down) plus label (booklet cover) on one side, 12 (2 across by 6 down) on other side, with horizontal peel-off strips between blocks of 4 on each side. Gravure printing cylinders printing 504 subjects per revolution (18 across, 28 around).

Gum Type: self-adhesive

Overall Stamp Size: 0.87 by 0.98 inches; 22.1 by 24.89 mm

Booklet Size: 1.74 by 6.2084 inches; 44.193 by 157.69 mm

Perforations: 10¼ by 10¾ (die-cut simulated perforations) (Comco custom rotary die cutter)

Selvage Markings: on peel-off strips: "© 2005 USPS" and cylinder numbers

Cover Markings: "Lady Liberty/and U.S. Flag/Twenty/First-Class/Self-adhesive/Stamps." Universal Product Code (UPC) "0 674400 7."

Designer, Art Director and Typographer: Terrence McCaffrey, USPS

Photographers: Carl and Ann Purcell of Alexandria, Virginia

Modeler: Donald H. Woo

Stamp Manufacturing: Stamps printed by American Packaging Corporation, Columbus, Wisconsin, for Sennett Security Products, Chantilly, Virginia, on Cerutti 950 gravure press. Stamps finished by Unique Binders, Fredericksburg, Virginia.

Quantity Ordered: 1,500,000,000 stamps

Cylinder Number Detail: 1 set of 4 cylinder numbers preceded by the letter S on 1 peel-off strip

Cylinder Number Combination Reported: S1111

Paper Supplier: Mactac

Tagging: phosphored paper

NONDENOMINATED (39¢) LADY LIBERTY AND FLAG VENDING BOOKLET OF 20

Date of Issue: December 8, 2005.

Catalog Number: Scott 3974, single stamp; 3974a, booklet pane of 4; 3974b, booklet pane of 6

Colors: black, magenta, cyan, yellow

First-Day Cancel: Washington, D.C.

First-Day Cancellations: 52,035 (includes all rate-change items issued December 8)

Format: Vending booklet of 20, vertical, arranged vertically, 2 across by 10 down, in 2 4-stamp segments (2 by 2) and 2 6-stamp segments (2 by 3). Offset printing plates printing 520 stamps per revolution (20 across, 26 around).

Gum Type: self-adhesive

Microprinting: none

Overall Stamp Size: 0.87 by 0.982 inches; 22.01 by 24.94 mm

Booklet Size: 1.74 by 10.275 inches; 44.2 by 260.99 mm

Perforations: 11¼ by 11 (die-cut simulated perforations) (Goebel Optiforma 26 rotary die cutter). Cover scored for folding.

Selvage Markings: none

Cover Markings: "Lady Liberty/and U.S. Flag/Twenty/First-Class/Self-adhesive/Stamps" on front of cover. Promotion for Postal Store Web site and Universal Product Code (UPC) "0 674300 8" on back cover. USPS logo, "© 2005 USPS" and plate numbers on tuck-in extension of back cover.

Designer, Art Director and Typographer: Terrence McCaffrey, USPS

Photographers: Carl and Ann Purcell of Alexandria, Virginia

Modeler: Donald H. Woo

Stamp Manufacturing: Stamps printed by Banknote Corporation of America, Browns Summit, North Carolina, for Sennett Security Products, Chantilly, Virginia, on Goebel Optiforma 26 offset press. Stamps processed by BCA.

Quantity Ordered: 750,000,000 stamps

Plate Number Detail: 1 set of 4 plate numbers preceded by the letter S on tuck-in extension of back cover

Plate Number Combination Reported: S1111

Paper Supplier: Mactac

Tagging: phosphored paper

NONDENOMINATED (39¢) LADY LIBERTY AND FLAG ATM-VENDED PANE OF 18

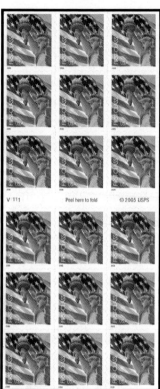

Date of Issue: December 8, 2005.

Catalog Number: Scott 3975, single stamp; 3975a, pane of 18

Colors: yellow, magenta, cyan, black

First-Day Cancel: Washington, D.C.

First-Day Cancellations: 52,035 (includes all rate-change items issued December 8)

Format: Pane of 18, vertical, arranged vertically 3 across by 6 down, with horizontal peel-off strip between horizontal rows 3 and 4. Gravure printing cylinders printing 30 panes per revolution (5 across, 6 around) manufactured by WRE ColorTech.

Gum Type: self-adhesive

Overall Stamp Size: 0.87 by 0.982 inches; 20.098 by 24.942 mm

Pane Size: 2.61 by 6.125 inches; 66.29 by 155.58 mm

Perforations: 8 (die-cut simulated perforations) (Comco Commander rotary die cutter)

Selvage Markings: "Peel here to fold" "© 2005 USPS" and cylinder numbers

Cover Markings: "Lady Liberty/and U.S. Flag/Eighteen First-Class/Self-adhesive Stamps" on front cover. Promotion for Postal Store Web site, USPS logo and Universal Product Code (UPC) "0 567600 0" on back cover.

Designer, Art Director and Typographer: Terrence McCaffrey, USPS

Photographers: Carl and Ann Purcell of Alexandria, Virginia

Stamp Manufacturing: Stamps printed by Avery Dennison Security Printing Division, Clinton, South Carolina, on a Dia Nippon Kiko 8-station gravure press. Stamps lacquer coated, front and back, die cut, processed and shipped by Avery Dennison.

Quantity Ordered: 720,000,000 stamps

Cylinder Number Detail: 1 set of 4 cylinder numbers preceded by the letter V on peel-off strip

Cylinder Number Combinations Reported: V1111

Paper Supplier: Fasson Division of Avery Dennison

Tagging: Unphosphored paper. Phosphor added to lacquer coating applied to front of pane.

The Stamps

In early December 2005, the Postal Service issued a nondenominated definitive stamp in several formats to cover the new first-class postage rate of 39¢ that would take effect the following January 8.

Its common design shows the Statue of Liberty's head, right arm with torch, left hand with book, and upper body against a portion of a waving American flag. It bears a 2006 year date.

Despite the fact that the statue and the flag are two of the most frequently depicted patriotic icons on U.S. stamps, they had not been previously pictured together on a definitive.

The stamp comes in 11 collectible varieties and was produced by three different printers, some using the offset process, some using gravure. Ten of the varieties received Scott catalog numbers. All were printed using the four standard process colors: cyan, magenta, yellow and black.

Their official nationwide first day of issue was December 8, and USPS provided a Washington, D.C., first-day postmark. However, for some of the formats there is no evidence that they were available on that day, and one format wasn't distributed until early January.

The 11 varieties are:

• Pane of 100 with water-activated gum (Scott 3965), printed by Sterling Sommer for Ashton-Potter (USA) Ltd. by the offset process. The perforations gauge 11¼. A microprinted "USPS" can be found at the top of the top red stripe of the flag where it meets the blue canton.

• Pane of 20, self-adhesive (Scott 3966), also printed by Ashton-Potter by offset. The die-cut simulated perforations gauge 11¼ by 11. The micro-

The microprinted "USPS" on the Ashton-Potter Lady Liberty and Flag stamps can be found near the upper right corner of the stamp. It is located at the top of the top red stripe of the flag where it meets the dark blue canton.

printing is the same as on Scott 3965.

• Coil of 3,000 with water-activated gum (Scott 3967), printed by American Packaging Corporation for Sennett Security Products by the gravure process. The perforations gauge 9¾. Four cylinder numbers preceded by the letter S are on every 14th stamp. Magenta counting numbers are on the back of every 10th stamp.

• Coil of 100, self-adhesive (Scott 3968), printed by Avery-Dennison Security Printing Division by gravure. The die cuts gauge 8½. Four cylinder numbers preceded by the letter V are on every 11th stamp.

• Coil of 100, self-adhesive (Scott 3969), printed by American Packaging Corporation for Sennett Security Products by gravure. The die cuts gauge 10¼. Four cylinder numbers preceded by the letter S are on every 14th stamp.

• Coil of 100, self-adhesive (Scott 3970), printed by Ashton-Potter by offset. The die cuts gauge 9½. Four plate numbers preceded by the letter P are on every 31st stamp. The microprinting is the same as on Scott 3965 and 3966.

• Double-sided convertible booklet of 20, self-adhesive (Scott 3966), printed by Ashton-Potter by offset. The die cuts gauge 11¼ by 11. Twelve stamps are on one side of the booklet, and eight stamps, plus a label that serves as a booklet cover, are on the other side. The stamps on one side are upside down relative to those on the other. The Scott catalog editors originally assigned this stamp the number 3971, but later determined that it is identical to the stamp on the Ashton-Potter self-adhesive pane of 20 in design details, including microprinting, and die-cut gauge. However, the pane stamp has no straight edges, while each booklet stamp has one or two straight edges.

• Double-sided convertible booklet of 20, self-adhesive (Scott 3972), printed by Avery-Dennison by gravure. The die cuts gauge 11¼ by 10¾.

Twelve stamps are on one side of the booklet, and eight stamps, plus a label that serves as a booklet cover, are on the other side. All the stamps have one or two straight edges.

• Double-sided convertible booklet of 20, self-adhesive (Scott 3973), printed by American Packaging Corporation for Sennett Security Prod-

ucts by gravure. The die cuts gauge 10¼ by 10¾. Twelve stamps are on one side of the booklet, and eight stamps, plus a label that serves as a booklet cover, are on the other side. All the stamps have one or two straight edges. Shipments of the stamp to Stamp Fulfillment Services and post offices did not begin until January 3, 2006, and the earliest known use is on a cover created by *Linn's Stamp News* that has a January 30, 2006, postmark from Sidney, Ohio. First-day covers bear the December 8, 2005, postmark from Washington, D.C., even though the stamp was not available then.

• Vending booklet of 20, self-adhesive (Scott 3974), printed by Banknote Corporation of America for Sennett Security Products by offset. The stamps are arranged in two panes of four and two panes of six. The die cuts gauge 11¼ by 11. All the stamps have one or two straight edges. A four-digit cylinder number preceded by the letter S is on a segment of the cover behind one of the panes of four. The microprinting that normally is required for stamps printed by the offset process is absent.

• Pane of 18, self-adhesive, for vending by automated teller machine (ATM) (Scott 3975). Like all the Postal Service's ATM-vended stamp

panes, this one was printed by Avery Dennison by gravure and has the dimensions and thickness of a currency bill. The stamps are arranged three across by six down. The 14 outer stamps have one or two straight edges, while the inner four have die cuts on all four sides. The die cuts gauge 8.

Stamp Fulfillment Services enabled collectors seeking coil stamps with cylinder or plate numbers to buy a strip of 25 from the Sennett coil of 3,000 with water-activated gum. However, stamps from the three coils of 100 with self-adhesive gum were available in full coils only, at $39 each.

The Design

"The art directors were so involved with other projects that the idea of designing new flag stamps kind of slipped through the cracks," said Terrence McCaffrey, manager of stamp development for USPS. "When the [Citizens' Stamp Advisory] Committee said, 'Where are the flag designs for the next rate change?' I had to get busy. PhotoAssist [the Postal Service's research firm] got me some stock photographs to look over."

McCaffrey was looking for something other than a simple picture of a waving American flag such as those that had been featured on the last two definitive flag designs, in 2001 (the post-September 11, 2001, United We Stand stamp) and 2002. After a composite photo of Lady Liberty and the flag from the Corbis service caught his eye, he developed it as a stamp layout, which he e-mailed to CSAC members. "They liked it, and we went forward with it," he said.

The image was a melding of two photographs taken by Carl Purcell in the early 1990s. Carl and his former wife, Ann Purcell, both of whom were credited by USPS for the stamp image, are travel journalists based in Alexandria, Virginia, and Florida. Their writing and photography have appeared worldwide in major travel publications, through syndication, on the Internet and in four books of text and pictures.

Purcell made his picture of the statue from a boat that takes visitors to Liberty Island. He shot the flag, which flies near the statue, while standing on the island. For both photographs he used a Nikon 35-millimeter camera with a 100-300-mm lens.

Bill and Ann Purcell combined Bill Purcell's photographs of the Statue of Liberty and an American flag flying on Liberty Island to produce this patriotic image. To adapt it for use on a vertically arranged definitive stamp, designer Terrence McCaffrey cropped the picture on the left and right sides and electronically darkened Lady Liberty to remove the "ghosting" effect on the original and make the statue's details more legible at stamp size.

"There was a very good wind that day," he said. "The flag was very large, but the wind was strong enough to pull it out almost all the way." From the lighting on the statue, Purcell guessed that the photo was taken in mid-afternoon.

He combined the two pictures into one patriotic image, with the blue-green statue superimposed over the flag so that the stars and stripes are visible through the arms and torch. The Purcells made the image available for reproduction royalty-free. They had created a similar blended picture of a flag and the World Trade Center with the caption "Lest We Forget" after 9/11.

Carl Purcell said he never expected the Lady Liberty and flag combination to be circulated worldwide on billions of postage stamps, however. "I was quite pleased that it was used that way, and very understandably flattered," he said. "All of my colleagues were thunderstruck when they realized that it was my picture."

Because the photograph was arranged horizontally, McCaffrey cropped both sides to fit it into a vertical stamp layout. He also had the photo electronically altered to show the statue as solid rather than transparent. "Otherwise, at stamp size you would have lost sight of the torch arm altogether," he said.

The words "FIRST-CLASS," in dropout white, were inserted vertically in the lower left corner. Beside them, horizontally, is "USA." The typeface is called Verdana.

Distinguishing the 11 varieties of the nondenominated Lady Liberty and Flag stamp can be done in several ways.

The easiest stamps to identify are those from the water-activated pane of 100 (Scott 3965), with perforations on all sides; the self-adhesive pane of 20 (Scott 3966), with die-cut simulated perforations on all sides; the water-activated coil of 3,000 (3967), with perforations on the two vertical sides; and the ATM pane (3975), with broad, undulating, pointed die cuts.

The three self-adhesive coil stamps from rolls of 100 are also fairly easy to tell apart. The Avery Dennison die cuts (Scott 3968) are much deeper than those on the Sennett stamp (Scott 3969), while the Ashton-Potter stamp (Scott 3970) has microprinting.

Identification is a somewhat more exacting task with the self-adhesive stamps from the various convertible booklets of 20 and the vending booklet. The Ashton-Potter stamp from a convertible booklet (Scott 3966) has microprinting, and can be distinguished from its counterpart on the pane of 20 by the presence of a straight edge or edges.

Gauging the die cuts is the best way to identify stamps from the other booklets, although there are some other distinguishing features. The stamp from the Sennett convertible booklet (Scott 3973) has a large 2006 year date beneath the design at the lower left. There is a visible triangle of blue sky in the lower left corner, and the left arm of the star at the upper left barely touches the frameline. On Sennett's vending-booklet stamp (Scott

P111   Peel here to fold

Shown here is a block of four with no die cuts, graphically cropped from a double-sided pane of 20 printed by Ashton-Potter (USA) Ltd.

3974), this blue area is missing or is merely a sliver, and less of the star's arm is visible.

A white shadow effect surrounds the Statue of Liberty on the Avery Dennison convertible-booklet stamp (Scott 3972), most noticeably where the red stripes meet the arm and breast of the statue. Neither of the Sennett booklet stamps has this effect.

Varieties

A double-sided convertible booklet printed by Ashton-Potter without die cuts on either side of the booklet was discovered in March 2006.

Linn's Stamp News reported that the pane was found at a post office in Ohio. James Kloetzel, Scott catalog editor, told *Linn's* that the stamp would be listed as a major error in the 2007 Scott *Specialized Catalogue of United States Stamps & Covers.*

First-Day Facts

No first-day ceremony was held.

Because the Postal Service formally announced the new stamps just before the December 8 issue date, collectors were given 60 days rather than the normal 30 to submit covers for first-day postmarks. For a limited time, Stamp Fulfillment Services sold uncacheted first-day covers of certain varieties of the stamp for 77¢ each.

REVISED DEFINITIVES

60¢ Acadia National Park, 2005 year date

Early in 2005, the Postal Service issued a third collectible variety of the 60¢ Acadia National Park self-adhesive definitive stamp that had first appeared in 2001 and was reprinted, with differences, in 2003. The stamp, part of the Scenic American Landscapes series, reproduces a photograph of a scene in Maine's Acadia park. Its denomination covered the rate in effect through 2005 for a letter weighing one ounce or less addressed to Canada or Mexico.

The original stamp was issued May 30, 2001, with a print order of 100 million from the printer, Banknote Corporation of America. In 2003, USPS ordered BCA to print an additional 100 million. Both versions were produced by offset lithography and have the same basic design, including a 2001 year date. The 2003 printing differs from the first, however, in the gauge of its die cuts, which are 11½ by 11¾ instead of 11¼ by 11½, and the paper, which is unphosphored with block tagging over the stamps rather than phosphored. The two printings also differ in their selvage markings and the markings on the back of their liner paper.

Shortly after the second variety was placed on sale, BCA lost its contract as a prime supplier of stamps for USPS. In 2005, when USPS needed an additional 60 million Acadia National Park stamps, it turned to a surviving contractor, Sennett Security Products. Sennett had acquired BCA in the meantime, so BCA again did the printing, using the same Roland 300 offset press with 240-subject plates it had used to produce the 2003 variety, and laying down the four process colors in the same order: cyan, magenta, yellow and black.

The new stamp has a 2005 year date, but in other respects it is identical to its 2003 predecessor, with the same gauge of die cuts and the use of unphosphored paper with block tagging. The microprinting in the design of all three varieties is the same, consisting of the letters "USPS" on the rocky outcropping near the center of the stamp, approximately one-half inch from the left side.

Scott assigned the catalog number C138 to the first variety, C138a to the reprint of 2003 and C138b to the new version with the 2005 year date. Scott lists the stamps in the Scenic American Landscapes series with the airmails (hence the C prefix on the catalog numbers) because they are primarily intended for international mail, which travels by air, and they incorporate a small silhouette of a jet airplane in their designs.

A pane of 20 of the 2005 year-date stamps that was mistakenly printed on the back of the backing paper rather than on the facing paper on the other side was shown to *Linn's Stamp News* in June 2005 by Arnold Selengut of Bejjco of Florida, a stamp firm in Temple Terrace, Florida. "The pane was purchased at a post office in upstate New York by a person interested in sending out wedding invitations," Selengut said. "Upon finding that the stamps would not stick to the envelopes, the pane was set aside, and substitute postage was obtained for the envelopes." Scott listed a single from the pane as C138c.

25¢ American Eagle coil, 2005 year date

On August 5, the Postal Service issued 10 nondenominated self-adhesive stamps, arranged in sequence in coil rolls of 3,000. Their simple, graphic common design depicts a portion of the eagle that is on the Great Seal of the United States. The stamps differ in appearance from each other only in their color combinations.

USPS had used the same design and color combinations for two previous 10-variety coils, in 2003 and 2004. All three sets were printed on a Rotomec 3000 gravure press by American Packaging Corporation for Sennett Security Products.

The first set, also self-adhesive, was issued in rolls of 10,000. The stamps bear a 2003 year date. The second set was issued in rolls of 3,000 and differs from the first in three additional respects: It has water-activated gum, its year date is 2004, and the stamps are arranged in a different sequence of color combinations. The newest stamps have a 2005 year date, which enables collectors to distinguish them from the 2003 set of self-adhesives. The print order was 90 million stamps.

With the new varieties, Sennett returned to the sequence of colors it had used with the first set: gold on dark blue, blue on gold, gold on green, gray on gold, gold on blue, dark blue on gold, gold on red, green on gold, gold on gray and red on gold.

As was the case with the first set, the seven-digit cylinder number combination is found on every other gold-on-green stamp, or every 20th stamp on the roll. Thus, collectors must save a strip of 21 stamps to have the ideal collectible, namely, a symmetrical strip, with the single PNC (plate number coil) in the center, containing every color-combination variety, including the gold-on-green stamp without cylinder numbers. Such a strip is too large to be displayed on a standard album page.

The 25¢ charged by the Postal Service for each stamp represents a credit for mailers of first-class bulk mail against the actual cost of mailing their pieces. The service inscription in the design, "PRESORTED FIRST-CLASS," is considered a precancel, and the untagged stamps bypass the canceling machines in post offices.

The 2005 American Eagle coil has a four-digit magenta counting number printed on the back of the liner paper of every 10th (gold-on-green) stamp. Thus, every other stamp with a counting number on the back also has cylinder numbers on the front.

Stamp Fulfillment Services required collectors to purchase a strip of 25 stamps at $6.25 to obtain a PNC. Stamp Fulfillment Services also sold strips of five for $1.25. Collectors wishing to use surplus stamps for postage were required to obtain a precancel permit from USPS and present it with each mailing.

Dealer-columnist Robert Rabinowitz, who specializes in PNCs, was critical of the fact that a new set of varieties was created. "Apparently the Postal Service is violating its own policy, wherein additional printings of the same stamps by the same printer always bear the original date," he wrote in a letter to *Linn's Stamp News.* "For example, the 37¢ Flag stamps in coil rolls of 100 printed by the Bureau of Engraving and Printing in at least 15 different press runs from 2002 to 2005 bear a '2002' year date.

"As a matter of fact, when Sennett Security Products printed the non-denominated (10¢) Lion Statue self-adhesive coil bearing plate number S55555, it mistakenly used '2002' instead of '2000,' which was used with the previous four printings. Apparently the Postal Service flagged and corrected this, because plate number S77777 returned to using the '2000' year date.

"I wonder why the decision was made to change the date on the Eagle stamps. Could it have been sheer greed? Because the Postal Service considers these 10 stamps to be different stamps from those issued in 2003, many collectors throughout the world will shell out $2.50 to own a mint set."

The stamps had their first-day sale at the American Philatelic Society Stampshow in Grand Rapids, Michigan. Because "the stamp image is a reprint," USPS announced, "there will not be a first-day-of-issuance ceremony."

Collectors were given 90 days to submit self-addressed envelopes franked with one or more of the stamps to the postmaster in Washington for first-day cancellations. If only one American Eagle stamp was affixed, additional postage sufficient to cover the 37¢ first-class rate was required. For a limited time, Stamp Fulfillment Services offered uncacheted first-day covers bearing two American Eagle stamps chosen at random for 88¢.

Scott assigned numbers 3792 through 3801 to the original 2003 self-adhesive Eagle stamps, and 3801a to a strip of 10. Of the new varieties, the first nine are numbered 3792a through 3800a and the 10th is numbered 3801b, while a strip of 10 is listed as 3801c.

37¢ Snowy Egret convertible booklet with microprinting

In 2003, the Postal Service issued a 37¢ coil stamp in rolls of 100 depicting a snowy egret in profile against a blue sky and water background. Because the Avery Dennison Security Products Division printed the stamp by the gravure process, which USPS considers to be a more secure printing method than offset lithography, it contained no microprinting in its design.

However, when a second variety of the Snowy Egret stamp (in a con-

On the left is a Snowy Egret convertible booklet stamp without microprinting. On the right is the variety with the microprinted letters "USPS."

vertible booklet of 20) was issued January 30, 2004, it also bore no microprinting, although it was offset-printed by Ashton-Potter (USA) Ltd. The omission was obviously an oversight, because USPS policy calls for the inclusion of microprinting on all single-design stamps that are produced by the offset method.

The lapse wasn't repeated in March 2004 when USPS issued a third Snowy Egret variety, also offset-printed by Ashton-Potter. On this variety, another coil stamp that came in rolls of 100, the microprinted letters "USPS" in black can be found at the edge of the white plumage at the base of the bird's neck.

Fast-forward to late 2005, when James Studer, an observant collector from Ohio, examined a stamp from a convertible booklet and discovered that its design contained a microprinted "USPS" in the same location as the microprinting on the 2004 Ashton-Potter coil stamp.

Studer notified *Linn's Stamp News* of his find in early November, and *Linn's* asked the Postal Service about the unannounced variety. "We did an initial printing of 750 million stamps [37.5 million panes] without microprinting," said USPS spokesman Mark Saunders. "Following that printing, we decided to add microprinting for more security."

Saunders said the microprinting "USPS" appeared on an additional printing of slightly more than 1.5 billion stamps. Plate-number combinations P11111 and P22222 were used to print the original variety, without microprinting, and P33333, P44444 and P55555 were used to print stamps with microprinting.

The Scott catalogs assigned the minor number 3830D to the microprinted version of the convertible booklet stamp.

$15 MIGRATORY BIRD HUNTING (DUCK) STAMP 2005-2006

Date of Issue: June 30, 2005

Catalog Number: Scott RW72, Type I; RW72c, Type II

Colors: black, cyan, magenta, yellow (offset); black (intaglio). Back: black (offset).

First-Day Cancel: Washington, D.C.

Format: Panes of 20, horizontal, 5 across, 4 down. Printing plates printing 80 stamps per repeat (10 across, 8 around). Also distributed in uncut press sheets of 80.

Gum Type: water-activated

Microprinting: "FWS" in water below reflection of second (rear) duck

Overall Stamp Size: 1.98 by 1.415 inches; 50.29 by 35.94 mm

Pane Size: 11.315 by 7.075 inches; 287.4 by 179.7 mm

Uncut Sheet Size: 24.0 by 16.0 inches; 609.6 by 406.4 mm

Perforations: 11 (Wista perforator)

Selvage Markings: "ARTIST:/MARK ANDERSON" in 4 locations. "DEPART-MENT OF THE INTERIOR/20 x $15.00" in 4 locations. "PLATE/POSI-TION" and diagram. 6 duck-shaped color bars in 2 locations.

Back Inscription (printed on top of gum): On stamp: "INVEST IN AMERI-CA'S FUTURE./BUY DUCK STAMPS./SAVE WETLANDS./SEND IN OR REPORT ALL/BIRD BANDS TO/1-800-327-BAND/IT IS UNLAWFUL TO HUNT WATERFOWL OR USE THIS STAMP/AS A PASS TO A NATIONAL WILDLIFE REFUGE UNLESS/YOU SIGN YOUR NAME IN INK ON THE FACE OF THIS STAMP." On selvage: Universal Product Code (UPC) "333400" in 4 locations.

Artist: Mark Anderson of Sioux Falls, South Dakota

Art Director and Modeler: Donald Woo of Sennett Security Products, Chan-tilly, Virginia

Designers and Engravers: Czeslaw Slania and Piotr Naszarkowski of Swe-den

Stamp Manufacturing: Stamps printed by Banknote Corporation of America, Browns Summit, North Carolina, for Sennett Security Products on Man Roland 300 offset press and TA intaglio press. Stamps finished by BCA.

Quantity Ordered: 1,000,000 stamps (regular panes) and 8,000 stamps (uncut press sheets)

Plate Number: 1 4-digit offset plate number preceded by the letter S and 1 intaglio plate number in selvage above or below each corner stamp

Plate Number Reported: S1111 1

Paper Supplier: Troy Laminating and Coating Inc., Troy, Ohio

Tagging: untagged

$15 MIGRATORY BIRD HUNTING (DUCK) STAMP
2005-2006 PANE OF 1

Date of Issue: June 30, 2005

Catalog Number: Scott RW72b

Colors: Black, cyan, magenta, yellow (offset); black (intaglio). Back: black. Artist's signature in black, blue or gold.

First-Day Cancel: Washington, D.C.

Format: Pane of 1, horizontal. Printing plates printing 18 stamps per repeat (6 panes across, 3 panes around).

Gum Type: water-activated

Microprinting: "FWS" in water below reflection of second (rear) duck

Overall Stamp Size: 1.98 by 1.415 inches; 50.29 by 35.94 mm

Perforations: 11 (Wista perforator)

Selvage Markings: "U.S. Fish & Wildlife Service"/2005-2006 Migratory Bird/ Hunting & Conservation Stamp/Artist: Mark Anderson."

Back Inscription (printed on top of gum): On stamp: "INVEST IN AMERI- CA'S FUTURE./BUY DUCK STAMPS./SAVE WETLANDS./SEND IN OR REPORT ALL/BIRD BANDS TO/1-800-327-BAND/IT IS UNLAWFUL TO HUNT WATERFOWL OR USE THIS STAMP/AS A PASS TO A NATIONAL

WILDLIFE REFUGE UNLESS/YOU SIGN YOUR NAME IN INK ON THE FACE OF THIS STAMP."

Artist: Mark Anderson of Sioux Falls, South Dakota

Art Director and Modeler: Donald Woo of Sennett Security Products, Chantilly, Virginia

Designers and Engravers: Czeslaw Slania and Piotr Naszarkowski of Sweden

Stamp Manufacturing: Stamps printed by Banknote Corporation of America, Browns Summit, North Carolina, for Sennett Security Products on Man Roland 300 offset press and TA intaglio press. Stamps finished by BCA.

Quantity Ordered: 1,000 stamps

Plate Number: none

Paper Supplier: Troy Laminating and Coating Inc., Troy, Ohio

Tagging: untagged

$15 MIGRATORY BIRD HUNTING (DUCK) STAMP
2005-2006 (SELF-ADHESIVE)

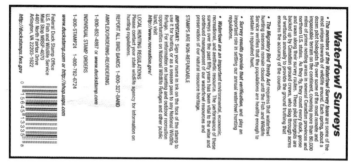

Date of Issue: June 30, 2005

Catalog Number: Scott RW72A

Colors: black, cyan, magenta, yellow (offset); black (intaglio)

City of Issue: Washington, D.C.

Format: Sold in single-stamp panes. Printed by offset plates printing 18 stamps per repeat (3 across, 6 around) with debossing. Also distributed in uncut press sheets of 18 panes.

Gum Type: self-adhesive

Microprinting: "FWS" in the water near the right frameline

Overall Stamp Size: 1.98 by 1.415 inches; 50.29 by 35.94 mm

Pane Size: 6.125 by 2.625 inches; 155.57 by 66.68 mm

Uncut Sheet Size: 23 by 19 inches; 584.2 by 482.6 mm

Perforations: 11 by 10¾ (die-cut simulated perforations) (Heidelberg 102 Speedmaster rotary die cutter)

Selvage and Back Markings: see illustrations above

Artist: Mark Anderson of Sioux Falls, South Dakota

Art Director and Modeler: Donald Woo of Sennett Security Products, Chantilly, Virginia

Designers: Czeslaw Slania and Piotr Naszarkowski of Sweden

Stamp Manufacturing: Stamps printed by Banknote Corporation of America for Sennett Security Products on Man Roland 300 offset press and Bobst 102 Die Press. Stamps finished by BCA.

Quantity Ordered: 3,000,000 stamps (single-stamp panes) and 1,800 stamps (uncut press sheets)

Plate Number: none

Paper Supplier: Mactac

Tagging: untagged

The Stamps

Two male hooded mergansers swimming on a pond turned golden by a setting sun are featured on the federal migratory bird hunting and conservation stamp that was issued for use by duck hunters during the 2005-2006 hunting season.

The image was adapted from an acrylic painting by wildlife artist Mark Anderson of Sioux Falls, South Dakota, that won the annual U.S. Fish and Wildlife Service duck stamp design competition October 4 and 5, 2004. The printer was Banknote Corporation of America for its parent company, Sennett Security Products.

As usual, the stamp was issued in two versions for general sale. One has water-activated gum and conventional perforations and comes in panes of 20. The other is a self-adhesive with die-cut simulated perfs and was distributed in currency-sized panes of one.

The 2005 stamp produced several firsts, however.

For the first time, a duck stamp was made with no intaglio printing. Although BCA printed the version with water-activated gum by the customary combination of offset lithography and intaglio, the self-adhesive stamp combines offset printing with a process called debossing. In debossing, parts of the image are recessed under heavy pressure, resulting in a textured surface that serves as a security element. The stamp was the first ever issued by the U.S. government to feature this technique.

Also for the first time, the Federal Duck Stamp Office offered a limited number of uncut press sheets of both varieties, complete with the color bars and registration marks that are trimmed off individual panes. One hundred press sheets containing four panes of the water-activated stamp (8,000 stamps), with a face value of $1,200, were sold for $1,320 each. Another 100 press sheets containing 18 single-stamp panes of the self-adhesive stamp (1,800 stamps), with a face value of $270, were sold for $297.

But the most striking innovation — an unannounced step that caused an uproar in the duck-stamp collecting community — was the duck stamp office's decision to order a printing of the water-activated stamp in what it called a souvenir sheet of one, to be signed by artist Anderson.

316

Only 1,000 of these panes were produced and signed. They were sold before collectors or the philatelic press were aware that they existed. The pane became an instant rarity, and the price escalated quickly after the Scott catalog editors certified its legitimacy by assigning it a minor listing. As of this writing, the going price for the panes has stabilized at between $1,700 and $2,000.

Collectors, dealers and stamp writers were nearly unanimous in criticizing the duck stamp office for breaching a long-standing government policy against creating collectibles that are not announced and not available to all customers on an equal basis.

A key player in the drama — and one whose role was widely misunderstood at first — was Bob Dumaine of the Sam Houston Duck Company of Houston, Texas, a leading dealer, collector, author and judge in the field of duck stamps.

The story of how the rarity came to be and how the news belatedly reached the collecting public was reported by *Linn's Stamp News* editor Michael Schreiber in his Open Album column for August 1, 2005. The column was based on interviews with Dumaine, Scott Publishing Company editors and Robert L. Williams, head of stamp development and marketing for the duck stamp office.

Schreiber's chronology follows:

"Prior to 2005: The Postal Service solicits bids to print the duck stamps. It does this on behalf of the issuer, the U.S. Fish and Wildlife Service of the Department of the Interior. Sennett Security Products wins the job, in either late 2004 or early 2005.

"The Sennett proposal includes the water-activated pane of one. Williams said the pane was the idea of Sandra Lane and Donald Woo, president and vice president, respectively, of Sennett Security Products.

"January 2005: The delivery order for the issue is signed January 19. The duck stamp office gets its copy on January 28.

"Mid-June: The duck stamp office receives the 1,000 panes of one water-activated stamp. Williams sends them to artist Mark Anderson in South Dakota for signatures. Anderson later tells *Linn's* that he used three different inks to sign black, blue and gold.

"Late June: About a week prior to the first day, the duck stamp office sends 250 signed panes to Amplex Corporation [the distributor that supplies duck stamps to wildlife refuges, gun shops and sport shops], and 750 signed panes to the Postal Service's Stamp Fulfillment Services mail-order center in Kansas City, Missouri. Williams said that he personally counted them (his previous job was with the Postal Service's stamps office, in quality assurance).

"June 29: Dumaine places an initial order of duck stamps with Amplex, as he routinely has done in prior years, 100 water-activated stamps, 50 self-sticks, 300 junior federal duck stamps, and 10 of what Dumaine says he was told was 'a souvenir card with a stamp.' He does not know what this is.

"June 30: The first-day ceremony for the duck stamps is held in the U.S. Senate's Russell office building, a sacred federal place where no sales are allowed. Outside the building, a Postal Service temporary post office truck sells the new duck stamp from the pane of 20, the single self-stick pane and the junior duck stamp. It sells no other items related to duck stamps.

"Down in Texas the same day, Dumaine receives his express order from Amplex and opens it. The 'souvenir card with a stamp' turns out to be the surprise water-activated pane of one.

"Dumaine's adrenaline level shoots up when he realizes that it is a stamp. Its back looks just like the back of the duck stamp issued in the pane of 20. He measures the perforations, and they also are the same. He later told *Linn's*, 'I knew immediately that this was a good product, a hybrid between the water-activated pane of 20 and the self-stick pane of one.'

"With his adrenaline surging, Dumaine calls Amplex again, learns of the 250 panes and tries to buy what is left. Amplex refuses but agrees to sell him 100. With 110 panes in the bag, Dumaine calls Stamp Fulfillment Services to order more. The telephone order taker does not know what Dumaine is talking about, and the pane of one is not in the computer system. Dumaine calls Williams at the duck stamp office to tell him that Kansas City is clueless, but Williams is out of the office.

"July 5: Dumaine frets over the holiday weekend, but he reaches Williams on Tuesday. Later that day, Williams eventually tells Dumaine the Kansas City inventory number. Dumaine orders 200 more. Later, Dumaine calls Scott Publishing to ask what the pane's catalog number would be, but Scott is unaware of the water-activated pane of one.

"July 6: Scott Publishing orders a couple of panes for its reference collection. Dumaine orders 150 more plus another 100 for a customer who asked. Dumaine then e-mails the officers of the National Duck Stamp Collectors Society about the surprise pane of one.

"He schedules a 'sold out' ad in the July 25 *Linn's*, saying later that he knew the pane of one would sell out quickly.

"Dumaine eventually acquires 'about 500' of the water-activated pane of one, he later said, adding 'I could have had them all.'

"July 8: Dumaine sends me by e-mail a copy of his ad offering a pane at $39 (very fine centering) or $55 (extra fine centering), limit two. Dumaine later said that he also offered the pane to his new-issue customers at a few dollars above the $20 cost. He said that many panes have perforations that are poorly centered around the stamp design, thus his two prices.

"Dumaine's July 8 e-mail sets *Linn's* off in search of the story, and the news was published in the July 25 issue that was put together July 11-12 and printed July 13."

The pane was sold out as of July 8, the same day *Linn's* found out about its existence and eight days after it went on sale, Schreiber wrote. *Linn's* learned of the sellout July 13 from the Postal Service, and posted basic information about it on the afternoon of July 14 on its free Web site at www.linns.com. The news of the sellout appeared in print in *Linn's* August 1 issue on page 1.

"Why were only 1,000 panes of one made?" Schreiber continued in his column. "Williams said that he wanted to limit the number that artist Mark Anderson would have to sign.

"The quantity was based on recent sales of other 'value-added products,' as he called them. These include cacheted duck-stamp first-day covers (1,000 produced), so-called artist cards that bear a mounted new duck stamp and the stamp of three years ago (900 cards produced), duck-stamp ceremony programs (950 produced, 800 of which were for sale).

"The duck stamp office considers the water-activated pane of one to be a value-added product, not a pure revenue stamp. What it failed to realize with the new stamp, however, is that collectors consider anything that waddles like a duck stamp to be a duck stamp. They care about the stamp, not semantics or some so-called product enhancement.

"For the duck stamp office, the autograph is the added value, and that is what allowed the item to be sold for more than face value.

"For many wildlife lovers, the autograph provides the impetus to collect duck stamps. The autograph helps to link the art, the artist, the stamp and the purpose of the stamp (helping wildlife survive). That some of the ducks eventually take buckshot does not matter.

"Williams said no additional 2005 water-activated panes of one will be issued. The 1,000 are it.

"The villain in this story is the duck stamp office. It should have issued about 500 numbered, artist-signed panes at $100 each and about 100,000 unsigned panes at $15 each.

"It also should have announced the issue."

Williams told *Linn's* that the $20 received for each signed pane would be distributed as follows: $2 to either the Postal Service or Amplex to cover expenses associated with selling them, and the remaining $18 to the Fish and Wildlife Service for the Migratory Bird Conservation Fund ($15.90) and the Federal Duck Stamp Marketing Fund ($2.10), "to help offset the cost of this and other stamp-related products used to generate additional revenue for the Migratory Bird Conservation Fund."

The value of the pane headed for the sky, like a duck flushed from cover. Bob Dumaine raised his price to $49 for very-fine centering and $75 for extra-fine centering, keeping his limit at two per customer. But in a July 23 e-mail to *Linn's*, Dumaine announced that he had exhausted his stock. Six days later, he sent another e-mail to the publication offering to buy back panes for $100, more than double his original selling price.

On July 16, a seller in Indiana auctioned a pane online on eBay for $41.80. The same seller sold a second pane July 24 for $220.30.

On August 16, a pane fetched $950. On August 22, Dumaine himself sold a pane on eBay for $1,034. Six days later, an eBay sale was consummated for $1,402.99.

In an additional twist to the story, the color of ink in which artist Anderson's signature appears on a pane became a factor in its desirability.

"The duck stamp office sent me 1,000 panes and said they needed them signed like yesterday," Anderson told *The Yearbook*. "I sat down and started signing them with a black ballpoint pen, and the pen ran out of ink. So I grabbed the next pen — I didn't think twice about it being blue — and kept signing, and went through a couple of hundred, and all of a sudden ran out of ink again.

"I was down to the last package, and I thought I would try my special gold metallic pen, so I signed the rest of them — roughly 100 — in gold, which really looked nice."

Dumaine estimates that Anderson originally signed between 100 and 200 panes in blue, and the majority of the panes in black. At the dealer's request, Anderson re-signed some of Dumaine's panes that he already had signed in black with additional autographs in blue and gold.

As the price of the pane was soaring, the letters columns of stamp publications were filled with collectors' complaints about the new variety and its unavailability, with several suggesting that Dumaine had benefited from favoritism and was improperly profiting from the item.

After the latter were published, they were answered by numerous letters strongly defending Dumaine, including one from the dealer himself.

"At no time was I aware of any special-interest deal or insider information," Dumaine wrote in the August 29, 2005 *Linn's*.

"For the record, to supply our customers, we need more than 1,000 of each duck stamp annually, so only buying about half of this issue was a sacrifice for my firm ... and eventually will cause some of our customers to pay more.

"We also sold 70 panes to a competitor, Michael Jaffe, because he had received an initial order of only 75 panes. Part of my purchase was also for another individual. In reality, I was working with about one-third of the 1,000. ...

"In cases of this nature, dealers function as for-profit brokers between collectors, as the laws of supply and demand dictate. ...

"Active duck-stamp collectors who are our customers and have a current e-mail address on file learned of the signed pane in a timely manner. These collectors were able to get in on the ground floor. ...

"The real irony of the story is that the 1,000 signed panes were issued simultaneously with only 100 sets of an announced item, namely the 100 uncut press sheets each of the water-activated and self-adhesive $15 Hooded Mergansers stamps. The press sheets are 10 times scarcer and sold out in the third week in July."

In an unusual action, the editor of *American Philatelist* printed a personal apology to Dumaine for having published a letter critical of the dealer "without first giving him a chance to respond to the implication that he had been anything less than completely aboveboard in his dealings with the Federal Duck Stamp Office."

"Mr. Dumaine throughout acted ethically and even generously, making the existence of the autographed pane known to others in the philatelic community, including Scott and *Linn's*," the editor's note concluded. "We deeply apologize for any distress caused by our having printed a letter that would seem to impugn his integrity in any way."

In February 2006, Pat Fisher, the new chief at the Federal Duck Stamp Office, told *Linn's* that the 2006-2007 duck stamp would be issued in the same formats as those of 2005-2006, but that quantities would be increased.

"We are planning to offer the same products as last year: full press sheets of both water-activated and self-adhesive stamps, and a signed souvenir sheet [pane of one] like last year, except that we will have more than 1,000 available for purchase," Fisher said.

She said the actual number had not been determined, but that it would be publicized before the pane was issued.

Although the sale of duck stamps in uncut sheets at a set price is unprecedented, uncut sheets were sold once before under unique circumstances. As the Scott catalog reports:

"After No. RW51 [the $7.50 duck stamp of 1984] became void, 15 uncut sheets of 120 (four panes of 30 separated by gutters) were overprinted '1934-84' and '50th ANNIVERSARY' in the margins and auctioned by the U.S. Fish and Wildlife Service.

"Bids were accepted from September 1 through November 1, 1985. Minimum bid for each sheet was $2,000. The face value of each sheet, had they still been valid, was $900. Each sheet also had the sheet number and pane position printed in the corner of each pane ('01 of 15-1,' '01 of 15-2,' etc.). Fourteen of the sheets were sold at this and one subsequent auction and one was donated to the Smithsonian.

"An individual sheet could be broken up to create these identifiable collectibles: four margin overprint blocks of 10; cross gutter block of four; six horizontal pairs with gutter between; eight vertical pairs with gutter between.

"Single stamps from the sheet cannot be distinguished from No. RW51. No used examples can exist."

The duck stamp program was established by the Migratory Bird Hunting Stamp Act of 1934, which requires all waterfowl hunters 16 years of age and older to annually buy and carry a federal duck stamp. Other purchasers include stamp collectors, art lovers and conservationists.

Proceeds from the sale of duck stamps — approximately 98 cents of each dollar raised — are used to purchase and conserve migratory bird habitat. Over the years, as the face value of the stamp has increased incrementally from the original $1 to the present $15, some $600 million has been collected and more than six million acres of habitat conserved.

The duck stamp competition is the U.S. government's only art contest. First place carries no cash award, but the winners earn substantial returns from the sale of limited-edition prints of the artwork and other ancillary products. A contest victory also carries great prestige that can pay off in painting commissions, as well as contracts to design the various wildlife stamps produced by state fish and game agencies.

The 224 artists who paid the $100 entry fee for the 2004 competition were required to choose their subjects from among five species: American widgeon, wood duck, gadwall, ring-necked duck and hooded merganser. More than half chose the colorful wood duck, while, at the other extreme, only 11 picked the gadwall.

The judges for the two-day competition were Kenn Kaufman, field editor for *Audubon* magazine and author of several books on birding, including the field guide titled *Birds of North America*; Richard Smoker of Maryland, a noted taxidermist and carver of waterfowl; Michael Jaffe of Washington, D.C., a veteran duck-stamp collector and dealer; Tom Hutchens of North Dakota, immediate past chairman of the Delta Waterfowl Foundation and a long-time director of Ducks Unlimited; and John Tomke of Indiana, serving his third term as Ducks Unlimited's president.

"After the first round of judging, which took almost all morning [October 5], the original 224 pieces of art were whittled down to fewer than 50," wrote Kenn Kaufman in *Bird Watcher's Digest*. "... Like the jury in a high-profile court case, we were sequestered during lunch, spirited away to an upper floor of the Interior building, so that no one could claim that artists had been lobbying the judges during this time ...

"In the second round, we voted again on the remaining 43 pieces by holding up cards to give each piece a numerical score from one to five. It was slow and painstaking work. By now, almost all the remaining paintings were accurate enough in the way they showed the birds, and we had to consider more subjective things. How attractive was the composition? How well would the design hold up when reduced to the size of a stamp? By the time the second round was over, the 43 excellent entries had been narrowed down to eight outstanding ones.

"Then the room was cleared so that the judges could study the finalists closely one more time. None of us tried to influence the votes of the others, but we were allowed to discuss technical aspects of the paintings. Rich Smoker, accustomed to looking at fine details, pointed out one wing feather that appeared to be upside down. Tom Hutchens raised a question about another painting in which two birds appeared to be in different stages of plumage (one fresh, one worn), as if seen at different times of year. I asked our attending consultant from the Postal Service about whether certain fine details in another painting would show up when reproduced. We all made good use of our reducing glass: the opposite of a magnifying glass, making each painting look smaller, so that we could visualize how it would look at stamp size."

This is Mark Anderson's painting of two male hooded mergansers that was adapted for use on the 2005-2006 federal duck stamp.

For the final round of voting, Interior Secretary Gale Norton and senior Fish and Wildlife Service officials joined the judges. "We'd been told that there are often ties at this point, and that voting has to continue until the tie is broken, but today the first, second and third-place finishers were all chosen in this round," Kaufman wrote. "Secretary Norton did the honors of revealing these winners, and then from the podium she placed a call to the winner, Mark Anderson."

Jim Hautman's male and female wood duck placed second in the competition.

A painting of a single male hooded merganser won third place for Don Moore.

Second place went to Jim Hautman of Chaska, Minnesota, one of a famous trio of brothers that collectively has won the federal competition seven times, for his acrylic painting of a pair of wood ducks. Don Moore of Monona, Wisconsin, took third place for an acrylic of a male hooded merganser.

Mergansers are fish-eating ducks that are characterized by comparatively long, narrow, cylindrical bills with saw-tooth edges that enable them to seize and devour fish of considerable size. The smallest and most beautiful of the group is the hooded merganser. The male has a thin semicircular crest that it can open or shut like a fan. The crest is mostly white, with a narrow black border behind and a wider black space in front. Its body is blackish with dull rusty flanks, and its breast is white with two black stripes down the side.

Hoodeds breed from southern Alaska south to Oregon and Montana, and from Manitoba and Nova Scotia south to Arkansas and northern Alabama, nesting in hollow trees or logs. They winter near the coasts from British Columbia to California and from New England to Florida and Texas.

The birds are most often seen along rivers and in estuaries during the fall and winter. In flight, they are among the fastest members of the duck family. They feed chiefly on small fish, which they pursue swiftly underwater, but also eat frogs and aquatic insects.

The hooded merganser had made two previous appearances on federal duck stamps. Albert Earl Gilbert's opaque watercolor painting of a solo male swimming was reproduced on the 1978 stamp, while a wash by Claremont Gale Pritchard of a male and female seated on a branch jutting out of the water was featured in 1968.

The Design

Mark Anderson grew up in South Dakota. A self-taught wildlife artist, he began painting in 1980 and made art his full-time vocation in 1993.

Although he has created the illustrations for numerous state wildlife stamps, his victory in the 2004 federal duck stamp competition was his first in 18 consecutive years of trying to win the "big one." His best showing during that time was a seventh-place finish in 2002.

Anderson had not painted hooded mergansers often, but he had an adequate supply of reference photographs he had taken at the local zoo in Sioux Falls, and his luck with the species had been good. "I won the Iowa Ducks Unlimited Artist of the Year competition with mergansers," he said. "The few merganser paintings I did after that sold right away.

"They're an easy duck to paint. I feel really comfortable painting them. There's not a whole lot of color to them; they're black and white and orange, and that's it."

His decision to depict two male mergansers was a "gamble," he said.

"The judges tend to like to see a male and female pair or a single bird," he said. "Each year, you try to figure out which species to do, and how to portray them. I was at the point where I didn't care any more. I was just going to paint what I wanted to paint.

"I had pulled out my best photographs of a male merganser, and my best photographs of a female, and I was sitting there playing with them, putting them together to see what looked good. For some reason, I put the two males together, and I thought, 'Man, that's striking,' because of their feather patterns. I thought to myself, 'I'm going to do two males.' "

The next question was how to portray the birds — flying, standing or swimming, and in which direction.

"I decided to show the two drakes swimming to the left, sitting on the water, and make it a very clean design. It was really important that there not be a lot of weeds or tree branches or leaves in the background.

"I had a hard time not putting in a few weeds! But I had looked at past winners, and a lot of them had nothing else in them, pretty much just a duck sitting on the water, and again I thought, 'What the heck, I'm just going to leave it plain.' Again, it was almost this I-don't-care attitude."

His key decision, Anderson believes, was to use warm colors in the painting.

"After I won, I went on the tour with the Federal Duck Stamp Office," he said. "They cart around the top 25 original paintings, and they always put the first-, second- and third-place paintings in the middle, surrounded by the others.

"And I tell you what, when you stood back 20 feet away and looked at them, mine just jumped out at you because of the warm golden yellowish colors. Your eye went right to it. The other entries were blues and grays, which are cool colors, and mine just seemed to have that extra snap.

"That's what you're trying to do when you're in competition. They say right there in the contest rules: You have to produce a painting that's going to capture the attention of the judges. In this contest, they were looking at 224 entries.

"I had never really used that color scheme before, and I was initially planning to do bluish or greenish water. Then I thought, 'I'm going to use golden water.' Again, something different. And it worked."

Anderson subtly varied the look of the two birds themselves. One has its crest raised slightly more than the other, exposing more of the white patch. The bird at the rear has turned its head slightly away from the viewer, while its companion is looking straight ahead.

The painting was completed in about three days. As is his custom, Anderson omitted the preliminary sketches and color studies that many artists consider a necessary step. "It's all visualized in my mind," he said. "I can do a painting in the time it would take most artists to make a pencil sketch. It saves me an immense amount of time. I can average about 70 original paintings a year."

"Anderson's painting … was simple but elegant, a striking composition," wrote contest judge Kenn Kaufman in *Bird Watcher's Digest*. "It had caught my eye on my first pass through all 224 entries. Any of the eight finalists would have made a great stamp, but Anderson's mergansers will make one of the most beautiful duck stamps ever."

Recent duck stamps had been designed by Postal Service art director Phil Jordan, and their intaglio portions had been created by a photochemical process. This time, Sennett Security Products contracted with world-famous stamp engraver Czeslaw Slania of Sweden to do both the design and engraving work.

Czeslaw Slania completed the preliminary design for the 2005 duck stamp, as shown here. The name of the species and the void date are incorrect and were included by Slania as placeholders. Also shown is his intaglio study for the engraved portion of the stamp.

This is Piotr Naszarkowski's line engraving, which is printed in black on the four-color offset-printed portion of the stamp with water-activated gum.

However, Slania was in failing health and died March 17, 2005, at the age of 83. He completed the preliminary design and an intaglio study for the stamp before the task had to be turned over to a protégé, Piotr Naszarkowski. In a similar manner, Naszarkowski had taken over from Slania the job of engraving the U.S. 37¢ Greta Garbo commemorative stamp and its 10-krona Swedish counterpart (see separate chapter).

On the version of the stamp with water-activated gum, Naszarkowski's engraving is much more detailed than the intaglio portions on previous duck stamps have been. It comprises the two hooded mergansers, their reflections in the water and the surrounding ripple patterns, and is printed in black.

On the self-adhesive variety, which has debossing instead of intaglio, the debossed area consists of the portions of the two mergansers — bodies, wings and tails — between their heads and their reflections in the water. The offset printing is much more detailed, darker and richer than on the water-activated stamp, a difference that is particularly noticeable in the birds' crests and the reflections of their bodies.

In Slania's design, the vignette is surrounded by a gray-green border that is tapered on the two sides. "MIGRATORY BIRD HUNTING AND CONSERVATION STAMP" and "U.S. DEPARTMENT OF THE INTERIOR" are in the top and bottom border panels, respectively. The "$15" and "Void after June 30, 2006" are superimposed on the water at the upper right, and "Hooded Merganser," in dropout white letters, is at the upper left.

Both the water-activated and self-adhesive varieties include in their designs the microprinted letters "FWS," for Fish & Wildlife Service, but in different locations. On the water-activated stamp, the microprinting can be found in the water below the reflection of the second (rear) duck. On the self-adhesive, it is in the water near the right frameline, about one-fourth of an inch below the "6" in "2006."

Varieties: Extra Frameline

A production oversight produced a constant plate variety on exactly one-half of the stamps with water-activated gum that were distributed in panes of 20.

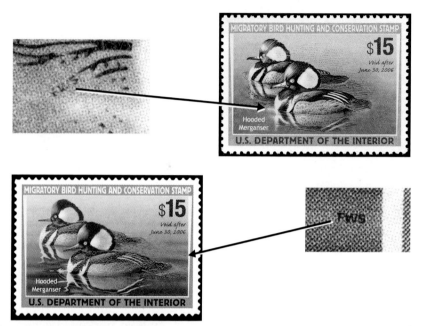

The microprinted letters "FWS" are in different locations on the two stamp varieties. On the water-activated stamp, they can be found in the water below the reflection of the second (rear) duck. On the self-adhesive, they are in the water near the right frameline, about one-fourth of an inch below the "6" in "2006."

The stamps on the right two panes of a four-pane printing sheet have a very thin black frameline at the top, right and bottom edges of the design. It can be seen with moderate magnification (10-power or greater). The stamps on the left side of the printing sheet do not have the frameline.

The Scott catalogs have designated the varieties Type I (no frameline) and Type II (frameline). Type II was assigned the minor catalog number RW72c.

Bob Dumaine told *Linn's* that Steve Rosen, an expertizer for Professional Stamp Experts of Newport Beach, California, first spotted the thin lines on some of the stamps that Dumaine had submitted to PSE for authentication. The Federal Duck Stamp Office's Robert Williams told Dumaine that the lines should have been removed before the stamps were printed.

"The lines on the edges of the stamps on the right side of the press sheet do not appear on the stamp model approved by the U.S. Fish and Wildlife Service," Williams told Dumaine. "According to the printer, the lines on the edges of some of the stamps are computer-generated holding lines.

"All of the lines should have been deleted when the offset printing film was processed. Some lines remain as a result of a process error in making the offset printing film.

"The lines do not impact the functionality or security features of the

A production mistake caused a thin frameline to be printed along three edges of the design on 500,000 of the 1 million 2005-2006 Hooded Mergansers duck stamps issued with water-activated gum. The magnified image of the top right corner of the stamp shows the unnecessary frameline.

stamp. Therefore, the U.S. Fish and Wildlife Service will not issue a recall."

Dumaine pointed out to *The Yearbook* that three of the position pieces that can be extracted from an uncut press sheet contain both Type I and Type II stamps. These are the cross-gutter block of 16, which consists of four plate number blocks, and the two pairs of plate number blocks that are linked by a vertical gutter, one pair from the top of the sheet, the other from the bottom.

Varieties: Partial Perforations

At least one specimen of the water-activated stamp in a pane of one is known without a row of perforations along the bottom. The perforations along the top and sides are normal.

First-Day Facts

The first day of sale ceremony for the 2005 Duck Stamp was held June 30 in the caucus room of the Russell Senate Office Building in Washington, D.C.

On hand were Matt Hogan, acting director of the Fish and Wildlife Service; U.S. Senator Tim Johnson, Democrat of South Dakota; members of the Migratory Bird Conservation Commission; and artist Mark Anderson.

The following day, a "Duck Stamp Celebration" was held at the National Postal Museum in Washington. Speakers were Allen Kane, director of the museum; Paul Schmidt, assistant service director for migratory birds; and Mark Anderson,

The traditional artist's hometown ceremony was held July 7 at the Washington Pavilion, an arts and sciences center in Sioux Falls, South Dakota,

July 7. On hand were the Fish and Wildlife Service's Matt Hogan and U.S. Senator John Thune, South Dakota Republican.

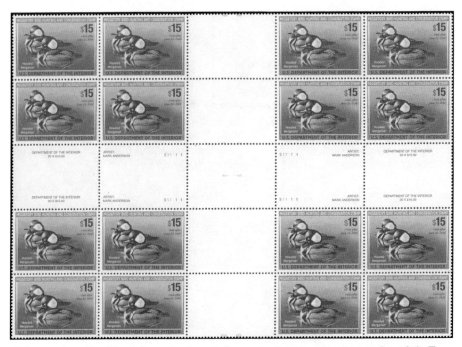

This cross-gutter block from the heart of an uncut press sheet contains eight Type I (no frameline) Hooded Merganser stamps on the left and eight Type II (frameline) stamps on the right. (Photo courtesy of Sam Houston Duck Company)

37¢ GARDEN BOUQUET STAMPED STATIONERY

Date of Issue: March 3, 2005

Price: $14.95 for a pack of 12 sheets

Catalog Number: Scott U657

Colors: cyan, magenta, yellow, black

First-Day Cancel: New York, New York

First-Day Cancellations: 235,593 (includes Northeast Deciduous Forest stamps)

Format: letter sheet, vertical, with rows of roulettes in two places for folding and an adhesive strip for sealing, printed in press sheets of 8 letter sheets each

Sheet Size: 5½ by 10⅜ inches; 139.7 by 263.53 mm

Pack Size: 5½ by 13 inches; 139.7 by 330.2 mm

Sheet Markings: "TO EXPOSE ADHESIVE, REMOVE LINER" in repeat pattern on liner

Pack Markings: On front: "Garden Bouquet/STAMPED STATIONERY." "TWELVE/SELF-MAILERS." "NEW PRODUCT!" USPS logo. "Stamp Products A/C 092/www.usps.com/1 800 STAMP-24." On back: "No Postage Required! Stamp is Pre-printed/1. Fold top flap down/2. Remove adhesive liner and fold bottom flap up to seal/3. Place clear seals one on each side of folded mailer/4. Address and mail." "Garden Bouquet/12 Stamped Stationery/Item No. 566294/Price: $14.95/A/C 092/Package Not Suitable for/Philatelic Archiving." Universal Product Code (UPC) "0 566294 8."

Designer, Art Director and Typographer: Richard Sheaff of Scottsdale, Arizona

Modeler: Donald Woo of Sennett Security Products, Chantilly, Virginia

Stamp Manufacturing: Printed by Banknote Corporation of America/Sennett Security Products, Browns Summit, North Carolina, on Man Roland 300 offset press. Sheets processed by Unique Binders, Fredericksburg, Virginia.

Quantity Ordered: 480,000 (40,000 packs)

Tagging: block tagging over imprinted stamp

The Letter Sheet

On March 3, the Postal Service issued a postpaid letter sheet bearing an imprinted reproduction of the 37¢ Garden Bouquet stamp of 2004. USPS sold the letter sheet in packs of 12 for $14.95, a price that represented a markup of 50.6¢ over the 37¢ postage value of each sheet.

"Writing a personal note on this beautiful stationery certainly shows the recipient you care," said David Failor, executive director, stamp services, in a USPS news release. "This prestamped stationery is ideal for thank-you notes, Mother's Day wishes and expressions of love and friendship. It's also easy to use. Just write a note, seal the stationery and drop it in the mail."

The first-day sale of the Garden Bouquet sheet followed by a little more than eight months the issuance of a set of four 37¢ letter sheets reproducing the 2004 Art of Disney: Friendship stamps. Those sheets also were sold in packs of 12 for $14.95 (three of each variety). In the case of the Disney sheets, the high premium drew strong criticism from the philatelic press and led to a formal challenge filed with the Postal Rate Commission by a customer and frequent postal critic.

Despite the controversy, USPS proceeded with plans to issue the Garden Bouquet letter sheet in 2004. It was listed as available for ordering in the Fall 2004 issue of *USA Philatelic*, the Postal Service's mail-order catalog, which was distributed in mid-July 2004. However, officials decided to delay the Garden Bouquet sheet's issuance after the Disney sheets turned out to be prone to damage in the mailstream.

When folded and sealed, the Disney sheets were like

envelopes with no sides, and *Linn's Stamp News* reported that they did not fare well in the Postal Service's automated, high-speed mail-processing equipment. "The heavy paper stock likely is the culprit, because when a given sheet is first folded and sealed, it bows out at the middle, instead of lying flat," *Linn's* said. "This bowing significantly increases the probability that the leading edge of the folded sheet will be bent, scraped, torn or otherwise mutilated as the sheet moves through a facer-canceler machine."

David Failor told a meeting of stamp journalists August 12, 2004, that questions were being posed to Banknote Corporation of America/Sennett Security Products, the printer of both the Garden Bouquet sheet and the Disney sheets. "We are trying to work with the printer to reduce the possibility of damage in the mail," Failor said. "One change being considered is the addition of side flaps to the sheet."

Ultimately, the Garden Bouquet sheet was issued without side flaps. Instead, each pack of 12 came with a separate sheet of 24 round, clear seals that could be used to close the open edges on the left and right sides of a folded sheet before mailing.

The Garden Bouquet sheet is narrower and shorter than the Disney sheets and the lined writing area on its message side is only about two-thirds as large. The outside is decorated on the top and bottom flaps with enlarged reproductions of the imprinted stamp's floral design, with the flaps' edges die-cut to follow the outline of petals and leaves. When the flaps are folded over to form the envelope, the floral image on the bottom flap overlaps and lines up with the image on the top flap.

The paper stock is thinner than the paper used to print the Disney sheets and has roulettes instead of grooves to facilitate folding. A pull-off strip exposes the pressure-sensitive sealing adhesive. Except for the message and address areas, the paper is coated with a thick, shiny laminate that wasn't found on the Disney sheets. As *Linn's* reported, this coating isn't particularly receptive to the inks used to apply cancellations and auxiliary markings, which tend to rub off.

Linn's conducted a test mailing of Garden Bouquet sheets and reported that, although the item "is a somewhat reluctant traveler through the mailstream … a given Garden Bouquet sheet is more likely to arrive intact at its destination" than is a Disney sheet.

One problem, wrote staff writer Charles Snee, was the ambiguity of the directions printed on the cardboard insert to which the 12 sheets are attached. Step 3 of a four-step process reads: "Place clear seals on each side of folded matter." This step "is decidedly unclear," Snee wrote. "What exactly is meant by 'each side'?

"The sender (spouse of a *Linn's* editor) of [a cover illustrated with the article] misinterpreted step 3 and affixed the seals on the left and right of the flap on the back side of the folded sheet. As a result, the folded sheet bowed out and was severely damaged during transit. A large chunk of paper was torn away at lower right."

These two Garden Bouquet sheets tell different stories of their trips through the mailstream. One, sent from Ohio to Denmark, had its two auxiliary seals correctly affixed to the left and right edges and arrived undamaged. The other, with the seals incorrectly placed on the back of the folded sheet, was severely damaged in transit, with a large chunk of paper torn away at lower right.

However, another sheet, sent by a *Linn's* editor to a relative in Oregon, arrived inact despite having the two seals affixed in the same manner as those on the damaged sheet, Snee reported.

Linn's examined two additional Garden Bouquet sheets that had passed through the mail without damage. One, with the seals correctly placed, was sent from Ohio to Denmark. The other was mailed to *Linn's* by a collector in California.

"It is difficult to draw any conclusions from these hit-or-miss results," Snee wrote. "The laminated paper stock and proper use of the seals, however, both seem to increase the likelihood that the Garden Bouquet sheet will avoid significant damage after being mailed."

The complaint that the premium charged by USPS for the Disney letter sheets — and, by inference, other letter sheets sold at the same price — was excessive was filed with the Postal Rate Commission June 24, 2004, by self-styled postal watchdog Douglas F. Carlson, a lawyer and assistant dean at the University of California/Santa Cruz who had contested other USPS policies in the past.

The commission should have been asked to approve the product and to set its price under the same standards it applies to postal stationery items, Carlson contended. He asked the panel to establish a new category of "stamped stationery" and to require such products to be sold at a "fair and consistent price."

On January 17, 2006, USPS filed a motion in response arguing that the Disney stationery is "a philatelic item" and therefore not comparable to "a utilitarian stamp envelope" that the commission regulates "based solely on the actual costs of the envelope." The Postal Service cited a 1976 commission ruling that disavowed authority over the sale of philatelic items because "providing philatelic services is not so closely related to the carriage of mail that it can be considered a special postal service" under the law that controls the Postal Service.

In its motion, USPS argued: "Most of the value the Disney stationery has above the face value of the stamps is due to the value placed by the public on the artwork and design, i.e., its philatelic value. Indeed, in order for the commission to properly discern the artistic and design values of such products, entirely new disciplines, namely the valuation of artwork and the appraisal of design features, would have to be introduced into commission proceedings."

The Postal Service contended that the heart of Carlson's complaint "actually undermines the other arguments he makes to support his contention that the sale of the stationery is so closely related to the transmission of mail that it is a 'postal service.' " It cited his allegation that the surcharge discriminates against stamp collectors who "may feel compelled to purchase" the stationery "to avoid a gap or omission in their stamp collections."

"The problem Mr. Carlson alleges is not that it costs too much to buy Disney stamped stationery to mail a letter," USPS said. "He does not, and cannot, allege that one is compelled to buy Disney stationery in order to send a letter. Mailers have many options to do so, all of which include the need for some level of expenditure above postage for paper, envelopes and the like.

"Mr. Carlson is apparently objecting to the price because he 'may feel compelled' to buy the stationery not to mail it, but in order to complete his philatelic collection. Regulating the philatelic value of items — beyond the original face value of the stamp itself — is not an area over which the commission exercises jurisdiction.

"Disney stationery does not replace other ordinary means of first-class mail letter postage, and is offered primarily for other reasons, including the heritage represented by the artwork and the encouragement of children to sit down, take out their pens, and engage in good old-fashioned letter writing."

The Design

The imprinted stamp on the letter sheet is a reproduction of the 37¢ Garden Bouquet stamp of 2004, which was offset-printed by Ashton-Potter (USA) Ltd. It was one of a pair of special stamps, 37¢ and 60¢ in denomination, that were issued for use in mailing wedding invitations and RSVPs. The 37¢ stamp depicts a bouquet of white lilacs and pink roses, from a chromolithograph probably printed in Germany circa 1880-1900. The source art is in the ephemera collection of the stamp's designer, USPS art director Richard Sheaff.

Both the imprinted stamp and the actual stamp are identical in size and appearance. The actual stamp, when superimposed on the imprinted stamp, fits its outline exactly, down to the peaks and valleys of the die-cut simulated perfs.

However, the image of the stamp on the letter sheet is not as clearly defined as that of its real counterpart. This is because BCA/Sennett used coarser screens to print the four process colors of the imprinted stamp than Ashton-Potter used for the real one.

The lilacs-and-roses illustration on the imprinted stamp is reproduced in enlarged form in three other places on the letter sheet.

First-Day Facts

The letter sheet was issued at the American Stamp Dealers Association's New York Postage Stamp Mega Event at Madison Square Garden in Manhattan. It was the same venue at which the 37¢ Garden Bouquet stamp itself had been dedicated one year earlier.

"Visitors to the show can obtain the first-day-of-issue postmark on this item, as March 3 will be the first day of issue dedication ceremony for the Deciduous Forest stamp [sic]," the Postal Service announced. "As the Garden Bouquet stamp was issued last year, there is no first-day ceremony for the Garden Bouquet stationery."

Collectors were given 90 days, until June 2, 2005, to submit self-addressed Garden Bouquet letter sheets to the USPS Special Events Unit in New York, New York, for first-day postmarks. Stamp Fulfillment Services didn't offer uncacheted first-day covers of the Garden Bouquet sheet, as it does for most new issues.

37¢ THE ART OF DISNEY: CELEBRATION PICTURE POSTAL CARDS (4 DESIGNS)

Date of Issue: June 30, 2005

Price: $9.75 for book of 20 cards

Catalog Numbers: Scott UX436-UX439, single cards; UX439a, book of 20 cards

Colors: cyan, magenta, yellow, black. Aqueous coating added to picture sides and book covers.

First-Day Cancel: Anaheim, California

First-Day Cancellations: 379,255 (includes Disney stamps)

Format: Book containing 20 cards, 5 of each design, with microperforations to permit removal of individual cards. Cards offset-printed in 18-subject sheets, 6 cards across by 3 cards down.

Size of Card: 6 by 4.25 inches; 152.4 by 107.9 mm

Size of Book: 6.75 by 4.25 inches; 171.45 by 107.95

Card Markings: On address side of each card: "Disney Materials © Disney," "© 2005 USPS." On individual cards: "Walt Disney's Mickey Mouse and Pluto/Anticipating a celebration can be half the fun. Mickey Mouse and his faithful/dog Pluto are experts when it comes to sharing cake and having good times./They're sure to help get your party started early!" "Alice and the Mad Hatter/A very merry tea party hosted by the Mad Hatter gives Alice a chance to/catch up on all the news in Wonderland. This cheerful postal card makes it/easy for you and your friends to stay in touch." "Ariel and Flounder/Wherever you are, just being in touch with pals can lead to merriment. Ariel,/a little mermaid, longs to enjoy life on land, but that doesn't stop her from/enjoying music with/Flounder and her other under-sea friends." "Snow White and Dopey/When it's time to celebrate, our best advice is to follow the lead of Snow/White and Dopey and dance! With this postal card, you can keep the 'silly/song' playing a little bit longer."

Cover Markings: On outside front: "The Art of Disney/Celebration/TWENTY STAMPED POSTAL CARDS • FOUR DESIGNS • $9.75." On outside back: "THE ART OF DISNEY: CELEBRATION/With these stamped postal cards, the U.S. Postal Service honors the art of celebration/as imagined by Walt Disney and his studio animators. Now, with help from a few/beloved Disney characters, it's easy to add some zest to your correspondence." Promotion for the Postal Store website. "Disney Materials © Disney."/"© 2005 USPS."/"Item No. 980600/Price: $9.75/AIC 092/Package Not Suitable for Philatelic Archiving." USPS logo. Universal Product Code (UPS) "0 980600 1."

Designer: David Pacheco, Burbank, California

Illustrator: Peter Emmerich, New York, New York

Art Director: Terrence McCaffrey

Modeler: Joseph Sheeran of Ashton-Potter (USA) Ltd., Williamsville, New York

Card Manufacturing: Cards printed by Ashton-Potter on Heidelberg SN102-8-PL offset press. Cards processed by Ashton-Potter.

Quantity Ordered: 48,700 books (974,000 cards)

Paper Type: Carolina 10 PT C1S

Paper Supplier: Xpedex, Chicago, Illinois

Tagging: Vertical bar to right of stamp

The Cards

On June 30, the Postal Service issued a set of four 23¢ picture postal cards illustrating The Art of Disney: Celebration. The cards were compan-

Walt Disney's Mickey Mouse and Pluto
Anticipating a celebration can be half the fun. Mickey Mouse and his faithful dog Pluto are experts when it comes to sharing cake and having good times. They're sure to help get your party started early!

Alice and the Mad Hatter
A very merry tea party hosted by the Mad Hatter gives Alice a chance to catch up on all the news in Wonderland. This cheerful postal card makes it easy for you and your friends to stay in touch.

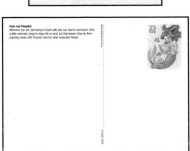

Ariel and Flounder
Wherever you are, just being in touch with pals can lead to merriment. Ariel, a little mermaid, longs to enjoy life on land, but that doesn't stop her from enjoying music with Flounder and two other undersea friends.

Snow White and Dopey
When it's time to celebrate, our best advice is to follow the lead of Snow White and Dopey and dance! With this postal card, you can keep the "silly song" playing a little bit longer.

ion pieces to four 37¢ self-adhesive stamps that were issued the same day (see separate chapter).

The two sets, stamps and cards, constituted the second entry in the Postal Service's three-year Art of Disney series and featured characters from the films of the Walt Disney Studios in festive settings.

The cards, like the stamps, had their first-day sale in Disneyland, which was observing its 50th anniversary in 2005. The Anaheim, California, theme park also had been the dedication site for the inaugural Disney stamps and cards, The Art of Disney: Friendship, in 2004.

The Postal Service's announced plan was to issue four stamps and four matching postal cards with the theme of Romance in 2006 to complete the series.

The postal cards are bound in a book of 20 cards, five of each variety, with microperfing for easy removal. USPS sold the book for $9.75, or 48.75¢ per card.

On the address side of each postal card is an imprinted stamp reproducing the design of one of the four Disney postage stamps. In the upper left corner is a paragraph of descriptive text, identical to the text on the back of the liner behind the corresponding stamp. An enlargement of the stamp design, without typography, fills the picture side of the card.

The cards were produced by offset lithography by Ashton-Potter (USA) Ltd., unlike the 2004 cards, which were offset-printed by Banknote Corporation of America/Sennett Security Products. The picture sides and the book covers were printed in the four process colors, black, cyan, magenta and yellow. An aqueous coating for protection against scuffing was applied to the picture sides and the covers.

USPS ordered a total of 48,700 books, or 974,000 cards, 243,500 of each variety. The print order for the first set of Disney postal cards in 2004 had been 68,000 books, or 1.36 million cards.

The Designs

The imprinted stamps and picture sides of the postal cards, like the corresponding postage stamps, depict Mickey Mouse and his dog Pluto; the Mad Hatter and Alice at the Mad Tea Party, from *Alice in Wonderland*; Snow White and Dopey, from *Snow White and the Seven Dwarfs*; and Ariel and her best friend, Flounder, from *The Little Mermaid*. Each illustration features a different way of celebrating, through food, drink, dance and music, respectively.

The imprinted stamp on each postal card is the same size as its postage-stamp counterpart and identical in design, except that the denomination is 23¢ rather than 37¢ and there is no tiny 2005 year date beneath the frameline. Their images are unusually crisp and well-defined for postal-card printing. The images on the picture sides are large and clear, and do full justice to the detail and texture of Peter Emmerich's acrylic paintings. Because the postal cards are slightly deeper and narrower than the stamp designs, more of the blue sky — or, in the case of the Little Mermaid stamp, blue water — shows at the top of the pictures on the cards; the cropping at the sides of the cards and of the stamps is virtually identical.

The cover of the postal-card book bears reproductions of each of the four designs, minus typography, against a gold background that reproduces the inscription, Tinker Bell image and stars from the header of the stamp pane.

When a card is removed from its book, a narrow strip of blue from the top of the picture-side image remains on the book stub.

First-Day Facts

Information on the first-day ceremony at Disneyland in Anaheim, California, can be found in the chapter on The Art of Disney: Celebration stamps.

23¢ AMERICA ON THE MOVE: 50S SPORTY CARS PICTURE POSTAL CARDS (5 DESIGNS)

Date of Issue: August 20, 2005

Price: $9.75 for book of 20 cards

Catalog Numbers: Scott UX440-UX444, single cards; UX444a, book of 20 cards

Colors: black, cyan, magenta, yellow

First-Day Cancel: Detroit, Michigan

First-Day Cancellations: 337,512 (includes Sporty Cars stamps)

Format: Book containing 20 cards, 4 of each design, with microperforations to permit removal of individual cards. Cards offset-printed in 18-subject sheets, 6 across by 3 down.

Size of Card: 6 by 4.25 inches; 152.4 by 107.9 mm

Size of Book: 6.75 by 4.25 inches; 171.45 by 107.95

Card Markings: On address side of each card: "© 2005 USPS." On individual cards: "Ford & Thunderbird™ Ford Motor Company." "General Motors Corvette Trademarks used under license to the USPS."

Cover Markings: On outside front: "AMERICA ON THE MOVE/50s Sporty Cars/$9.75/Twenty Stamped Postal Cards • Five Separate Designs." On outside back: Images of the 5 card designs. Promotion for The Postal Store website. "Ford & Thunderbird™ Ford Motor Company/General Motors Corvette Trademarks used under license to the USPS"/© 2005 USPS." "Item No. 980700/Price: $9.75/AIC 092." "Package Not Suitable/ for Philatelic Archiving." USPS logo. Universal Product Code (UPC) "0 980700 0."

Artist and Designer: Art M. Fitzpatrick of Carlsbad, California

Art Director and Typographer: Carl Herrman of Carlsbad, California

Modeler: Joseph Sheeran, Ashton-Potter (USA) Ltd., Williamsville, New York

Card Manufacturing: Cards printed by Ashton-Potter on Heidelberg SN102-8-PL offset press. Cards finished by Ashton-Potter.

Quantity Ordered: 48,700 books (974,000 cards)

Paper Type: Carolina 10 pt, C1S

Paper Supplier: Xpedex, Chicago, Illinois

Tagging: vertical bar to right of stamp

The Cards

On August 20, the Postal Service issued a set of five 23¢ picture postal cards illustrating what it called "sporty cars" of the 1950s. The cards were companion pieces to five 37¢ self-adhesive stamps that were issued in double-sided convertible-booklet form on the same day (see separate chapter).

The postal cards are bound in a book of 20 cards, four of each vari-

1955 Ford Thunderbird

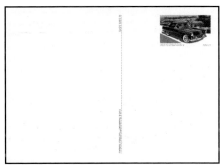

1952 Nash Healey

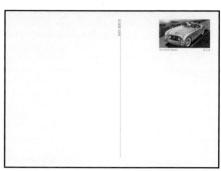

1953 Chevrolet Corvette

1953 Studebaker Starliner

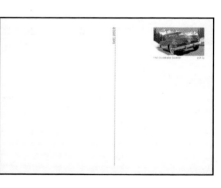

1954 Kaiser Darrin

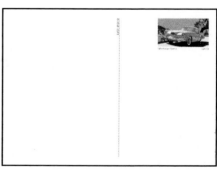

ety, arranged in five-card sequences. The cards are microperfed for easy removal. USPS sold the book for $9.75, or 48.75¢ per card.

On the address side of each postal card is an imprinted stamp reproducing the design of one of the five Sporty Cars postage stamps, which depict a 1955 Ford Thunderbird, 1952 Nash Healey, 1953 Chevrolet Corvette, 1953 Studebaker Starliner and 1954 Kaiser Darrin. An enlargement of the stamp design, with identifying typography, fills the picture side of the card.

Carl Herrman, the art director for the Sporty Cars project, pointed out that the cards contain no subject information, although brief textual material normally is an integral part of USPS picture postal cards. There would have been ample room on the cards for the "fascinating little stories" that could have been told about each featured automobile, he said, "but no one ever did it."

The cards were produced by offset lithography by Ashton-Potter (USA) Ltd., which also printed the stamps. The picture sides and the book covers were printed in the four process colors: black, cyan, magenta and yellow. An aqueous coating for protection against scuffing was applied to the picture sides and the covers.

The Designs

The imprinted stamp on the address side of each postal card is slightly smaller than its postage-stamp counterpart, but otherwise is identical, except that the denomination is 23¢ rather than 37¢ and there is no tiny 2005 year date included in the design. The images are less crisp than those on the stamps because the screening is coarser and the postal-card stock is a lower grade than the stamp paper.

However, the images on the picture sides are large and clear, and do full justice to the detail and texture of Art M. Fitzpatrick's computer paintings, which evoke the glamorous automobile illustrations he made for General Motors' advertisements in the 1950s and 1960s. Because the postal cards are slightly deeper and narrower than the stamp designs, there is more of each design at top and/or bottom of the cards and less on one or both sides. This is most noticeable on the card depicting the Nash Healey, on which two moored yachts can be seen at the top of the picture that are cropped from the stamp illustration.

The cover of the postal-card book reproduces the Chevrolet Corvette illustration, the same Fitzgerald art that Carl Herrman chose for the cover of the convertible booklet containing the Sporty Cars stamps.

First-Day Facts

Information on the first-day ceremony at the Michigan State Fair in Detroit, Michigan, can be found in the chapter on the Sporty Cars stamps.

23¢ LET'S DANCE/BAILEMOS
PICTURE POSTAL CARDS (4 DESIGNS)

Date of Issue: September 17, 2005

Price: $9.75 for book of 20 cards

Catalog Numbers: Scott UX445-UX448, single cards; UX448a, book of 20 cards

Colors: black, cyan, magenta, yellow

First-Day Cancel: Miami, Florida; New York, New York, and nationwide

First-Day Cancellations: 192,337 (both locations) (includes Let's Dance/Bailemos stamps)

Format: Book containing 20 cards, 5 of each design, with microperforations to permit removal of individual cards. Cards offset-printed in 18-subject sheets, 6 across by 3 down.

Size of Card: 6 by 4.25 inches; 152.4 by 107.9 mm

Size of Book: 6.75 by 4.25 inches; 171.45 by 107.95

Card Markings: On address side of each card: "© 2005 USPS." On individual cards: "Derived from Cuba's danzón and taking its name from the last three beats in its/1-2, 1-2-3 rhythm, cha-cha-cha became a dance craze in the 1950s." "A partir del danzón cubano y adoptando su nombre del sonido de los tres tiempos/seguidos del ritmo 1-2, 1-2-3, el cha-cha-chá hizo furor en los años 50." "An elaboration of the lively rhythms added to the Cuban son and danzón, mambo/became an international dance craze in the 1950s." "El mambo es un ritmo musical derivado del son y danzón-cubanos que se convirtió/en un baile de moda en los años 50 a nivel inter-nacional." "Popularized in the 1960s by New York Puerto Rican musicians, salsa integrates/rhythm and blues and jazz into Afro-Cuban rhythms." "El ritmo salsa, que músicos puertorriqueños hicieron popular en Nueva York en los/años 60, combina la música de jazz y blues con ritmos afrocuba-nos." "A blend of European and African-derived styles, merengue, with its cross-class/appeal, is the national dance of the Dominican Repúblic." "El merengue, co su combinación de estilos europeos y africanos y su encanto para/todas las clases sociales, es el baile nacional de la Repúb-lica Dominicana."

Cover Markings: On outside front: "Let's Dance Bailemos/Four Designs/Twenty Stamped Postal Cards/$9.75/Cuatro Diseños/Veinte Tarjetas Postales Prefranqueadas." On outside back: "Mambo/Cha Cha Cha/Salsa/Merengue/With these stamped postal cards, Latino artists/present their personal interpretations of the dances./En estas tarjetas postales pre-franqueadas, artistas latinos/ofrecen su interpretación personal de estos ritmos." Promotion for The Postal Store website in English and Spanish. "Item No. 980800/Price: $9.75/AIC 092/Package Not Suitable/for Philatelic Archiving." USPS logo. "© 2005 USPS." Universal Product Code (UPC) "0 980800 9."

Artist-Typographers: Edel Rodriguez of Mount Tabor, New Jersey; Sergio Baradat of New York, New York; Rafael López of San Diego, California; José Ortega of Toronto, Ontario, Canada

Designer and Art Director: Ethel Kessler of Bethesda, Maryland

Modeler: Joseph Sheeran, Ashton-Potter (USA) Ltd., Williamsville, New York

Card Manufacturing: Cards printed by Ashton-Potter on Heidelberg SN102-8-PL offset press. Cards finished by Ashton-Potter.

Quantity Ordered: 48,700 books (974,000 cards)

Paper Type: Carolina 10 pt, C1S

Paper Supplier: Xpedex, Chicago, Illinois

Tagging: vertical bar to right of stamp

The Cards

On September 17, the Postal Service issued a set of four 23¢ picture postal cards featuring dances that trace their origins to the islands of the Caribbean: merengue, salsa, cha-cha-cha and mambo.

The cards were companion pieces to four 37¢ self-adhesive stamps that were issued in a pane of 20 that same day (see separate chapter). They reproduced the stamp designs in their imprinted stamps and the illustrations on their picture sides.

Both cards and stamps were placed on sale nationwide, with official dedication ceremonies in New York, New York, and Miami, Florida.

The postal cards are bound in a book of 20 cards, five of each variety, arranged in four-card sequences. The cards are microperfed for easy removal. USPS sold the book for $9.75, or 48.75¢ per card.

On the address side of each postal card is an imprinted stamp reproducing the design of one of the four Let's Dance postage stamps, and a brief text message, in both English and Spanish, describing the dance that is illustrated. An enlargement of the stamp design fills the picture side of the card.

The cards were produced by offset lithography by Ashton-Potter (USA) Ltd. The picture sides and the book covers were printed in the four process colors, black, cyan, magenta and yellow. An aqueous coating for protection against scuffing was applied to the picture sides and the covers.

As it had done with the stamps, USPS destroyed the original print run of 48,700 books of postal cards (974,000 cards) because of mistakes in the Spanish text, and ordered a reprinting with corrections. The total cost of the Postal Service's failure to get it right the first time was $172,000.

The Designs

The imprinted stamp on the address side of each postal card is identical to its postage-stamp counterpart, except that the denomination is 23¢ rather than 37¢ and no tiny 2005 year date is included. The images are less crisp than those on the stamps because the screening is coarser than that used on the stamps and the postal-card stock is a lower grade than the stamp paper.

However, the illustrations on the reverse are large and clear, and reproduce the artwork of the four Latino artists, Edel Rodriguez, Sergio Baradat, Rafael Lopez and Jose Ortega, to excellent advantage. The vertical images are placed laterally and do not extend to the edges, but are of the same aspect ratio as the stamps, so no cropping was necessary.

The cover of the postal-card book bears reproductions of the four illustrations, without denominations, against a black background.

First-Day Facts

Information on the first-day ceremonies in New York, New York, and Miami, Florida, can be found in the chapter on the Let's Dance/Bailemos stamps.

VARIETIES

37¢ Flag

A die-cut variety of the 2002 37¢ Flag stamp issued in self-stick panes of 10 (Scott 3634) came to light in late December 2005.

Collector Rob Loeffler of New Jersey informed *Linn's Stamp News* of the discovery of the variety, which measures 11.3 on three sides, a slightly larger gauge than the gauge 11 stamp listed in the Scott *Specialized Catalogue of United States Stamps & Covers*. Scott catalog editor James Kloetzel told *Linn's* that the variety would be listed in the 2007 edition of the U.S. specialized catalog.

The accompanying illustration shows close-up images of horizontal die cutting between two rows of stamps on intact panes of 10. Stamps in the left pane have gauge 11.3 die cuts, while the die cuts of the stamps in the right pane measure 11.0. The tops of the die-cut peaks of stamps with gauge 11.3 die cuts are noticeably more pointed than are the tops of the die-cut peaks of stamps with gauge 11.0 die cuts.

About a year earlier, an observant collector in California found several used examples on mail, Loeffler told *Linn's*. Dealer Victor Bove of New Jersey checked his stock and found a mint block of four from the top of a booklet. The top selvage bore a plate number with a V prefix, so a positive identification of Avery Dennison as the printer was determined.

Close-up images of the die cutting between two rows of 37¢ Flag stamps in a pane of 10 with gauge 11.3 die cuts, left, and in a pane with gauge 11 die cuts, right. The gauges are distinguishable by the shape of the die-cut peaks.

37¢ Snowy Egret

A convertible booklet of 20 of the 37¢ Snowy Egret stamps that were issued January 30, 2004, was found with no die cutting between the stamps. A collector who wished to remain anonymous bought the pane at his local post office after a discussion with a postal clerk who told him that another customer had returned the stamps because they couldn't be removed from the backing paper.

The pane was consigned to Jacques C. Schiff Jr. of Ridgefield Park, New Jersey, who included it in his August 18, 2005, auction. On December 9, 2004, Schiff had auctioned a similar die-cut-missing error pane of Snowy Egret stamps with its bottom left stamp removed. That pane sold for $1,320, including a 10 percent buyer's premium.

The stamps were printed by Ashton-Potter (USA) Ltd. A normal pane is listed by Scott as 3830a. An error pair is listed as 3830b and a full pane without die cuts is listed as 3830c.

1¢ Kestrel

A pane of 50 self-adhesive 1¢ American Kestrel stamps with no trace of die-cutting was sold March 23, 2005, for $1,430, including a 10 percent buyer's premium, at a Jacques C. Schiff Jr. public auction. The stamp was printed by Banknote Corporation of America and issued in 2000. A pair without die cutting is listed by Scott as 3031Ab.

45¢ Future Mail Transportation Souvenir Sheet

A souvenir sheet containing four 45¢ airmail stamps depicting hypothetical future modes of mail transportation, with the tagging missing, was discovered by dealer Victor Bove of New Jersey among other tagging-omitted errors in a collection he purchased in January 2005. The imperforate souvenir sheet, printed by the Bureau of Engraving and Printing, was issued in 1989 to commemorate the 20th Universal Postal Union Congress.

On March 11, 2005, the error sheet received certificate No. 160,978 of the American Philatelic Expertizing Service stating that it is an "untagged error, unused, full original gum, never hinged, genuine in all respects." The pane is listed by Scott as C126e.

90¢ World Stamp Expo '89 Souvenir Sheet

In May 2005, after collector Roland Austin of Oklahoma read in *Linn's Stamp News* about the untagged Future Mail Transportation souvenir sheet cited above, he realized the significance of a different untagged souvenir sheet, also issued in 1989, that he had owned since the early 1990s. The imperforate sheet commemorated World Stamp Expo '89 and consists of reproductions of the 90¢ carmine and black Abraham Lincoln stamp of 1869 and three so-called trial color proofs of the same stamp with different color combinations.

Austin told *Linn's* that the error sheet was one of a small number of Expo '89 sheets he had bought from two small-town post offices in Oklahoma. After inspecting their tagging with a shortwave ultraviolet stamp, he found one without tagging. The error sheet was certified as genuine July 12, 2005, by the American Philatelic Expertizing Service. Scott lists it as 2433e.

20¢ Thomas H. Gallaudet

A tagging-omitted error of the 20¢ Thomas H. Gallaudet stamp of 1983 was discovered in February 2005 by collector Steve Unkrich of Ohio, who found it while examining tagging varieties of Great Americans definitive stamps in his collection. The error stamp is listed by Scott as 1861a.

37¢ Official Mail Envelope

In the fall of 2005, the Postal Service made available to specialist collectors of postal stationery a variety of the 37¢ Great Seal official mail stamped envelope (Scott UO91) of 2002.

The variety first was listed in the summer 2006 issue of *USA Philatelic*, the Postal Service's mail-order catalog, and has been given a minor listing in the Scott *Specialized Catalogue of U.S. Stamps & Covers* (Scott UO91a).

The first version of the envelope was printed on paper supplied by Manistique Paper Company of Manistique, Michigan. The paper looks gray because it was produced using 100 percent recycled paper. Text on the back of the envelope indicates the paper content.

After supplies of Manistique paper ran out, additional quantities of the envelope were printed on Weyerhaeuser Paper Company paper. This envelope looks white because it has a lower percentage of recycled content.

The new envelope also can be distinguished by the characteristics of its imprinted stamp. On the first version, the Great Seal blue panel measures 29 mm by 28 mm, the "USA" is even with the bottom of the eagle's neck, and "Official Mail" is not centered and slightly to the left. All of these elements are printed in the same blue ink. On the second version, the blue panel measures 27½ mm by 27½ mm, the top of "USA" is even with the olive branch, and "Official Mail" is centered over the panel.

USA Philatelic typically does not offer paper varieties of stationery, but because Official envelopes are not available to collectors through post offices, USPS made an exception.

On the left is the imprinted stamp of the 2002 envelope (Scott UO91). On the right is the variety (UO91a) printed on whiter paper. Differences include the size of the blue field forming the Great Seal and the position of the blue "USA."

BEP prints its last U.S. stamp

The year 2005 saw the private sector complete its takeover of the U.S. stamp printing business. On June 10, workers at the Bureau of Engraving and Printing in Washington, D.C., pulled a final roll of 37¢ Flag stamps from the Andreotti gravure press, concluding 111 years of postage stamp production by the Bureau. "In the end," wrote *Linn's Stamp News* Washington correspondent Bill McAllister, "the Bureau, with its elaborate security system, unionized printers and large government payroll, declared it could not compete with private printers."

First-class rate rises to 39¢

The Postal Service Board of Governors approved new postal rates and fees, to take effect January 8, 2006. Major changes approved were: first-class letter (one ounce), increase from 37¢ to 39¢; each additional ounce, 23¢ to 24¢; postcard, 23¢ to 24¢; priority mail (one pound), $3.85 to $4.05; express mail (one-half pound), $13.65 to $14.40; certified mail, $2.30 to $2.40. New international rates include: letter to Canada or Mexico (one ounce), 63¢; letter to all other countries, 84¢; postcard to Canada or Mexico, 55¢; postcard to all other countries, 75¢; aerogram to all countries, 75¢.

GAO finds U.S. semipostals successful

The Government Accountability Office reported September 30, 2005, that the nation's first three semipostal stamps were successful at raising funds for their respective causes.

The semipostals, all nondenominated, were the Breast Cancer Research stamp of 1998 (Scott B1), the Heroes of 2001 stamp (Scott B2) and the Stop Family Violence stamp of 2003 (Scott B3).

There are clear reasons why the Breast Cancer Research stamp was the most successful of the three, producing $44 million of the more than $56 million raised by the semipostals, the GAO said. The agency cited the stamp's strong support from the public, the efforts of the advocacy groups promoting it, its appealing design and its effective promotion by the Postal Service.

In November 2005, Congress completed action on a bill to extend the life of the Breast Cancer Research stamp an additional two years, and President George W. Bush signed it into law. Without the legislation, the stamp would have expired at the end of 2005. At the time, USPS had sold more than 657.5 million stamps — 6.9 million in September 2005 alone — and raised $47.9 million for breast cancer research.

During the year, Hungarian postal officials sought and received permission from USPS to use the U.S. Breast Cancer Research design on a new semipostal that Magyar Posta (the Hungarian postal authority) issued to raise money for the same cause. The design, by Ethel Kessler, a USPS art director, features artist Whitney Sherman's line drawing of Artemis, the Greek goddess of the hunt, against a background of pastel colors.

Turnover at CSAC

C. Douglas Lewis, chair of the Citizens' Stamp Advisory Committee, stepped down from CSAC in October 2005 under the term-limit policy instituted by Postmaster General John E. Potter. Lewis, a retired curator at the National Gallery of Art in Washington, D.C., had been named to CSAC in 1979 by Postmaster General William F. Bolger and served as chair of its Design Subcommittee for 20 years. He was appointed chair of the full committee in 2004. He was succeeded in the latter post by Ron Robinson, a CSAC member since 1993 and a retired Arkansas marketing-firm executive.

Meredith Davis, a professor and director of graduate programs in graphic design at North Carolina State University, departed from CSAC after 12 years' service. Postmaster General Potter appointed two new members to the panel: Joan Adams Mondale of Minneapolis, Minnesota, an artist who was honorary chairwoman of the Federal Council of the Arts and Humanities under President Jimmy Carter, and James Miho of Pasadena, California, an art director for Champion Papers and Container Corporation of America and an award-winning graphics artist and photographer. Mondale is the wife of former Vice President Walter Mondale. Miho is a Japanese-American who was interned in a federal camp with members of his family for four years during World War II.

"Scrambled Indicia" terminated

The Postal Service terminated its contract with Graphic Security Systems of Florida to produce "Scrambled Indicia," the concealed images, visible only through a special plastic decoder, that had been placed in the designs of selected commemoratives and high-value definitives since 1997.

"It was a nice security feature," said USPS spokesman Mark Saunders, "but we simply decided not to move forward with the program. Cost, ease of use and overall contribution to the program were some of the many factors in our decision. We have no plans to use hidden images at this time."

The first use of the marketing and security device was on the 32¢ U.S. Department of the Air Force stamp issued September 18, 1997 (Scott 3167). The last was on the 37¢ World War II Memorial commemorative of 2004 (Scott 3862). In all, the company says it provided hidden images for 43 U.S. stamps.

Stamp development officials and art directors were not unhappy to see Scrambled Indicia discontinued. Its use required placement of the concealed image on one or more of the four process-color plates that are used to print multicolor stamps, which sometimes caused a distortion of the colors on the finished stamp. For example, on the Early Football Heroes block of four of 2003, the image was on the magenta and blue plates, which "dramatically changed the color of the stamps," officials told *The Yearbook*. The faces of the players became an unnatural pink, and what was meant to be the deep blue of Red Grange's jersey came out "a kind of bright teal."

Deaths:

George W. Brett, the philatelic hobby's foremost authority on United States stamp production, died January 14, 2005, in Spirit Lake, Iowa, from complications following pneumonia. He was 92. No other U.S. stamp collector has received as many awards and accolades, or contributed so many articles and reports to the hobby's publications.

Brett was a 72-year member of the United States Stamp Society, which in 2000 made him the only person to be inducted into its hall of fame while living, and a 69-year member of the American Philatelic Society. He was an early member of the Citizens' Stamp Advisory Committee, serving under Postmaster General J. Edward Day from 1961 to 1963.

Czeslaw Slania, the world's most prolific and best-known stamp engraver, died in Stockholm, Sweden, March 17, 2005, after a long illness. He was 83.

The court engraver for Sweden, Denmark and Monaco, Slania engraved stamps for 29 other postal services, including USPS. Of the 1,070 stamps he engraved, approximately 400 were for Sweden. His 1,000th stamp was issued March 17, 2000, by Sweden Post, and is the world's largest engraved stamp, measuring 81 by 61 millimeters (Scott 2374).

Czeslaw Slania (pronounced CHESS-wav SWAN-ya) was born October 22, 1921, near Katowice, Poland. As a child, he demonstrated a talent for drawing. After Germany invaded Poland in 1939, he joined the underground and helped forge documents.

While a student at the Academy of Fine Arts in Krakow, he worked for the Polish Stamp Printing Works, where he learned the art of steel engraving. In 1951, Poland issued the first stamp containing a Slania engraving (Scott 499). He engraved 23 stamps for Poland before leaving the Communist-dominated country in 1956 and gaining political asylum in Sweden.

His first U.S. stamp was the 20¢ U.S.-Sweden Treaty joint issue of 1983 (U.S. Scott 2036, Sweden Scott 1453). His final illness prevented him from engraving the portrait of Greta Garbo for the 2005 U.S.-Swedish joint issue honoring the actress, and it was done by his protege, Piotr Nazsarkowski (see separate chapter).

Preston Robert Tisch, a billionaire who served as the nation's 69th postmaster general, died at age 79 in New York City November 15, 2005.

Tisch was born April 29, 1926, in New York City. He built an extensive business empire before being named by President Ronald Reagan to head the Postal Service. He served as postmaster general from August 16,

1986, until February 1988. During his tenure, he created a department of philatelic affairs, separating the stamp program from the USPS marketing department, and named Gordon C. Morison to head it as an assistant postmaster general. Morison told *Linn's Stamp News* that Tisch helped create the modern retail look of post offices by pushing for sales areas that displayed prepackaged stamps. He also introduced stamp sales by telephone.

Mary Ann Aspinwall Owens, an 18-year member of CSAC who became stamp collecting's firmest liaison with the Postal Service, died November 21, 2005, at age 77.

Owens may well have been the world's best-known topical collector. She won many awards for her exhibits, with topics and themes that included elephants, umbrellas, parasols and ladybugs, the Danube River, the U.S. Transportation coil stamps, the states of Wisconsin and New York, badgers and the Order of the Eastern Star. She was a long-time accredited judge of the American Topical Association and American Philatelic Society.

She was born June 24, 1928, in Fort Atkinson, Wisconsin. Her husband, John C. Owens, preceded her in death. In 1980, she moved to Brooklyn, New York, where she worked as a bookkeeper. She began collecting stamps in 1960, when an acquaintance gave her the 1957 elephant stamps of Laos to accompany her established collection of elephant miniatures.

In 1979, Owens was appointed to CSAC by Postmaster General William F. Bolger. She served until 1997. During her tenure, she brought a dedicated collector's perspective to designing the U.S. stamp program, and her personal interests were reflected in some of its elements, such as the Ladybug stamp that she insisted be included on the 1987 North American Wildlife pane.

Terrence McCaffrey, USPS manager of stamp development, said that Owens "continually sought to make the U.S. stamp program the best in the world, which is reflected in the stamps she helped bring to reality. ... Her philatelic experience and knowledge was one of the mainstays of the committee."

Ronald Reagan stamp tops Linn's poll

The 37¢ Ronald Reagan stamp was chosen as the overall favorite issue in the 2005 United States Stamp Popularity Poll conducted by *Linn's Stamp News*. This was only the second time *Linn's* readers and others selected a single-design issue as their overall favorite since that category was established in the 1984 poll. In the 2004 poll, the 37¢ Lewis and Clark stamp was voted the overall favorite.

The 37¢ Ronald Reagan stamp received 319 paper and online votes, 31 more than the second-place issue — the 10 37¢ American Advances in Aviation stamps (288 votes). The 37¢ Greta Garbo commemorative finished third with 250 votes.

Following are the top three finishers, in order, in each of the other poll categories:

Commemoratives: Best Design: Northeast Deciduous Forest, Greta Garbo, Advances in Aviation. Worst Design: Let's Dance Bailemos, To Form a More Perfect Union, Presidential Libraries. Most Important: Ronald Reagan, To Form a More Perfect Union, Distinguished Marines. Least Necessary: Let's Dance Bailemos, Art of Disney: Celebrations, Happy New Year.

Definitives and Special Stamps: Best Design: Spring Flowers, Silver Coffeepot, Christmas Cookies. Worst Design: Bouquet Love, Christmas Cookies, Silver Coffeepot. Most Important: Christmas Cookies, Bouquet Love, Spring Flowers. Least Necessary: Silver Coffeepot, Bouquet Love, Spring Flowers.

Postal Stationery: Best Design: Sporty Cars postal cards, Art of Disney postal cards, Garden Blossoms letter sheet. Worst Design: Let's Dance Bailemos postal cards, Garden Blossoms letter sheet, Art of Disney postal cards. Most Important: Sporty Cars postal cards, Art of Disney postal cards, Garden Blossoms letter sheet. Least Necessary: Let's Dance Bailemos postal cards, Garden Blossoms letter sheet, Art of Disney postal cards.

PLATE NUMBER COILS, SHEET, BOOKLET AND SELF-ADHESIVE STAMPS

Page guide for plate number groups

Changes to the plate number listings that appeared in the 2004 *Linn's U.S. Stamp Yearbook*, as well as all new listings, are shown in bold typeface.

Great Americans sheet stamps

Scott number	Stamp	Plate number	Perf type	Tagging type
1844	1¢ Dix	1 floating	bull's-eye	block
1844c, **d**	1¢ Dix	1, 2 floating	L perf	block
2168	1¢ Mitchell	1	bull's-eye	block
1845	2¢ Stravinsky	1, 2, 3, 4, 5, 6	electric-eye	overall
2169	2¢ Lyon	1, 2	bull's-eye	block
2169a	2¢ Lyon	3	bull's-eye	untagged

Scott number	Stamp	Plate number	Perf type	Tagging type
1846	3¢ Clay	1, 2	electric-eye	overall
2170	**3¢ White**	**1, 2, 3**	**bull's-eye**	**block**
2170a	3¢ White	4	bull's-eye	untagged[17]
1847	4¢ Schurz	1, 2, 3, 4	electric-eye	overall
2171	4¢ Flanagan	1	bull's-eye	block
2171a	4¢ Flanagan	1, 2	bull's-eye	untagged
2171b	**4¢ Flanagan**	**2**	**bull's-eye**	**block**
1848	5¢ Buck	1, 2, 3, 4	electric-eye	overall
2172	5¢ Black	1, 2	bull's-eye	block
2173	5¢ Munoz	1	bull's-eye	overall
2173a	5¢ Munoz	2	bull's-eye	untagged
1849	6¢ Lippmann	1 floating	L perf	block
1850	7¢ Baldwin	1 floating	L perf	block
1851	8¢ Knox	3, 4, 5, 6	L perf	overall
1852	9¢ Thayer	1 floating	L perf	block
1853, a	10¢ Russell	1 floating	L perf	block
2175	10¢ Red Cloud	1	bull's-eye	block
2175a	10¢ Red Cloud	1, 2	bull's-eye	overall
2175c	10¢ Red Cloud	2	bull's-eye	prephosphored[17]
2175d	10¢ Red Cloud	2	bull's-eye	prephosphored[18]
2175e	**10¢ Red Cloud**	**2**	**bull's-eye**	**prephosphored[18]**
1854	11¢ Partridge	2, 3, 4, 5	L perf	overall
1855	13¢ Crazy Horse	1, 2, 3, 4	electric-eye	overall
1856, a	14¢ Lewis	1 floating	L perf	block
2176	14¢ Howe	1, 2	bull's-eye	block
2177	15¢ Cody	1, 3	bull's-eye	block
2177a	15¢ Cody	2, 3	bull's-eye	overall
2177b	15¢ Cody	1	bull's-eye	prephosphored
1857	17¢ Carson	1, 2, 3, 4, 13, 14, 15, 16	electric-eye	overall
2178	17¢ Lockwood	1, 2	bull's-eye	block
1858	18¢ Mason	1, 2, 3, 4, 5, 6	electric-eye	overall
1859	19¢ Sequoyah	39529, 39530	electric-eye	overall
1860	20¢ Bunche	1, 2, 3, 4, 5, 6, 7, 8, 10, 11, 13	electric-eye	overall
1861	20¢ Gallaudet	1, 2, 5, 6, 8, 9	electric-eye	overall
1862	20¢ Truman	1 floating	L perf	block
1862a	20¢ Truman	2	bull's-eye	block
1862b	20¢ Truman	3	bull's-eye	overall
1862d	20¢ Truman	4	bull's-eye	prephosphored[18]
2179	20¢ Apgar	B1, B2, B3	bull's-eye	prephosphored

Scott number	Stamp	Plate number	Perf type	Tagging type
2179a	**20¢ Apgar**	**B2**	**bull's-eye**	**prephosphored**
2180	21¢ Carlson	1	bull's-eye	block
1863, **a**	22¢ Audubon	1 floating	L perf	block
1863d	22¢ Audubon	3	bull's-eye	block
2181	23¢ Cassatt	1	bull's-eye	block
2181a	23¢ Cassatt	1, 2	bull's-eye	overall
2181b	23¢ Cassatt	2, 3	bull's-eye	prephosphored[19]
2181c	**23¢ Cassatt**	**3**	**bull's-eye**	**prephosphored[19]**
2182	25¢ London	1, 2	bull's-eye	block
2183	28¢ Sitting Bull	1	bull's-eye	block
2184	29¢ Warren	S1, S2 (six positions)	bull's-eye	prephosphored
2185	29¢ Jefferson	S1, S2 (six positions)	bull's-eye	prephosphored
1864	30¢ Laubach	1 floating	L perf	block
1864a	30¢ Laubach	2	bull's-eye	block
1864b	30¢ Laubach	2	bull's-eye	overall
2933	32¢ Hershey	B1, B2	bull's-eye	prephosphored
2934	32¢ Farley	B1	bull's-eye	prephosphored
2935	32¢ Luce	B1	bull's-eye	prephosphored
2936	32¢ Wallaces	P1	bull's-eye	prephosphored
1865	35¢ Drew	1, 2, 3, 4	electric-eye	overall
2186	35¢ Chavez	S1, S2 (six positions)	L perf	prephosphored
1866	37¢ Millikan	1, 2, 3, 4	electric-eye	overall
1867	39¢ Clark	1 floating	L perf	block
1867c	39¢ Clark	2	bull's-eye	block
1868	40¢ Gilbreth	1 floating	L perf	block
1868a	40¢ Gilbreth	2	bull's-eye	block
2187	40¢ Chennault	1	bull's-eye	overall
2187a, **b, c**	40¢ Chennault	2	bull's-eye	prephosphored[17]
2188	45¢ Cushing	1	bull's-eye	block
2188a	45¢ Cushing	1	bull's-eye	overall
2938	46¢ Benedict	1	bull's-eye	prephosphored
1869	50¢ Nimitz	1, 2, 3, 4	L perf	overall[18]
1869a	50¢ Nimitz	1, 2	bull's-eye	block
1869d	50¢ Nimitz	2, 3	bull's-eye	overall
1869e	50¢ Nimitz	3	bull's-eye	prephosphored[17]
2189, **a**	52¢ Humphrey	1, 2	bull's-eye	prephosphored[20]
2940	55¢ Hamilton	B1, B2, B3	bull's-eye	prephosphored
2941	55¢ J. Morrill	B1, B2	die-cut	prephosphored
2190	56¢ Harvard	1	bull's-eye	block
2191	65¢ Arnold	1	bull's-eye	block

360

Scott number	Stamp	Plate number	Perf type	Tagging type
2192	75¢ Willkie	1	bull's-eye	prephosphored[17]
2942	77¢ Breckinridge	B1, B2	die-cut	prephosphored
2943, **a, b**	78¢ Paul	B1, B2	bull's-eye	prephosphored
2193	$1 Revel	1	bull's-eye	block
2194	$1 Hopkins	1	bull's-eye	block
2194b	$1 Hopkins	1	bull's-eye	overall
2194d, **e, f**	$1 Hopkins	2	bull's-eye	prephosphored[17]
2195	$2 Bryan	2	bull's-eye	block
2196	$5 Bret Harte	1	bull's-eye	block
2196b	$5 Bret Harte	2	bull's-eye	prephosphored

Great Americans sheet stamps notes
17 Shiny gum and dull gum
18 Shiny gum
19 Plate number 3 shiny gum
20 Plate number 1 shiny and dull gum, plate number 2 shiny gum

General notes
Plate positions: Floating plate number positions are left or right, either blocks of six or strips of 20 (number must be centered in selvage in a block of six). All other plate number positions consist of upper left, upper right, lower left and lower right, with the following exceptions: 29¢ Warren, 29¢ Jefferson and 35¢ Chavez, which have positions of upper left, center upper right, upper right, lower left, center lower right and lower right. (Traditional corners have plate numbers to the side of the stamps; center positions have plate numbers above or below stamps.)

Tagging types
Block: tagging block centered over design of stamp; no tagging in selvage.
Overall: tagging applied to entire pane, often leaving an untagged strip at outer edge of large margin selvage.
Prephosphored: paper that has phosphorescent taggant applied to the paper by the paper supplier prior to printing. On some stamps, under shortwave UV light, the appearance of the phosphorescent tagging is smooth and even (surface taggant), while on others, the taggant appears mottled (embedded taggant). Examples that exhibit both are the 10¢ Red Cloud, 23¢ Cassatt, 40¢ Chennault, 52¢ Humphrey, 75¢ Willkie and $1 Hopkins from the Great Americans and the 23¢ Lunch Wagon, 29¢ Flag Over Mount Rushmore and the variable-denomination coil (Scott 31, 31a, 31b and 31c) from the plate number coils.

Transportation coil stamps

Scott number	Stamp	Plate number	Tagging type
1897	1¢ Omnibus (1983)	1, 2, 3, 5, 6	overall
2225	1¢ Omnibus (1986)	1, 2	block
2225a	1¢ Omnibus (1991)	2, 3	untagged[2]
2225a	1¢ Omnibus (1997)	3	untagged[19]
1897A	2¢ Locomotive (1982)	2, 3, 4, 6, 8, 10	overall
2226	2¢ Locomotive (1987)	1	block
2226a	2¢ Locomotive (1993)	2	untagged
2226a	2¢ Locomotive (1997)	2	untagged[20]

Scott number	Stamp	Plate number	Tagging type
1898	3¢ Handcar (1983)	1, 2, 3, 4	overall
2252	3¢ Conestoga Wagon (1988)	1	block
2252a	3¢ Conestoga Wagon (1992)	2, 3, 5, 6	untagged[15]
2123	3.4¢ School Bus (1985)	1, 2	overall
2123a	3.4¢ School Bus (1985)	1, 2	untagged
1898A	4¢ Stagecoach (1982)	1, 2, 3, 4, 5, 6	overall
1898Ab	4¢ Stagecoach (1982)	3, 4, 5, 6	untagged
2228	4¢ Stagecoach (1986)	1	block
2228a	4¢ Stagecoach (1990)	1	overall
2451	4¢ Steam Carriage (1991)	1	overall
2451b	4¢ Steam Carriage (1991)	1	untagged
2124	4.9¢ Buckboard (1985)	3, 4	overall
2124a	4.9¢ Buckboard (1985)	1, 2, 3, 4, 5, 6	untagged
1899	5¢ Motorcycle (1983)	1, 2, 3, 4	overall
2253	5¢ Milk Wagon (1987)	1	block
2452	5¢ Circus Wagon (1990)	1	overall
2452a	5¢ Circus Wagon (1991)	1, 2	untagged[33]
2452B	5¢ Circus Wagon (gravure) (1992)	A1, A2	untagged
2452Bf	5¢ Circus Wagon (gravure) (1992)	A3	untagged[32]
2452D	5¢ Circus Wagon (gravure) (1995)	S1, S2	untagged[12]
2452Dg	5¢ Circus Wagon (gravure) (1995)	S2, S3	untagged[32]
2453	5¢ Canoe (1991)	1, 2, 3	untagged
2454	5¢ Canoe (gravure) (1991)	S11	untagged
1900	5.2¢ Sleigh (1983)	1, 2, 3, 5	overall
1900a	5.2¢ Sleigh (1983)	1, 2, 3, 4, 5, 6	untagged
2254	5.3¢ Elevator (1988)	1	untagged
2125	5.5¢ Star Route Truck (1986)	1	block
2125a	5.5¢ Star Route Truck (1986)	1, 2	untagged
1901	5.9¢ Bicycle (1982)	3, 4	overall
1901a	5.9¢ Bicycle (1982)	3, 4, 5, 6	untagged
2126	6¢ Tricycle (1985)	1	block
2126a	6¢ Tricycle (1985)	1, 2	untagged
2127	7.1¢ Tractor (1987)	1	block
2127a	7.1¢ Tractor (1987)	1	untagged[3]
2127b	7.1¢ Tractor (1989)	1	untagged[4]
1902	7.4¢ Baby Buggy (1984)	2	block
1902a	7.4¢ Buggy (1984)	2	untagged
2255	7.6¢ Carreta (1988)	1, 2, 3	untagged
2128	8.3¢ Ambulance (1985)	1, 2	overall
2128a	8.3¢ Ambulance (1985)	1, 2, 3, 4	untagged

362

Scott number	Stamp	Plate number	Tagging type
2231	8.3¢ Ambulance (1986)	1, 2	untagged
2256	8.4¢ Wheel Chair (1988)	1, 2, 3	untagged
2129a	8.5¢ Tow Truck (1987)	1, 2	untagged
2129	8.5¢ Tow Truck (1987)	1	block
1903a	9.3¢ Mail Wagon (1981)	1, 2, 3, 4, 5, 6, 8	untagged
1903	9.3¢ Mail Wagon (1981)	1, 2, 3, 4, 5, 6	overall
2257	10¢ Canal Boat (1987)	1	block
2257a	10¢ Canal Boat (1991)	1, 4	overall
2257b	10¢ Canal Boat (1992)	1, 2, 3, 4	prephosphored[1]
2257c	10¢ Canal Boat (1999)	5	prephosphored[25]
2457	10¢ Tractor Trailer (1991)	1	untagged
2458	10¢ Tractor Trailer (gravure) (1994)	11, 22	untagged
2130	10.1¢ Oil Wagon (1985)	1	block
2130a	10.1¢ Oil Wagon (1985)	1, 2	untagged[5]
2130a	10.1¢ Oil Wagon (1988)	2, 3	untagged[6]
1904a	10.9¢ Hansom Cab (1982)	1, 2, 3, 4	untagged
1904	10.9¢ Hansom Cab (1982)	1, 2	overall
1905	11¢ Caboose (1984)	1	block
1905a	11¢ Caboose (1984)	1	untagged[7]
1905a	11¢ Caboose (1991)	2	untagged
2131	11¢ Stutz Bearcat (1985)	1, 2, 3, 4	overall
2132	12¢ Stanley Steamer (1985)	1, 2	overall
2132a	12¢ Stanley Steamer (1985)	1, 2	untagged
2132b	12¢ Stanley Steamer (1987)	1	untagged
2133a	12.5¢ Pushcart (1985)	1, 2	untagged
2133	12.5¢ Pushcart (1985)	1, 2	block
2258	13¢ Patrol Wagon (1988)	1	untagged
2259	13.2¢ Coal Car (1988)	1, 2	untagged
2134	14¢ Iceboat (1985)	1, 2, 3, 4	overall
2134b	14¢ Iceboat (1986)	2	block
2260	15¢ Tugboat (1988)	1, 2	block
2260a	15¢ Tugboat (1988)	2	overall
2261	16.7¢ Popcorn Wagon (1988)	1, 2	untagged
1906	17¢ Electric Auto (1981)	1, 2, 3, 4, 5, 6, 7	overall
1906a	17¢ Electric Auto (1981)	1, 2, 3, 4, 5, 6, 7	untagged
2135	17¢ Dog Sled (1986)	2	block
2262	17.5¢ Racing Car (1987)	1	block
2262a	17.5¢ Racing Car (1987)	1	untagged
1907	18¢ Surrey (1981)	1, 2, 3, 4, 5, 6, 7, 8, 9, 10, 11, 12, 13, 14, 15, 16, 17, 18	overall

Scott number	Stamp	Plate number	Tagging type
1908	20¢ Fire Pumper (1981)	1, 2, 3, 4, 5, 6, 7, 8, 9, 10, 11, 12, 13, 14, 15, 16	overall
2263	20¢ Cable Car (1988)	1, 2	block
2263b	20¢ Cable Car (1990)	2	overall
2463	20¢ Cog Railway (1995)	1, 2	prephosphored
2264	20.5¢ Fire Engine (1988)	1	untagged
2265	21¢ Railroad Mail Car (1988)	1, 2	untagged
2464	23¢ Lunch Wagon (1991)	2, 3	prephosphored[17]
2464a	23¢ Lunch Wagon (1993)	3, 4, 5	prephosphored[2]
2464b	23¢ Lunch Wagon (1991)	2, 3	prephosphored
2266	24.1¢ Tandem Bicycle (1988)	1	untagged
2136	25¢ Bread Wagon (1986)	1, 2, 3, 4, 5	block
2466	32¢ Ferryboat (1995)	2, 3, 4, 5	prephosphored[13]
2466b	32¢ Ferryboat (1995)	5	prephosphored
2468	$1 Seaplane (1990)	1	overall[28]
2468b	$1 Seaplane (1993)	3	prephosphored[1]
2468c	$1 Seaplane (1998)	3	prephosphored[19]

American Transportation coil stamps

Scott number	Stamp	Plate number	Tagging type
2905	(10¢) Auto (1995)	S111, S222	untagged[12]
2905a	(10¢) Auto (1996)	S333	untagged
2906	(10¢) Auto (1996)	S111	untagged[12]
3229	(10¢) Green Bicycle (1998)	S111	untagged[23, 25]
3228	(10¢) Green Bicycle (1998)	111, 221, 222, 333, 344, 444, 555	untagged[21, 23, 24]
3228a	(10¢) Green Bicycle (1998)	666, 777, 888, 999	untagged

Special services self-adhesive panes

Scott number	Stamp	Denomination	Number of subjects	Total value	Date of issue	Plate numbers	Notes
3261	Shuttle Landing	$3.20	20	$64.00	11/9/98	B1111, B2222, B3333	15
3262	Shuttle Piggyback	$11.75	20	$235.00	11/19/98	B11111, B22222, B33333	15
3472	Capitol Dome	$3.50	20	$70.00	1/29/01	B1111, B2222	
3647	Jefferson Memorial	$3.85	20	$77.00	7/30/02	B1111	
3647A	Jefferson Memorial	$3.85	20	$77.00	12/03	S11111	
3473	Washington Monument	$12.25	20	$245.00	1/29/01	B1111	
3648	Capitol at Dusk	$13.65	20	$273.00	7/30/02	B1111	

National Symbols coil stamps

Scott number	Stamp	Plate number	Tagging type
3615	3¢ Star (2002)	S111	untagged
2602	(10¢) Eagle & Shield (1991) "Bulk Rate USA"	A11111, A11112, A12213, A21112, A21113, A22112, A22113, A32333, A33333, A33334, A33335, A34424, A34426, A43324, A43325, A43326, A43334, A43335, A43426, A53335, A54444, A54445, A77777, A88888, A88889, A89999, A99998,	untagged
2602	(10¢) Eagle & Shield (1991) "Bulk Rate USA" (continued)	A99999, A1010101010, A1011101010, A1011101011, A1011101012, A1110101010, A1110101011, A1110111110, A1111101010, A1111111010, A1211101010, A1411101010, A1411101011, A1412111110, A1412111111	
2603	(10¢) Eagle & Shield "USA Bulk Rate" (1993)	11111, 22221, 22222, 33333, 44444	untagged[9]
2603b	(10¢) Eagle & Shield "USA Bulk Rate" (1993)	11111, 22221, 22222	tagged error
2604	(10¢) Eagle & Shield (gold) "USA Bulk Rate" (1993)	S11111, S22222	untagged[16]
2907	(10¢) Eagle & Shield (1996)	S11111	untagged[12]
3270	(10¢) Eagle & Shield "USA Presorted Std" (1998)	11111	untagged
3270a	(10¢) Eagle & Shield "USA Presorted Std" (1998)	22222	untagged
3271	(10¢) Eagle & Shield "USA Presorted Std" (1998)	11111, 22222	untagged[21, 22, 24]
3271a	(10¢) Eagle & Shield "USA Presorted Std" (1998)	33333	untagged[21, 22, 24]
3271b	(10¢) Eagle & Shield "Presorted Std"	11111	tagged error[21, 22, 24]
2149	18¢ Washington (1985)	1112, 3333	block
2149a	18¢ Washington (1985)	11121, 33333, 43444	untagged[10]
3475	21¢ Bison (2001)	V1111, V2222	prephosphored
3263	22¢ Uncle Sam (1998)	1111	prephosphored[21]
3353	22¢ Uncle Sam (1999)	1111	prephosphored[21]
2606	23¢ USA Presort (1992) (dark blue)	A1111, A2222, A2232, A2233, A3333, A4364, A4443, A4444, A4453	untagged
2607	23¢ USA Presort (1992) (light blue)	1111	untagged[2]
2608	23¢ USA Presort (1993) (violet blue)	S111	untagged

Scott number	Stamp	Plate number	Tagging type
3475A	23¢ George Washington (2001)	B11	prephosphored
3617	23¢ George Washington (2002)	V11, V13, V21, V22, V24, V35 , V36, V45, V46	prephosphored
3801a	(25¢) American Eagle (2003)	S1111111, S2222222, S3333333	prephosphored
3801c	**(25¢) American Eagle (2005)**	**S1111111**	**prephosphored**
3853a	(25¢) American Eagle (2004)	S1111111	prephosphored
3452	(34¢) Statue of Liberty (2000)	1111	prephosphored
3453	(34¢) Statue of Liberty (2000)	1111	prephosphored
3466	34¢ Statue of Liberty (2001)	1111, 2222	prephosphored
3476	34¢ Statue of Liberty (2001)	1111	prephosphored
3477	34¢ Statue of Liberty (2001)	1111, 2222, 3333, 4444, 5555, 6666, 7777	prephosphored
3550	34¢ United We Stand (2001)	1111, 2222, 3333	prephosphored
3550A	34¢ United We Stand (2001)	1111	prephosphored
3967	**(39¢) Liberty/Flag**	**S1111**	**prephosphored**
3968	**(39¢) Liberty/Flag**	**V1111**	**prephosphored**
3969	**(39¢) Liberty/Flag**	**S1111**	**prephosphored**
3970	**(39¢) Liberty/Flag**	**P1111, 2222**	**prephosphored**

National Symbols panes

Scott number	Stamp	Denomi-nation	Number of subjects	Total value	Date of issue	Plate numbers	Notes
3613	Star	3¢	50	$1.50	6/7/02	B111, B222, B333, B444	
3614	Star	3¢	50	$1.50	6/7/02	B111	
3482a	George Washington	20¢	10	$2.00	2/22/01	P1, P2, P3	
3483c/f	George Washington	20¢	10	$2.00	2/22/01	P1, P2, P3	
3484d	Bison	21¢	10	$2.10	2/22/01	P111111, P222222, P333333, P444444, P555555	
3484Ag/j	Bison	21¢	10	$2.10	2/22/01	P111111, P222222, P333333, P444444, P555555	
3467	Bison	21¢	100	$21.00	9/20/01	P111111	
3468	Bison	21¢	20	$4.20	2/22/01	V1111, V1112, V2222	
3259	Uncle Sam	22¢	20	$4.40	11/9/98	S1111	15
3468A	George Washington	23¢	20	$4.60	9/20/01	B111, B222, B333	
3616	George Washington	23¢	100	$23.00	6/7/02	P1	
3618c	George Washington	23¢	10	$2.30	6/7/02	P1, P2, P3, **P4**	

Scott number	Stamp	Denomi-nation	Number of subjects	Total value	Date of issue	Plate numbers	Notes
3619e-f	George Washington	23¢	10	$2.30	6/7/02	P1	
3819	George Washington	23¢	20	$4.60	10/03	V11	
2431a	Eagle & Shield	25¢	18	$4.50	11/10/89	A1111	1, 2, 3
2595a	Eagle & Shield	29¢	17	$4.93	9/25/92	B1111-1, B1111-2, B2222-1, B2222-2, B3333-1, B3333-3, B3434-1, B3434-3, B4344-1, B4344-3, B4444-1, B4444-3	3, 6, 7
2596a	Eagle & Shield	29¢	7	$4.93	19/25/92	D11111, D21221, D22322, D32322, D32332, D32342, D42342, D43352, D43452, D43453, D54561, D54563, D54571, D54573, D54673, D61384, D65784	3, 6, 7
2597a	Eagle & Shield	29¢	17	$4.93	9/25/92	S1111	3, 6, 7
2598a	Eagle	29¢	18	$5.22	2/4/94	M111, M112	5
2599a	Statue of Liberty	29¢	18	$5.22	6/24/94	D1111, D1212	5
3122a	Statue of Liberty	32¢	20	$6.40	2/1/97	V1111, V1211, V1311, V2122, V2222, V2311, V2331, V3233, V3333, V3513, V4532	13, 14, 16
3122E	Statue of Liberty	32¢	20	$6.40	2/1/97	V1111, V1211, V2122, V2222	14, 16, 18
3451a	Statue of Liberty	(34¢)	20	$6.80	12/15/00	V1111, V2222	
3485a	Statue of Liberty	34¢	10	$3.40	2/7/01	V1111, V1221, V2222	
3485b	Statue of Liberty	34¢	20	$6.80	2/7/01	V1111, V1211, V1221, V2111, V2121, V2122, V2212, V2222	
3549a	United We Stand	34¢	20	$6.80	10/24/01	B1111, B2222, B3333, B4444	
3549Be	United We Stand	34¢	20	$6.80	1/?/02	S1111	
3965	**Liberty/Flag**	**(39¢)**	**100**	**$39.00**	**12/8/05**	**P1111**	
3966	**Liberty/Flag**	**(39¢)**	**20**	**$7.80**	**12/8/05**	**P1111**	
3971a	**Liberty/Flag**	**(39¢)**	**20**	**$7.80**	**12/8/05**	**P1111**	
3972a	**Liberty/Flag**	**(39¢)**	**20**	**$39.00**	**12/8/05**	**V1111**	
3973a	**Liberty/Flag**	**(39¢)**	**20**	**$7.80**	**12/8/05**	**S1111**	
3974	**Liberty/Flag**	**(39¢)**	**20**	**$7.80**	**12/8/05**	**S1111**	
3471	Art Deco Eagle	55¢	20	$11.00	2/22/01	S11111	
3471A	Art Deco Eagle	57¢	20	$11.40	9/20/01	S11111	
3646	Coverlet Eagle	60¢	20	$12.00	7/12/02	P1111, P2222, P3333, P4444, **P5555**, P6666, P7777, **P8888**	

Flag coil stamps

Scott number	Stamp	Plate number	Tagging type
1891	18¢ Sea to Shining Sea (1981)	1, 2, 3, 4, 5, 6, 7	block
1895	20¢ Flag Over Supreme Court (1981)	1, 2, 3, 4, 5, 6, 8, 9, 10, 12, 13, 14	block
1895e	20¢ Flag Over Supreme Court precanceled (1984)	14	untagged
2115	22¢ Flag Over Capitol Dome (1985)	1, 2, 3, 4, 5, 6, 7, 8, 10, 11, 12, 13, 14, 15, 16, 17, 18, 19, 20, 21, 22	block
2115a	22¢ Flag Over Capitol Dome (1985)	1, 3, 5, 7, 8, 11, 12, 17 18, 19, 20, 22	prephosphored
2115b	22¢ Flag Over Capitol Dome (1985)	18, 20, 22	block
2115c	22¢ Flag Over Capitol Dome (1987)	1	prephosphored
2605	23¢ Flag Presort (1991)	A111, A112, A122, A212, A222, A333	untagged
2280	25¢ Flag Over Yosemite (1988)	1, 2, 3, 4, 5, 7, 8, 9	block
2280	25¢ Flag Over Yosemite (1989)	1, 2, 3, 5, 6, 7, 8, 9, 10, 11, 12, 13, 14, 15	prephosphored
2523	29¢ Flag Over Mount Rushmore (1991)	1, 2, 3, 4, 5, 6, 7, 8, 9	prephosphored
2523A	29¢ Flag Over Mount Rushmore (1991) (gravure)	A111111, A222211	prephosphored
2609	29¢ Flag Over White House (1992)	1, 2, 3, 4, 5, 6, 7, 8, 9, 10, 11, 12, 13, 14, 15, 16, 18	prephosphored
2913	32¢ Flag Over Porch (1995)	11111, 22221, 22222, 22322, 33333, 34333, 44444, 45444, 66646, 66666, 77767, 78767, 91161, 99969	prephosphored[14]
2914	32¢ Flag Over Porch (1995)	S11111	prephosphored[12]
2915	32¢ Flag Over Porch (1995)	V11111	prephosphored
2915A	32¢ Flag Over Porch (1996)	11111, 22222, 23222, 33333, 44444, 45444, 55555, 66666, 78777, 87888, 87898, 88888, 88898, 89878, 89888, 89898, 89899, 97898, 99899, 99999, 11111A, 13211A, 13231A, 13311A, 22222A, 33333A, 44444A, 55555A, 66666A, 77777A, 78777A, 88888A	prephosphored[1, 2]
2915B	32¢ Flag Over Porch (1996)	S11111	prephosphored[12]
2915C	32¢ Flag Over Porch (1996)	55555, 66666, 88888	prephosphored
2915D	32¢ Flag Over Porch (1997)	11111	prephosphored
3133	32¢ Flag Over Porch (1997)	M11111	prephosphored
3280	33¢ Flag Over City (1999)	1111, 2222	prephosphored

Scott number	Stamp	Plate number	Tagging type
3280a	33¢ Flag Over City (1999)	3333	prephosphored
3281	33¢ Flag Over City (1999) (large date)	6666, 7777, 8888, 9999, 1111A, 2222A, 3333A, 4444A, 5555A, 6666A, 7777A, 8888A, 1111B, 2222B	prephosphored
3281c	33¢ Flag Over City (1999) (small date)	1111, 2222, 3333, 3433, 4443, 4444, 5555, 9999A	prephosphored
3282	33¢ Flag Over City (1999)	1111, 2222	prephosphored
3622	(37¢) Flag (2002)	1111, 2222	prephosphored
3631	37¢ Flag (2002)	S1111	prephosphored
3632	37¢ Flag (2002)	1111, 2222, 3333, 4444, 5555, 6666, 7777, 8888, 9999, 1111A, 2222A, 3333A, 4444A, 5555A	prephosphored
3632A	37¢ Flag (2003)	S1111, S2222, S3333, S4444	prephosphored
3632Ae	37¢ Flag (2003)	S1111, S3333, S4444	prephosphored
3632C	37¢ Flag (2004)	S1111	prephosphored
3633	37¢ Flag (2002)	B1111	prephosphored
3633A	37¢ Flag (2003)	B1111	prephosphored
3633B	**37¢ Flag (2005)**	**P1111**	**prephosphored**

Flag panes

Scott number	Stamp	Denomi-nation	Number of subjects	Total value	Date of issue	Plate numbers	Notes
2920a	Flag Over Porch	32¢	20	$6.40	4/18/95	V12211, V12212, V12312, V12321, V12322, V12331, V13322, V13831, V13834, V13836, V22211, V23322, V23422, V23432, V23522, V34743, V34745, V36743, V42556, V45554, V54663, V56663, V56665, V56763, V57663, V65976, V78989	5, 9, 10, 11, 16
2920c	Flag Over Porch	32¢	20	$6.40	4/18/95	V11111	16
2920De	Flag Over Porch	32¢	10	$3.20	1/20/96	V11111, V12111, V23222, V31121, V32111, V32121, V44322, V44333, V44444, V55555, V66666, V66886, V67886, V68886, V68896, V76989, V77666, V77668, V77766, V77776, V78698, V78886, V78896, V78898, V78986, V78989, V89999	10

Scott number	Stamp	Denomination	Number of subjects	Total value	Date of issue	Plate numbers	Notes
3278	Flag Over City	33¢	15	$6.60	2/25/99	V1111, V1211, V2222	14, 15
3278d	Flag Over City	33¢	10	$3.30	2/25/99	V1111, V1112, V1113, V2222, V2322, V2324, V3433, V3434, V3545	14
3278e	Flag Over City	33¢	20	$6.60	2/25/99	V1111, V1211, V2122, V2222, V2223, V3333, V4444, V8789	14, 16
3278Fg	Flag Over City	33¢	20	$6.60	2/25/99	V1111, V1131, V2222, V2223, V2227, V2243, V2323, V2423, V2443, V3333, V4444, V5428, V5445, V5446, V5576, V5578, V6423, V6456, V6546, V6556, V6575, V6576, V7567, V7663, V7667, V7676, V8789	14, 16
3278j	Flag Over City	33¢	10	$3.30	1999	V1111, V1112, V1113, V2222	
3449	Flag Over Farm	33¢	20	$6.60	12/15/00	P1111, P2222, P3333	
3469	Flag Over Farm	34¢	100	$34.00	2/7/01	P1111, P2222	
3470	Flag Over Farm	34¢	20	$6.80	3/6/01	P1111, P2222, P3333, P4444, P5555	
3620	Flag	(37¢)	100	$37.00	6/7/02	P1111	
3621	Flag	(37¢)	20	$7.40	6/7/02	P1111, P2222, P3333	
3623a	Flag	(37¢)	20	$7.40	6/7/02	B1111, B2222, B3333, B4444, B5555	
3624c	Flag	(37¢)	**20**	$7.40	26/7/02	S1111	
3629F	Flag	37¢	100	$37.00	11/24/03	P1111	
3630	Flag	37¢	20	$7.40	6/7/02	P1111, P2222, P3333, P4444, P5555	
3634a	Flag	37¢	10	$3.70	6/7/02	V1111	
3635a	Flag	37¢	20	$7.40	6/7/02	B1111, B2222, B3333, B4444, B5555, B6666, B7777	
3636c	Flag	37¢	20	$7.40	6/7/02	S1111, S2222, S3333, S44444, S5555	
3636D	Flag	37¢	20	$7.40	7/04	V1111, **V1112, V2222**	

Nondenominated rate-change coil stamps

Scott number	Stamp	Plate number	Tagging type
2112	D (22¢) Eagle (1985)	1, 2	block
O139	D (22¢) Official (1985)	1	block

Scott number	Stamp	Plate number	Tagging type
2279	E (25¢) Earth (1988)	1111, 1211, 1222, 2222	block
2518	F (29¢) Flower (1991)	1111, 1211, 1222, 2211, 2222	prephosphored
2893	G (5¢) Old Glory (1995) nonprofit	A11111, A21111	untagged
2888	G (25¢) Old Glory (1994) presort	S11111	prephosphored
2886	G (32¢) Old Glory (1994)	V11111	prephosphored
2889	G (32¢) Old Glory (1994)	1111, 2222	prephosphored
2890	G (32¢) Old Glory (1994)	A1111, A1112, A1113, A1211, A1212, A1222, A1311, A1313, A1314, A1324, A1417, A1433, A2211, A2212, A2213, A2214, A2223, A2313, A3113, A3114, A3314, A3315, A3323, A3324, A3423, A3426, A3433, A3435, A3436, A4426, A4427, A4435, A5327, A5417, A5427, A5437	prephosphored
2891	G (32¢) Old Glory (1994)	S1111	prephosphored[11]
2892	G (32¢) Old Glory (1994)	S1111, S2222	prephosphored
3264	H (33¢) Hat (1998)	1111, 3333, 3343, 3344, 3444	prephosphored[25, 26]
3265	H (33¢) Hat (1998)	1111, 1131, 1141, 2222, 3333	prephosphored[21]
3266	H (33¢) Hat (1998)	1111	prephosphored[21, 22, 23, 27]

Nondenominated rate-change panes

Scott number	Stamp	Denomi-nation	Number of subjects	Total Value	Date of issue	Plate numbers	Notes
2883a	G	(32¢)	10	$3.20	12/13/94	2222	5
2886a	G	(32¢)	18	$5.76	12/13/94	V11111, V22222	5
3268a	H (Hat)	(33¢)	10	$3.30	11/9/98	V1111, V1211, V2211, V2222	
3268b	H (Hat)	(33¢)	20	$6.60	11/9/98	V1111, V1112, V1113, V1122, V1213, V1222, V2113, V2122, V2213, V2222, V2223	16

American Scenes coil stamps

Scott number	Stamp	Plate number	Tagging type
2902	(5¢) Butte (1995)	S111, S222, S333	untagged[12]
2902B	(5¢) Butte (1996)	S111	untagged[12]
2903	(5¢) Mountains (1996)	11111	untagged
2904	(5¢) Mountains (1996)	S111	untagged
2904A	(5¢) Mountains (1996)	V222222, V333323, V333333, V333342, V333343	untagged[12]

Scott number	Stamp	Plate number	Tagging type
2904B	(5¢) Mountains (1997)	1111	untagged[11, 21, 23, 24]
3207	(5¢) Wetlands (1998)	S1111	untagged
3207A	(5¢) Wetlands (1998)	1111, 2222, 3333, 4444, 5555, 6666	untagged[11, 21, 22, 23]
3207Ab	(5¢) Wetlands (1998)	5555, 6666	untagged
3693	(5¢) Sea Coast (2002)	B111	prephosphored
3775	(5¢) Sea Coast (2003)	B111	untagged
3785	(5¢) Sea Coast (2003)	P1111	untagged
3785a	(5¢) Sea Coast (2004)	P2222	untagged
3864	(5¢) Sea Coast (2004)	S1111	untagged
3874	(5¢) Sea Coast (2004)	P2222, P3333	untagged
3874a	(5¢) Sea Coast Small "2003"	P3333, **P5555, P6666, P7777**	untagged
3875	(5¢) Sea Coast (2004)	S1111	untagged

American Design coil stamps

Scott number	Stamp	Plate number	Tagging type
3757	1¢ Tiffany Lamp	S11111	untagged
3759	**3¢ Silver Coffeepot**	**S1111**	**untagged**
3612	5¢ American Toleware	S1111111	untagged

American Design panes

Scott number	Stamp	Denomination	Number of subjects	Total value	Date of issue	Plate number	Notes
3749	**Navajo Necklace**	**2¢**	**20**	**$0.40**	**8/20/04**	**V11111**	
3749A	**Navajo Necklace**	**2¢**	**20**	**$0.40**	**12/8/05**	**S11111**	
3749B	**Navajo Necklace**	**2¢**	**20**	**$0.40**	**12/8/05**	**P11111**	
3750	Chippendale Chair	4¢	20	$0.80	3/5/04	P1111	
3750A	American Toleware (2004)	5¢	20	$1.00	6/25/04	S1111111	
3751	American Clock	10¢	20	$2.00	1/24/03	P1111, P2222 **P3333, P4444**	

American Culture coil stamps

Scott number	Stamp	Plate number	Tagging type
3447	(10¢) Lion Statue (2000)	S11111, S22222 S33333, S44444, S77777	untagged
3447a	(10¢) Lion Statue (2004)	S55555, **S66666**	untagged
3769	(10¢) Lion Statue (2003)	S11111, S22222, S33333, S44444, S55555	untagged

Scott number	Stamp	Plate number	Tagging type
3520	(10¢) Atlas Statue (2001)	B1111	untagged
3770	(10¢) Atlas Statue (2003)	V11111, V11222, V12111, V12222, **V13222**, V21111, **V21211**, V22111, **V22211**, V22222, **V23113, V32332, V33333**	untagged
2908	(15¢) Tail Fin (1995)	11111	untagged
2909	(15¢) Tail Fin (1995)	S11111	untagged[12]
2910	(15¢) Tail Fin (1996)	S11111	untagged[12]
3522	(15¢) Woody Wagon (2001)	S11111	untagged
2911	(25¢) Jukebox (1995) "Presorted First-Class"	111111, 212222, 222222, 332222	untagged
2912	(25¢) Jukebox (1995) "Presorted First-Class"	S11111, S22222	untagged[12]
2912A	(25¢) Jukebox (1997) "Presorted First-Class"	S11111, S22222	untagged[21, 22, 23, 24, 27]
2912B	(25¢) Jukebox (1997) "Presorted First-Class"	111111, 222222	untagged[21, 22, 23, 24, 27]
3132	(25¢) Jukebox (1997)	M11111	untagged
3208	(25¢) Diner (1998) "Presorted First-Class"	S11111	untagged[23, 25]
3208A	(25¢) Diner (1998) "Presorted First-Class"	11111, 22211, 22222, 33333, 44444, 55555	prephosphored untagged[21, 22, 23, 24, 27]

American Culture panes

Scott number	Stamp	Denomi-nation	Number of subjects	Total value	Date of issue	Plate numbers	Notes
3766	Wisdom	$1	20	$20.00	2/28/03	P11111, P22222, P33333, P44444, P55555	

Flora and Fauna coil stamps

Scott number	Stamp	Plate number	Tagging type
3044	1¢ Kestrel (1996)	1111	untagged[29]
3044	1¢ Kestrel (1996-99)	1111	untagged[30]
3044a	1¢ Kestrel (1999)	1111, 2222, 3333, 4444	untagged[31]
3045	2¢ Woodpecker	11111, 22222	untagged
3053	20¢ Blue Jay (1996)	S1111	prephosphored
3055	20¢ Pheasant (1998)	1111, 2222	prephosphored[21]
2281	25¢ Honey Bee (1988)	1, 2	block
2525	29¢ Flower (1991)	S1111, S2222	prephosphored
2526	29¢ Flower (1992)	S2222	prephosphored
2491	29¢ Pine Cone (1993)	B1	prephosphored
2598	29¢ Eagle (1994)	111	prephosphored

Scott number	Stamp	Plate number	Tagging type
2599	29¢ Statue of Liberty (1994)	D1111	prephosphored
2492	32¢ Pink Rose (1995)	S111	prephosphored
2495-95A	32¢ Peach/Pear (1995)	V11111	prephosphored
3054	32¢ Yellow Rose (1997)	1111, 1112, 1122, 2222, 2223, 2233, 2333, 3344, 3444, 4455, 5455, 5555, 5556, 5566, 5666, 6666, 6677, 6777, 7777, 8888	prephosphored[1, 2]
3302-05	33¢ Four Fruit Berries (1999)	B1111, B1112, B2211, B2221, B2222	prephosphored[1, 2]
3404-07	33¢ Four Fruit Berries (2000) linerless	G1111	prephosphored
3462-65	(34¢) Four Flowers (2000)	B1111	prephosphored
3478-81	34¢ Four Flowers (2001)	B1111, B2111, B2122, B2211, B2222	prephosphored

Flora and Fauna panes

Scott number	Stamp	Denomination	Number of subjects	Total value	Date of issue	Plate numbers	Notes
3031	Kestrel	1¢	50	$0.50	11/19/99	1111, 2222, 2322, 4444, 5555, 5655, 6666, 6766, 7777, 8888, 9999, 1111A, 2222A, 3222A, 3322A, 4322A, 4333A, 4433A, 5433A, 5544A, 5644A, 6755A, 6766A, 7777A, 8888A, 9999A, 1111B, 2222B, 3333B, 4444B, 5555B, 8888B, 9999B, 1111C	15
3031A	Kestrel	1¢	50	$0.50	10/2000	B111111, B222222, B333333, B444444, B555555	
3048a	Blue Jay	20¢	10	$2.00	8/2/96	S1111, S2222	10, 14
3050a	Pheasant	20¢	10	$2.00	7/31/98	V1111, V2222, V2232, V2342, V2343, V3232, V3233	14
3050c	Pheasant	20¢	10	$2.00	7/31/98	V2232, V2332, V2333, V2342, V2343, V3232, V3243, V3333	
3051A	Pheasant	20¢	10	$2.00	7/31/98	V1111	
2489a	Red Squirrel	29¢	18	$5.22	6/25/93	D11111, D22211, D22221, D22222, D23133	3
2490a	Red Rose	29¢	18	$5.22	8/19/93	S111	3, 4
2491a	Pine Cone	29¢	18	$5.22	11/5/93	B1, B2, B3, B4, B5, B6, B7, B8, B9, B10, B11, B12, B13, B14, B15, B16	5

Scott number	Stamp	Denomi-nation	Number of subjects	Total value	Date of Plate numbers		Notes
2492a	Pink Rose	32¢	20	$6.40	6/2/95	S111, S112, S333, S444, S555	5, 9, 10
2494a	Peach/Pear	32¢	20	$6.40	7/8/95	V11111, V11122, V11131, V11132, V11232, V12131, V12132, V12211, V12221, V12232, V22212, V22221, V22222, V33142, V33143, V33243, V33323, V33333, V33343, V33353, V33363, V33453, V44424, V44434, V44454, V45434, V45464, V54365, V54565, V55365, V55565	5, 9, 10
3127a	Botanical Prints	32¢	20	$6.40	3/3/97	S11111, S22222, S33333	14, 16
3049a	Yellow Rose	32¢	20	$6.40	10/24/96	S1111, S2222	
3052d	Coral Rose	33¢	20	$6.60	8/13/99	S111, S222	14, 16
3052Ef	Pink Coral Rose	33¢	20	$6.60	4/7/00	S111, S222, S333	14, 16
3297b	Fruit Berries	33¢	20	$6.60	4/10/99	B1111, B1112, B2211, B2222, B3331, B3332, B3333, B4444, B5555	14, 16
3297d	Fruit Berries	33¢	20	$6.60	3/15/00	B1111	
3457e	Four Flowers	(34¢)	20	$6.80	12/15/00	S1111	
3461b	Four Flowers	(34¢)	20	$6.80	12/15/00	S1111	
3461c	Four Flowers	(34¢)	20	$6.80	12/15/00	S1111	
3490e	Four Flowers	34¢	20	$6.80	2/7/01	S1111, S2222	
3492b	Apple & Orange	34¢	20	$6.80	3/6/01	B1111, B2222, B3333, B4444, B5555, B6666, B7777	
3036	Red Fox	$1	20	$20.00	8/14/98	B1111, B3333	15
3036a	Red Fox	$1	20	$20.00	2002	B1111	

Holiday and Love coil stamps

Scott number	Stamp	Plate number	Tagging type
2799a	29¢ Snowman (1993)	V1111111	prephosphored
2813	29¢ Sunrise Love (1994)	B1	prephosphored
2873	29¢ Christmas Santa (1994)	V1111	prephosphored
3014-17	32¢ Santa/Children with Toys (1995)	V1111	prephosphored
3018	32¢ Midnight Angel (1995)	B1111	prephosphored
3683a	37¢ Snowmen (2002)	G1111, G1112	prephosphored

Holiday and Love panes

Scott number	Stamp	Denomination	Number of subjects	Total value	Date of Plate numbers		Notes
2802a	Christmas	29¢	12	$3.48	10/28/93	V111-1111, V222-1222, V222-2112, V222-2122, V222-2221, V222-2222, V333-3333	5
2813a	Sunrise Love	29¢	18	$5.22	1/27/94	B111-1, B111-2, B111-3, B111-4, B111-5, B121-5, B221-5, B222-4, B222-5, B222-6, B333-5, B333-7, B333-8, B333-9, B333-10, B333-11, B333-12, B333-14, B333-17, B334-11, B344-11, B344-12, B344-13, B434-10, B444-7, B444-8, B444-9, B444-10, B444-13, B444-14, B444-15, B444-16, B444-17, B444-18, B444-19, B555-20, B555-21	5
2873a	Christmas	29¢	12	$3.48	10/20/94	V1111	5
2949a	Love Cherub	(32¢)	20	$6.40	2/1/95	B1111-1, B2222-1, B2222-2, B3333-2	16
3011a	Santa/Children with Toys	32¢	20	$6.40	9/30/95	V1111, V1211, V1212, V3233, V3333, V4444	5, 16
3012a	Midnight Angel	32¢	20	$6.40	10/19/95	B1111, B2222, B33333	5, 10, 16
3030a	Love Cherub	32¢	20	$6.40	1/20/96	B1111-1, B1111-2, B2222-1, B2222-2, B3333-1, B3333-3, B3434-1, B3434-3, B4344-1, B4344-3, B4444-1, B4444-3	16
3112a	Madonna and Child	32¢	20	$6.40	11/1/96	1111-1, 1211-1, 2212-1, 2222-1, 2323-1, 3323-1, 3333-1, 3334-1, 4444-1, 5544-1, 5555-1, 5556-1, 5556-2, 5656-2, 6656-2, 6666-1, 6666-2, 6766-1, 7887-1, 7887-2, 7888-2, 7988-2	16
3116a	Family Scenes	32¢	20	$6.40	10/8/96	B1111, B2222, B3333	16
3118	Hanukkah	32¢	20	$6.40	10/22/96	V11111	15, 17
3123a	Love Swans	32¢	20	$6.40	2/4/97	B1111, B2222, B3333, B4444, B5555, B6666, B7777	16
3175	Kwanzaa	32¢	50	$16.00	10/22/97	V1111	15
3176a	Madonna and Child	32¢	20	$6.40	10/27/97	1111, 2222, 3333	14, 16

Scott number	Stamp	Denomination	Number of subjects	Total value	Date of	Plate numbers	Notes
3177a	American Holly	32¢	20	$6.40	10/30/97	B1111, B2222, B3333	14, 16
3203	Cinco de Mayo	32¢	20	$6.40	4/16/98	S11111	15
3244a	Madonna and Child	32¢	20	$6.40	10/15/98	11111, 22222, 33333	16
3252c	Wreaths	32¢	20	$6.40	10/15/98	B222222, B333333, B444444, B555555	14, 16
3252e	Wreaths	32¢	20	$6.40	10/15/98	B111111, **B222222**	
3274a	Victorian Love	33¢	20	$6.60	1/28/99	V1111, V1112, V1117, V1118, V1211, V1212, V1213, V1233, V1313, V1314, V1333, V1334, V1335, V2123, V2221, V2222, V2223, V2324, V2424, V2425, V2426, V3123, V3124, V3125, V3133, V3134, V3323, V3327, V3333, V3334, V3336, V4549, V5650	15
3309	Cinco de Mayo	33¢	20	$6.60	4/27/99	B111111	15
3352	Hanukkah	33¢	20	$6.60	10/8/99	V11111	15
3355a	Madonna and Child	33¢	20	$6.60	10/20/99	B1111, B2222, B3333	19
3359a	Deer	33¢	20	$6.60	10/20/99	B111111	14, 15
3363a	Deer	33¢	20	$6.60	10/20/99	B111111, B222222, B333333, B444444, B555555, B666666, B777777, B888888, B999999, B000000, BAAAAAA, BBBBBBB	14
3368	Kwanzaa	33¢	20	$6.60	10/29/99	V1111	15
3496a	Rose and Love Letter	(34¢)	20	$6.80	1/19/01	B1111, B2222	
3497a	Rose and Love Letter	34¢	20	$6.80	2/14/01	B1111, B2222, B3333, B4444, B5555	
3532	Eid	34¢	20	$6.80	9/1/01	V111	
3536a	Madonna and Child	34¢	20	$6.80	10/10/01	B1111	
3537-40	Four Santas	34¢	20	$6.80	10/10/01	S1111	
3540d	Four Santas	34¢	20	$6.80	10/10/01	S1111, S3333, S4444	
3540g	Four Santas	34¢	20	$6.80	10/10/01	S1111, S3333, S4444	
3546	We Give Thanks	34¢	20	$6.80	10/19/01	P1111, P2222	
3547	Hanukkah	34¢	20	$6.80	10/21/01	V11111	
3548	Kwanzaa	34¢	20	$6.80	10/21/01	V11111	
3558	**Happy Birthday**	**34¢**	**20**	**$6.80**	**2/8/02**	**V1111**	

Scott number	Stamp	Denomination	Number of subjects	Total value	Date of	Plate numbers	Notes
3657	Stylized Love	37¢	20	$7.40	8/16/02	B11111, B22222, B33333, B44444, B55555, B66666, B77777	
3658	Stylized Love	60¢	20	$12.00	8/16/02	V11111	
3672	Hanukkah	37¢	20	$7.40	10/10/02	V11111	
3673	Kwanzaa	37¢	20	$7.40	10/10/02	V1111	
3674	Eid	37¢	20	$7.40	10/10/02	V111	
3675a	Madonna and Child	37¢	20	$7.40	10/10/02	B1111, B2222 , B4444	
3679a	Snowmen	37¢	20	$7.40	10/28/02	V1111	
3687b	Snowmen	37¢	20	$7.40	10/28/02	S1111, S1113, S2222, S4444	
3695	Happy Birthday	37¢	20	$7.40	10/25/02	V1111	
3820a	Madonna and Child	37¢	20	$7.40	10/23/03	P1111, P2222, P3333, P4444	
3824b	Music Makers	37¢	20	$7.40	10/23/03	S1111, S2222	
3833a	Candy Hearts Love	37¢	20	$7.40	1/14/04	V1111	
3836	Garden Bouquet	37¢	20	$7.40	3/4/04	P11111, P22222, P33333 P44444, P55555, P66666, P77777, P88888	
3879a	Madonna and Child	37¢	20	$7.40	10/14/04	P1111	
3880	Hanukkah (Dreidel)	37¢	20	$7.40	10/15/04	S1111	
3881	Kwanzaa	37¢	20	$7.40	10/16/04	P111111	
3886a	Holiday Ornaments	37¢	20	$7.40	11/16/04	S1111	
3886b	Holiday Ornaments	37¢	20	$7.40	11/16/04	S1111, S2222	
3890b	Holiday Ornaments	37¢	20	$7.40	11/16/04	S11111	
3898a	**Bouquet Love**	**37¢**	**20**	**$7.40**	**2/18/05**	**V1111, V1112**	
3952a	**Christmas Cookies**	**37¢**	**20**	**$7.40**	**10/20/05**	**S1111**	
3956a	**Christmas Cookies**	**37¢**	**20**	**$7.40**	**10/20/05**	**S1111**	
3960b	**Christmas Cookies**	**37¢**	**20**	**$7.40**	**10/20/05**	**S1111**	
2960a	Love Cherub	55¢	20	$11.00	5/12/95	B1111-1, B2222-1	9, 16
3124a	Love Swans	55¢	20	$11.00	2/4/97	B1111, B2222, B3333, B4444	16
3275	Victorian Love	55¢	20	$11.00	1/28/99	B1111111, B2222222, B3333333	15

Scott number	Stamp	Denomi-nation	Number of subjects	Total value	Date of Plate numbers		Notes
3499	Rose and Love Letter	55¢	20	$11.00	2/14/01	B1111	
3551	Rose and Love Letter	57¢	20	$11.40	11/19/01	B11111	
3837	Garden Blossoms	60¢	20	$12.00	3/4/04	S11111	

Distinguished Americans stamps

Scott number	Stamp	Denomi-nation	Number of subjects	Total value	Date of issue	Plate numbers	Notes
3420	Joseph W. Stilwell	10¢	20	$2.00	8/24/00	B11-1	
3422	Wilma Rudolph	23¢	20	$4.60	7/14/04	P11-1, P22-1, **P33-1**	
3436c	Wilma Rudolph	23¢	10	$2.30	7/14/04	P11, P22	
3426	Claude Pepper	33¢	20	$6.60	9/7/00	B11-1	
3330	Billy Mitchell	55¢	20	$11.00	7/30/99	B11111, B11211	15
3431	Hattie Caraway	76¢	20	$15.20	2/21/01	B11-1	
3432	**Hattie Caraway**	**76¢**	**20**	**$15.20**	**2/21/01**	**B11-1**	
3433	Edna Ferber	83¢	20	$16.60	7/29/02	B11-1	
3434	Edna Ferber	83¢	20	$16.60	8/03	P11-1, P22-1, **P33-3**	

Scenic American Landmarks panes

Scott number	Stamp	Denomi-nation	Number of subjects	Total value	Date of Plate numbers		Notes
C134	Rio Grande	40¢	20	$8.00	7/30/99	V11111	15
C133	Niagara Falls	48¢	20	$9.60	5/12/00	V11111, V22111, V22222	15
C135	Grand Canyon	60¢	20	$12.00	1/20/00	B1111	
C138	Acadia National Park	60¢	20	$12.00	5/30/01	B1111	
C138a	Acadia National Park	60¢	20	$12.00	**3/?/03**	B2222	
C138b	**Acadia National Park**	**60¢**	**20**	**$12.00**	**1/?/05**	**S1111**	
C136	Nine Mile Prairie	70¢	20	$14.00	3/6/01	P11111, P22222, P33333, P44444	
C137	Mount McKinley	80¢	20	$16.00	4/17/01	V11111	

Regular issues 1982-85

Scott number	Stamp	Plate number	Tagging type
2005	20¢ Consumer Education (1982)	1, 2, 3, 4	overall
2150	21.1¢ Letters (1985)	111111, 111121	block
2150a	21.1¢ Letters (1985)	111111, 111121	untagged

379

Regular issue coil stamps, 1991-94

Scott number	Stamp	Plate number	Tagging type
2529	19¢ Fishing Boat (1991)	A1111, A1112, A1212, A2424	prephosphored
2529a	19¢ Fishing Boat (1993)	A5555, A5556, A6667, A7667, A7679, A7766, A7767, A7779	prephosphored
2529c	19¢ Fishing Boat (1994)	S11	prephosphored

Regular issue coil stamps 2002-04

Scott number	Stamp	Plate number	Tagging type
3640	37¢ Antique Toys (2002)	B11111, B12222	prephosphored
3829	37¢ Snowy Egret (2003)	V1111, V2111, **V2121,** V2222, V3211, V3212, **V3221,** V3222	prephosphored
3829A	37¢ Snowy Egret (2004)	P11111, P22222, P33333, **P44444,** P55555	prephosphored

Regular issue panes 2002-04

Scott number	Stamp	Denomi- nation	Number of subjects	Total value	Date of Plate numbers		Notes
3629e	Antique Toys	(37¢)	20	$7.40	6/7/02	V1111, V1112, V2222	
3645e	Antique Toys	37¢	20	$7.40	7/26/02	V1111, V2221, V2222	
3645h	Antique Toys	37¢	20	$7.40	9/3/03	V1111, V1112, V2222	
3784	Purple Heart	37¢	20	$7.40	5/30/03	B1111	
3784A	Purple Heart	37¢	20	$7.40	5/30/03	P1111, P2222, P3333, P4444, P5555, **P6666,** P7777	
3830a	Snowy Egret	37¢	20	$7.40	1/30/04	P11111, P22222, P33333, P44444, P55555	

Official coil stamps

Scott number	Stamp	Plate number	Tagging type
O135	20¢ Official (1983)	1	block
O159	37¢ Official (2002)	S111	prephosphored

Variable-denomination coil stamps

Scott number	Stamp	Plate number	Tagging type
CVP31 and CVP31a	variable-denomination coil (1992)	1	prephosphored[8]
CVP31b and CVP31c	variable-denomination coil (1994) (new font)	1	prephosphored[8]

Scott number	Stamp	Plate number	Tagging type
CVP32	variable-denomination (1994)	A11	prephosphored
CVP33	variable-denomination (1996)	11	prephosphored

Test coil stamps

Scott number	Stamp	Plate number	Tagging type
TD123	Eagle linerless coil **(1992)**	1111	untagged
TD126	For Testing Purposes Only self-adhesive coil (1996) black on blue printing paper	1111	untagged[12, 18]
TD127	For Testing Purposes Only self-adhesive coil (1996) black on white	V1	untagged
TD133	**For Testing Purposes Only self-adhesive coil black on white**	**1111**	**untagged**
TD135	**South Carolina Flag self-adhesive coil light blue on white**	**V1**	**untagged**
TD137	**For Testing Purposes Only self-adhesive coil black on white**	**S1**	**untagged**
TDB87	For Testing Purposes Only self-adhesive ATM booklet **(1997)** straight-line die cut black	V1	untagged
TDB86	For ATM Testing (blue temple) self-adhesive ATM booklet **(1997)**	V1	untagged
TDB88-89	For Testing Purposes Only self-adhesive ATM booklet **(1997)** serpentine die cut gauge 7.8 black	V1	untagged
Not Listed	Eagle Over Forest sheet (World Stamp Expo 2000)	S1111	untagged
TDB89	For Testing Purposes Only self-adhesive ATM booklet magenta stamps/blue back cover	V1	untagged
TDB90	NCR For ATM Testing paper ATM booklet	V1	untagged
Not Listed	29¢ red-rose paper ATM booklet	V1	untagged

Automated teller machine (ATM) panes

Scott number	Stamp	Denomination	Number of subjects	Total value	Date of Plate numbers		Notes
2475a	Stylized Flag	25¢	12	$3.00	5/18/90	—	
2522a	F	(29¢)	12	$3.48	1/22/91	—	
2531Ab	Liberty Torch (revised back)	29¢ 29¢	18 18	$5.22 $5.22	6/25/91 10/??/92	— —	8

Scott number	Stamp	Denomination	Number of subjects	Total value	Date of Plate numbers		Notes
2719a	Locomotive	29¢	18	$5.22	1/28/92	V11111	
2803a	Snowman	29¢	18	$5.22	10/28/93	V1111, V2222	
2874a	Cardinal	29¢	18	$5.22	10/20/94	V1111, V2222	
2887a	G	(32¢)	18	$5.76	12/13/97	—	
2919a	Flag Over Field	32¢	18	$5.76	3/17/95	V1111, V1311, V1433, V2111, V2222, V2322	
3013a	Children Sledding	32¢	18	$5.76	10/19/95	V1111	
3117a	Skaters	32¢	18	$5.76	10/8/96	V1111, V2111	
3269a	H	(33¢)	18	$5.94	11/9/98	V1111	
3283a	Flag Over Chalkboard	33¢	18	$5.94	5/13/99	V1111	
3450a	Flag Over Farm	(34¢)	18	$6.12	12/15/00	V1111	
3495a	Flag Over Farm	34¢	18	$6.12	12/17/01	V1111	
3625a	Flag	(37¢)	18	$6.66	6/7/02	V1111	
3637a	Flag	37¢	18	$6.66	2/4/03	V1111	
3894a	Holiday Ornaments	37¢	18	$6.66	11/16/04	V11111	
3975a	Liberty/Flag	39¢	18	$7.08	12/8/05	V1111	

Plate number coil notes

1 Shiny gum
2 Plate number 3 shiny and dull gum
3 Service inscribed in black "Nonprofit Org."
4 Service inscribed in black "Nonprofit Org. 5-Digit ZIP+4"
5 Service inscribed in black "Bulk Rate" (between two lines)
6 Service inscribed in red "Bulk Rate Carrier Route Sort"
7 Has two black precancel lines
8 Shiny gum and dull gum
9 22222 shiny and dull gum, 33333 dull gum
10 11121 shiny gum, 33333 and 43444 dull gum
11 Rolls of 3,000 and 10,000 have back numbers
12 Has back numbers
13 2 and 4 shiny gum, 3, 4 and 5 low gloss and shiny gum
14 22221 shiny only and 11111, 22222 shiny and low gloss gum; others low-gloss gum only
15 2 dull gum, 3 dull and shiny gum, 6 shiny gum
16 S22222 has back numbers
17 Plate number 2 dull gum, 3 shiny dull, 4 shiny
18 Tagged paper printed with three layers of opaque white
19 3 low-gloss gum
20 Shiny gum, new white paper on 2¢ Locomotive
21 Die cut, equivalent to perf 10
22 Stamps spaced on backing paper
23 Back numbers, can be both top and bottom
24 Self-adhesive
25 Water-activated gum
26 Roll of 100, has shinier gum, plate numbers (1111) nearly touch "st-Cl" of "First-Class" on roll of 100, 1998 is ½mm farther to right of perforations as compared to roll of 3,000
27 Rounded corners (all four) are found only on spaced self-adhesive stamps

28 New white paper and shinier gum on $1 Seaplane with plate number 3
29 Process-color plate number digits ordered black, yellow, cyan and magenta
30 Process-color plate number digits ordered black, cyan, yellow and magenta
31 Process-color plate number digits ordered yellow, magenta, cyan and black
32 Luminescent ink
33 Plate number 1 dull gum, plate number 2 low-gloss gum

Notes for self-adhesive panes

1 Selling price was $5, which included a 50¢ surcharge. On September 7, 1990, the USPS announced it was sending 400,000 Eagle & Shield stamps to the U.S. Forces in the Persian Gulf Area. The selling price would be $4.50, thus eliminating the surcharge.
2 Plate numbers are in two positions, upper left and lower right.
3 Also available in coil format.
4 There are two different UPC bar codes on the back of the liner. The correct one is 16694. The other one, 16691, is the number for the African Violets booklet.
5 Also available in coil format with plate number.
6 When originally issued, the selling price was $5 (7¢ surcharge). The Postal Bulletin dated February 18, 1993, announced that beginning March 1, 1993, the new selling price would be $4.93, thus removing the surcharge.
7 The pane contains 17 stamps and one label the same size as the stamps.
8 Originally printed on prephosphored paper with and without a lacquer coating. When reissued with the revised back in October 1992, the panes were tagged on press (overall tagged). See Linn's Stamp News December 7, 1992, issue.
9 The Peach/Pear, Flag Over Porch, and the Pink Rose all have reorder labels in the lower right corner of the pane. To discourage the use of these labels as postage, later printings had a target and x die cut into the label. The Peach/Pear V12131, V33323 and V33333 exist both plain & die cut, while V33353 and higher numbers exist die cut only. The Flag Over Porch V23322 and V23422 exist both plain and die cut, while V12331, V13831, V13834, V13836, V23522, V34743, V34745, V36743, V42556, V45554, V56663, V56665, V56763, V57663, V65976 and V78989 exist die cut only. The Pink Rose S444 exists both plain and die cut while S555 exists die cut only. The 55¢ Love Cherub B2222-1 exists die cut only.
10 In 1996, to lower costs, USPS instructed printers that printing on the inside of the liners was no longer required. Several sheetlets that were originally issued with printed liners had unprinted liners on later releases. The following issues can be found with both printed and unprinted liners: 20¢ Blue Jay (S1111 and S2222 both ways); 32¢ Love Cherub (B2222-1 and B2222-2 both ways); 32¢ Pink Rose (S555 both ways); 32¢ Flag Over Porch (V23322, V23422, V42556 and V45554 both ways; V13831, V13834, V13836, V23522, V34745, V36743, V56663, V56763, V57663, V65976 and V78989 with unprinted liners only). The Flag Over Porch panes of 10 have unprinted liners on any panes with plate number V44322 or higher. The original Midnight Angel (B1111 and B2222) have printed liners while the reissue (B3333) has an unprinted liner.
11 In 1997 the printing on the back of the pane was changed to "NATIONAL DOMESTIC VIOLENCE HOTLINE." The original inscription was "Stamps etc." Plate V34745 exists with both backings, while V36743, V56663, V56763, V57663 and V78989 exist only with the new backing. All other plates were printed with the original "Stamps etc." inscription.
12 There are three different back printings: "108th Tournament of Roses Parade," "Kids! Start Stampin!" and "Delivering the Gift of Life The National Marrow Donor Program." Both S1111 and S2222 are available with all three printings.
13 There are two different back printings: "Stamps etc." and "NATIONAL DOMESTIC VIOLENCE HOTLINE." Plate number V3333 exists with "Stamps etc." only; V1311, V2222, V2311, V2331, V3233, V3513 and V4532 are found with "NATIONAL DOMESTIC VIOLENCE HOTLINE" only. Plate numbers V1111, V1211 and V2122 can be found with both.
14 Also available in a folded version for vending-machine use: Blue Jay ($2.00), Ring-Necked Pheasant ($2.00), Yellow Rose ($4.80 and $9.60), Statue of Liberty ($4.80 and $9.60), Botanical Prints ($4.80) and American Holly ($4.80 and $9.60), Wreaths ($4.80), Flag Over City ($4.95), Fruit Berries ($4.95), Coral Rose ($4.95) and Deer ($4.95).
15 Each pane contains four plate numbers, in selvage adjacent to corner position stamps.
16 The pane contains 20 stamps and one label the same size as the stamps.
17 The reissue has a different style die cut in the backing paper than the original.

18 There are two different back printings: "Stamps etc." and "National Domestic Violence Hotline." Plate numbers V1111 and V2222 exist with "National Domestic Violence Hotline" only. Plate numbers V1211 and V2122 can be found with both.
19 Stamps are printed on both sides of the pane (single liner between them). Plate number is only present on one of two sides. Also includes a label identifying issue and the price of the pane.
20 Initially, the Breast Cancer semipostal stamp was valued at 32¢ for postage and 8¢ for cancer research. Effective with the 1999 rate change, this changed to 33¢ for postage and 7¢ for cancer research.
21 Exists with and without a special die cut for philatelic purposes.

Booklets with plate numbers

Scott booklet number	Booklet	Scott pane number	Denom- ination	Plate numbers	Notes
137	$3.60 Animals	2 panes 1889a	18¢	1-16	1, 2
138	$1.20 Flag	1 pane 1893a	two 6¢ & six 18¢	1	
139	$1.20 Flag	1 pane 1896a	20¢	1	3, 4
140	$2 Flag	1 pane 1896b	20¢	1, 4	3, 4
140A	$4 Flag	2 panes 1896b	20¢	2, 3, 4	3, 4
140B	$28.05 Eagle	1 pane 1900a	$9.35	1111	2
142	$4 Sheep	2 panes 1949a	20¢	1-6, 9-12, 14-26, 28, 29	1, 2, 5
142a	$4 Sheep	2 panes 1949d	20¢	34	5
143	$4.40 D	2 panes 2113a	D (22¢)	1-4	5
144	$1.10 Flag	1 pane 2116a	22¢	1, 3	3
145	$2.20 Flag	2 panes 2116a	22¢	1, 3	
146	$4.40 Seashells	2 panes 2121a	22¢	1-3	
147	$4.40 Seashells	2 panes 2121a	22¢	1, 3, 5-8, 10	
148	$32.25 Eagle	1 pane 2122a	$10.75	11111	3
149	$32.25 Eagle	1 pane 2122a	$10.75	22222	
150	$5 London	2 panes 2182a	25¢	1, 2	6
151	$1.50 London	1 pane 2197a	25¢	1	
152	$3 London	2 panes 2197a	25¢	1	
153	$1.76 Stamp Collecting	1 pane 2201a	22¢	1	
154	$2.20 Fish	2 panes 2209a	22¢	11111, 22222	
155	$2.20 Special Occasions	1 pane 2274a	22¢	11111, 22222	
156	$4.40 Flag	1 pane 2276a	22¢	1111, 2122, 2222	6
157	$5 E	2 panes 2282a	E (25¢)	1111, 2122, 2222	
158	$5 Pheasant	2 panes 2283a	25¢	A1111	
159	$5 Pheasant	2 panes 2283c	25¢	A3111, A3222	